GERRY GOLDSM

COMP

through Case Studies

Nelson

Nelson Blackie
Westercleddens Road
Bishopbriggs
Glasgow
G64 2NZ UK

Thomas Nelson and Sons Ltd
Nelson House Mayfield Road
Walton-on-Thames Surrey
KT12 5PL UK

Front cover courtesy of Electronic arts
Illustrations by Terry Forrest Illustration, Ian Foulis Associates and David Gardner

First published by Blackie and Son Ltd 1991
ISBN 0-216-92937-7

This edition published by Thomas Nelson and Sons Ltd 1993

ISBN 0-17-448230-2
NPN 9 8 7 6 5 4 3 2

Printed in Hong Kong

ACKNOWLEDGEMENTS

The authors and publishers would like to thank the following for permission to reproduce copyright material:

Photographs

Edinburgh Zoo 3; Royal Botanic Gardens Kew 13 (top and bottom); Climate Controls Limited 16 (top and bottom); The Post Office 19; Sainsbury's plc 27 and 31 (left and right); St Dunstan's 35; Electronic Arts 88 and 218 (right); IBM UK Ltd 202, 211 and 218 (left); Kimball Ti Systems UK Ltd 202 and 203; Data & Research Services Ltd 206 (left and right); Bank of Scotland 207; Nationwide Anglia 208 (top and bottom); Science Photo Library 212; NEC (UK) 215 and 216; Apple Computer UK Ltd 219 (top left and right); Calcomp Limited 219 (left); Toshiba Information Systems (UK) Ltd 219 (right).

Other copyright material

The Guardian Reader (page 95), Reader 1, Reader 4a) and b) and Reader 5a); *Computing* Reader 3 and Reader 5c); *Computer Weekly* Reader (page 148), Reader 2, Reader 5b) and Reader 6a).

Exam Questions

The Associated Examining Board (AEB); Joint Matriculation Board (JMB); Oxford and Cambridge Schools Examination Board (COSSEC); Scottish Examination Board (SEB); University of Cambridge Local Examinations Syndicate (UCLES); University of London School Examinations Department (ULSED); University of Oxford Delegacy of Local Examinations (OLE); Welsh Joint Education Committee (WJEC).

Filmset by Advanced Filmsetters (Glasgow) Ltd

CONTENTS

PART 1
Case Studies

PART 2
Information Chapters

Readers

PREFACE

To the reader

What this book is about:

- the practical uses of computers
- what the main parts of a computer are called and their functions
- principles of programming a computer
- the storage and handling of information in computers
- the design and development of computer systems in organisations
- the impact of computers on people and the jobs they do.

The book is in two main parts. Part 1 is a set of Case Studies. Part 2 contains Information Chapters. The Case Studies provide detailed descriptions of the use of computer systems in actual applications. The Information Chapters explain the principles and provide the background knowledge in relation to the Case Studies. When a topic arises in a Case Study which needs further explanation you may refer to the relevant Information Chapter with the help of the index.

However, reading a book is not enough. To understand computers and computer programming fully you need to get your hands on a computer to gain practical experience. You need to write your own programs and try them out. You will also need to visit offices, banks, police stations, libraries, shops, businesses, factories or any other place where computers are used, to see at first hand the jobs they can (and cannot) do. No book on computers can explain all their uses and possibilities. You will need to look out for newspaper stories, TV programmes, and magazine articles which show the ways in which computers are affecting the world you live in.

To the teacher

This book is designed to cover most A and AS level syllabuses in Computing; it will also be useful for Scottish Highers and BTEC courses. A set of Case Studies describing real-life applications is provided, along with Information Chapters giving the theoretical background. Cross-referencing is used extensively between the two types of material to help relate theory to practice.

The aim is to promote a greater depth of understanding of syllabus material. Exercises and questions, including questions taken from A and AS level examination papers, are provided. You may wish to supplement the Case Studies with others of your own or with those published by the examination boards.

The authors would like to thank the following for providing information for the case studies:

Dr Peter Bennett and the National Federation of Zoos (Arks & Noah); Dr Bridson and Davina Simmonds (SCBU); Ricky Russell and Steve Shaughnessy (Sainsburys); Mr P Dowel and Ms S Licorish (Datapost); Mr Peter Jones B.E.M. (Audiocalc); Dr John Woodhams (Princess of Wales Conservatory, Kew); Mr John Kennedy (Millhouses Travel).

The front cover is a computer-generated illustration which has been produced using the Apple Macintosh paint program.

PART 1
Case Studies

CASE STUDY 1

Arks and Noah

Siberian tiger

INTRODUCTION

Zoos all over the world are becoming more aware of their role in the conservation of endangered species. Animals can be bred in zoos and then reintroduced into the wild to avoid extinction of the species. It is not an easy process; the animals have to be trained to find food and to avoid predators before they can be left in the wild; some animals adapt to the wild better than others.

When there are only a few animals of a particular species in a zoo, there is sometimes a lot of inbreeding. This produces young animals which are less strong and therefore have a lower chance of survival if they are put into the wild. To reduce the problems of inbreeding, the zoologists practise what they call 'genetic management' to increase the genetic diversity of the animals being bred. This involves planning the breeding programme with the help of 'studbooks' which record information on the pedigree of a zoo animal, much the same as one might do for dogs or horses.

The Siberian tiger, for example, is an endangered species; there are probably no more than three hundred roaming the wilds of Siberia. There is an international zoo breeding programme to preserve the species until they can be reintroduced gradually into the wild. Zoos have to decide which descendants recorded in the international Siberian tiger 'studbook' will live and breed to keep the genetic stock evenly balanced.

Zoos often borrow or swap animals from other zoos to mate with one of theirs. Finding a suitable male or female partner for an animal can involve lengthy correspondance with other zoos. This case study looks at how computerised information systems can help.

Why use a computer?

Most large zoos have a computerised **database**, which helps them to manage their stock, much the same as a shop or a factory warehouse does. The database also contains important information for zoologists who use it to help them study animals and to organise breeding programmes.

To see a zoo's database system in action we talked to Peter, a zoologist and conservation coordinator working for the National Federation of Zoos, based at London Zoo. We asked him about the advantages of using a computer. This was his answer.

"From my point of view there are three main advantages:

- *speed of access to information. Searching a database is much faster and more convenient than using a card index.*
- *better and more accurate information. Computers can provide all sorts of* ***reports*** *and analyses that took a long time to do manually. Computerised records are less prone to error, though of course errors can still occur if data is entered wrongly initially.*
- *the ability to share information with zoos all over the world. With computers and modern* ***telecommunications*** *we can create national and even international databases which can be accessed from anywhere in the world."*

There are four different systems in use at London Zoo:

▲ The Animal Record Keeping System (ARKS) is a database system for individual zoos to keep their records.

▲ The National Online Animal Histories (NOAH) is a national database for British zoos.

▲ A national stocktaking system.

▲ A studbook system which is under development.

Arks

We asked Peter to tell us about ARKS.

"ARKS is a ***software package*** *produced specifically for zoos by the International Species Information System (ISIS). It is used by about 160 zoos worldwide, including 16 British zoos. ISIS is an organisation based in the United States which collects information from zoos all over the world. Fig. 2 shows the zoos which contribute information to ISIS and the zoos which have the ARKS computer package."*

"We use ARKS to keep a record of all our animals. When a new animal arrives at the zoo, we enter its details which are stored in the database. This includes its name; species; date of birth and its parents' names (if known, ie. if it was born in captivity); its transaction history (ie. the different zoos it has lived in and when). When the animal is loaned or sold to another zoo or it dies, this is recorded on the database. We use the information for predicting population changes and planning ahead."

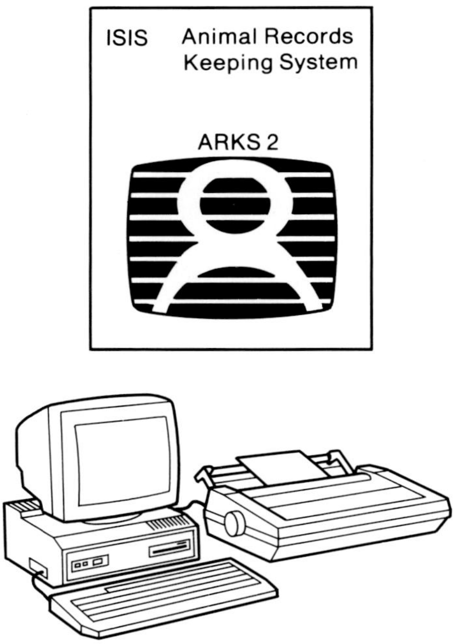

Figure 1 ARKS package and computer system

Figure 2 Map of ISIS participants

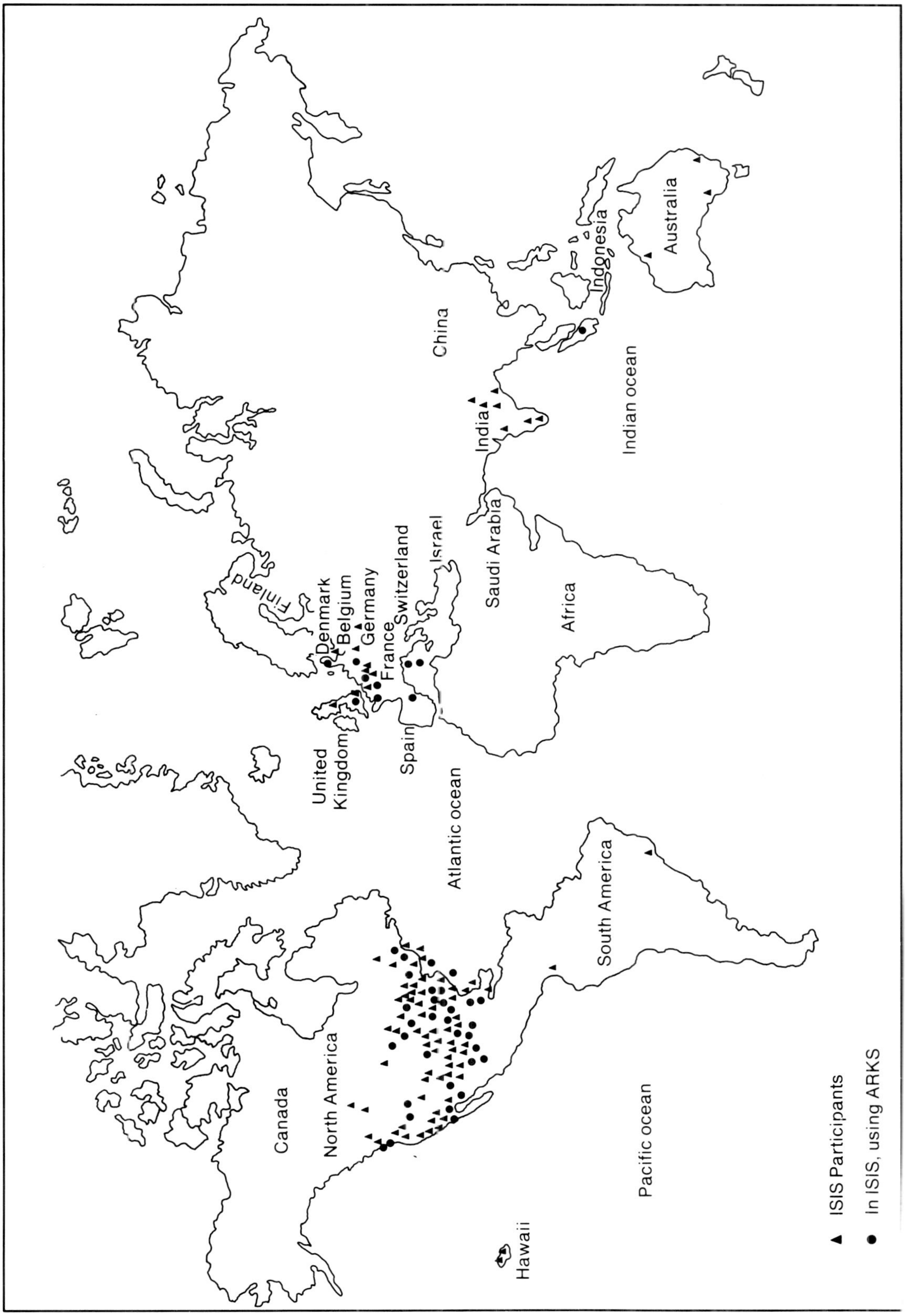

Canada
North America
Hawaii
Pacific ocean
South America
Atlantic ocean
United Kingdom
Spain
Denmark
Belgium
Germany
France
Switzerland
Israel
Finland
Saudi Arabia
Africa
India
China
Indian ocean
Indonesia
Australia
▲ ISIS Participants
● In ISIS, using ARKS

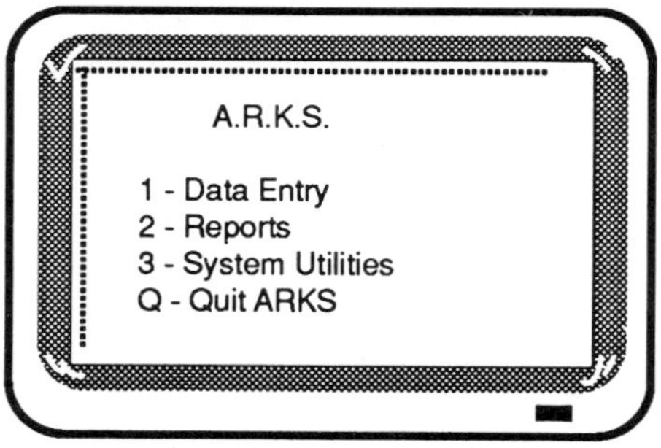

Figure 3 ARKS main menu

Report Start Date: 20 Jan 1989	**Taxon Report** LONDON, ZOOL. SOCIETY OF	Report End Date: 20 Jan 1989

Taxon Name: **GORILLA GORILLA GORILLA**
Common Name: **WESTERN LOWLAND GORILLA**

ID's: Spec. Id	House/Tag/Tattoo/ Studbook/Cage	Sex/Age	Dates: Birth/In/Out	Terms:	Origin/ Party:	Dam-Sire Their Id
A1	SALOME///620/ 129/SOBELL/	Female 12Y, 6M, 9D	16 Jul 1976 16 Jul 1976	Captive born Birth		
A2	KUMBA II///330/ X/	Male ~20Y	~11 Jun 1968 7 Jun 1984	Wild born Loan from	CAMEROONS CHESINGTON	
A3	ZAIRE///557/96/ SOBELL/	Female 14Y, 3M, 2D	23 Oct 1974 26 Jul 1984	Captive born Loan from	JERSEY JERSEY	M.405
A4	KAMILI//// SOBELL/	Female 1Y, 7M, 22D	31 May 1987 31 May 1987	Captive born Birth	A3	A2
A212	ASALI (HONEY)/ ///SOBELL/	Female 9M, 19D	2 Apr 1988 2 Apr 1988	Captive born Birth	A1	A2

Current Inventory Summary as of Report End Date: 20 Jan 1989

Totals: 1.4.0 Animals (5)	4 Captive Born
2 In on Loan	1 Wild Born
0 Out on Loan	0 Birth Type Unknown

Acquisition Summary:

0.3.0 by birth (3)
1.1.0 from elsewhere (2)

Figure 4 Taxonomic report

Peter started up the ARKS system on the **microcomputer** and a **menu** of options appeared on the screen (Fig. 3). Peter chose option 2.

*"**S**uppose I want to plan a breeding programme for our Western Lowland gorillas (a gorilla which lives in West Africa). First I'd look at the family of gorillas kept here at London Zoo. To do this I select the option from the next menu for a report on this particular species (it's called a Taxonomy report). I type in the species name and the report comes up on the screen. I'll get a printout of it as well (Fig. 4).*

As you can see, there are currently five gorillas of this species in the zoo, one male called Kumba and four females. (The male is often referred to as the silver-back because of the silver stripe down the back). Kumba is about 20 years old (we don't know exactly because he was born in the wild in Cameroons, West Africa) and he came to London on loan from Chessington Zoo in 1984. Kumba has two 'wives' called Salome, 12 years old, and Zaire, 14 years old. There are two daughters called Kamili and Asali."

We asked Peter to explain some of the other data on the report.

*"**T**he taxonomic name is the official species name; Western Lowland Gorilla is the common name. This name is fairly simple but some species have long complicated names, for example* 'Leontopithecus rosalia'. *That's the Golden Lion Tamarin, another endangered species. When we enter the data, the computer checks the name with the ISIS list of species to make sure we've entered it properly.*

The basic data is entered in a standard ISIS format so that it is compatible with other zoos' data. Each zoo adds its own local data, such as the name of the animal's enclosure. You can see that the gorillas at London Zoo are housed in the Sobell pavillion. Each animal is given a unique identification code (Salome's is A1, for example). The other numbers are the studbook numbers. The numbers at the bottom of the page summarise the data. For example, it tells us we have five gorillas of this species, one male and four females. Two are on loan and three were born here."

This report tells us about a particular species, the Western Lowland Gorilla family, and we could get a similar report for any other species (for example the Golden Lion Tamarin). What other sorts of information can we obtain from the system?

*"**A**RKS can provide answers to queries about individual animals or produce reports based on your requirements. Here are some examples.*

- *If we want to find all the data available on an animal we'd ask for a specimen report. In addition to the data shown in Fig. 4 we'd get more details of the animal's parents, the zoos it has been loaned to or from and the enclosures it has lived in at this zoo.*
- *A collection inventory report provides the curator with a complete list of animals for a particular timespan in the zoo, giving for each type of animal the number of births, deaths, arrivals and departures. Many zoos generate this report annually.*
- *Suppose the curator wants to know which animals were loaned to other zoos during the last two years. A transaction report would supply this information.*
- *Similarly an enclosure report tells the curator which animals have lived in a particular enclosure."*

Presumably the system is also used to generate statistics for zookeepers and zoologists?

*"**Y**es, the collection inventory I've just mentioned gives us some annual statistics. ARKS also produces reports that provide statistical information needed by the International Zoo Yearbook census of rare animals. This saves the zoo having to fill in forms by hand.*

Because details of each animal's parents are stored, it is possible to generate the 'family tree' for a particular species. (ARKS call this a 'pedigree chart'.) An example is shown in Fig. 5; it's not our gorilla family, but comes from a test database set up by ISIS.

Statistics on the age and sex of types of animals and a local inbreeding report can also be produced. All this information is useful to zoologists who are managing the animals."

Pedigree Chart
ISIS DATA BASE TEST USE ONLY

Taxon Name: GORILLA GORILLA GORILLA — Accession Number: 217
Common Name: GORILLA — Acq. Date: 10 Oct 1978

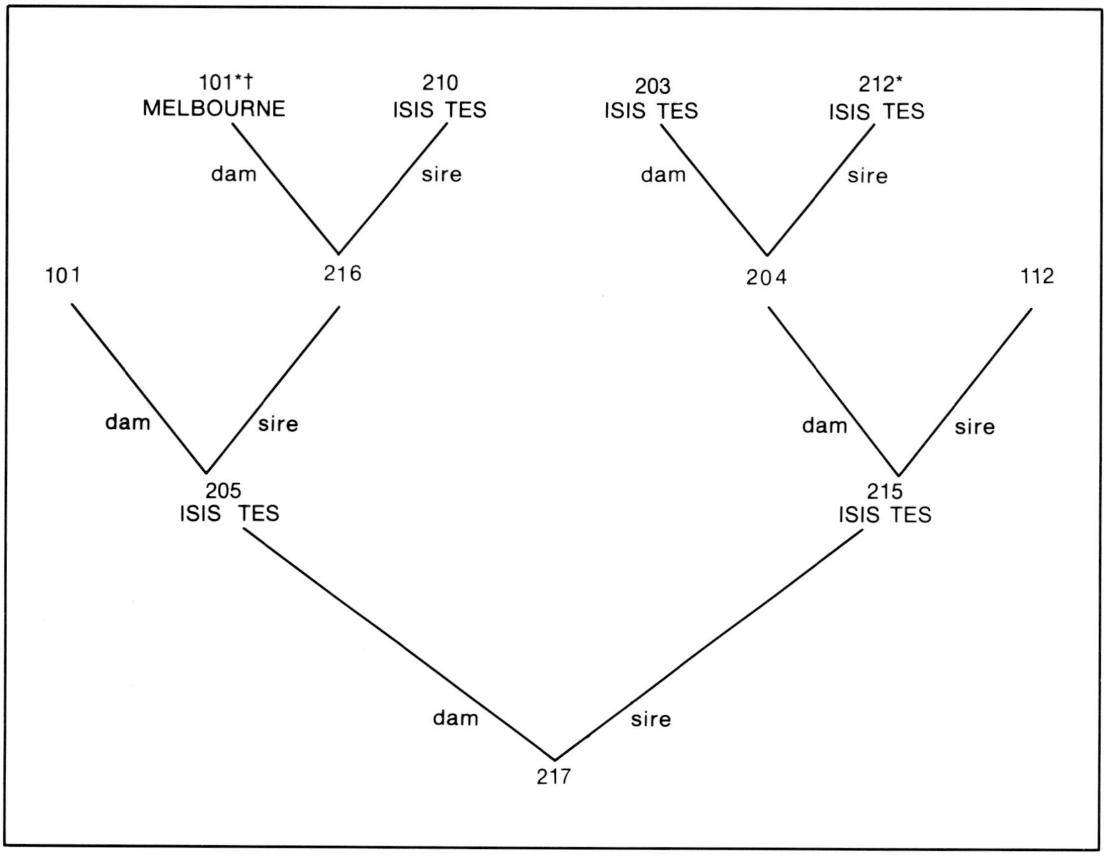

Sex: Male
House Name: HUBERT
Tattoo:
Tag/Band:
Studbook Number: 443

† Specimens known to be obtained from the wild . . .
* Specimen Id's appearing more than once . . .
^Pedigree Chart continues beyond top of page . . .

ISIS/ARKS
8 Jan 1987

Figure 5 Pedigree chart

NOAH

There are a few countries with a national zoo database, but the British system (NOAH) was the first one to go **online**. Noah can be accessed by anyone who has permission and the necessary equipment. NOAH is based at London Zoo and Peter runs the system.

Peter first explained the origins of the NOAH system.

"British zoos often contact each other to arrange to loan or swap their animals. For example, in the future it will be advantageous to send our baby gorillas to other zoos to avoid inbreeding – Kumba is the only male at London zoo. I need to find out about gorillas in other zoos so I can decide where to send these two young females to mate. It's a sort of computer dating for animals!

In the past I'd have to telephone or write to all the other British zoos for information about their gorillas but that was very time consuming. We decided we needed a computer system to help the zoos to communicate with each other. Remember that my ARKS system only stores data about this zoo so I can't use it to get information about other zoos.

What we needed was a software package that would collect ARKS data from all the zoos and store it in a central database, which other people could then retrieve information from. We decided that users would have ***online access*** *to the central database (here in London) via the telephone system. This meant that the software had to handle the communications between the central database and the users. It had to be a* ***multi-user*** *system as several users may need to access it at the same time and it had to be available all the time."*

Why couldn't you use ARKS to do this?

"The ARKS package was originally designed to be a ***single user*** *system and had to be adapted to run under a* ***multi-user operating system****. So we had the NOAH package written specially for us by a* ***software house****. If you're interested in the technical details, they used a database package called Informix, which runs under an operating system similar to* ***UNIX****."*

How does the NOAH system work?

"There are 16 British zoos contributing to the NOAH database. Each zoo has its own ARKS system for storing its local data. All the changes and additions the zoo enters into its ARKS system are automatically recorded on a floppy disk as well as in the database. Each month the zoo sends its floppy disk to me at London Zoo. I then run a special program (part of NOAH) to convert the ARKS data into the format needed for NOAH and to transfer the data to the NOAH database."

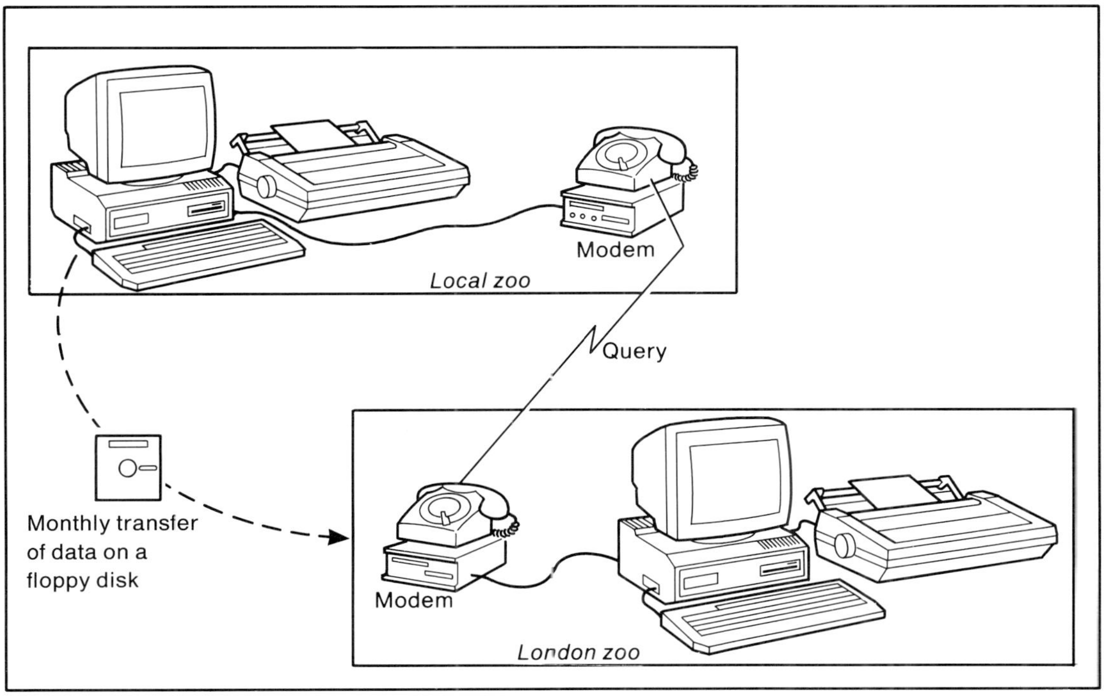

Figure 6 Data transfer and online access

It occurred to us that NOAH would only contain data from those zoos that were using the ARKS package and that might exclude the smaller zoos. Had Peter considered this?

"Yes, the alternative was to key in the data from forms that zoos fill in. But this would be very time consuming, both for the zoos and for us, apart from the possibility of introducing errors. It doesn't make sense to key in the same data twice, does it? The most convenient method would be for zoos to transmit their data over the telephone line, but that requires more equipment."

We asked Peter to show us NOAH. How would another zoo access it?

"If I was accessing NOAH from somewhere else, like Chessington Zoo, I'd have a ***modem*** *to send my messages to this computer here and to receive information from NOAH. I'd dial up the NOAH telephone number (or my modem might dial it automatically). From that point on, it's the same as accessing NOAH from here. NOAH asks me for my* ***password****."*

Peter **logged on** to NOAH by typing in his user code and then his password. NOAH accepted these and displayed the main menu (Fig. 7). Peter selected option B and entered 'Gorilla'. This produced a list of zoos in Britain that have gorillas, with a limited amount of detail about them. Part of the list is shown in Fig. 8. Browsing through this list, Peter found several zoos which may have suitable companions for the young gorillas, Kamili and Asali. He printed the information and **logged off**. The next step would be to contact these zoos for further information.

■ The national stocktaking system

"This is a simple database of the locations of animals in all British zoos (including small zoos which do not have a computer). It is essentially a stock check system and is stored on a portable personal computer, using a database package called Delta. The data is entered at London Zoo from data sent in by all the zoos. Annual reports are then produced showing the numbers of animals in each species and their location so that changes can be monitored.

You may wonder why we need this as this information could be extracted from the zoos' ARKS data which they send us each month for NOAH. The problem is that not all zoos have ARKS and our stock records would be incomplete. We need an annual report on all the animals in captivity in Britain so we have to use a separate system. Fortunately it is simply a question of numbers of animals and not all the details of individual animals, so there is not a large amount of data to enter."

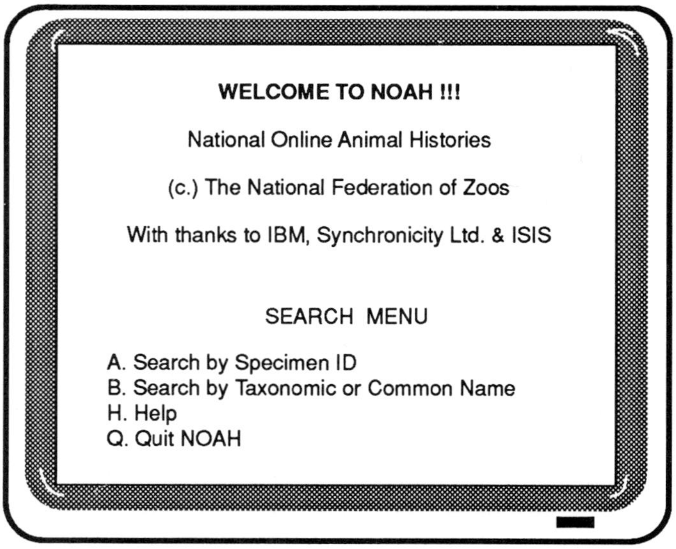

Figure 7 NOAH main menu

WELCOME TO NOAH!!!
National Online Animal Histories
Search by taxonomic or common name

Taxon name: **GORILLA GORILLA GORILLA**
Common Name: **WESTERN LOWLAND GORILLA**

Zoo	Id	Name	Sex	Father's Id	Mother's Id	DOB
Chessington	A26	Jenny	F	Wild	Wild	Jan 1972
Chessington	A50	Mukera	M			May 1969
Chessington	A59	Cora	F	A50	A26	Feb 1980
Jersey	A4	Dao	M	M20	M42	Aug 1986
Jersey	A5	Constance	F	Wild	Wild	Dec 1988
London	A1	Salome	F			
London	A2	Kumba	M	Wild	Wild	June 1968

Figure 8 Part of a NOAH report

■ A studbook system

This is a new microcomputer based package which is being developed. We asked Peter to explain what it does and why it is needed.

*"**A** lot of work is involved in producing a studbook for a particular species (imagine the work required to find out your ancestors and to prepare your family tree). Consequently, British studbooks have only been compiled for about 20 species and there are international studbooks for around 80 species. Computer systems like ARKS and NOAH can only help with a small amount of the research because they only store recent data; they haven't been in use for long.*

The package helps to trace the family tree back to the original animals from the wild. When there is sufficient data, the program can analyse it and make predictions on, for example, population trends."

A WORLDWIDE SYSTEM

You mentioned earlier that an advantage of using computers is the sharing of data. We've seen how NOAH collects data from British zoos and provides an online service for people to access the data. What about a worldwide service?

*"**Y**es. The next step forward is online access to an international database. It's feasible now – there are plenty of examples of commercial databases which are online to the public. ISIS already has an international database, but it's not yet online. It requires a large database system capable of handling online access by a number of users at the same time. This takes up a lot of computer time. Buying the software and running the central system is expensive. It is also costly for the users."*

Tell us more about the ISIS database. How is the data collected?

*"**F**or zoos which have ARKS it's easy. Any updates (ie. new data or changes to our data) are automatically recorded on a floppy disk as well as on our hard disk and we post the floppy disk to ISIS, where the data is input and stored on their mainframe computer. ISIS use the data for international breeding programmes. It would be useful if we all had direct access to the data.'*

So what of the future?

*"**W**e rely on the help of funding organisations and sponsorship to develop our systems and therefore work has to be done gradually. For example, a new system called MedARKS, designed to keep animals' medical records is being developed in phases as funding becomes available.*

NOAH is to be used by other countries for their national databases and eventually we will all be linked to the international database. Ideally all the data kept in different systems (animal records, stocktaking and studbooks) should be combined. It's a question of time and money."

QUESTIONS

1 (a) Draw a family tree for Kumba's family.
(b) Explain how you would find out the number of Siberian tigers at London Zoo.

2 List the likely **fields** which would make up a typical animal **record**.

3 (a) What equipment would a zoo, based in Wales for example, need to access NOAH?
(b) Why would they have to get permission to use NOAH?
(c) Suppose that the international database could be accessed online from anywhere in the world. Explain the process by which data would be transmitted between the database and a zoo situated in your home town.
(d) Currently all zoos which have the ARKS system send their updates on a floppy disk to ISIS who store the data on their mainframe computer. What alternative method might be used to update the international database?

4 What happens when some new animals arrive at London Zoo and the ARKS database needs to be updated? Suggest how the mainframe database in the United States might be updated from the zoos' floppy disks. Compare the two processes. (You may find it helpful to draw systems flowcharts.)

5 Discuss the benefits and advantages of integrating the various applications described in this case study and of linking all zoos to a central database.
What difficulties need to be overcome in order to do this? Are there any disadvantages of having a common, linked system for zoos?

FURTHER INFORMATION

Chapter 2 Systems Analysis and Design
Chapter 3 Files and Database Systems
Chapter 5 Operating Systems and Systems Software
Chapter 7 Data Transfer and Communications

CASE STUDY 2

Controlling the Princess of Wales Conservatory at Kew

Princess of Wales conservatory

INTRODUCTION

The botanic garden at Kew near Richmond in London was founded in 1759 by Princess Augusta, the then Princess of Wales. Since then many glasshouses and great conservatories have been built there. The newest conservatory, the Princess of Wales Conservatory, was opened in 1987. It is the latest in a series of great conservatories that have been built at Kew since its foundation.

The gardens and houses contain collections of plants from all over the world and it is a centre for research in botanical science. The conservatories have been built to provide environments in which plants may thrive and be viewed in attractive surroundings. The great glasshouses built in the Victorian era are splendid examples of glass and iron architecture.

Princess Augusta

The New Conservatory

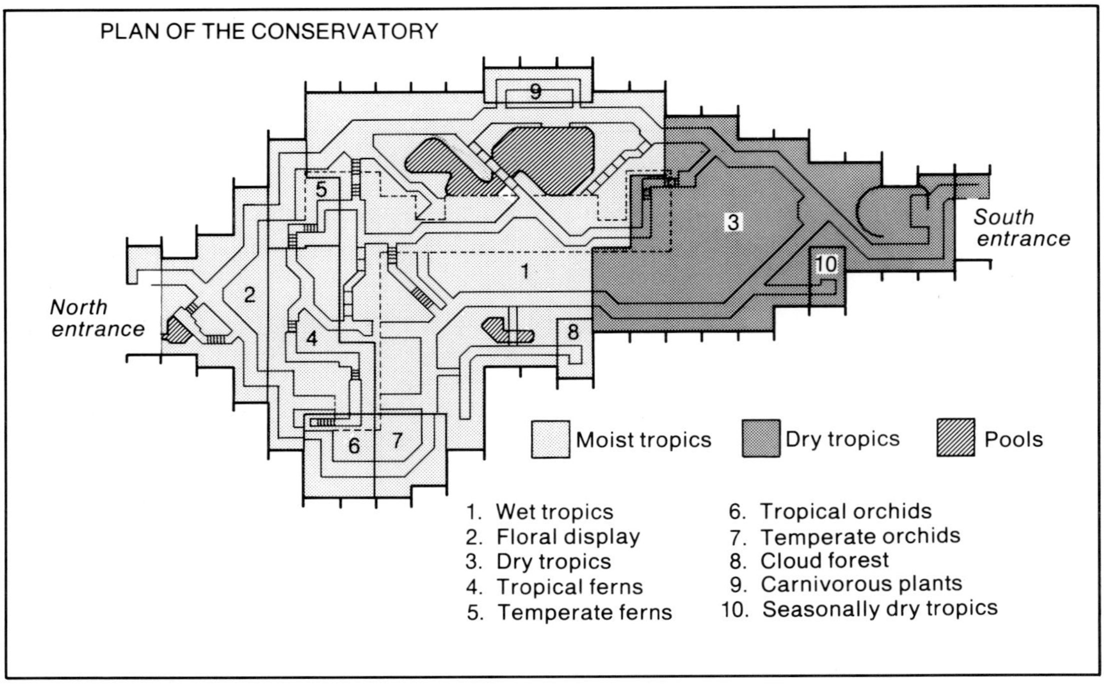

Figure 1 Plan of the conservatory

The Princess of Wales Conservatory is designed to house plants which originate in a variety of climates. These climates range from tropical rain forests to arid deserts. One of the main objectives in the designing of the house was to provide a range of climates under one roof. And all this in Britain!

Fig. 1 shows a plan of the house with a list of climates. As you can see, the house is divided into two main divisions; moist tropics and dry tropics. Within these divisions are a total of ten smaller climatic zones. Each zone provides an environment best suited for particular groups of plants.

The environments are designed to keep the plants healthy and also to display them to their best effect.

■ Glasshouses and climates

The point about conservatories or any glasshouse is that the 'climate' inside the glasshouse is controllable. There are various factors which may be varied to produce different climates. These are:

temperature

humidity

light levels

soil moisture content.

Other factors such as type of soil also affect the growth of plants. But the soil content doesn't usually vary from day to day.

By controlling these components the right way, the correct conditions for particular plants can be provided.

- ▲ Temperature – may be controlled by providing heating or opening ventilators.
- ▲ Humidity – the amount of moisture in the air may be varied by spraying or 'misting' with water.
- ▲ Light levels – may be lowered by shading, and raised by removing shades or providing artificial light.
- ▲ Soil moisture content – may be varied by watering.

■ Controlling climates – the old way

The controlling of the variables listed above can be a very labour intensive activity, especially in a large conservatory. Controlling temperature, humidity and light levels is done by opening and closing vents and blinds, by lowering or raising boiler output levels and by spraying.

Decisions about whether to open or close vents and blinds, use a spray etc. are taken as a result of consulting various **monitoring** devices, for example, a thermometer. If you consider this process you will realise that it involves someone consulting the various measuring devices and carrying out some activity at regular intervals. In the older houses this is done manually. These houses usually contain plants which all require a similar 'climate' and although time consuming, control is possible.

In the New Princess of Wales house, the job would be almost impossible to do manually because of the variety of 'climates' required.

■ Computerised control – the new way

The Princess of Wales house uses computers to help in the creation of the micro-climates required. This section describes the design of the **computer system** used and its use at Kew.

We spoke to Dr. John Woodhams, Assistant Curator of the Tropical Section at Kew, who gave us a description of the system.

"The house is divided into ten zones, each zone has a supervisor, a person in charge of the plants in that zone. Each zone has a set of ***sensors*** *and equipment to vary the climatic conditions. The controlling computer requests information from the sensors every two minutes for all zones. According to the information received from the sensors, the computer may decide to switch on the misting system, operate fans, open windows etc. The heating is an important element in the system and is, in fact, controlled by its own computer."*

The outline of the computer system is shown in Fig. 2.

As you can see from the diagram, each zone has its own separate set of **controllers**. These can be set individually, or from the central computer, via the keyboard. All zones require temperature control and humid zones also require humidity control.

Before going on to describe the system in detail, let's have a look at the equipment used in the system.

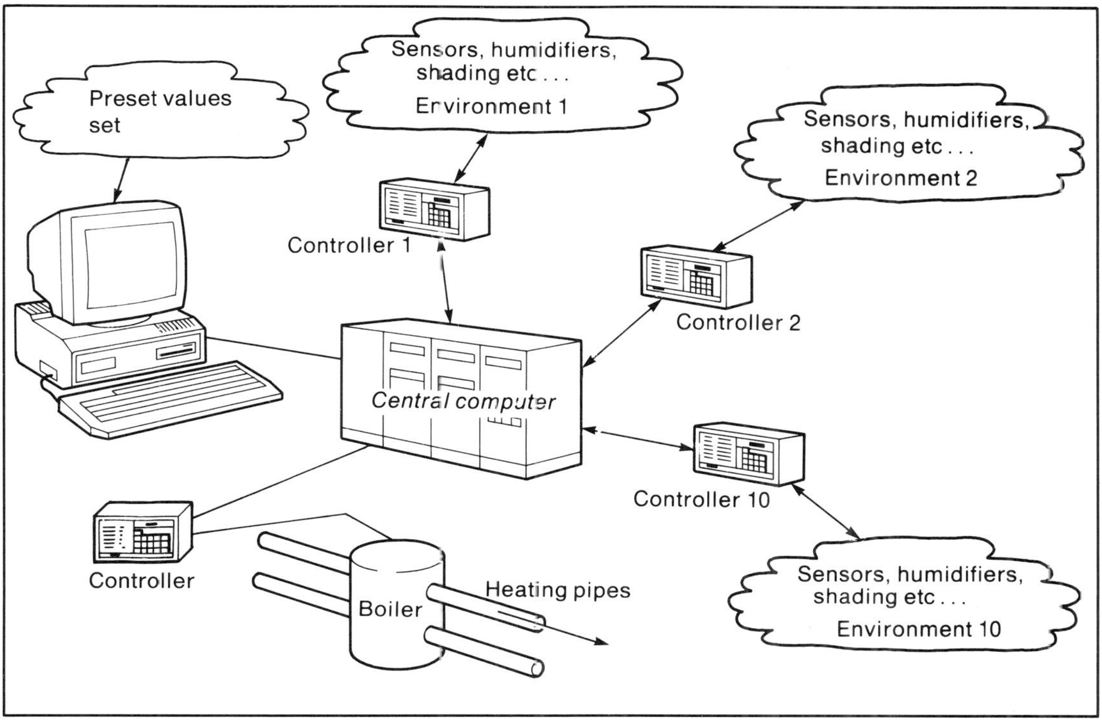

Figure 2 The outline control system

■ Climate control equipment

As was described earlier, climate can be changed by varying components such as temperature, humidity etc. The following set of pictures illustrate some equipment used in climate control.

The particular equipment used at Kew was supplied by a company called Climate Controls Ltd., who also supplied the computer system. As Dr. Woodhams said:

"We went for a commercially available ***package****, since the cost of getting our own system development would have been too high."*

Climate Controls Ltd. are based in Jersey where their systems are used in glasshouses for the commercial production of tomatoes and other salad products. This experience has made them experts in the development of climate control technology. Kew Gardens also uses equipment developed in Holland in some of the other glasshouses. Again, Holland is a big producer of plants under glass and the Dutch also have a lot of experience in developing and using computer control in glasshouses.

"So Kew went for tried and trusted technology and adapted it to our requirements, rather than involve the risk and expense of specially developed technology."

■ Using the system

Fig. 3 is a simple **printout** from the central controlling computer. There is a column of figures for each zone (seven out of the ten zones are shown). The bottom of the printout shows some figures which are measurements, taken from outside the conservatory, of weather factors which may affect the climate inside. At the top of the printout is the date and time at which values have been measured. Remember, the system accepts a new set of values every two minutes. Some of the values listed are **preset values**, that is, values entered by the supervisor to act as a **control**. Other values are direct readings from the monitoring devices, either in the zone or outside the conservatory.

Let's look at some of these values and what they represent.

First of all we can see that the values were obtained at 13.00 on Thursday 26th June, 1989. By looking at the bottom set of figures we can tell what the weather was generally like. The figures tell us the wind strength and direction, the temperature and the radiation levels. Before you get too worried – these figures are not measurements of nuclear fallout, but measurements of the sunlight available. The figures are obtained from **sensors** on the conservatory roof. Sunrise and sunset times are preset by the supervisor. These factors affect the control of the internal climate in the following way.

- *Wind speed and direction*

To reduce the temperature in a zone ventilators are opened. If the wind is blowing into a ventilator then it should not be opened as much as if the wind is not blowing into it.

- *Radiation*

Glass buildings obtain a lot of heat from outside by an effect known as solar gain. If the sun is shining, even hazily, the house will be heated by it. This could make the house too hot. Without some form of control, a glasshouse will become much hotter than the outside temperature. To control the temperature rise due to solar gain blinds are used to block out the sun's rays.

- *Sunrise and sunset*

The general requirements of the control system change at night. The solar gain factor disappears at night, therefore shading is irrelevant. Also some zones require very different night-time conditions. For example, the arid zone requires a very cold temperature compared with its daytime temperature, simulating desert conditions.

Measurements					Thursday	26/06/89	13:00	
Zones	A	B	C	D	E	F	G	
Night temp.	17.0	13.0	9.0	18.0	11.0	18.0	12.0	C
Clock temp.	21.0	15.0	15.0	20.0	12.0	20.0	12.0	C
Day temp.	24.0	17.0	17.0	21.0	15.0	25.0	18.0	C
Ventilation temp.	28.0	20.0	20.0	30.0	18.0	28.0	23.0	C
Indoor temp.	27.1	20.3	21.6	23.6	21.0	25.2	21.9	C
Humidity	74	71	39	92	74	83	87	%
Lower pipe temp.	25.6	20.8	21.2	25.2	23.1	41.8	23.1	C
Upper pipe temp.	53.3	53.5	54.1	53.1	53.1	54.1	54.0	C
Left vent	0	31	99	0	30	0	0	%
Right vent	0	0	99	0	20	0	0	%
Screen	0	0	0	0	0	0	0	%

Radiation	232	Wh/m2	Wind speed	5	m/s
Outdoor temp.	17.6	C	Wind direction	53	
Rain	OFF		Sunrise	4.03	clk
Radiation amount	629	Wh/m2	Sunset	20.19	clk

Figure 3 Control computer printout

Having looked at the factors measured outside the conservatory which may affect the individual zones, let's consider the individual zone settings and measurements. By the way, notice that the system could measure rainfall, but the supervisors at Kew choose not to.

■ Control in a zone

Let's look at the figures for one zone. Remember, the design of the system is such that the controlling values may be entered at a **distributed control** unit, or at the central computer. This printout is from the central computer.

The first four values in the column are all preset temperature.

- ▲ Night temperature – is the temperature the zone should be kept at during night-time.
- ▲ Day temperature – the temperature for daytime.
- ▲ Ventilation temperature – the temperature at which the vents in that zone should be opened to reduce the temperature.
- ▲ Clock temperature – needs a little more detailed explanation.

In very simple terms, daytime starts at sunrise and ends at sunset. However, as we know the change from night to day is more gradual. The system has preset day and night temperatures and these can be quite different. For instance, the third column, the arid zone, has a temperature difference of 8°C (Night temp. 9°C; Day temp. 17°C).

To suddenly demand that the boilers increase output at sunrise (4.03 am) would put a strain on them. Also, in daylight, heat will be gained from outside as the sun rises because of solar gain. To enable a smooth transition from night to day time temperature requirements, the clock temperature is a target temperature for the system during the transitional period.

The remainder of the values in the columns represent the readings from the various sensors. They represent the **current state** of the system, and may vary as they are **updated** every two minutes.

- ▲ Indoor temperature and humidity – the readings from sensors located in the zones.
- ▲ Lower and upper pipe temperature – the heating system provides heat at two heights in the conservatory. These values represent the temperatures of the heating pipes.
- ▲ Left and right vent – cooling is provided by opening vents located on either side of the house. These figures represent the percentage opening of these vents.
- ▲ Screen – cooling may also be achieved by increasing shading. The package allows for automatic shading. However, Kew operate the shades independent of the control system.

■ The user and the control system

By presetting values and monitoring the system state the computer system and its associated climate control equipment can provide the right environment for the plants. That is the simple objective. If the control system can achieve this without human intervention, then the computer could be left to run the conservatory on its own.

All that is required of the user is to set the **system objectives** by setting the presets correctly and leaving it at that. We asked Dr. Woodhams if that was how the system is used.

*"**W**ell, no, each zone supervisor has the ability to override decisions made by the computer. A special case is humidity versus temperature. If the temperature rises above the vent temperature the control system would open the vents. However, opening the vents reduces humidity because moist air escapes. This causes the humidifying system to increase output, but it may not be able to achieve target humidity."*

So how does the supervisor deal with this?

*"**T**he supervisor makes a decision based on assessing the relative importance of too high a temperature against too low humidity."*

So if the system starts to open the vents, he might close them again.

*"**Y**es, loss of humidity can be far more damaging to some plants than too high a temperature."*

Do the supervisors check that the control system is behaving according to expectations?

*"**T**he system produces printed reports every twelve hours. For example, we can get a graph of temperature against humidity for a given zone. By looking at these reports we can check that the system is keeping things within reasonable limits."*

Do you keep any long-term storage of this information?

*"**N**o. It is possible, by adding a disk drive to the computer to do that, but we don't. We use the system as a basic control system which we work with. We see it as helping us to provide the right environment, rather than expecting it to take **total control**."*

■ Computer or curator – who's in charge?

Through thinking about this question we can get a clearer understanding of the use of the control system at Kew. We can see that the control system is sophisticated and operates in a situation which is extremely delicate rather than dangerous. In a nuclear power station or chemicals factory loss of control may result in disaster. At Kew, loss of control may result in the loss of rare and valuable plants. That is still a disaster, but of a different order.

The use of a computer system at Kew allows the labour intensive activities of running a greenhouse to be automated. The control system is also, theoretically, capable of running the greenhouse on its own. The only demands it makes are that the correct presets are input and updated every so often. However, the system is not allowed to do this. The example of the temperature versus humidity is one where the user overrides the system.

We could ask: why is this so? Is it because the system is not sophisticated enough? Couldn't the designer have allowed for another sort of preset, linking temperature and humidity? Or would the curator always want to have the ability to finally be in control?

Questions

1 Compare the requirements of the control system at Kew with such systems in chemical plants. In what way are they similar and in what ways do they differ?

2 The system used at Kew is a commercially available package. What advantages does this give and what possible disadvantages have arisen?

3 Describe how a systems analyst might set about arriving at a system specification for a control system. Compare this with the same task for a data processing system.

Further information

Chapter 1 The Systems Cycle
Chapter 2 Systems Analysis and Design
Chapter 6 Computer Architecture
Chapter 7 Data Transfer and Communications
Chapter 8 Hardware Selection

CASE STUDY 3

The Datapost Parcels System

Datapost airplane

INTRODUCTION

The British Post Office is a very large organisation, split into two main business areas – Counters (the Post Offices where customers buy stamps, collect pensions, etc.) and Mails, which is divided into Letters and Parcels. The Parcels business delivers about 180 million parcels per year. Datapost is one of the Parcels services, handling about 10 million parcels per year, and it is constantly expanding.

Datapost is an Express Mails Service (EMS). Although it's more expensive than the ordinary postal service, companies use it because delivery is guaranteed by a certain time the same day or the next day. Also it is more secure as each parcel is checked through the stages of its journey.

This case study describes the development of a computerised system for tracking and tracing Datapost parcels. It illustrates the different stages of development of a large computer system (the **systems cycle**), the people involved and the benefits for the organisation.

THE DATAPOST SERVICE

We asked Mr. Smith, Datapost systems manager, to tell us more about Datapost.

*"**We** transport all sorts of items (except, in the interests of safety, live animals and dangerous or poisonous materials). For example, oil tankers at sea have to send engine oil samples back to the UK for inspection by the authorities – they use Datapost. So does a company which repairs cash card tills – we deliver spare parts to their engineers so that the repairs can be carried out quickly.*

You can phone for your parcel to be collected or you can take it to one of the Post Offices that accepts Datapost. There are 1165 acceptance points in the UK. The larger offices (about 300) deal with collecting and despatching the parcels and delivering them. There are also 17 Datapost network centres which are switching points for parcels en route.

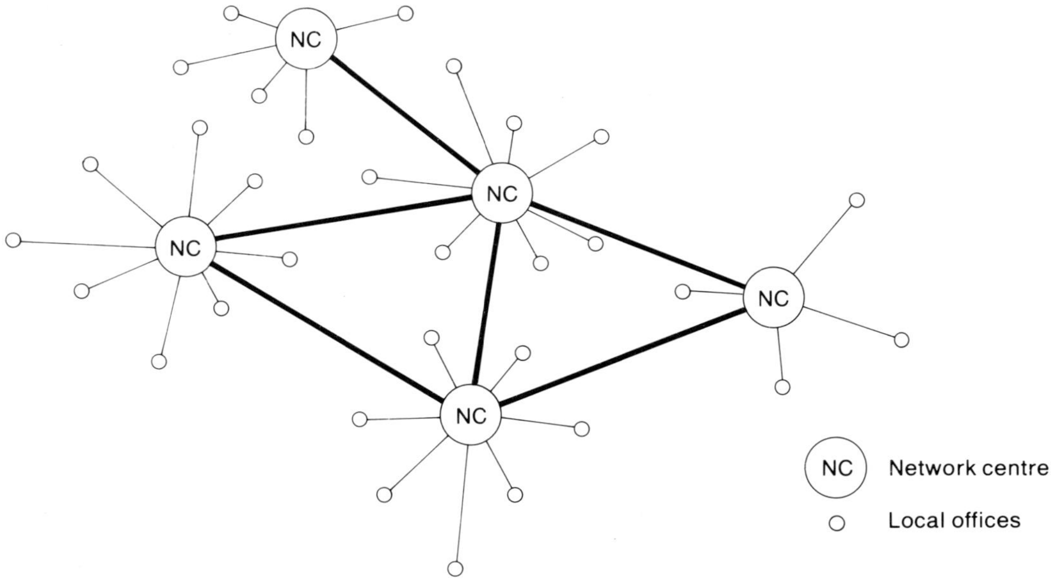

Figure 1 Datapost network configuration

Parcels are delivered everywhere, from Lands End to the Shetland Isles in the far North. There are other companies who deliver parcels but not many of them deliver to such remote places! We also have International Datapost which delivers door-to-door in over 100 countries throughout the world. As you can see, Datapost is a very large operation."

The need for a computerised system

Mr. Smith went on to explain why Datapost management had decided that a computerised system was required.

"The planning of routes for the delivery vans was already done by computer but recording of the parcels themselves was done manually. This worked well when we were delivering a smaller number of parcels, but as we expanded we had to computerise. We needed a computer system to help us to operate more efficiently, to help us with planning and budgeting. We wanted to expand the business and increase our share of the market (and thus our profits too!).

We wanted to minimise the paperwork – in the old manual system a lot of time was spent on it – so that the operators could get the parcels through more quickly. We also needed to be able to identify bottlenecks, so delays could be avoided.

As well as speeding up operations, we knew that the computer would be able to trace parcels quickly – doing this manually used to be very time consuming. For example, if a customer rings up to ask when their parcel will arrive the computer system knows where the parcel was last tracked, and so the people at the enquiry centre can estimate its time of arrival.

The computer also provides the customers with quicker proof of delivery, if they need it. Some companies want to know as soon as possible that their parcel has been delivered so that they can send out the bill to their client.

It's important for us (the management) to monitor the delivery system to make sure that it works efficiently and to plan for the future. We used to monitor by counting the number of parcels travelling through particular offices at certain times and by following a small sample of individual parcels from posting to destination, but this only provided us with a limited amount of information. The computer automatically monitors how quickly parcels are delivered etc.

We wanted the computer system to produce ***reports*** *and statistics promptly and regularly. For example, our marketing departments want statistics on the areas where customers are based and the areas where parcels are delivered so that they can target and monitor their advertising.*

We knew what we wanted the system to do and what we could afford to spend on it. It was then a matter of finding the best way of achieving it."

THE FEASIBILITY STUDY

A proposal for a computerised system was put forward and the Post Office management board agreed that the project should go ahead. We interviewed Jill Knight, a business **consultant** in the IT (Information Technology) department, who was involved in preparing the feasibility report.

"The Post Office has various systems running on its large ***mainframe*** *computers and numerous* ***minicomputers****. The IT department develops programs and maintains the computer systems for many departments in the Post Office.*

My job involves liaising with people who need computer systems and discussing how a computer system can help them to run their part of the business more effectively. The IT department also has ***systems analysts****,* ***programmers*** *and* ***computer operators****. I was one of a team investigating the feasibility of the new Datapost system they were proposing, to see how they could computerise and what the likely costs would be.*

We looked at several software packages on the market but there was nothing suitable for this particular job. So we decided on ***in-house*** *development, ie. the software would be written by our IT department.*

Barcoding *was the obvious choice for identifying parcels and recording them at points on their journey. There is already a standard international code for Express Mails Services for parcels sent abroad and rather than have two sets of codes, we kept with the international standard for all our deliveries. We didn't decide on the type of barcode equipment at this stage. We knew that there were a number of different types and that these would need to be thoroughly trialled before making a final decision."*

The barcode equipment simply reads the barcodes. What other **hardware** was needed?

"The mainframe at the Post Office Computer Centre would store and process the data. Each office would be connected to this computer by telephone lines, via a ***modem****.*

There was a lot of discussion about the ***configuration*** *of the equipment and the number of Datapost sites we were going to computerise. We knew that the 17 network centres where parcels were checked en route had to be computerised. We considered computerising all 1165 acceptance offices but decided this would be far too costly; also some of these offices only accepted small numbers of parcels. Therefore we recommended that the 300 offices where parcels were dispatched and delivered should be computerised.*

Each office needed barcode readers and decoders to record the parcels. Small offices only needed one reader but larger offices needed several. The readers and decoders would be connected to a local computer which would accept and validate the barcodes, transmit data to the central computer and receive lists of parcels shortly to arrive. A printer would be required to print the lists.

We estimated the costs and timescale for analysing requirements, designing and developing the software for the system, implementing it, purchasing and installing the equipment and training users. We knew that, with so many sites, installation of the equipment and user training could not be done all at once; it would need to be ***phased*** *and this would lengthen the timescale. We estimated that the whole project was likely to last three years, from initial planning to final operation, and the total costs would be around £5 million."*

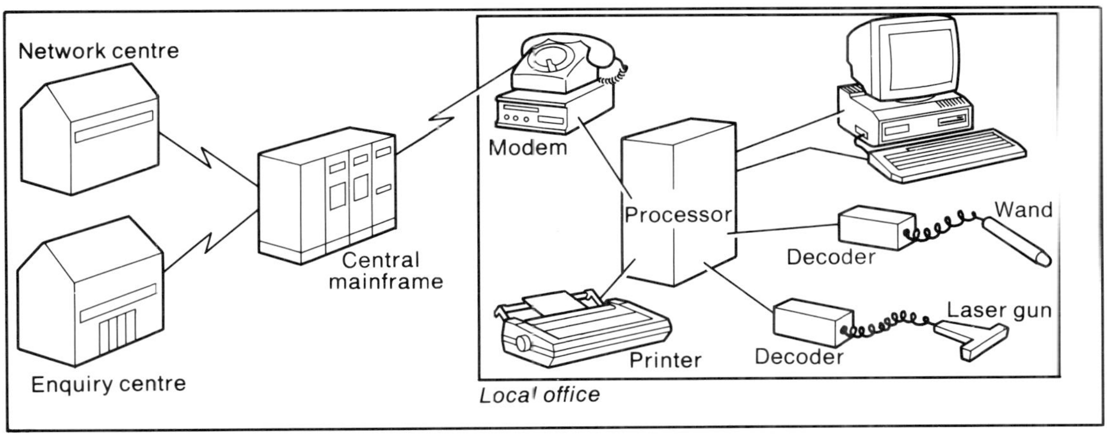

Figure 2 Datapost communication network

The results of the study and the recommendations were written in the **feasibility report**, which was presented to the Datapost director, Mr. Smith. Management accepted the report and gave the go-ahead for the next stage of the proposed system – the analysis.

Analysis – Investigating the System

Before deciding exactly how the new system should work, it was necessary to understand the operation of the manual system. The systems analysts interviewed users and observed the work practices, procedures and organisation of Datapost.

We talked to two systems analysts in the IT department. Jane Stevens has a degree in Business Studies and Computing and has been working for some years as an analyst. Bob Jones left school with few qualifications and started work as a computer operator. Since then he has attended several courses and has worked his way up through programming to systems analysis.

We asked Jane what she had found out about Datapost.

"Although I'd worked for the Post Office for several years I knew very little about Datapost – I'd not been involved with this particular business before. So the first step was to go and talk to the people who run Datapost – from the managers to the postmen and women who sort and deliver the parcels.

To explain how Datapost works let's follow a parcel containing urgent medical supplies on its journey from a company called Medicaid in Exeter to Linda Jones in Sheffield. The parcel's journey is shown in Fig. 4. Medicaid telephones Datapost who send a courier to collect the parcel. Medicaid fills in the Datapost label (Fig. 3) with their name and address, the date, the name and address of the recipient (Linda Jones) and Medicaid's account number. Medicaid, like many companies, have an account with Datapost. Our staff fill in the parcel weight and cost.

The courier takes Medicaid's parcel to a collection office nearby in Exeter where the parcels are bagged and distributed. The postman or woman reads the address on the parcel, decides which destination office it should go to and puts it into a bag labelled 'Sheffield'. (In fact the bag could be a container or even a lorry if there are lots of parcels!)

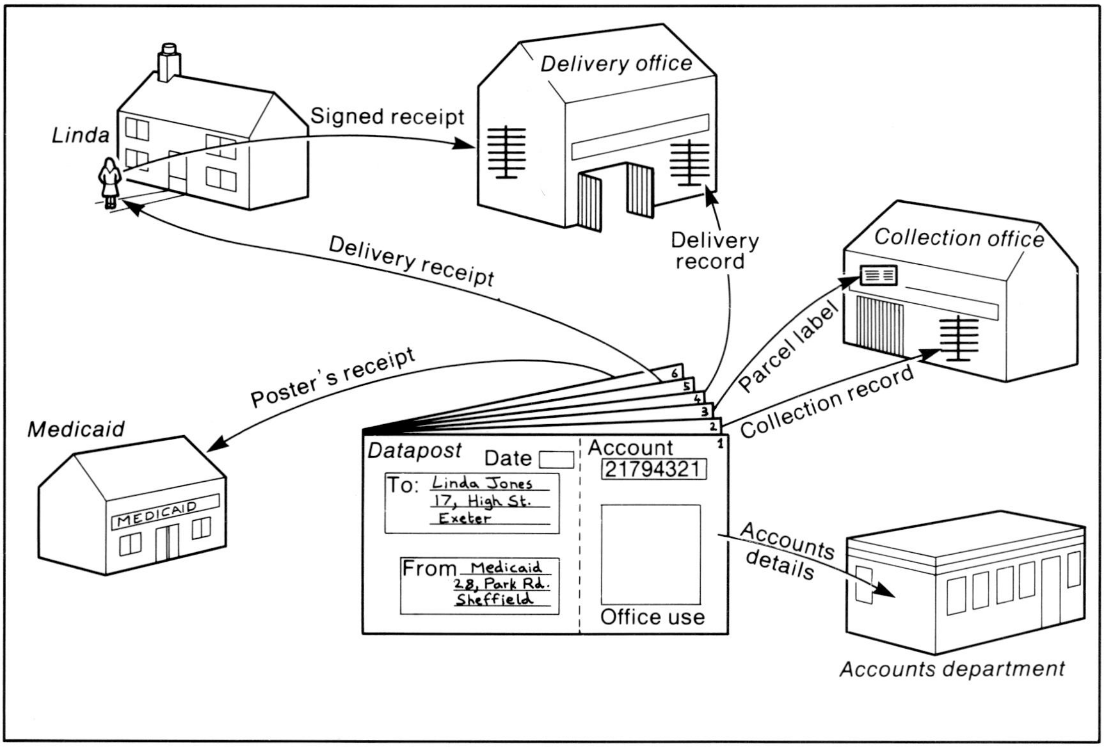

Figure 3 What happens to a docket set?

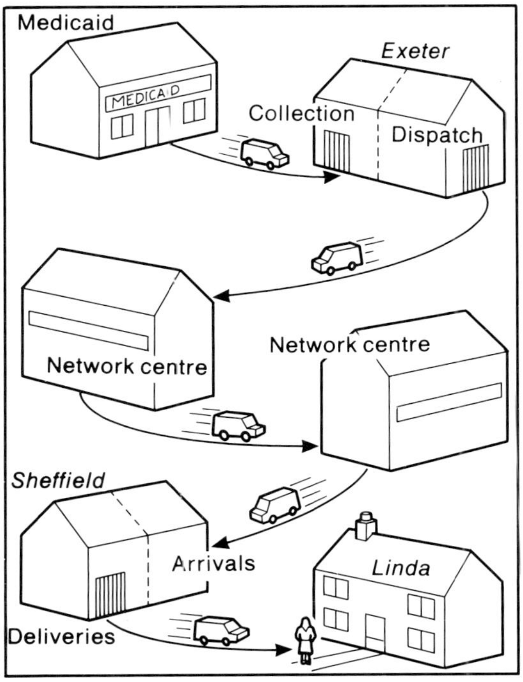

Figure 4 Collection and delivery of Linda's parcel

From the collection office, the bags are taken to a network centre and from there to the network centre nearest to the parcel's destination. From the network centre, the bag goes to the local delivery office and the parcels are delivered. Linda, the recipient, signs to say she has received her parcel and the date and time are recorded. If there is no-one to receive the parcel, the Datapost courier takes it back to the office and it has to be included in the next delivery."

How do they keep a record of each parcel?

"There are six copies of the label (we call it a 'docket set'). One copy goes to the accounts department so that they can send a bill to the customer (Medicaid). One copy stays at the collection office. The customer (Medicaid) gets a copy as a receipt for the parcel. The three remaining copies stay with the parcel; one is the label to say where the parcel is going, one is for the delivery office records and the last one is signed by the person who receives the parcel.

Under the old system, a list of items in each bag was handwritten and put in the bag. A list of bags was written out for the driver. When the bags were emptied at the delivery office, the parcels were recorded in the delivery book, delivered to the recipient and noted as 'delivered' or 'attempted delivery'. The signed docket slips for delivered parcels were then bundled together and checked against the delivery office record."

What were the problems with this manual system?

"Firstly, processing all the paperwork was very time consuming and slowed operations down. Secondly, the managers said they weren't getting the information they needed fast enough.

The docket set provided a record of the parcel's collection and delivery, but there was no check on the bags of parcels as they passed through the network centres en route for their destination; if a bag went astray it was difficult to trace."

ANALYSIS – SPECIFYING THE NEW SYSTEM

The analysts had to decide what the new computer system would do and how it would be different from the manual system. This involved specifying requirements, data and procedures. Bob explained:

"Firstly, I'll summarise the main requirements of the new system:

- *store a parcel's details*
- *keep a record of where each parcel is in the network*
- *send a delivery office a list of parcels due to arrive*
- *handle customer enquiries (when was the parcel sent, has it been delivered, when will it arrive, etc.)*
- *trace a parcel and say where it was last tracked*
- *report on average parcel delivery times*
- *report on bags or parcels which go astray*
- *report on the number of parcels handled at each office at various times of day*
- *report on parcels business in various categories (eg. how many parcels collected in each location).*

To satisfy these requirements the main operational procedures of Datapost (ie. collection, distribution and delivery) did not need to be altered. The difference was the recording of parcels and bags of parcels on the computer system; they must be recorded at each stage of their journey. We'd already decided that parcel labels should be barcoded using the international standard. Bags would also have a barcoded label showing their destination. (If we know where each bag is we know where the parcels in it are.)

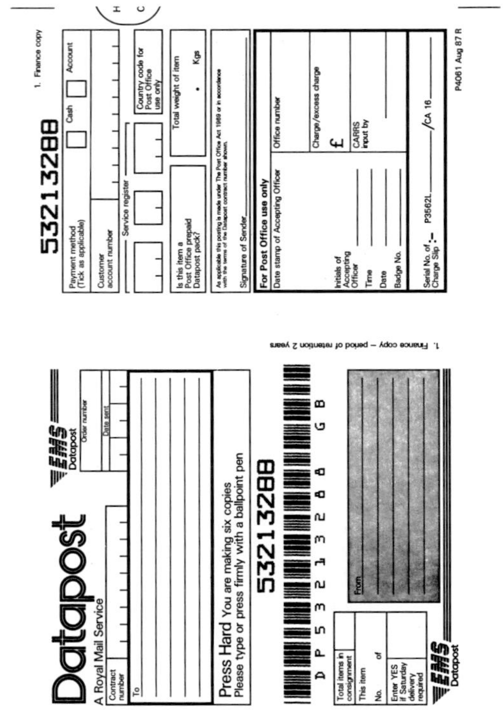

Datapost label

To handle customer enquiries, we need a central telephone service. Staff enter the parcel identification number (supplied by the customer from their receipt) and the system tells them whether the parcel has been delivered, is an 'attempted delivery' or is still in transit.''

Bob went on to explain the **data analysis** and how they specified the data and procedures required for the computer system:

*''**We** identified the things we needed to store data about on the computer (eg. parcels, routes, collection and delivery offices) and drew diagrams to show the relationships between these. Then we listed the items of data needed for each thing (eg. for a parcel: sender name and address, recipient name and address, time of posting, etc.).*

We specified the procedures staff should follow for recording bags and parcels and what the staff should do when errors occur (parcels off route, torn parcel label, etc.). We discussed with management the reports they wanted and the benefits of each one – it's not worth the computer producing a report if there's no benefit. Also a list was made of types of queries that customers would be likely to make and that the system should be able to answer.

*This stage took a long time because we consulted people as we went along and there was a lot of cross-checking to do. We finally put the information together in a **requirements report** for management. This formed the basis for the next stages of development.''*

SELECTING EQUIPMENT

The feasibility report outlined the hardware required but there remained work to be done on equipment selection. Barcodes can be read by **laser readers** or **wands** and different models were available. There were also plenty of microcomputers and minicomputers to choose from. A number of companies **tendered** for the equipment and a group of Datapost managers, analysts and technical staff selected the most suitable and cost-effective equipment.

Before making a final decision, equipment trials took place to ensure that the equipment would do the job required. The postmen and women were asked to use the equipment and give their opinion of its ease of use. For example, they preferred a lighter, smaller laser gun to a heavier one. They liked certain keypads because the keys were easier to press when wearing gloves. The colours on the decoder keypad were altered because red wasn't easily visible in darker areas.

DESIGNING THE NEW SYSTEM

Having specified what the system should do and what data should be stored, the systems analysts' next task was to design the programs and the **user interface**. Bob explained:

*''**The** design stage involved writing **program specifications**, which consisted of detailed descriptions of each process. Some of this work had been done during the analysis stage and we simply added the detail, but there were some extra procedures we hadn't thought of. It's always like that – however careful you are with the analysis, there's always something you didn't think of!*

Another important job was to design all the input and output screens for the users and the layout of the reports the system had to produce. The designs were discussed with the users – after all they're the ones who have to use the system when it's completed.''

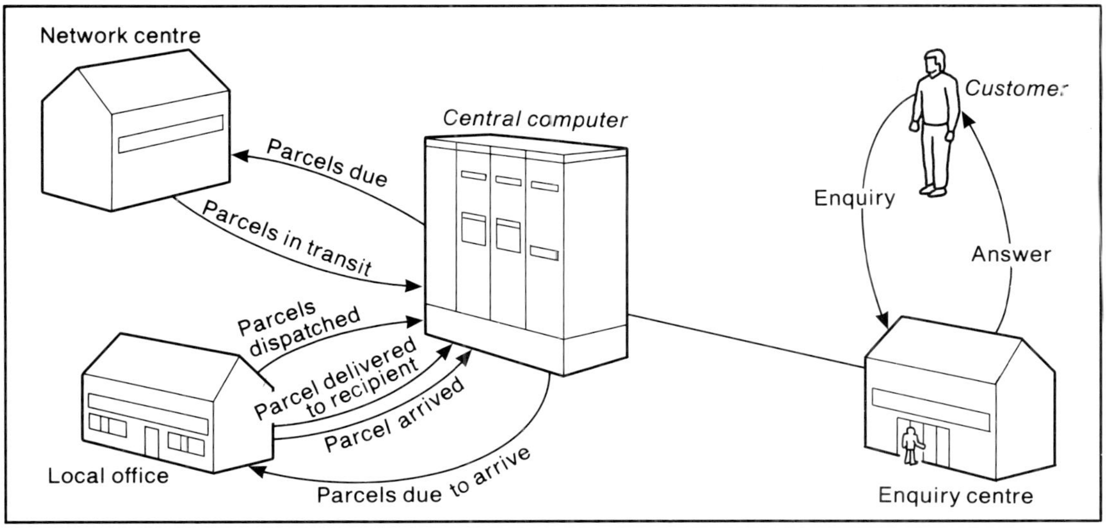

Figure 5 Data flows

The new system

How does the new system work?

"Let's start with bagging the parcels. The operator has an identification (id) card which he 'swipes' with the wand or 'fires' the laser gun at. When the local computer has accepted his id, he can start. He presses a function key on the decoder keypad to indicate that a new bag is to be filled and to record each parcel put in that bag. He can use the keypad to manually record a barcode that can't be read due to a torn label; screwed up labels are OK – they can be read if they're flattened.

The local computer keeps track of which parcels have been put in which bag. After bagging up the parcels for a particular destination, it prints a dispatch note which goes with the bags on their journey.

Once the dispatch note has been printed, the data is automatically sent to the mainframe computer which stores it. When the data has been received from all the offices (usually about 11 pm) the mainframe starts processing it. It works out which bags (and therefore which parcels) are going on which routes. It then produces a list of parcels due to arrive at each office next day and transmits this data to the local offices. The local computer stores the information and the manager uses it to plan the work for the day.

Bags are automatically checked at the network centres by barcoding them in and out. If any bags have been put on the wrong van, they are detected; the computer recognises they are off route. When bags arrive at their final destination they are again recorded and automatically checked against the local computer's list of expected arrivals (see Fig. 5).

When the parcel has been delivered, the postman or woman returns the docket copy, signed by the recipient, and the delivery is recorded using the barcode on the docket slip. The recipient's name has to be typed in, with the time of delivery.

Data about parcels arriving and parcels delivered to recipients is transmitted to the mainframe so that it has an up-to-date picture of what has happened to every parcel in the system.

As you can see, the local computer keeps records of the parcels it has handled, while the mainframe collates all the data it receives from local offices to provide a complete picture of what has happened to each parcel."

Implementing, testing and installing the new system

All the information from the design stage was given to a team of programmers in the Post Office IT department. We spoke to Alison Taylor, one of the team, about the program development.

*"We use a **database package** which runs on our **mainframe** computer. I've helped develop several systems using the package so I know it pretty well. We write programs in **COBOL** and we also use a database language called **SQL** to access the database.*

Programs were also needed for the local computers for checking the barcodes, producing despatch notes, sending data to the mainframe, receiving lists of parcels due to arrive and recording deliveries. These programs were written in a different language called ***C****."*

We asked Alison about the testing of the system they had developed and how it was installed:

"The system consists of many programs, which we tested individually and gradually linked together for testing, using a set of ***test data*** *that we had generated on the mainframe. The local computer programs were tested separately. We then linked a local computer to the mainframe and tested the programs that transmitted data between the two machines.*

The hardware and software were installed in a few local offices to start with and the people there were trained. The system ran for a trial period and as a result some minor modifications were made, for example, to the format of reports produced or screen messages that weren't quite clear to the operators.

Don't forget that at this stage the system was not complete; it only recorded a small number of parcels passing through the trial offices. As more offices started to use the system, we monitored its performance. Even if the final capacity (ie. number of parcels) doubled, the response time for recording each parcel should not be noticeably different.

With so many offices the installation and training was a major job. The most we could cope with was six offices per week. As soon as the installers had set up and tested the hardware and software in an office, the local trainer would train the postmen and women to use the barcode readers and the managers to use the local computer to get daily reports and information.

A help desk was set up to refer problems to the relevant experts. All problems were logged and analysed to see whether they were caused by hardware faults or inadequate training or whether the system needed to be changed. I'm pleased to say that everything went quite smoothly except for a little bug in the local computer software which took us some time to figure out – not my fault of course!

Eventually the system was fully operational. My role then changed and I moved on to supporting the system and adding enhancements."

Summary

We asked Mr. Smith, Datapost systems manager, to tell us about the new system.

"The main benefit is that our operation is far more efficient and as a result we are able to offer our customers a better service. Management at all levels use the information provided by the computer to identify areas where they can make cost savings and to plan and budget more effectively.

Our network planners, who decide on new routes for transporting parcels, use the computer to model alternative routes and associated problems – for example they can simulate what happens if there is delay due to fog at Luton Airport and find alternative routes.

Of course, development does not stop here. We will always be looking at ways of improving the Datapost service."

Questions

1 Suppose that Linda's parcel doesn't arrive. Eventually Linda rings Medicaid who say they have sent the parcel via Datapost.
(a) What might have caused Linda's parcel to be misdirected?
(b) Explain how Datapost might have traced the parcel using the old manual system.
(c) Suggest how the new computer system might deal with Linda's parcel and how it would trace the parcel.

2 According to Jill, barcoding was the 'obvious choice' for data collection. Explain why she said this. What other data collection methods might have been considered? List the advantages and disadvantages of each and say why these would not be suitable for Datapost.

3 Many people are involved in developing, operating, maintaining and using a large computer system such as the one used by Datapost. Make a list of these people. Describe, briefly, their jobs and the skills they require.

Further information

Chapter 1 The Systems Cycle
Chapter 2 Systems Analysis and Design
Chapter 8 Hardware Selection

Since the time of writing this Case Study, the Royal Mail Parcels division has now been relaunched as Parcelforce.

CASE STUDY 4

Supermarket Stock Control

Old Sainsburys' store

INTRODUCTION

Sainsburys is one of the largest companies in the UK and Britain's largest food retailer. Rapid development has placed increased reliance on their computer systems and the staff who develop and run them. This case study looks at Sainsburys' modern computer systems and how they benefit both the company and their customers.

Before describing the modern computer systems, we will briefly look at the gradual introduction of computers into large supermarkets and stores.

In Sainsburys' first shop, descriptions of items for sale, prices and number in stock would have probably been written in a book. A regular stock count would tell the manager how many of each item to buy from the suppliers. Many small shops still operate this way. Someone goes round the shelves, counts the stock and writes down the orders.

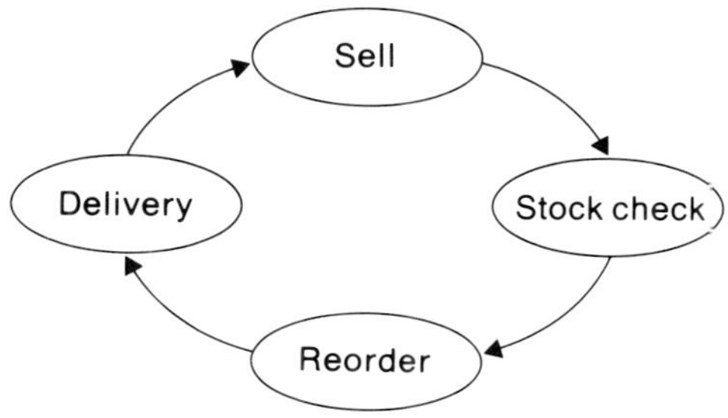

Figure 1 The ordering cycle

Tills of various types have been developed to keep a record of the money taken for each item; initially this was on a paper roll and later electronically. Amounts can be totalled and the cash in the till checked against the total. Some tills have special keys to record the category of each item sold (eg. fresh produce, drinks, groceries, household) or, in a department store to record the individual department, so that the manager has a breakdown of the money taken for each type of goods. However, the cash register receipts only tell the manager the prices and category of what is sold, not exactly which items have been sold.

In the 1970's, chain stores and supermarkets were installing large **mainframe** computers at their head offices, to help with stock control, accounts, payroll, etc. Branches did not have their own computers, all data was processed centrally. However, they could communicate with the central computer via a **modem**, for example to transmit how much money the branch had taken each day.

The link with the central computer also helped to speed up the ordering process and the following system is used in some stores (see Fig. 2 overleaf).

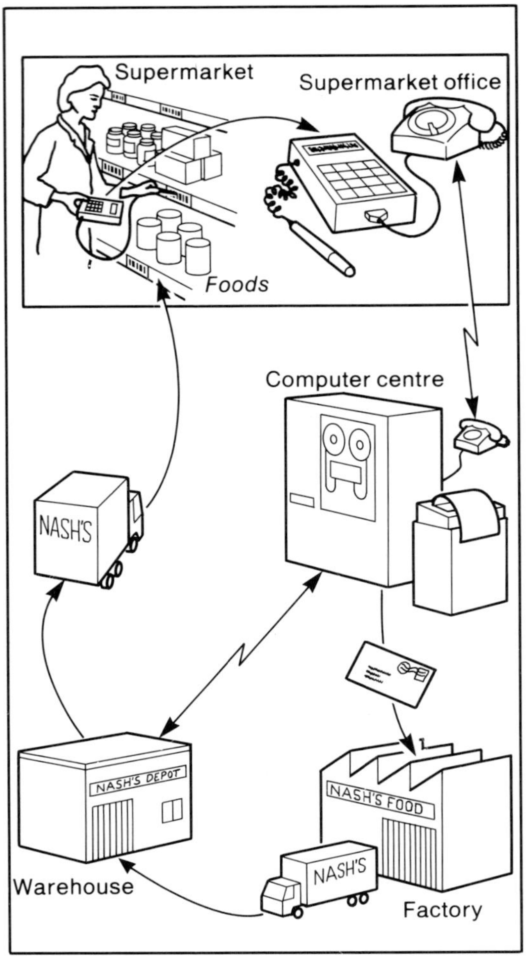

Figure 2 Ordering via a central computer

- Staff go round the store with a hand held data recorder, counting the stock and entering their orders.
- The recorder is then connected to the modem and the order transmitted to the central computer.
- The computer processes the order and transmits instructions to the warehouse to deliver the goods to the local branch.

Counting stock manually is very time consuming, particularly in a large store, and this delays the ordering. The alternative is to record each item sold and subtract it from the number in stock. Reordering can then be done automatically. However, the method of recording items sold must be fast and accurate.

Many chain shops, particularly clothes shops, use a **Kimball tag** system, where part of the label is detached from the item when it is sold. The tags are sent to the central office where they are fed into the central computer. This **offline** process does not require branches to have their own computers. (Chapter 8 discusses these systems in more detail). However, tag systems are impractical for food shops.

The next stage of development was to record each item directly at the point of sale. To do this an **electronic point-of-sale (EPOS) terminal** with a **magnetic stripe** or **barcode** reader is required to record the item. Most supermarkets use **laser scanners** at the checkouts. Each branch store also needs its own computer to store the data from the terminals and to keep track of its stock. This local computer transmits data to the central computer.

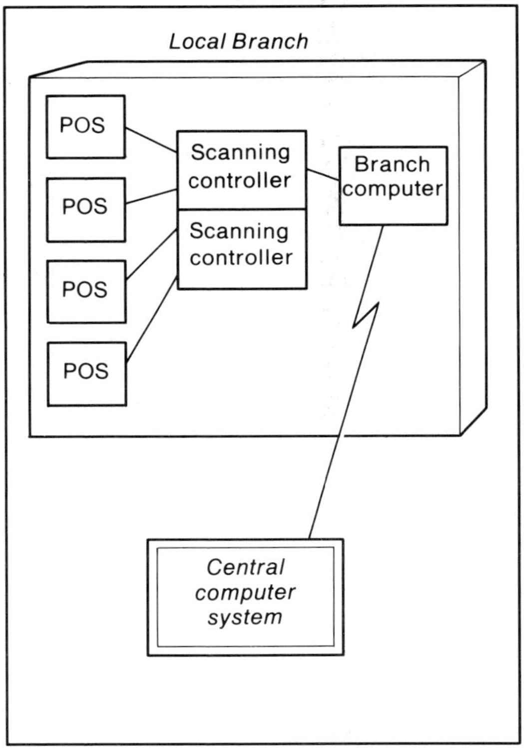

Figure 3 An EPOS system

An international barcoding system

Each product for sale must have a unique identifying number. Different sizes and colours all need a separate number. Manufacturers, wholesalers and retailers need to communicate with each other about their products (orders, invoices, deliveries, sales and market research).

Therefore they need a common numbering system. To coordinate this, there is an organisation called the Article Numbering Association (ANA) which allocates the numbers used on a wide range of goods including foods, books, records, pharmaceuticals and DIY products. Many companies, both retailers and manufacturers, are members of the ANA. Members include well known names such as Tesco, Boots, EMI, ICI, Unilever, W.H. Smith and Sainsburys.

There is an international ANA to coordinate numbering in different countries. They chose barcoding as being the best labelling system for products. Barcoding is reliable and cheap and can be produced by any normal printing process. Barcodes are printed on the labels by the manufacturer or supplier of the item. Over 98% of grocery items and over 50% of general merchandise are now barcoded.

Have a look at the barcodes on tins and packets in your kitchen cupboards.

Systems to support business needs

Sainsburys has had large mainframe computers for some time. All processing used to be carried out centrally, with orders sent over the telephone line from small handsets in the stores. Although at the time this system was considered to be quite advanced, Sainsburys were looking for something better. In 1982–3, they decided to install computers in the branches and trials took place in six stores, using ICL System 25 minicomputers. The trials were very successful and gradually minicomputer systems were installed at all branches.

Once each branch had a computer, linked to the central computer, the next step was the introduction of laser scanning systems. Sainsburys installed their first scanning system in 1980. Trials of various types of equipment took place and in 1984 the company decided to proceed with a mass installation programme using ICL equipment.

There are about 500 staff working in the data processing division, designing and developing new systems, maintaining and improving current systems and operating the systems. We spoke to Jane, a senior project manager who has worked for the company for several years and Brian, a senior project manager in charge of the branch computer systems. First Jane told us about Sainsburys' main computer systems.

*"We have two major data processing centres employing some of the most powerful equipment installed in the UK. The mainframe computers in these centres are linked to **minicomputers** in the stores (the branches) and the warehouses are **online** to the central mainframes too. The computer centres work 24 hours a day, seven days a week.*

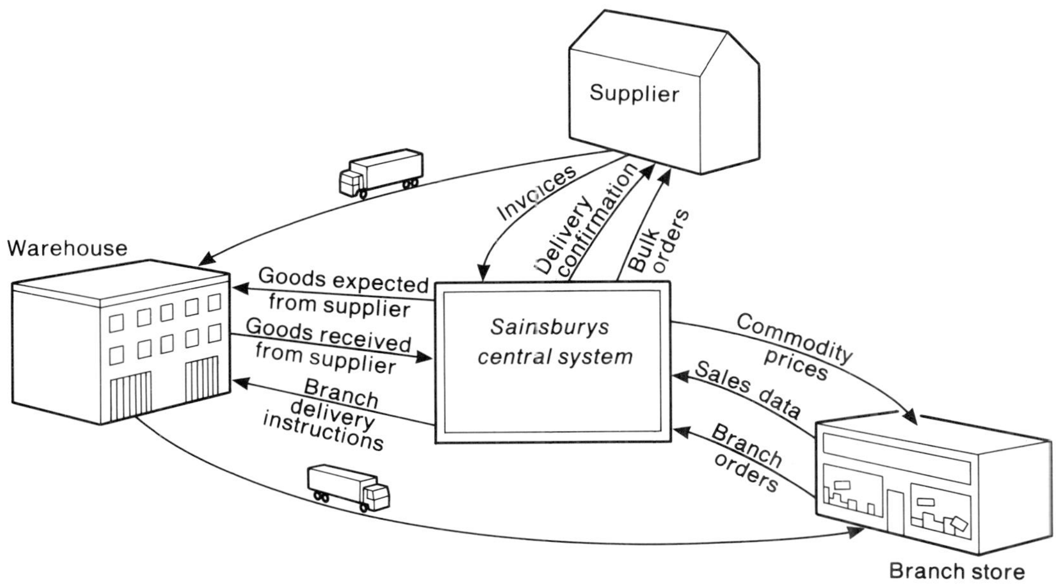

Figure 4 Sainsburys' network

At the computer centres, there are several systems.

- *Our central database system supports all other systems with facts about products, depots, suppliers and branches.*
- *The purchasing system puts our buyers into contact with suppliers for ordering queries, maintaining delivery schedules and predicting the demand for products.*
- *The warehousing system helps to manage warehouse space effectively.*
- *The branch ordering system enables branches to place orders for delivery the following day.*
- *The* ***Electronic Data Interchange (EDI)*** *system enables us to transmit orders to our suppliers and to receive electronic invoices.*
- *The payroll systems handle the wages of over 80 000 staff.*
- *Management information and accounting systems help to administer the company and to plan ahead.''*

THE BRANCH SYSTEM

■ Configuration

We asked Brian to describe the computer system used in the branch stores.

"Each Sainsburys branch has three mini-computers (Fig. 5). The ICL System 25 stores the current prices and descriptions of all the products we sell (we call them commodities) and it decides the orders for the next day. The other two computers (DRS) are linked via a ***high speed interface*** *to the point-of-sale tills. These two computers are identical and provide* ***backup*** *for each other. The software system they run is called the General Merchandising System (GMS) which was provided with the computers by ICL.''*

What is backup and why is it needed?

"Imagine if we only had one computer in a branch and it breaks down. That store couldn't operate because the computer stores all the prices, etc. So we have two computers in each branch, both storing all the information. If one breaks down the other one can take over.''

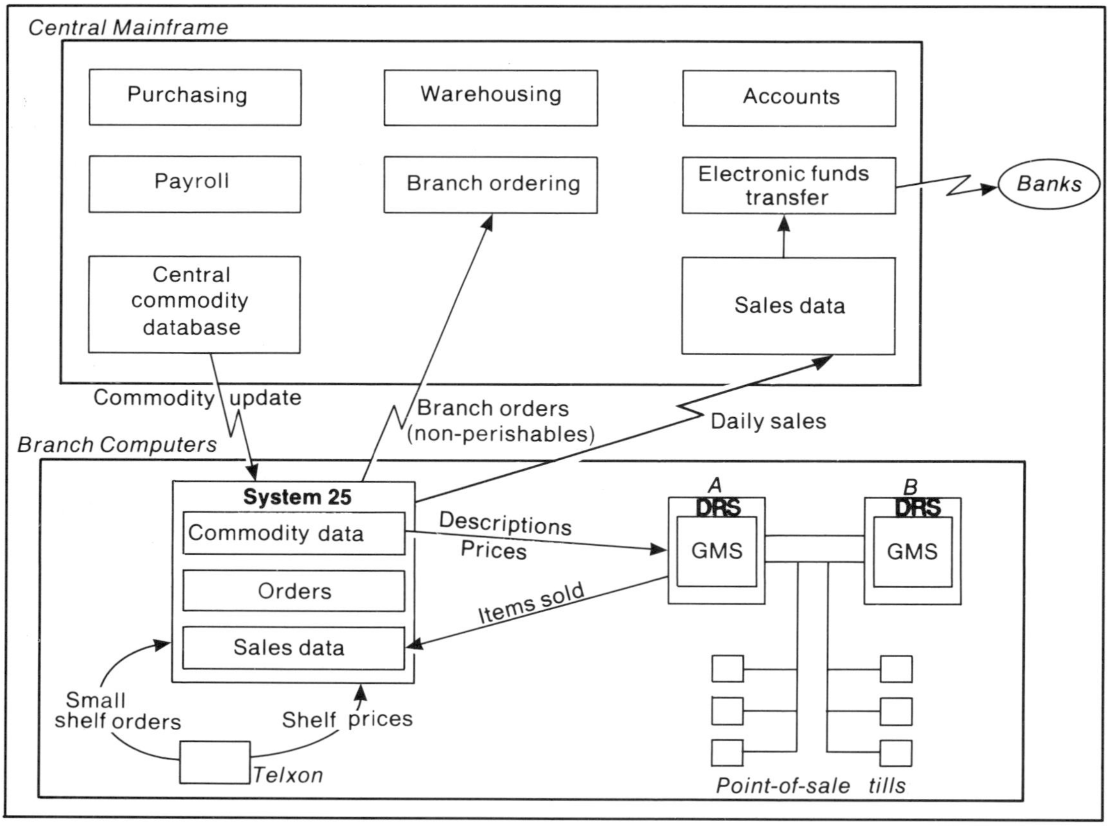

Figure 5 The branch system

Scanner

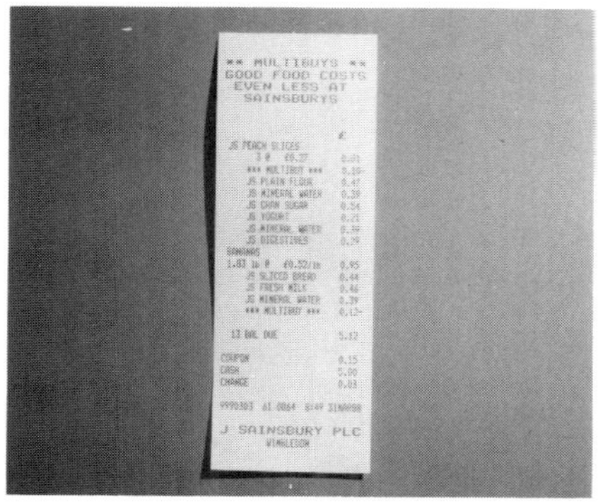

Multibuy receipt

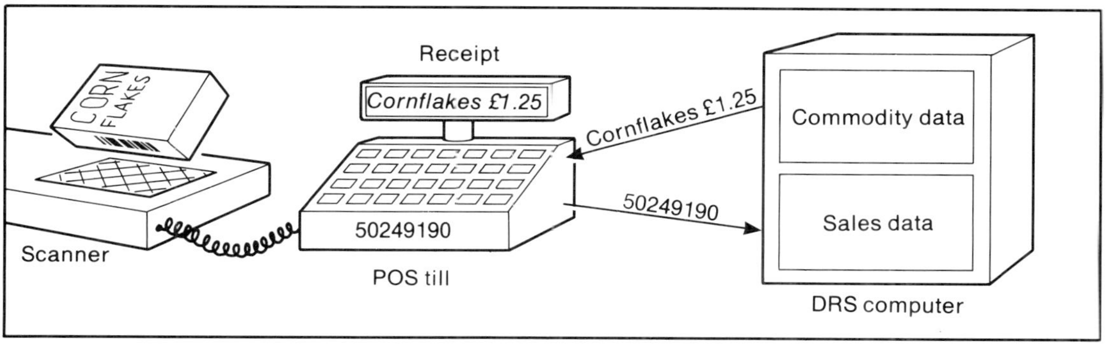

Figure 6 Scanner and data recorder

The point-of-sale terminal (so called because it captures data about products at the point where they are sold) has a laser scanner, an electronic till and a **microchip** which communicates with the branch computer.

■ Prices and point-of-sale

Brian explained how the system works.

*"**L**et's look at what happens in a typical day. Overnight the mainframe sends the updated commodity prices and descriptions to the System 25 computer in each branch. In the morning, the staff have to make sure that their shelf edge prices match the ones sent. They use a small handheld data entry device (Telxon) and go round the store, entering shelf edge prices. These are compared with the central prices. It's important to ensure that what is displayed is what the customer will get charged. The store manager can change the price of a commodity locally on the DRS computer, for example, if a mistake has been made in the central price. Checks are incorporated in the computer program so that the price can't be changed by more than so many percent. Customers would not like to be charged £12 for something costing £1.20.*

When you buy an article at the checkout the barcode is read by the scanner and the article number is sent to the DRS computer. It looks up the price and description of the article and sends these back to the till, where they are printed on your receipt. The DRS also stores the article number to record the sale and adds the price to a total. Finally, the total amount is printed on your receipt. The details of your purchases are stored on both computers at this point, for backup, as I explained just before. (See Fig. 6.)

Multibuy, a special discount on selected multiple purchases, is a new benefit to customers which Sainsburys has introduced through scanning. The appropriate discount is calculated automatically whenever the correct number of items has been scanned. The receipt shows how this works for two products – mineral water and canned peach slices.

At the end of the day, details of the sales (how many of each article) are sent from the DRS computer to the System 25 computer so that it knows how many of each article it must order for the branch." (See Fig. 5.)

■ Branch ordering

Fig. 4 and Fig. 5 show orders being sent from the branch to the centre. How is this done and how do they know how many of each item to order?

"Orders for non-perishable commodities are automatically sent from the branch System 25 computer to the central computer in the evening. Most of these commodities are stored in the stock room at the back of the shop and the orders are worked out by the computer, based on what the branch should have in stock and what was sold during the day. For example, if the branch has 400 tins of beans in stock at the start of the day, sells 150 tins and has a normal stock level of 500, it will need to order 250 tins.

Goods that are kept in very small quantities are stored on the shelves, not in the stock room. These are ordered by the staff using the Telxon data recorder.

Perishable goods are ordered centrally, and the store is informed of what it will receive, based on what it usually sells. This is done via a terminal linked directly to the central mainframe. The branch manager can request a change to what they've been allocated if necessary."

Presumably these orders are delivered the next day. Do stores sometimes run out of certain items?

"That can happen if a delivery is late or if customers buy more than usual of the item in question. It's always a delicate balance between holding minimum stocks (to save space and storage costs) and still having enough on the shelves to satisfy demand. The business managers are responsible for making these sorts of decisions."

THE CENTRAL SYSTEM

■ Central ordering

Presumably the central system has to be very powerful to coordinate all of these branch systems?

"Yes. The scanning equipment is what the customer sees. But behind the scenes there is a lot more. We have very advanced warehousing, ordering and delivery systems. They have to be able to supply goods quickly to the branches. Having collected all the branch orders, the system sorts and totals them. It then sends the bulk orders to the manufacturers or suppliers, who send back the goods and invoices requesting payment."

To improve the efficiency of such exchanges of information, the ANA set up standard formats for documents such as orders and invoices. It also sets up standard ways of communicating data between manufacturers, wholesalers and retailers; these standards are called Tradacoms.

Many of the large suppliers are linked to a network called Tradanet, which uses the Tradacoms standards. It's rather like an electronic postal service; users submit data with an address and Tradanet routes the data to the recipient's electronic mailbox. This is the Electronic Data Interchange which we mentioned earlier.

Sainsburys sends its orders and delivery instructions to the Tradanet computer which sends each one to the relevant supplier. (Suppliers who aren't on Tradanet have to be contacted by phone.) The supplier then delivers the products to the Sainsburys warehouse as requested. Finally the suppliers send their invoices electronically through Tradanet to Sainsburys.

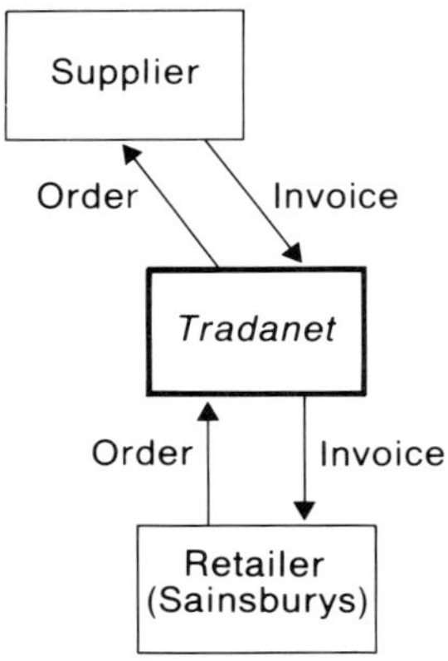

Figure 7 Tradanet

■ Warehouse deliveries

So the goods are delivered the next day?

"Yes. Some goods are delivered directly to the branch that ordered them, but most goods are delivered to the branch from the nearest warehouse. If the warehouse has transport problems or it doesn't have the stock to supply the branch, the delivery request can be rerouted to a different warehouse. This is done using the distribution system on the central computer.

Each warehouse is informed of what goods it should expect from the supplier and when the goods are delivered, they are recorded on the computer. The computer automatically checks the delivery with the original order.

At head office we have a microcomputer system called Spaceman which plans where in each warehouse goods should be stored, according to the space available and the ordering and delivery cycle. Shelf space is planned graphically on screen, using colours and shapes to represent shelves and goods."

THE BENEFITS OF THE SYSTEM

■ Benefits for the customer

We discussed with Brian the benefits of the new computer systems. From our point of view, as customers, we could see some of the benefits of the scanning system. These are as follows.

- The customer gets faster service at the checkout because the operator doesn't have to key in the price of each item. Moving items across the scanner is quick and easy. So queues move more quickly.
- Scanning also increases checkout accuracy because there are no keying mistakes. Prices at the checkout come from the branch computer.
- The itemised receipt is very useful to customers to see what they have bought and the price of each item.
- Special offers such as Multibuy are available. These aren't possible without a scanning system and give Sainsburys an advantage over competitors.
- Produce weighing is incorporated at the checkout, saving time.
- A greater variety of goods can be on display.

■ Benefits for the retailer

We asked Brian what are the benefits for Sainsburys.

"Checkout operations are more efficient because the price of each item doesn't need to be keyed in. They are faster and less error-prone. So customers don't have to queue for as long. Also, because the computer records every item which passes through each till, we can monitor the performance of checkout operators.

Prices are easily updated on the central computer and fed to the branches daily. All the branch has to do is to check its shelf edge prices. There is no longer any need to price each item separately. This saves a great deal of time and labour costs.

Prices can be changed more easily than under the old system, where price labels had to be stuck on every single tin or packet.

Our stock control is more efficient. Because the computer records every item sold, ordering is done automatically and promptly, we don't have to wait for someone to count the stock. Also our online ordering systems are fast. Therefore we can keep the minimum levels of stock, saving money and space.

Now that all items are recorded, we know exactly what has been sold in each branch and the time it was sold. Such information is useful to buyers and management. For example, it helps our buyers to track new products to see if they are selling well and to measure the impact of special promotions. They can also react more quickly to seasonal or unexpected demands. Local managers can see the effects of reorganising their store plan. Sales figures for certain times (eg. Friday evening) may help the manager to ensure that shelves are well stocked with popular goods at that time."

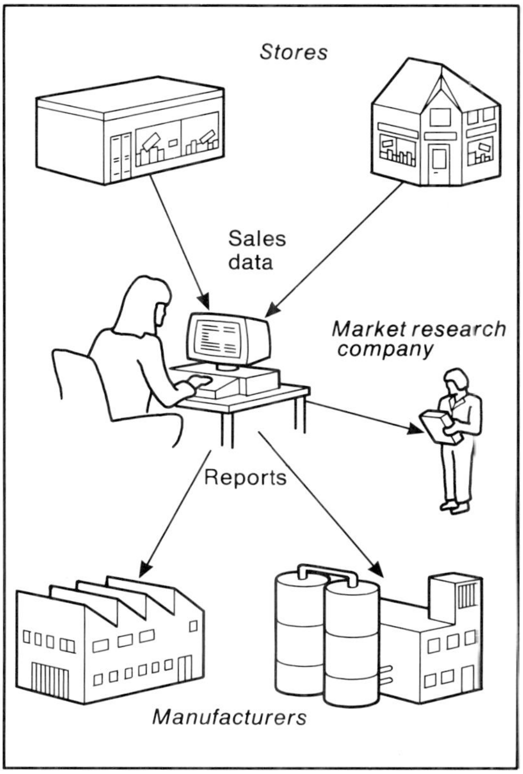

Figure 8 Market research

■ **Benefits for the manufacturer**

"Retailers like Sainsburys are now able to provide accurate, detailed sales data about individual items and when and where they were sold. This helps the manufacturer to refine the product and to package it and advertise it more successfully." *(see Fig. 8.)*

Looking to the future

We asked Jane about the difficulties involved in this automation project and the future of EPOS systems.

"The development and installation of sophisticated scanning systems is very costly. It has taken us years to get all of our 286 stores equipped. With perhaps 300 or 400 staff working in a store, training everyone to use new equipment and planning how to switch on the operation is a demanding task.

However many companies like Sainsburys consider it to be worthwhile, both financially and because it provides management with a wealth of extra information about sales and stock levels. Our systems reduce running costs and cut losses. We can provide more efficient and convenient services for customers and hopefully increase our sales.

And the future? We are always looking at ways of improving and developing our systems. For example, the central system we've talked about here is really a **batch** *system. The EPOS terminals are online to the local branch computer, but the data is only transmitted to the central computer once a day. The central computer therefore processes batches of sales data from all the branches. The next stage is to link the EPOS terminals in the branches directly to the central computer so that its sales data will be completely up-to-date, rather than a day old.*

Electronic Funds Transfer at the Point of Sale (EFTPOS) is an area which we are experimenting with at present. You'll be able to pay for your purchases with a special card which will automatically debit your bank account!"

Questions

1 What are the disadvantages to the consumer of the system described?

2 Study the different checkout systems in use in supermarkets, departmental stores, do-it-yourself stores, etc. Describe in as much detail as you can how each system works and discuss its advantages and disadvantages.

3 Find out more about EFTPOS systems. Discuss the advantages and disadvantages of EFTPOS, for the customer and for the retailer. What might be the difficulties involved in setting up these systems in shops?

4 Customers purchasing products in a modern hypermarket usually gather a number of items, each marked with a barcode, in a trolley. The trolley full of purchases is then presented to a checkout point. The checkout point operator passes each of the items through a laser beam and eventually the customer is given a detailed bill listing all the purchases by name. The bill also indicates the costs of each of the items and the total sum of cash needed.
Describe thoroughly the computing steps required to produce the bill for each customer. Indicate what other related computing processes are taking place within the hypermarket, of which the customer may be unaware.
Under what circumstances would the operator use manual entry?
[*WJEC 1987*]

5 In recent years computers have become commonly used in sales/stock control. For example, although customers may not necessarily be aware of it, computers are increasingly being used in supermarkets.
Discuss the use of computers and describe the technological developments that have made it possible. Illustrate your answer by considering a particular application you have studied. Comment on the benefits to the customers and the organisation.
[*WJEC 1988*]

Further information

Chapter 7 Data Transfer and Communications
Chapter 8 Hardware Selection

CASE STUDY 5

Audiocalc – The Speaking Spreadsheet

Audiocalc in use

INTRODUCTION

Microcomputers have proved very useful in helping people with special needs. By attaching special **input/output devices**, the computer can be used to help with communication problems associated with people who have lost (or never had) the ability to use their hands, eyes or ears. The photographs show some of the special devices that have been developed for use with computers by handicapped people.

This case study looks at the development of a **package of software** and special hardware for use by the visually handicapped – a speaking **spreadsheet** called Audiocalc.

The package was produced by a student, Philip Jennings, as a project whilst taking a degree in Computer Studies at Sheffield City Polytechnic. The work was supervised by his tutor and he worked in close collaboration with a blind person, Peter Jones. Peter was totally blinded in the Second World War and is very interested in the use of computers for helping the visually handicapped.

THE VISUALLY HANDICAPPED AND COMPUTERS

Microcomputers are used to help the visually handicapped in the following general ways:

- ▲ By attaching special printers to print braille output.
- ▲ By displaying large size text on the screen.
- ▲ By attaching a speech synthesiser to provide spoken output.
- ▲ By attaching specially adapted braille typing machines as input keyboards.

These options are useful in different ways for different situations. Braille printers may be used to produce **hard copy** which may be distributed in the same way as the printed page. However, reading braille is a difficult skill to acquire and many visually handicapped people don't master it. Large sized character display is useful for the partially sighted when they use the computer directly. Spoken output is more generally useful because both the partially sighted and the totally blind can understand the output. However, displayed output is quicker to understand than spoken output. This is because displayed information may be visually scanned. For a standard screen displaying double sized characters, a total of 480 characters may be displayed at the same time. Spoken output is uttered one word at a time, therefore most of the message has to be spoken before the message is understood. The braille typing machines may be used with a computer as an aid to teaching braille writing.

SPREADSHEET PROCESSING – AUDIOCALC

■ The background

The idea for a speaking spreadsheet processor arose out of looking at the way in which **word-processors** had previously been developed for the visually handicapped. If you have ever used a word processor or any other piece of software, you will know that the computer screen is used to display the information being processed (the words) and to display **prompts**, that is, instructions to the user indicating what may be done next.

In the word processor for the visually handicapped all the displayed outputs are replaced by spoken output. This is done by connecting a speech synthesiser which is used to 'speak' the information displayed on the screen and to speak the prompts. Any text typed in can be checked and heard by moving the cursor around the text and then output through the speech synthesiser.

A spreadsheet processor for the visually handicapped would allow users to process tables of figures in the same way. If the software could be developed for cheap computers then it would be available to more people for use at home.

■ The analysis

Both Philip and his supervisor had a good understanding of spreadsheets. There are lots of commercially available spreadsheet packages, and the initial part of the **analysis** was to investigate what functions these packages provided. Audiocalc could then be designed to provide at least some of these functions. Amongst the packages looked at were **Lotus 1-2-3** and **Supercalc**.

The more difficult area of the analysis was in finding out the needs of the visually handicapped.

The supervisor had some background knowledge about this area from the work done with the speaking word processor. This had provided some experience in the use of audible prompts, simple error recovery and consistent command sequences. It had also provided some knowledge about the potential users and the uses they might put a spreadsheet to.

Both Philip and his supervisor thought that one of the most useful facilities provided by a spreadsheet was the ability to 'go to' a predefined part of the spreadsheet with a simple command. It would allow for text to be 'read' in a non-sequential way. However, since neither the student nor his supervisor was visually handicapped, it was decided to carry out a survey of the sort of people who might be interested in using the potential software.

Mr. Jones, the blind person, was asked what he thought a spreadsheet was and how he might use it.

*"**A** sort of chessboard I suppose. I could get at the bit of information I wanted very quickly, without having to churn through loads of unwanted information before I got to it. I could keep track of my bank balance with it. I have a friend who has to keep tables of statistics in his job. He could use this to help him."*

His friend was also blind and had great difficulty in producing and handling tables of information, which he required in his job.

The student and his supervisor thought it would also be a good idea to consider other potential users.

*"**W**hat about schools for the visually handicapped?"*

A Sheffield school for the visually handicapped, which takes children from all over England was contacted and visited.

The school makes extensive use of BBC microcomputers to support their teaching, using adapted braille input devices and braille printers. Whilst visiting the school the student and his supervisor discovered that although they were in a school for the 'blind', most of the pupils could in fact see. This fact was made plain to them by a crowd of pupils who came into the room in which they were talking to Mr. Dorney, the teacher, and began reading from the computer screens, avoiding furniture and so on. This puzzled the rather naive student and supervisor. Some explanation was called for!

The answer to the puzzle was that the definition of visual handicap is very broad. Most 'registered blind' people can see, although their ability to see is impaired to an extent which causes them to be 'registered blind'.

This discovery lead to a rethink about the requirements of the **user interface**. The totally blind would need sound for every aspect of the system usage. However, for a lot of potential users, enlarged display would also make the system more useful.

But what would a school use the software for?

*"**I**'m sure we would use it to create tables of results from our own project work, I think there are lots of ways in which we could use it."*

What about the display?

*"**K**eep it simple and use contrasting colours to help with making out the different parts of the display. It's no good trying to take account of all the different types of visual handicap specifically. Enlarged characters, good use of colour and using sound will help in most cases. By the way, what about allowing the user to use the package as a speaking calculator?"*

A speaking calculator. Now, that was a good idea! There are other speaking calculators, but that's all they are. The computer could be used to process the spreadsheet, but could also be used to carry out instant calculations when required, without breaking off from using the spreadsheet.

AN OUTLINE SPECIFICATION

As a result of the very broad analysis of requirements described above, the designers decided that the spreadsheet processor should have the following **outline specification:**

- ▲ Displayed characters should be of at least double height.
- ▲ Colour should be used to create different areas of concentration on the screen, but the number of colours used should be kept to a small number.
- ▲ The users should always be allowed to 'find out where they are' in the system by pressing one key. Sighted users can usually tell what they have just done by looking at the results left on the screen. Unsighted users can't see and must therefore get the system to tell them.
- ▲ All system prompts must be spoken.
- ▲ If users make a mistake, the system should always allow corrections to be made very quickly and simply. The system must not leave them in a state where they are unsure of what to do next.
- ▲ The **command structure** must be very straightforward and consistent.
- ▲ Features such as 'crashing' sounds being emitted if the user moves outside the spreadsheet area should be included. Noises confirming that lengthy activities, such as reading from a disk are taking place would also be useful.
- ▲ The ability to link the package to a range of speech synthesisers would be useful. This could be done by allowing the users to specify the characteristics of their particular synthesiser.
- ▲ The computer used to develop and run the package should be a BBC microcomputer, because this computer was the one most in use in schools and in the home.

These are very broad requirements based upon the background knowledge about the needs of the visually handicapped and detailed discussions with Peter Jones and Mr. Dorney. They are mainly to do with the general requirements of computer systems for the visually handicapped. With these requirements in mind, a **system design** for the spreadsheet package was developed.

SYSTEM DESIGN

Using the information set out in the above outline specification, Philip and his supervisor set about defining the system design. **Structured, top down design** (see Chapter 4) was used to define the overall structure of the software and the detailed design of the **algorithms** used in the code. The code was written mainly in BBC BASIC, with some **routines** written in **assembler level** code.

The package is designed around a main user screen. The display is designed for sighted users who may have difficulties with their vision, or for people with normal sight. Double height characters are used, and one cell of the spreadsheet is displayed at a time. Most spreadsheets display a grid of several cells at once. For the purposes of Audiocalc, however, the characters on such a display would be too small.

The information displayed on the main screen is as follows:

spreadsheet name

current cell location (row, column)

current cell type (ie. blank, number, formula, text)

current cell value (the value used in any calculations)

calculation switch setting, this indicates the calculation sequence for the spreadsheet (ie. column then row or row then column – the initial setting is column then row and may be changed)

width of the column in which the current cell is located

the cell reference for the last cell in the spreadsheet.

The spreadsheet **functions** are made available by selecting an option from a list of one character commands on the screen. The list provides a set of the most commonly used spreadsheet functions. These are listed as follows:

'A' – Autoread – Allows the user to read through the spreadsheet using the cursor control keys.

'B' – Blank entry – Sets the current cell to zero.

'C' – Calculate spreadsheet – Forces the recalculation of the entire spreadsheet.

'D' – Data printout – Prints the spreadsheet, cell by cell.

'F' – File sheet – Saves the spreadsheet to disk or tape.

'G' – Goto cell – Changes the current cell to the cell specified by the user.

'I' – Immediate mode – Allows for a formula to be entered and calculated. The result is spoken. This provides a speaking calculator function.

'J' – Justify numbers – The user may specify that columns of numbers are to be aligned right or left justified, or on the decimal point.

'N' – Change name – Specify a new name for the spreadsheet.

'O' – Change output type – Change the voice synthesiser being used.

'P' – Print the spreadsheet – Print the spreadsheet in a formatted form.

'Q' – Quit – Leave Audiocalc without saving the spreadsheet.

'R' – Replicate – Copy the contents of the current cell to another cell.

'S' – Change calculation sequence – Changes the sequence used to calculate the spreadsheet from 'row then column' to 'column then row' or vice versa.

'W' – Change the column width (range allowed is 60–132 characters).

The software is designed so that if the user makes a mistake an error message is spoken and he or she may try again. The set of control functions listed below includes a 'speak available options' facility. This allows the user to find out what options are available at any time. On selecting an option, a user may be presented with another set of options ie. a hierarchical **menu-driven** system is used (see Chapter 2).

Remember, a sighted user can usually read these from the screen, a blind person can't.

The set of special control functions mentioned above are available at any time. These produce information about the system status through the speech synthesiser. The information is obtained by holding down the ⟨control⟩ key on the keyboard and pressing another key. The list of keys and the information they output is as follows:

⟨CTRL⟩ + ⟨C⟩ current cell contents

⟨CTRL⟩ + ⟨L⟩ current cell location

⟨CTRL⟩+⟨N⟩ spreadsheet name

⟨CTRL⟩+⟨O⟩ options available at this time

⟨CTRL⟩+⟨P⟩ current input prompt

⟨CTRL⟩+⟨S⟩ sequence of calculation (row then column or column then row)

⟨CTRL⟩+⟨T⟩ current cell type (number, text, formula)

⟨CTRL⟩+⟨V⟩ current cell value (calculated for formulae)

⟨CTRL⟩+⟨W⟩ current cell width

Chapter 4 on computer programming contains a sample algorithm showing the overall structure of the software design. Note that, to allow for the special control characters to be detected at any time, the program has to periodically test for the input of a **control character**, and respond accordingly. See Chapter 6 for information on **interrupt handling** for more detail on this sort of processing.

Using a speech synthesiser

There are a wide variety of speech synthesisers, varying in complexity, sophistication and price. The specification for Audiocalc includes the requirement that the speech synthesiser be cheap and relatively unsophisticated. There are several examples of this type and Audiocalc was required to run on different models. This description is based on the VOTRAX 'Type N Talk' (TNT) speech synthesiser. The VOTRAX TNT may be interfaced to a computer via an **RS432 serial link** and contains a VOTRAX SCO1 **phoneme** synthesiser chip and a text-to-speech system. The text-to-speech synthesis is done within the unit and so the connected computer does not need to do any text-to-speech conversion.

Figure 1 Hello!

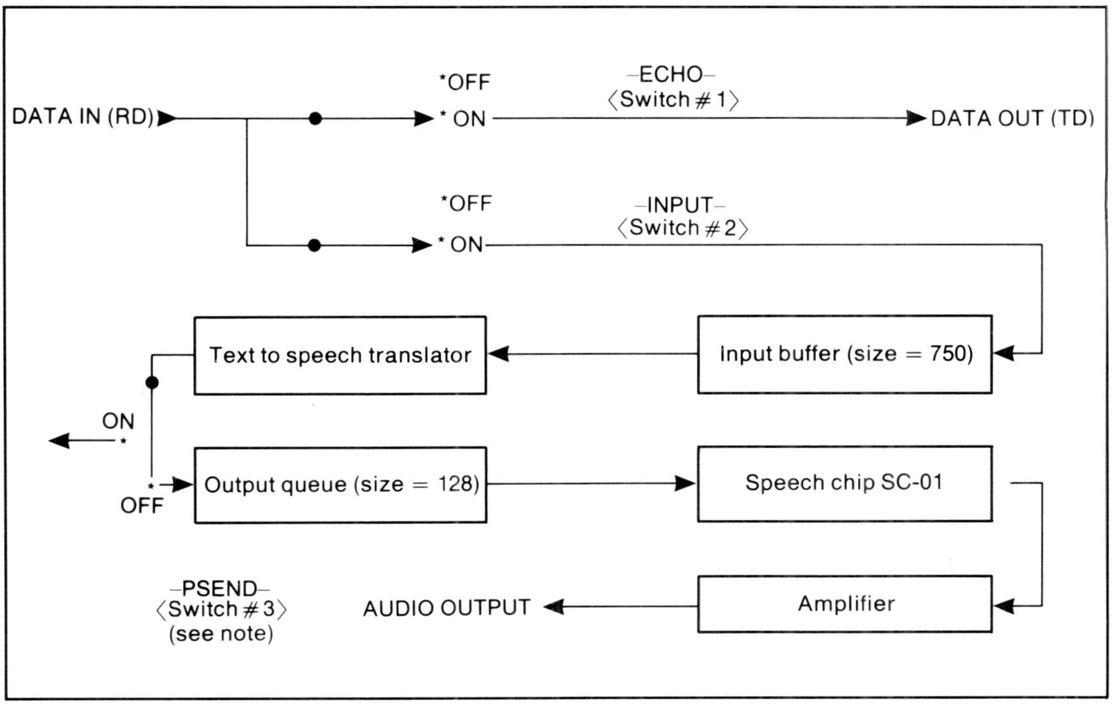

Figure 2 Text-to-speech conversion circuit

The speech output is generated according to a set of rules which describe what sort of sound should be generated for a given string of characters. This gives a more flexible output ability than if pre-stored utterances were used. The rules are applied to strings of characters as they arrive from the computer through the RS432 link. The program in the computer, in this case Audiocalc, may be used to drive the synthesiser directly.

Although some speech synthesisers contain their own speaker, the VOTRAX requires a separate speaker to be attached. When sound output is required, a string of **ASCII** codes (see Chapter 6) is sent from the computer to the synthesiser. The Audiocalc program is written in BBC BASIC and the message to be spoken is sent to the speech synthesiser using an ordinary PRINT statement.

For example:

```
300 PRINT "audiocalc is ready"
```

The synthesiser stores the string of characters or text (up to 750 characters) in an **input buffer** (see Chapter 5). The text is then passed to the text-to-speech translator, which in turn passes the converted text to a speech chip, and finally to the amplifier and speaker. There is also a buffer between the translator and the speech chip, which stores the phonemes ready for output. Phonemes are explained in more detail below The diagram in Fig. 2 illustrates the layout of the system.

■ Phonemes

The text-to-speech translator is a program stored in a **chip** which uses rules about the English language to convert text into phonemes. Phonemes are the speech sounds that are associated with a set of letters in a word. If you look in a dictionary you will find for each word, in addition to the description of its meaning, other information about how the word sounds when spoken. For example, here is the entry for the word '**computer**':

Computer (Kəm'pju:tər) *n.* **1**. a device, usually electronic, that processes data according to a set of instructions . . .

[from the Collins Dictionary]

The peculiar looking symbols in brackets following the word being defined tell you how to say the word. They are part of the international Phonetic alphabet. If you have a large dictionary have a look at the 'Pronunciation key' which is usually printed at the front of the dictionary. It gives information on the sound, the length and stress to be given to parts of a word.

In this example, the pronunciation guide tells us that the 'c' should be spoken as a hard 'c', like a 'k', that the 'o' should be spoken as in p<u>o</u>t and not in p<u>o</u>ke, and so on.

Every word in the English language and most other languages has a similar phonetic description. It is also worth noting that English is the standard language in several other countries, such as the USA. As you probably know there are several words which sound very different when spoken by an American than when spoken by a Briton. Think of, for example, the word 'tomato'. Also, there are great regional variations in dialect and accent. The phonetic description for words in English dictionaries refers to 'Standard' English.

There is a set of rules which can be used to decide what a string of letters will sound like when found in a word. This set of rules, which applies to standard English, are the rules which are programmed onto the text-to-speech chip However, there are a large number of exceptions to these rules. The program is not capable of handling these exceptions and has to be 'deceived' into producing the right sound for a given word by mis-spelling it. The basic idea is to spell the word in the text sent from the computer so that the nearest pronunciation is produced.

For example, the word 'English' spelt this way produces the wrong pronunciation. By mis-spelling it 'Inglish', the correct pronunciation is produced. Some consonants have more than one pronunciation. The table in Fig. 3 shows examples of these.

There are other considerations, such as short and long vowel sounds, diphthongs, stress etc. All these characteristics have to be considered when producing sound from text. This section has introduced you to some of the aspects of sound production, but a more detailed description is outside the scope of this book. However, it does provide an idea of how difficult it is to produce artificial speech.

VOCABULARY PROGRAMMING

Pronunciation Correction Guide

Word List	Correction
advertisement	advertise ment
baseball	base ball
beautiful	butiful
break	brake
breakfast	brekfest
bringing	bring ing
calculation	cal culation
capacity	cuppacity
cassette	case et
certain	certin
character	kerekter
children	chilldren
circuit	cirkit
clients	clyents
clothes	cloze
close	near by
color	cuhler
comfortable	comfterble
customer	custummer
data	dayta
definition	deffinition
delete	deleet
easiest	easy est
english	inglish
equivalent	eequivalent
error	airor
error	mistake
everyone	every one
extensive	extensiv
generator	generayter
goto	go to
item	ightem
machine	mosheen
machinery	mosheenery
output	out put
paste	payst
phoneme	phone eem
procedures	prowceejers
program	prowgram
promise	promiss
pronunciation	pronunsiation
radio	radeo
replace	reeplace
requirement	require ment
rodeo	rowdeo
scissors	scizors
shoes	shooz
singer	sing er
software	softwayr
specify	specifuy
today	tuday
typewriter	type writer
vocabulary	vowcabulary
ware	wair

Figure 3 Pronunciation guide

CONCLUSIONS

This case study has introduced a variety of topics. To summarise, these are:

- ▲ Using computers as an aid for the handicapped at work and leisure.
- ▲ Creating a computer system from the 'idea' stage to a final working package.
- ▲ How important the design of the human-computer interface is in aiding the success of a system.
- ▲ How synthetic speech is created and how it may be used.
- ▲ And last, but not least, it has shown that a very useful software package may be produced from a student project.

Spoken communication is a very subtle and complex business. To match the capability of humans with a computer system is probably virtually impossible. However, this does not stop people trying. To achieve a result which is close to speech used by humans requires the use of some powerful and sophisticated computing techniques. These are expensive. One of the requirements for the Audiocalc package was that it should be cheap and obtainable on commonly available microcomputers. To achieve this requirement a simple text-to-speech system is used. The output is nowhere as realistic sounding as more expensive systems, and some 'tricks' have to be performed with the programming. But, even with a cheap synthesiser and a BBC microcomputer, a very useful package was produced.

The package has proved very useful to visually handicapped users for direct use as an aid to managing business, home accounts etc. It has also found a use as a teaching package for organisations involved in providing training in the use of spreadsheets for the visually handicapped. Its 'simple' approach allows for the principles of the spreadsheet use to be taught, allowing users to move on to more complex versions if required.

Questions

1 Investigate and report on the facilities provided in a spreadsheet processing package you know. Compare these facilities with those described for Audiocalc.

2 What applications are spreadsheets used for?

3 In what ways could software such as Audiocalc help job prospects for the visually handicapped?

4 In what other ways are computers used to help the handicapped?

5 Extend the outline algorithm given for the structure of Audiocalc in Chapter 4 (Computer Programming), by providing a detailed description for one of the options listed.
Consider how you might design the program to deal sensibly with input errors.

Further information

Chapter 2 Systems Analysis and Design
Chapter 4 Computer Programming
Chapter 5 Operating Systems and Systems Software
Chapter 6 Computer Architecture
Chapter 8 Hardware Selection

CASE STUDY 6

Information on Newborn Babies

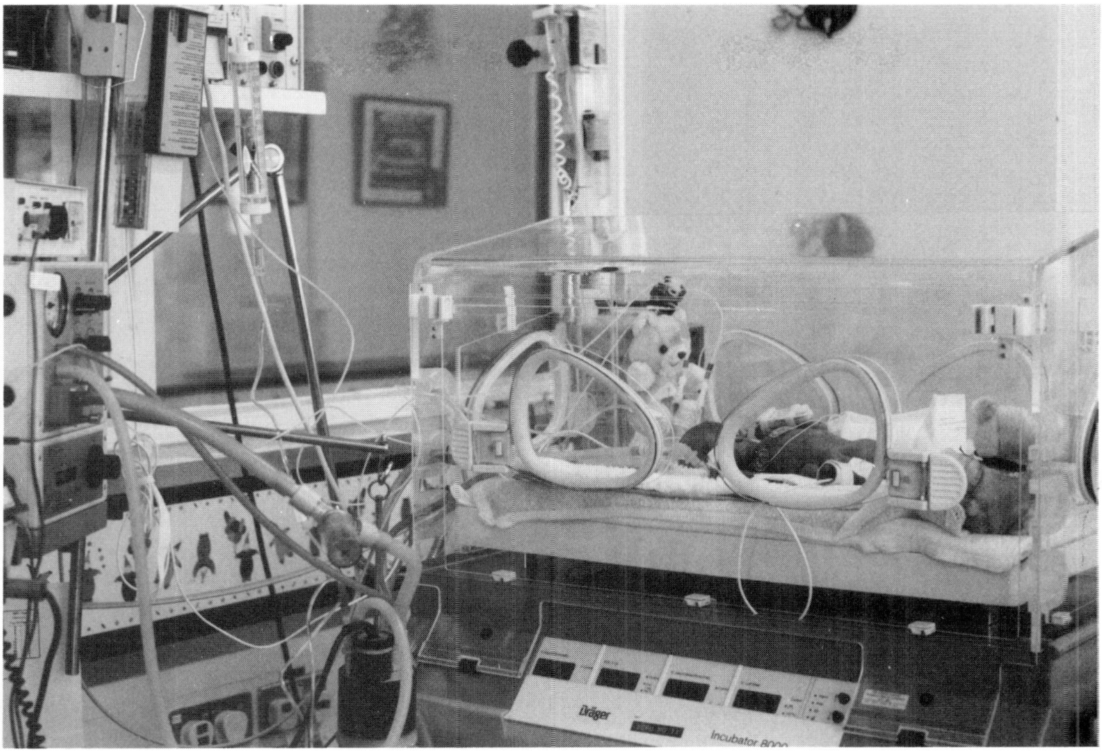

Special Care Baby Unit

INTRODUCTION

Barnsley Hospital, like many other hospitals, has a unit for babies who need special care called the Special Care Baby Unit (SCBU). Depending on how ill he or she is, a baby's stay varies from a few hours to a few months. As soon as they improve and no longer need special care, babies are sent back to a normal hospital ward or back home.

Some newborn babies may have an illness (for example, jaundice is quite common) or they may have difficulty in breathing or feeding. In particular, babies born prematurely are often smaller than the average baby and need constant, careful monitoring of their heartbeat, breathing, temperature, etc. Some babies need intensive care and special machines to provide life support. Babies are placed in incubators to maintain a constant temperature and to reduce the risk of infection. A ventilator machine helps them breathe and they may be given oxygen too.

Doctors and researchers are always looking for better ways of treating newborn babies for specific illnesses. Also it is useful to follow up some babies to see whether or not their illness has affected them in later life.

Barnsley Hospital uses a computer system in its Special Care Baby Unit to keep records on all newborn babies. This case study looks at the design of the system and how it is used to provide information for research.

DATA AND INFORMATION

We spoke to Davina who was responsible for the development of the system and asked her why the project was set up.

*"**A** large amount of data is recorded on these newborn babies in intensive care. Every time their heartbeat and breathing is monitored the data must be recorded. Laboratory tests (eg. blood tests) are all recorded and charted so that the consultants and nurses can see the baby's progress. All food and medicines given are recorded, as well as the consultant's notes on the baby's problems and treatment. We also keep data about the baby's mother and her family because it can give useful information about things like hereditary illnesses.*

All this recording is done manually, handwritten or typed, and put in a file for each baby. For some babies the file is enormous!

The size of the file, and the sheer number of files presents a real problem in correlating the data for large numbers of babies for research. For example, if the researchers wanted to find out what treatment was best for a particular illness, they had to sift through all the data in the files, first sorting out which babies had the illness, then what treatments they were given and what effects the treatments had. Everything was written on separate sheets and it took time to find the relevant pieces of paper.

*The process was so time consuming that it was rarely done and important information was missed. The **data** was there but extracting useful **information** from it was very difficult.*

The consultants need a baby's data in one file so that they can assess the baby's progress. But for research the data needs to be organised differently. For statistics it is the trends which are important and these can only be obtained by analysing large numbers of babies' records. This is where the computer comes in. Once all the data is entered, provided it is organised properly, it can be accessed in many different ways to give people the information they want."

REQUIREMENTS OF THE SYSTEM

We asked Davina how she had started the project.

*"**T**he first thing was to familiarise myself with the work of the Special Care Baby Unit and watch how they recorded the data on the various bits of paper. Then I discussed the proposed system with the users (the consultants, the nurses and the hospital managers) and drew up a list of requirements. I also worked out the costs of developing the software and of buying the hardware.*

There were two options:

- ▲ *The first was to use the **database** system for producing **reports** and for doing research. The data could be entered by any of the staff when convenient and it didn't matter where in the unit the computer was situated.*
- ▲ *The second option was to have a computer **terminal** actually in the baby room so that the nurses and doctors would enter data immediately. The advantage of this was that the database would always be up-to-date and it could be used to assess a baby's progress at any time.*

The second option may sound ideal but in fact, by law, most things have to be double checked and written down by hand, for example when medicines are given. Typing the data into a computer is therefore an extra job and may prove too time consuming. We decided to give this a short trial period to find out how much time and effort was involved.

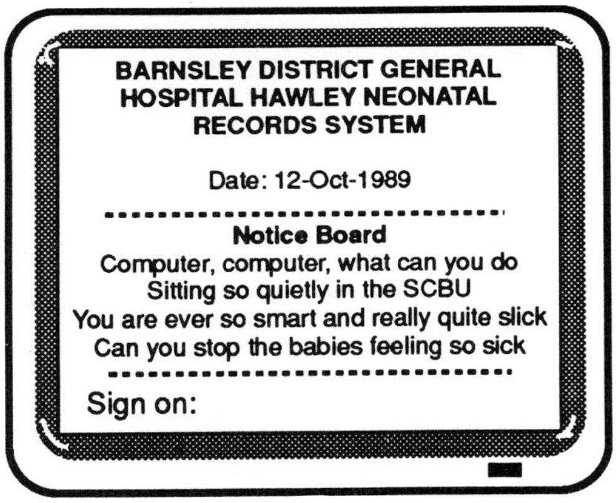

Figure 1 SCBU notice board

I knew that the cooperation of staff was vital to the success of the whole project. It was clear at the start that the most important thing was to make the system easy and quick to use so that people would use it in the normal course of their job. I was well aware that if I designed a system that was difficult to use, they would avoid using it! Also I felt it was important for the staff to gain some advantage as well; there would be less paperwork, faster access to information, and automatically produced, up-to-date reports.

The discharge report is one example of how the computer can help staff. This report is produced when the baby leaves, and is for sending to the family doctor and the midwife who visits the baby at home. It used to take a long time to prepare manually, extracting the information from the baby's papers and then writing the report. Now it is produced automatically from the computer's stored data, ready for the consultant to check the printout and sign it, saving time and effort for all concerned.

When considering the requirements of the system we also had to think about ***security*** *and* ***backup****. I'll explain these later."*

Design of the system

We asked Davina to show us the system and to tell us about the way it was designed to be easy to use.

■ System structure

"Let's look at the demonstration system which I set up for training the users. It's exactly the same system but it contains some made-up data so we can play around with it without altering the real data files. First I have to enter a ***password*** *to get access. For obvious reasons we don't want anyone, wandering round the ward, to be able to tamper with the system.*

The system is all based on ***menus*** *which are in a tree structure. Fig. 2 shows the menu structure.*

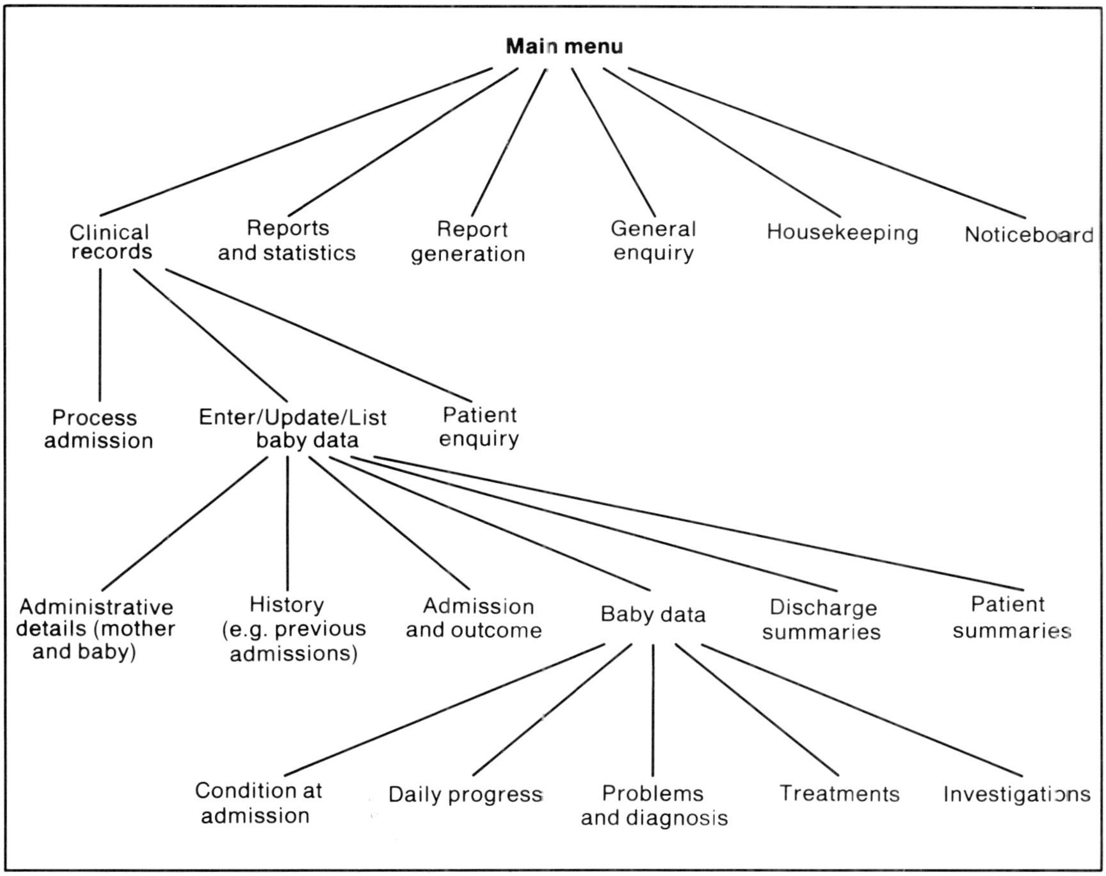

Figure 2 Menu structure

Fig. 3 shows the main menu which we have here on the screen, now the system has accepted my password. You select from a menu by moving the menu pointer (a square) up or down to the option you want and pressing ENTER. Some options take you to another menu and you may have to go through a few menus before you get to the function you want. There's an option to go back to the previous menu (shown in less bright text) and you can always return to the main menu by pressing the HOME key. I think it's important for the user to be able to get back easily.

*If you're in a hurry, you can **log off** the system by just pressing a special key. It leaves the system ready for someone else to use. People find this useful when they're dashing round doing several different jobs."*

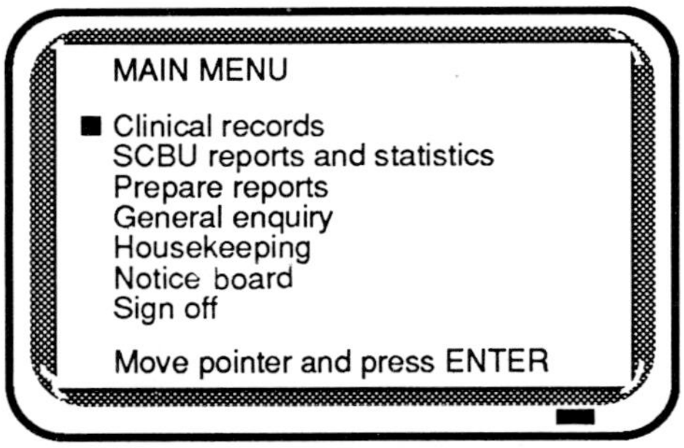

Figure 3 Main menu

Note that this menu system makes it easy for the programmer to use **structured programming** techniques. Each function shown in Fig. 2 becomes a program module or procedure.

■ The six main options

We asked Davina to explain the six options on the screen.

- *The clinical records subsystem*

"This is where we look at or enter data. For example, admitting a new baby; adding data to a baby's record about its feeds, heartbeat, etc; amending data; discharging a baby. I'll show you this later."

- *The reports and statistics subsystem*

"This displays and prints a variety of reports. For example, each time the consultant does a ward round, he/she gets a report on the recent problems and treatments of each baby. It also produces monthly and yearly statistical reports, for example on the number of babies admitted in certain birthweight categories (Fig. 4)."

- *The prepare reports subsystem*

"We use this to prepare the monthly statistical reports before they're printed. Some reports require a search of a large part of the database, as well as calculations, and can take several minutes to prepare. Once prepared, each report is stored and can be printed whenever it's needed, using the reports and statistics subsystem. Monthly reports are usually kept for a year."

- *The enquiry subsystem*

"This is what they use for research. It's a very powerful facility which can answer almost any question about the babies in the database. We'll look at this later on."

- *The housekeeping subsystem*

*"This is used by the staff responsible for the operation of the system and consists of routine procedures necessary for maintaining the database and to ensure the smooth running of the system. For example, there is a procedure to **archive** a baby's record after it has been discharged and the discharge report has been checked. The baby's record is stored in an archive file and can be recalled for information later if needed.*

We can delete any record that has been added accidentally and update the lists of codes that we use and their explanations. You'll see these codes when I show you the data entry. We also update passwords when new staff arrive or staff leave.

There are a few other facilities related to system operation which we only use occasionally. For example, there is one called system shutdown which we use when the computer has to be turned off for repair. There's another which allows us to alter the current date or the type of stationery that is loaded on the printer."

- *The notice board*

"This is simply a facility for any user to leave a message on the title screen. You can see my message in Fig. 1."

BARNSLEY DISTRICT GENERAL HOSPITAL

SCBU Admissions by Birth-Weight Group

YEAR: 1988

Month	500 & under	501–1000	1001–1500	1501–2000	2001–2500	2501–3000	3001 & over	Total
Jan	2	0	0	4	2	5	7	20
Feb	0	1	0	2	5	4	7	19
Mar	0	0	2	2	4	6	8	22
Apr	0	0	0	5	1	2	8	16
May	0	0	3	4	5	11	4	27
Jun	0	1	2	5	7	2	12	29
Jul	1	1	2	6	1	1	8	20
Aug	0	1	0	1	2	4	4	12
Sep	1	1	0	3	4	5	9	23
Oct	0	1	9	2	3	5	11	25
Nov	0	0	0	2	2	2	3	9
Dec	0	0	0	3	2	3	6	14
Adm n/k	0	0	0	0	0	0	0	0
Totals	4	6	12	39	38	50	87	236

Figure 4 Report on admissions by birthweight

THE DATA STRUCTURE

We asked Davina to show us some of the data held in the demonstration database.

"Let's choose the option 'clinical records' from the main menu and ask to look at a particular baby's record. It gives us a list of all the babies in the unit (Fig. 5); we'll select one (Ashok Patel) by moving the cursor and pressing ENTER.

Date: 12-10-89
Time: 13:00

BABY MENU

Unit No	Baby	DoB	DoL	Gest	Bwt	Consultant
492961	Mathew Simmonds Buckley	01-10-89	12	28/4	2905	Dr Bridson
492962	Melanie Simmonds Buckley	01-10-89	12	28/4	2465	Dr Bridson
493191	Amy Tofield	11-10-89	1	34/1	2133	Dr Jones
492993	Daniel Webster	10-10-89	2	35/3	2610	Dr Bridson
491056	Marie-Louise Yale	25-09-89	18	27/6	890	Dr Bridson
490923	Ashok Patel	10-09-89	33	33/0	1565	Dr Bridson

■ Return to previous menu
1 Admin 2 Admit 3 History 4 SCBU 5 Discharge 6 Summaries 7 Charts

Figure 5 Baby menu

Let's print his admission summary (Fig. 6). This gives us details of his admission, he hasn't been discharged yet so that part is blank. You can see that he was in the incubator for a few days because he was born early. He was put on a ventilator and given oxygen.

BARNSLEY DISTRICT GENERAL HOSPITAL

SCBU Admission

BABY		**ADMISSION**	
Unit No:	4352	Date:	10-09-89
Forename:	Ashok	Time:	10:00
Surname:	Patel	Consultant:	Dr. Bridson
Date of Birth:	10-09-89	Admitted From:	Postnatal Ward
Time of Birth:	09:44	Admission Reason:	Pre-Term or other LBW
Sex:	M		
Birthweight:	1565 grams		

Number of Admissions: 1

DISCHARGE

Date:
Time:
Weight:
Discharged to:
Outcome:

CONDITION AT ADMISSION

Time Obs. Done:	10:00	Incubator:	Yes
Temperature:	34.8 C	Incubator Temp:	C
Apex:	132/min	Oxygen Given:	Yes
Respiration:	32/min	Oxygen:	40%
Colour:	Pale	Ventilated:	Yes
Jaundice	No		
Grunting:			
Recession:			
Oedema:			

BLOOD GLUCOSE

	Mg%	*Mm/L*	*Time*
(Cot)	02	0.1	10:00
(Lab)			

Figure 6 Admission details on Ashok Patel

We can also get a special care summary (Fig. 7) which records the diagnosis the consultant made, the treatments the baby was given and the blood tests, etc. Another summary shows the data stored about the mother and the delivery. These summaries are very convenient; the relevant information is neatly presented on one or two sheets of printout and it saves looking at several different pieces of paper."

BARNSLEY DISTRICT GENERAL HOSPITAL

Special Care Report

BABY

Unit No: 4352
Forename: Ashok
Surname: Patel
Date of Birth: 10-09-89
Time of Birth: 09:44
Sex: M
Birthweight: 1565 grams
Gestation: 33/0 (A1)

Number of Admissions: 1

ADMISSION

Date: 10-09-89
Time: 10:00
Consultant: Dr. Bridson
Admitted From: Postnatal Ward
Admission Reason: Pre-Term or other LBW

DISCHARGE

Date:
Time:
Weight:
Discharged to:
Outcome:

CLINICAL PROBLEM LIST

Date	*Time*	*Diagnosis*	*Ceased*
10-09-89	09:44	Pre-term (under 37/52 but not under 28/52)	- -
	09:44	Severe birth asphyxia (Apgar 0-3/1; 0-6/5)	- -

TREATMENTS

Started		*Treatment*	*Stopped*	
10-09-89	09:45	Oxygen	- -	:
	10:10	Ventilation	- -	:
	10:45	IV glucose	- -	:
	10:45	Other transfusion (plasma etc)	10-09-89	11:00
	11:00	Penicillin	- -	:
	11:00	Gentamicin	- -	:
	11:45	Sodium bicarb.	- -	:
	16:00	Phenobarbitone	- -	:
	20:00	Frusemide	- -	:
11-09-89	11:00	Phototherapy	- -	:
	16:00	Diazepam	- -	:
	18:00	Phenytoin	- -	:

Figure 7 Special care report

Was it easy to decide what data the system had to store and how to structure the data?

*"**N**o. I spent a good deal of time looking at the babies' files, observing the nurses and consultants working in the unit and finding out from them what they used the data for. The data structure I came up with is a tree structure, which looks quite complicated (Fig. 8). The **primary key** is the baby's unit number, a unique identification number allocated by the hospital. For example, Ashok's unit number is 4352. However, the staff don't have to remember each baby's number because the computer displays a list of all the babies in the ward for them to choose from." (See Fig. 5.)*

Note that defining the **data structure** (see Chapter 3) needs thought and careful design so that the database can provide the information people need from the data. It is not an easy task; **data analysis** techniques can help.

DATA ENTRY

You said earlier that the system had to be easy to use. There's obviously lots of data to be entered. How did you design the data entry?

*"**I** used separate entry screens for entering the different sets of data: baby's admission; mother's details; baby's condition when admitted; treatments; investigations and observations. You can see that these correspond to the data structure (Fig. 8). Staff are used to recording data under these headings so it wasn't new to them.*

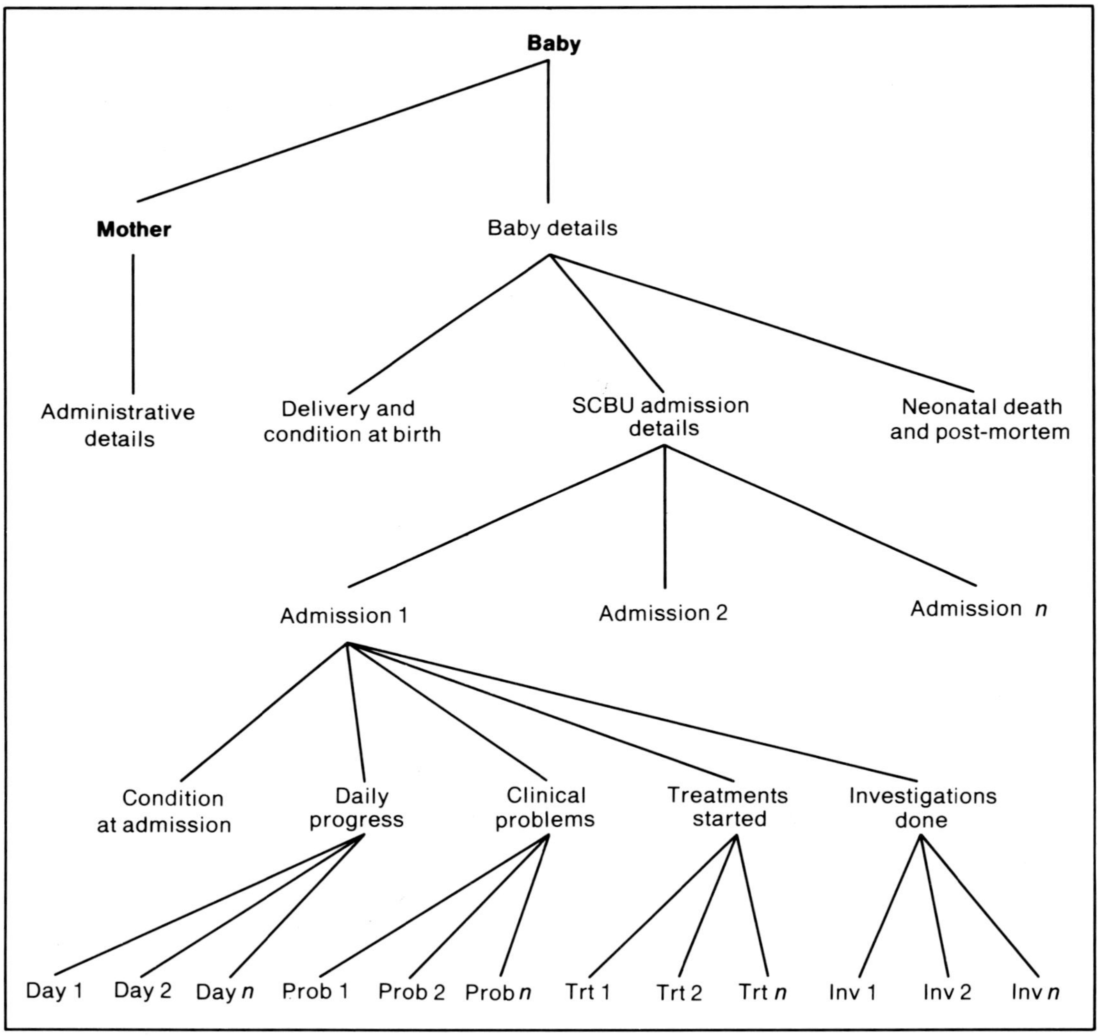

Figure 8 Structure of a single baby's computer record

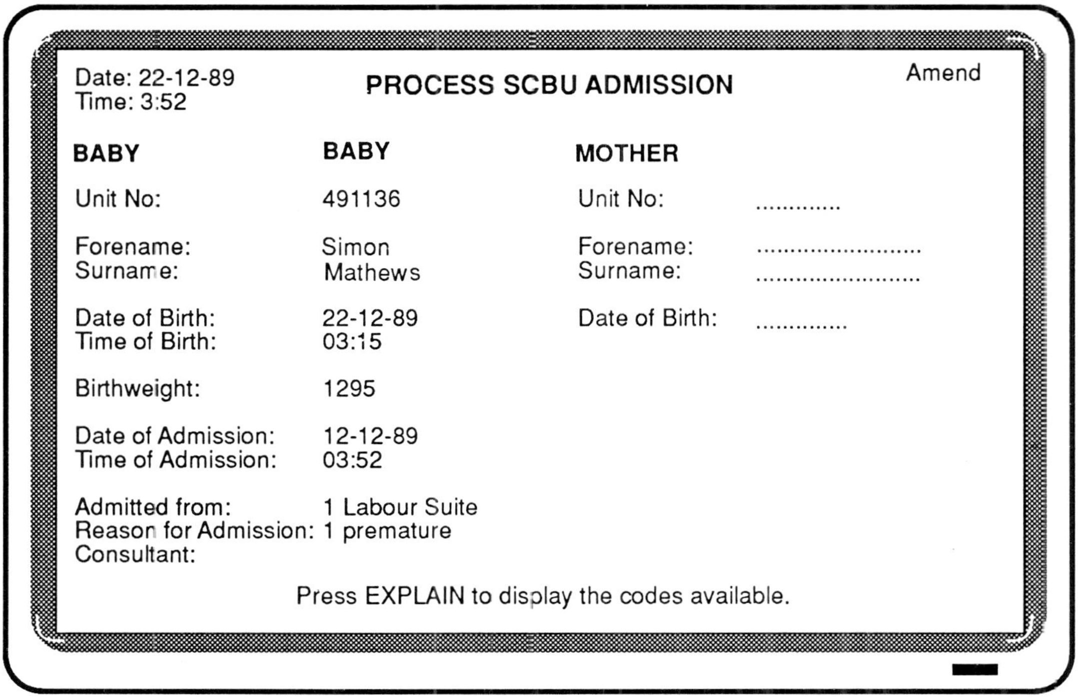

Date: 22-12-89 Time: 3:52 — PROCESS SCBU ADMISSION — Amend

BABY	BABY	MOTHER	
Unit No:	491136	Unit No:	....
Forename:	Simon	Forename:	....
Surname:	Mathews	Surname:	....
Date of Birth:	22-12-89	Date of Birth:	....
Time of Birth:	03:15		
Birthweight:	1295		
Date of Admission:	12-12-89		
Time of Admission:	03:52		
Admitted from:	1 Labour Suite		
Reason for Admission:	1 premature		
Consultant:			

Press EXPLAIN to display the codes available.

Figure 9 Admission summary

I decided to use a ***form fill*** *approach; it's a fairly standard method. As an example, let's look at what we enter when a baby is admitted (Fig. 9).*

First we enter his name and details such as date of birth. Apart from personal details like this, most of the data consists of numerical codes. They are quick to type in and the more common codes are fairly easily remembered. If you can't remember a code, you can step through the codes in the entry box by pressing the EXPLAIN key. The explanation of each code appears next to the entry box as shown in Fig. 9.

I enter 1 for where the baby came to us from (labour suite) and 1 for the reason for admission (premature). If there are a lot of possible codes for an entry, stepping through them is tedious and so instead of displaying each code in the box the whole list of codes is displayed down the screen.''

What if you make an error when entering the code?

*''**M**y system checks your code with the list of valid codes for that item. If it doesn't recognise what you've entered, you get an error message at the bottom of the screen and a beep to draw your attention to it.''*

Are people likely to make mistakes with the code if they don't remember it? Or by simply mistyping the code, could they enter the wrong one?

*''**V**ery rarely. You see, when I type in a code its explanation is automatically displayed next to the code. So if it's not the one I want I either enter the right code or I step through the possible codes to find the one I want. If I enter a unit number that's already there, the system tells me it's a duplicate and asks me if that baby is being re-admitted (it might have been discharged but has become ill again).*

When staff enter numerical data for things like blood counts, it's possible to make a mistake. Errors in an amount rather than a code are harder to detect on the computer. However, everything is checked by the consultant and anything unusual is quickly spotted. In fact, a researcher did a survey of the data entered by all the staff and found a very low error rate.''

Is all the data entry done in a similar way?

*''**Y**es, it's important to be consistent. Once the staff get used to this sytem, they can enter data very quickly, whether it's a baby's daily progress, problems and treatments, admissions or discharges.''*

Making an Enquiry

What if I'm doing medical research and I want to know how many of the babies on the database have had jaundice?

*"**O**ne of the options in the general enquiry sub-system is intended to do just this as people frequently make this type of enquiry. The system tells you how many babies have had jaundice and you can get a list of these babies if you want to follow them up."*

Is that all the enquiry system does?

*"**N**o. I knew the researchers would want to make all sorts of different enquiries so I designed a facility for specifying your own* ***search****. This is more complicated than the simple question you just asked about jaundice and it takes some time to learn how to correctly formulate your search. But it's a very powerful facility.*

Suppose we want to find out how many babies, weighing between 1000 and 2500 grams at birth, were put on a ventilator machine or given oxygen or an intravenous injection of glucose. We might want to follow up these babies to see whether they have problems later in life.

First we enter a name for our search, we'll call it DSVENTIL, the first two letters are my initials. All searches are saved, so they need a recognisable name. Then we enter a short title for the printout of results. We'll use the 1988 data.

Now we have to define our search. The criteria are:

> *birth weight is from 1000 to 2500;*
>
> *treatment is 13 or 11 or 31 (those are the codes for ventilator, oxygen and glucose);*
>
> *we'll narrow it down to babies born prematurely (alleged gestation between 28 and 38 weeks).*

BARNSLEY DISTRICT GENERAL HOSPITAL

General Enquiry Definition Report

ENQUIRY:— DSVENT Survival Rates Among Babies
Receiving Intensive Care in 1988

CATEGORY:— Enquire on results of JB/JN6
Intensive care on SCBU in 1988

SELECT ON:—

	Birthweight		from: 1000	to: 2500
AND	Treatment		from: 13	to:
		or	from: 11	to:
		or	from: 31	to:
AND	Alleged Gestation—weeks		from: 28	to: 38

REPORT ON:—

Selection fields		*Report fields*	
BTHWT	Birthweight	IDOB	Infant's Date of Birth
TRT	Treatment	MODE	Mode of Delivery
GESTAL	Alleged Gestation —weeks	MULT	Singleton/Multiple Birth
		APGAR1	Apgar Totals (1 min)
		DISCAT	SCBU Discharge Category
		OUTCOM	Outcome

Data sets

Figure 10 General enquiry definition report

Notice in Fig. 10 that the criteria are joined with AND.

Finally we specify the report fields (ie. the data items we want printed out). These are shown in Fig. 10. The system matches each baby's record against our search criteria and if it matches, the baby is included in the report. This search only takes one or two minutes because I'm using a subset of the 1988 data. Searching the whole database takes longer.

The report (Fig. 11) tells that there are 27 babies that match our criteria and it lists them (one line of data for each). Notice that the fields printed are the ones requested in the enquiry definition; other data fields aren't shown."

BARNSLEY DISTRICT GENERAL HOSPITAL

General Enquiry Report

Enquiry:— DSVENT Survival Rates Among Babies Receiving Intensive Care — 1988

Count:— 27
Processed:— 14-Sep-89 11:57
Results:—

BTHWT	TRT	GEST	IDOB	MODE	MULT	APGAR1	DISCAT	OUTCOM
1850	IV gluco	35/1	25/01/88	C/Sect	1	09	Home	Survived
2490	Oxygen	32/0	07/02/88	C/Sect	1	07	Transfer	Died
2270	Oxygen	35/5	09/02/88	Normal	1	07	Home	Survived
1955	Oxygen	32/0	09/02/88	C/Sect	1	08	Home	Survived
1730	Ventilat	33/0	21/03/88	C/Sect	1	09	Home	Survived
1380	Oxygen	29/0	29/03/88	C/Sect	1	04	Home	Survived
1875	Oxygen	34/0	16/04/88	C/Sect	2	05	Home	Survived
1575	Oxygen	34/0	16/04/88	C/Sect	2	09	Home	Survived
1760	Oxygen	31/5	20/04/88	C/Sect	1	04	Home	Survived
2440	Ventilat	34/0	02/05/88	Normal	1	07	Home	Survived
1440	Oxygen	31/5	16/05/88	Normal	2	08	Home	Survived
1615	Oxygen	31/5	16/05/88	Normal	2	08	Home	Survived
1340	Ventilat	29/0	22/05/88	Normal	1	02	Home	Survived
1545	Ventilat	31/0	31/05/88	C/Sect	2	03	Home	Survived
1635	Ventilat	31/0	31/05/88	C/Sect	2	08	Home	Survived
1170	Ventilat	28/0	04/06/88	Normal	1		Transfer	Died
1620	IV gluco	31/0	06/06/88	C/Sect	1	06	Home	Survived
1285	Ventilat	30/6	15/06/88	C/Sect	1	07	Home	Survived
2100	Ventilat	32/0	23/06/88	C/Sect	1	04	Home	Survived
2415	Oxygen	34/0	17/07/88	Normal	2	08	Home	Survived
1965	IV gluco	30/0	06/09/88	C/Sect	2	03	Home	Survived
2245	Ventilat	34/5	14/09/88	C/Sect	1	07	Home	Survived
1655	IV gluco	32/5	30/09/88	Normal	1	04	Home	Survived
2420	Oxygen	35/3	11/10/88	C/Sect	1	05	Home	Survived
1745	Oxygen	32/0	22/10/88	Other Fo	1	09	Home	Survived
1090	Ventilat	29/0	27/10/88	Breech	2	02	Died	Died
1700	Ventilat	31/6	15/11/88	C/Sect	1	05	Home	Survived

Figure 11 General enquiry report

A User-Friendly System

Can you sum up the aspects of the design of your system which you think are important to create a system that is user-friendly?

*"Getting around the system must be easy so I used a tree structured **menu** system. The selection of an option from the menu was also designed to be easy, using the space bar to move up/down the menu and the ENTER key to select. I included ways of going back to previous menus and to the main menu. There are also shortcuts provided for the experienced user so that they don't get frustrated having to go through several menus to get to the option they want.*

*A **help** on demand system, where you press a special HELP key, is really useful, particularly for new users. In my system every menu option is linked to a help screen which explains what that option does and what you need to do. The EXPLAIN key helps the user select codes.*

*The **data entry** method had to be quick and as easy as possible. I limited the amount of typing to the absolute minimum by using numeric codes. Also I programmed some of the keys to do special things, such as HELP, and labelled the key accordingly.*

I consider screen presentation to be very important. The layout must be clear and uncluttered but screens must also give enough information. Consistency is important too. For example, I always use the top line as a status line and the bottom line for displaying error and help messages. Menus all have the same format, with a title so you know where you are in the system."

A Flexible Design

What was the most difficult part of the design?

*"Structuring the system very carefully and making it very flexible so that it could be modified or added to very easily. There were two reasons for doing this. Firstly it made my job easier during the development of the system. I **prototyped** screens, menus and reports for the users to look at and comment on and I was constantly modifying these. Secondly, when the system was up and running there was a need for maintaining it and making changes quickly if people requested them.*

My solution was to create special programs for designing data entry screens and report layouts and creating or modifying menus and code lists. The main programs included general procedures for displaying any menu, printing any report and handling any data entry screen.

I knew that the enquiry system would have to be able to cope with virtually any query, because the research done in hospitals is so varied. I had to design a method of achieving this, but one which wasn't too difficult to use."

Security and Backup

If I walk in here and use the computer, can I get access to confidential information?

"No. As you saw when I started the demonstration I had to enter a secret password. There are also different levels of password for different members of staff. For example, I have access to all the data because I am responsible for the system operation, but some people are allowed to only read the data."

What happens if the disk 'crashes' or the computer breaks down. Do you lose all your data?

"No. An important housekeeping routine is system backup. Every day we use this to create a backup copy of the software and the database. It copies the entire contents of the Winchester disk onto floppy disks. If the Winchester disk or the computer breaks down we get it repaired (or replaced) and then copy everything back from the floppies. We may lose the data for the day when the disk broke down but that can quickly be reentered from recent ward reports, etc."

Use of the System

It was decided not to have a terminal in the ward because of the extra time and effort involved in entering data while caring for the babies. So the computer resides in an adjacent room and data is entered daily. Each day a ward round report is produced for the consultant's visit. Monthly reports are produced like the one shown earlier.

The main use of the system is for research. The enquiry system is frequently used to extract data from the database. Researchers can then analyse the data to find out more about the diagnosis of illnesses in babies and the best methods of treatment and care.

As you can see, the Special Care Baby Unit system is an **information retrieval system**, storing data and enabling users to retrieve data according to their requirements. It is not an intelligent system; it can't diagnose an illness or decide what treatment to give. To do this an **expert system** is needed.

EXPERT SYSTEMS IN MEDICINE

■ What is an expert system?

An expert system is a computer system which contains certain knowledge and expertise and can reason and draw conclusions from that knowledge, with a view to solving problems and giving advice. It usually deals with a small, well-defined area of expertise where substantial knowledge connects situations to actions. Expert systems are often referred to as **knowledge based systems**.

Like a human expert, an expert system has to go through an apprenticeship stage where it builds up its knowledge and expertise to create a knowledge base. This stage is called **knowledge acquisition**; a **knowledge engineer**, a person with similar skills to a systems analyst, talks to people who are experts in the area to find out how they reason and draw conclusions. For example, to create an expert system about premature babies, the knowledge engineer would interview the hospital consultants who treat these babies.

The most common way of representing knowledge in the knowledge base is with a set of rules. For example, a rule about premature babies might look like this:

IF birth weight < 2500 g AND blood glucose low
THEN there is 50% probability of jaundice

The knowledge engineer builds up a set of rules and then tests them by entering data about some premature babies. Here the consultant can help by judging the correctness of the expert system's conclusions. The rules will probably need modifying or adding to and the process continues until the system demonstrates the required level of expertise.

The **inference engine** receives data from the user about a particular baby; it works through the rules, testing all the conditions to see which ones match the data, and finally draws some conclusions and presents these to the user. It should also be able to explain its reasoning to the user (ie. which rules it has used).

The expert system is developed using a programming language, such as **PROLOG**, or using an **expert system shell**, a package which provides the inference engine, the user interface and an empty knowledge base into which the rules are entered.

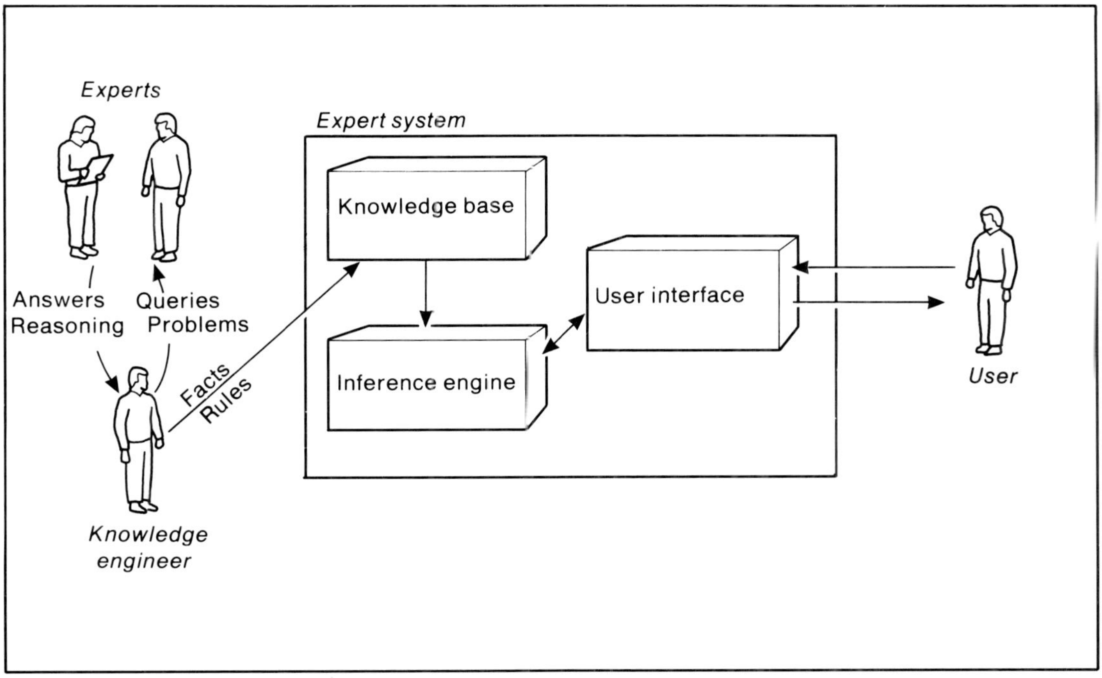

Figure 12 The expert system

■ Applications of expert systems

MYCIN (started in 1972) was one of the earliest expert systems, giving advice on diagnosis and treatment of blood infections. There are a number of medical systems in hospitals, each concerning the diagnosis and treatment of a particular type of illness. There is one which advises general practitioners on how to help diabetes patients and when to refer them to a specialist.

Expert systems are also in use in a variety of other areas. For example: assessing fire risks for insurance companies; selecting package holidays and travel routes; matching people to a job and identifying a person's individual training needs; choosing a suitable herbicide for weed control; configuring computers; detecting faults in a computer system. The ability to explain reasoning is also useful for educational purposes (eg. medical students can enter data about a patient and discuss the conclusions reached by the expert system).

■ Expert systems and Artificial Intelligence

Expert systems provide useful tools to assist people but they are not likely to replace the human expert. For one thing they lack the human characteristic of commonsense and the ability to handle inconsistencies. Also an expert system is limited to a small domain of expertise.

Expert systems are part of the larger field of **Artificial Intelligence (AI)**, which started in the 1950's when researchers programmed machines to prove theorems and to play games, such as chess. Later people tried to develop machines which could display characteristics of human intelligence, understand natural language and recognise objects. Research in these areas continues, investigating different ways of representing knowledge and human understanding, The field of AI is still very much in its infancy and there is still a lot to be learned.

QUESTIONS

1 (a) Why is it important to use a separate demonstration system with its own data for training new staff?
(b) Why does record deletion appear in the housekeeping section of the system, rather than in the clinical records section?

2 There are many applications of computers within medicine and the health service. Find out about some of these (what they do, who uses them and what hardware is required). For each application, discuss the advantages and disadvantages of using a computer.
It would be feasible to integrate all these health care systems, but it is a massive task. What would be the benefits to be gained from integrating the systems? What difficulties would be involved in implementing this?

3 Ms. Jones and Ms. Sahni are discussing the introduction of a new expert system. "They say it's better than a junior doctor and as good as a senior." "I think it's just not necessary." Discuss these statements.

4 A hospital consultant who specialises in liver disease is interested in developing an expert system to assist in diagnosis. A computer specialist is contacted with a view to creating an appropriate system.
(a) (i) Report on the types of issues they would need to discuss.
(ii) Indicate the steps the computer specialist would need to take to design the expert system.
(b) Suggest how such an expert system could be of benefit
(i) to patients,
(ii) to hospital doctors.
[*UCLES 1989*]

FURTHER INFORMATION

Chapter 2 Systems Analysis and Design
Chapter 3 Files and Database Systems

CASE STUDY 7

Millhouses Travel

Millhouses Travel Agency

INTRODUCTION

Millhouses Travel is a small independent travel agency, which is based in a suburb of Sheffield and provides a holiday booking service for its customers.

This case study looks at how the business uses information technology – how '**office automation**' affects the business operation.

THE BUSINESS

Millhouses Travel is run by one man and two assistants. It provides a holiday booking service, acting as an agent for approximately 35 holiday companies. These companies offer:

Inclusive tours (holiday and travel)

Ferry services

Flights

Cruises.

The agency works on the basis of displaying the brochures and advertising material for each company, and making bookings for customers who select their requirements from the brochures. The agent may also offer advice on various aspects of a holiday, and help customers in choosing a package. He receives a commission (a percentage of the price of each holiday sold) from the tour operators.

Most travel agencies now use an **online** computerised enquiry and booking system. Millhouses Travel is no exception, and the next section describes how they use the **ISTEL** booking system.

Using the online booking system

ISTEL is an online **remote** holiday booking system. It provides access to a large number of tour operator's booking systems, as well as the British Telecom PRESTEL service.

All these systems are **databases** containing information about holidays advertised in the brochures. Agents may make firm or provisional bookings by entering data into the database from a keyboard on the desk in their office. The system responds through a **VDU screen**. The agency and the database are connected by the telephone **network**.

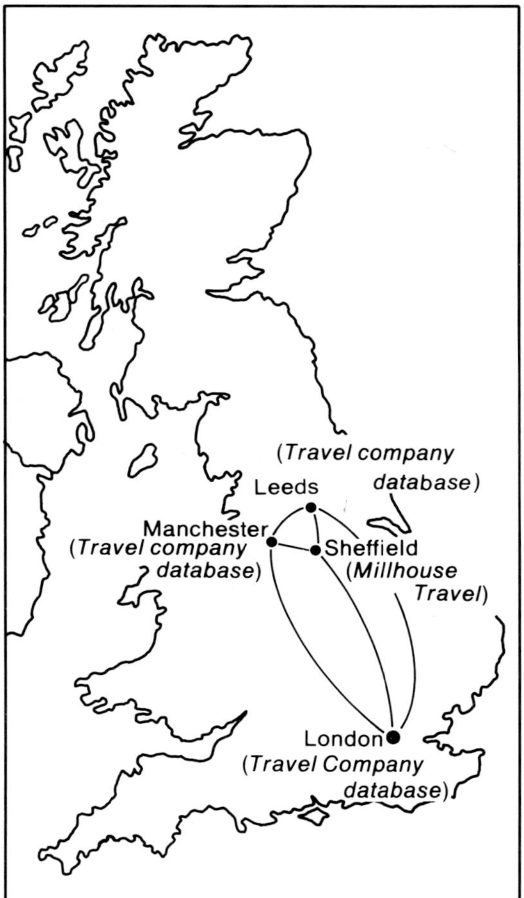

Figure 1 The travel agency is linked to holiday company databases in other cities

With these booking systems there is no need for people to answer the telephone when an agent wishes to make a booking or enquiry, the agent communicates directly with the database.

Booking a holiday

The following describes how you might enquire about or book a holiday using the online system. The pictures are printouts of the information displayed on the **terminal screen** at various points during the booking or enquiry sequence at the agency.

Figure 2 "Good morning" screen

Fig. 2 shows the screen displayed when the agency switches on their terminal in the morning. After entering an **identity code** and **password** the next screen is displayed (Fig. 3), which lists the databases available.

You can see that a number of database services are available, including PRESTEL and FASTRAK. PRESTEL is the general database system provided by British Telecom, FASTRAK is another general holiday booking system.

You can see that most of the options listed provide a telephone number – Option 'D', however, doesn't. This highlights an important difference in the way that the services are provided. If the agent uses any option other than 'D', the terminal dials the telephone number shown, and the charge for the time used will appear on the next telephone bill. Option 'D' causes the 'ISTEL DIRECT' service to be accessed. This still uses the telephone network but in this case, the time used doesn't appear on the telephone bill. The agent pays a yearly subscription, for the service, to the ISTEL company. The company pays for the telephone usage and provides access to individual travel companies' databases.

DATABASE DIRECTORY

DIR	Name	TEL No.
1	THOMSON HOLIDAYS	92371255
2	INTASUN HOLIDAYS	92375065
3	ISTEL	728474
4	AIRTOURS plc	750424
5	FASTRAK	750424
6	P.R.E.S.T.E.L.	701616
7	HORIZON TRAVEL	728474
8	YUGOTOURS LTD.	728474
9	GRECIAN/CYPRIANA	728474
0	REDWING	728474
A	COSMOS HOLIDAYS	728474
B	KUONI TRAVEL LTD	728474
C	POUNDSTRETCHER	728474
D	ISTEL DIRECT■ ■ ■ ■	
E	CITALIA HOLIDAYS	728474
F	NATIONAL/SMITHS	728474

Press 1–F or # for Manual Dialling

DISCONNECTED

Figure 3 Databases available

Having accessed the ISTEL direct system (Fig. 4), the agent is asked to enter a code for the required tour, ferry, flight or cruise company. The agent has a list of codes for companies on the system.

In this example we have chosen Thompson's holidays. Their booking system is called T.O.P. Fig. 5 shows the display for the T.O.P. system. Notice that the display offers various ways of using the database. This allows a customer and the agent to '**browse**' through the database

Figure 4 The ISTEL system

before choosing a holiday. Using the database like this is similar to reading the brochure – except that the database can be kept up to date with holiday availability information, special offers etc.

In this way the customer and the agent can choose and book a holiday directly with the database through the terminal. Once the holiday is booked, the travel company will send an invoice for payment.

T.O.P. 23JAN90 1134 0001a MANA06

GOOD MORNING

MILLHOUSES TRAVEL

WELCOME TO T.O.P.

BOOK
1 SPECIFIC HOLIDAY
2 CITIES HOLIDAY
3 AVAILABILITY SEARCH
4 ACCOMMODATION SEARCH
5 LATE DEAL SEARCH

ADMIN
6 DISPLAY/CONFIRM/EXTEND
7 AGENT DIARY
8 CANCEL

GENERAL
9 LATEST OFFERS/NEWS
0 HORIZON FACT FILE

ENTER NUMBER FOR FUNCTION REQUIRED

Figure 5 Thomson Holiday's database menu

COMPUTERS ON HOLIDAYS

■ How is the travel business affected?

To get answers to this question, we asked the owner of Millhouses Travel, John Kennedy. First of all we asked how using the holiday booking databases had affected the running of his office.

*"**W**ell, it means that instead of spending hours using the telephone ringing the tour operators, we now use our terminals. The database is available 24 hours every day, so, although we are not open all night, we can make bookings after 5 o'clock. Because we are in the suburbs, people often call in on their way home from work to make enquiries or bookings. It used to be that the travel operators would stop answering the phone at 5 o'clock or sooner, so we could lose business."*

Next, we asked how he thought the tour operator's end of the business had been affected.

"It must save them a lot of money because far fewer telephone operators are required. A lot of workers in the business must have lost jobs, that goes for the agents as well of course. Also, if a company is available on the ISTEL system it makes it more attractive to us."

Why's that?

"We prefer to use the ISTEL system because we have already paid the subscription. Dialling direct can be very expensive because we have to pay for each telephone call. It also means that we don't know how much the dialling charges are until we get our telephone bill. The travel business is very competitive and the travel companies could lose business through not being available to agents through the cheaper system."

We went on to ask Mr. Kennedy what other use he made of computers and information technology. Did he, for instance, use **word-processors**?

*"No, we don't use computers at all. I suppose they might be useful for doing '**mailshots**'. We do like to keep in touch with previous customers but we get their names and addresses from our manual filing system. We don't own a photocopier or a fax machine, I can't justify the cost against the benefits we might gain."*

SUMMARY

We can see from this case study that almost all the activity in this travel agency is based around using the **remote online databases** of the travel companies. These systems provide a very effective and efficient service. The agents and the operators obviously trust the system to keep a correct record of bookings.

However, computers don't figure at all in the running of the agent's office itself. This might be different if the number of customers handled by the agency increased. This seems to be a case of using technology as far as it is needed, and no further.

QUESTIONS

1 Visit a travel agent in your area and compare its activities with Millhouses Travel.
Does it: Use the same types of **online** booking systems?
Use computers in the office itself. If so, how and why?

2 We have looked at the way the agent uses the databases. What sort of operations would the tour operators carry out on the databases?

3 What implications does the introduction of these databases have for:
(a) the industry
(b) people working in the industry?

4 In what other ways might computers assist in the running of the business if, for instance, the number of customers increased?

5 (a) Describe some essential features of an automated office environment that uses up-to-date information technology facilities.
(b) What factors have worked against the more widespread use of home computing in areas such as direct shopping and banking?
[*UCLES 1989*] *AS*

6 The term *office automation* has been widely used during the last few years to cover the use of computers in the office. Describe recent advances in computer hardware and software including communications and networks which have made possible this transformation of working practice within some offices. By choosing examples from various fields, such as medicine, journalism or police work, discuss how the advent of office automation has:
(i) affected the nature of the work carried out;
(ii) affected the tasks performed by the office worker in such offices.
Comment on how society has responded to the use of computers in the office.
[*WJEC 1988*]

FURTHER INFORMATION

Chapter 3 Files and Database Systems
Chapter 5 Operating Systems and Systems Software
Chapter 7 Data Transfer and Communications

PART 2

Information Chapters

The Systems Cycle

INTRODUCTION

Computers are used in all areas of life and new computer systems are being developed for all sorts of applications. The organisation requiring a new computer system may be a large company, a small business, a government or local authority department, a hospital or a school. But whatever the size of the organisation and the type of application involved, the new system needs careful planning and development if it is to be successful.

Computer system development goes through several different stages, from the initial ideas to the final working system. This chapter explains these stages, why they are necessary, what happens at each stage and the people involved. The reasons for having a new computer system and the crucial decisions that must be made are also discussed.

The more detailed aspects of systems analysis and design are covered in Chapter 2.

DEVELOPING A NEW COMPUTER SYSTEM

■ What is a system?

The word **system** is probably the most over-worked word in the area of computing. There are also control systems, systems of government, the solar system and so on. Generally, a system is a complex whole made up of connected parts arranged to work together for a common purpose.

In this chapter we discuss systems in organisations and how they are designed to fit computers and people's jobs together to produce a more efficient organisation. The computer itself is only part of the system.

■ System development and the people involved

Each computer system has its own requirements and is developed accordingly. For example the Kew Gardens control system is very different from the Datapost parcels system. However, all systems go through certain stages of development as shown in Fig. 1. Note that people may use different names for some of these stages and that new methods may alter the details of what happens at each stage, but the basic cycle is the same.

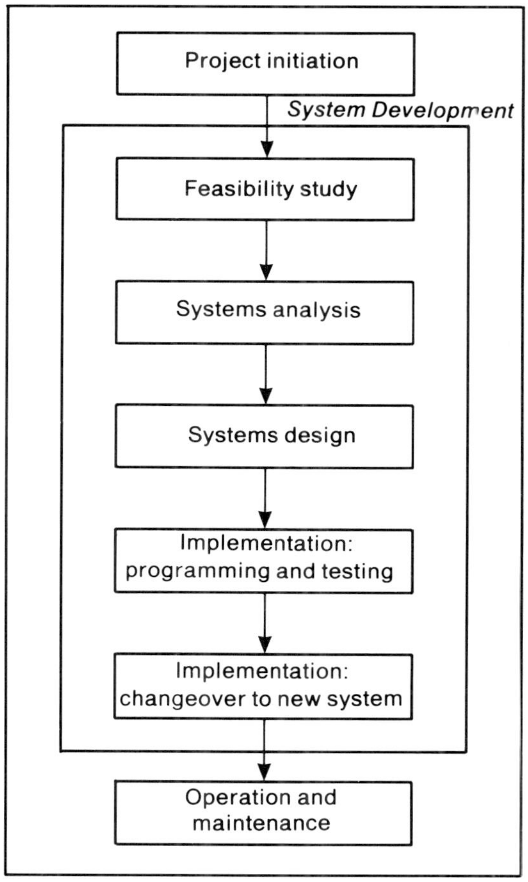

Figure 1 The system life cycle

This approach can be applied to most problems: analyse the problem; design a solution; put it into practice; review results. You probably use this approach for project work. At each stage, progress is reviewed and you may need to go back to a previous stage to alter something that doesn't work or could be done better. That's why it is called the **system life cycle**.

If the system is very small there may be only one person to do all the tasks. Suppose, for example, that someone who runs a theatre club asks you to develop a system to store information about club members and to mail letters and news-sheets to them. You have to assess the feasibility of the project, do the analysis, design, programming and testing as well as installing the hardware and training people to use the system. To do this well you need a variety of different skills, technical and communication. You need to be both analyst and programmer.

In large organisations, like Sainsburys and the Post Office, there are teams of **systems analysts** and **programmers**. Some systems analysts may act as **consultants**, advising management on the planning of their computer systems and doing feasibility studies. Consultants from an outside consultancy firm are sometimes hired to help, particularly if the organisation lacks the expertise in a particular area.

Let's not forget the users. In the theatre club the main user is the secretary who enters data but members are also users; they receive letters, etc. from the computer system. A large computer system has many users including managers at various levels who receive **reports** (information from the computer), **computer operators** who run the machines, **data preparation operators** who enter data and people who deal with enquiries.

■ The need for standards

With so many people involved in the system there is a need for standard ways of doing things and of recording them. **Standards** make it much easier for people to work together. Most organisations have their own standards for **analysis** and **design** (Chapter 2), for **programming** and for **documentation**.

■ Reasons for a new system

The project (ie. the development of a new system) starts when management decide that they need a new computerised system for a particular application. The new system replaces a manual system or an older computer system. Their aim may be to reduce costs, to increase efficiency, to make their business more competitive or to introduce some new manufacturing, monitoring or control process.

For example, the Datapost manual system of recording parcels involved an enormous amount of paperwork. Also it was difficult for management to monitor and control all operations because the information was either not available or took too long to obtain. With their new tracking and tracing system, Datapost aimed to:

- improve speed and efficiency
- provide a better service for customers
- expand the business
- provide up-to-date management information to help management in decision making, planning and budgeting.

Figure 2 People and computer systems

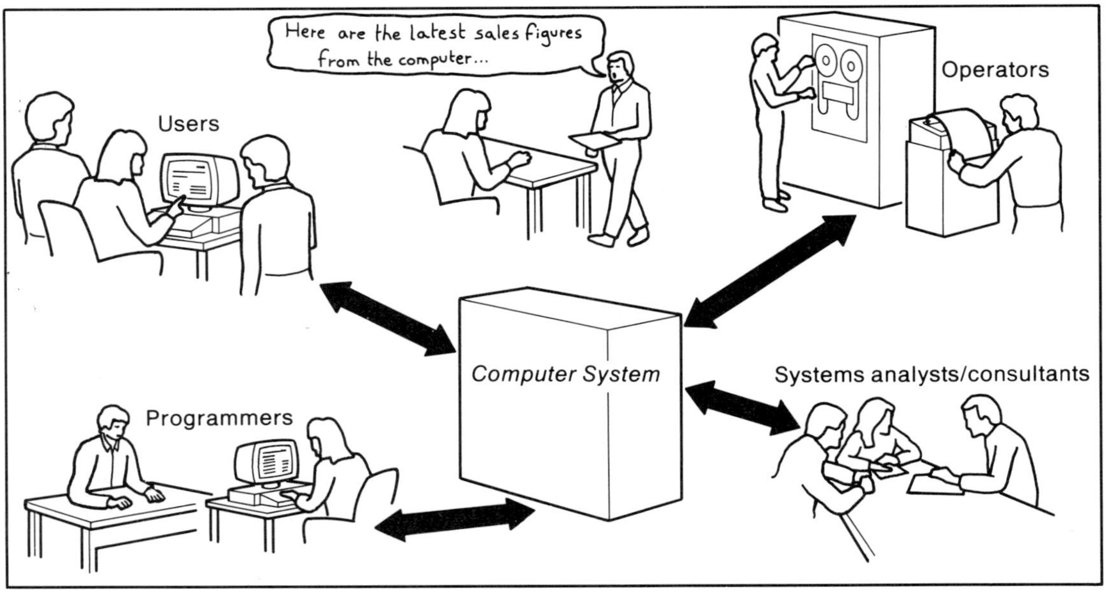

An organisation which already has a computer system may decide to replace it with a new one because:

- it is too slow
- it has insufficient capacity (the computer can't store all the data)
- the equipment is old and becoming too expensive to maintain
- new technology is available which will do a better job
- the system needs to be integrated with other new systems the company has installed.

A new system is likely to be expensive but is worthwhile if it helps the company become more competitive and more profitable or if it helps the organisation to provide better, more cost-effective services.

■ Who decides?

The go-ahead for a new system is given by the appropriate level of management. The finance for the project must be available and if there are several proposed projects competing for limited finances, top management have to decide on priorities. In large organisations these decisions are made by the directors.

Whatever the size of an organisation (from the local theatre club to the national Post Office) the purchase of a computer system is relatively costly and a wrong decision may have drastic consequences. Before committing themselves, management need to ask some important questions:

- ▲ Is it possible to develop the system they want?
- ▲ How can it be done (what are the options)?
- ▲ How much is it going to cost and how long will it take?
- ▲ How will it affect people's jobs?
- ▲ Will changes have to be made to the structure of the organisation?
- ▲ What are the benefits of a new system?
- ▲ What are the risks involved?
- ▲ Is it worth it?

■ Feasibility study

• *Investigating the options*

To help management make their decisions, a systems analyst is asked to conduct a preliminary study and to prepare a **feasibility report**. This report should present a set of options and enough information about each option for management to make a decision about what sort of computer system should be installed and how it should be used.

The report may vary in length from a few pages for the theatre club to a very thick report for a large system. It contains the following sort of information:

- the aims of the new system and its main functions
- the options considered, their advantages and disadvantages
- the recommended option, its costs, benefits and effects on the organisation
- a suggested plan for development of the new system (and the changeover from the old one).

• *Software options*

If a **software package** is available to do the job it may be the best solution. A package is a set of programs designed to do a particular job, such as payroll, stock control, accounts or word-processing (you are probably familiar with some microcomputer packages). A package is written for general use by a **software house** (a company that produces and sells software) and it is usually cheaper to buy one of these rather than develop a new system from scratch.

The disadvantage is that the package may not do exactly what's required. It is impossible for a package to meet everybody's individual needs – it must be designed to suit the majority. Some packages can be tailored to suit the organisation's requirements but only to a limited extent.

If no suitable package is available, the software must be written. Developing new software is more expensive and time consuming than buying a package but it is more likely to fit the organisation's requirements. Many large systems like Sainsburys and Datapost are developed **in-house** by their own analysts and programmers. The alternative is to get a software house to develop the software.

• *Hardware options*

At this stage we are just looking at what type of **hardware** is needed; the selection of the equipment is done later. We are making a 'shopping list' of computers, disk storage, printers, terminals, telecommunications equipment and any specialised equipment required, such as the temperature monitors for the Kew Gardens conservatory.

Hardware and software must be selected at the same time so that they are compatible. Some people make the mistake of choosing a computer and then finding that the software they want does not run on that computer! Most packages are designed to run under a particular **operating system**.

An organisation which already has computer equipment may decide to use it for the new system, provided it is suitable. For example, the Post Office use their **mainframe** computer to run the Datapost system because the data needs to be held centrally. However, they needed to purchase other equipment – barcode readers/decoders, local computers and the **communications network** to link the offices to the mainframe computer.

An organisation which doesn't want to buy its own computer equipment may decide instead to pay a **computer bureau** to run its programs. For example, some companies use a bureau to run their payroll. A bureau provides a computing service for its customers. Data is delivered to the bureau and output is collected. Alternatively, data is transferred over telephone lines. The advantage of using a bureau is that the organisation doesn't have to buy and maintain its own hardware and software. The disadvantages are that charges may be high; time may be lost transferring data; there may be difficulties dealing with errors.

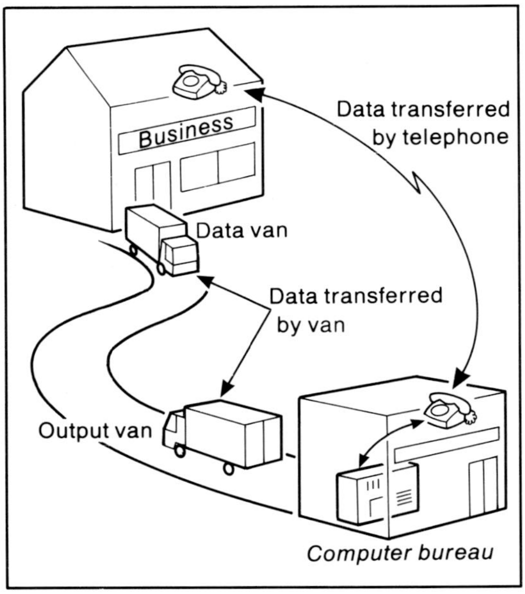

Figure 3 A computer bureau hires out time on its computer to a business

- *Effects on the organisation*

It is important to consider how the new system will affect employees. Some new systems require completely new methods of working. People's jobs change, the organisation may need to be restructured and redundancies are possible. Such changes have to be carefully planned and the management has to negotiate with the trade unions at an early stage to make sure that the new system can work effectively when it is installed. Otherwise user resistance may cause the system to fail.

- *Recommendations, costs and schedule*

The analysts consider all the options and make recommendations to management, who make the final decision. An option may be rejected for a variety of reasons: it is too costly; it is unsuitable for the needs of the organisation; it is unacceptable to operators or users; it would take too long to implement; it would cause too much disruption; it is incompatible with the organisation's other computer systems. The whole project might be dropped because none of the options is acceptable. In some cases the conclusion is that a new system is not needed and that some changes to existing procedures will do the job. A new system is not always the answer.

Estimates of the costs involved help management to reach a final decision. Costs include the initial setup costs (software development, hardware purchase and installation, training) and running costs (salaries, maintenance of hardware and software and consumables, such as listing paper and disks).

A development schedule is needed so that management can plan ahead. In addition to the time needed for analysis, design and programming, time is required for installation of equipment, testing the system and training users. This all has to be carefully planned.

The feasibility report describes the recommended options, their costs, benefits and effects on the organisation. Management then have to make the final decision – whether to go ahead with a particular option, or shelve the project or investigate other possibilities.

Specifying and Designing

If management decide to go ahead with the project the next stage is the detailed investigation and analysis of the system. This is done by a **systems analyst** (or team of analysts if the project is large).

■ Understanding the current system

Before specifying the new system, the analyst finds out how the current system works and what its problems and shortcomings are. A thorough understanding of what goes on is essential so that the analyst can discuss the requirements of the new system with management and users.

The analyst needs to know:

- what the system does
- what documents are involved (eg. forms for data entry, invoices, reports produced)
- what data is stored, input and output
- information flows – who sends and receives messages and documents and when
- problems experienced by users, such as delays or information that is difficult to obtain.

For Datapost, Jane talked to the managers at Head Office about the information they received, whether they were satisfied with it and what they felt they needed. Day to day matters, such as organisation of collections and deliveries and problems of bottlenecks (lots of parcels arriving at once), were discussed with the managers of the local offices. She observed staff sorting parcels and delivering them and discussed their work, how they used the six-part labels and how they coped with problems such as undelivered parcels or parcels with missing labels.

Talking to people involved in the current system is important. These people know best about what they do and will feel they should be involved in any changes being made. They will be the users of the new system. Individuals may only understand the part of the system they are involved in and so different points of view will emerge. The analyst has to take account of all of these; the analyst must understand the whole system.

Techniques for fact finding and for recording and analysing information collected are explained in Chapter 2.

■ Specifying the requirements of the new system

Having built up a picture (a model) of the current system, the analyst can discuss the requirements of the new system with the people involved. They need to discuss the main functions of the new system and the information the system should provide for management and users.

As well as specifying general requirements, the analysts have to plan exactly what jobs the system has to do. This means specifying the data to be input, output and stored, and the procedures to be followed (both manual and computer). This is a lengthy process as there is a lot of cross-checking to do to make sure that the system can meet the users' requirements.

The product of the investigation and analysis is a **requirements report**, sometimes referred to as a systems proposal or functional specification. It specifies in detail what the new system should do and includes revised estimates of costs and timescales. Management check that what is planned meets their needs and any necessary changes are made. It is important to get things right at this stage otherwise the system will not work the way that people want it to and the further into the development the harder it is to make changes.

■ Hardware and software selection

If a **software package** is to be used, suppliers who offer packages of the appropriate type are invited to **tender**. They have to show how their package matches the requirements of the organisation (or can be tailored to do so) and estimate the costs involved. The organisation then selects the most suitable package and draws up a contract with the supplier.

If the organisation has decided to use a **computer bureau**, it is selected by a similar tender process and a contract to supply services is drawn up.

If new hardware is required, the organisation invites manufacturers or suppliers to tender for equipment to suit their requirements. This was done for the Datapost equipment and a number of suppliers offered suitable equipment. Tests were carried out to select the best and most cost effective equipment for the job.

The factors the Datapost team considered were:

- ▲ Ease of use by the operators.
- ▲ Cost, both of the initial purchase and the daily running costs.
- ▲ Performance – could it do the job required, had it the speed and capacity to handle large numbers of bulky parcels of different sizes?
- ▲ Response times – would terminals respond quickly enough when several barcode readers were connected?
- ▲ Reliability – how often was the hardware likely to break down and what were the arrangements for repair and maintenance? What percentage of barcodes were read incorrectly?
- ▲ Security – if there was a disaster such as a fire, what **backup and recovery** procedures were there?
- ▲ Compatibility – would the equipment fit in with other hardware being used?

Large organisations often have an agreed **hardware strategy** (i.e. a policy for buying equipment). Compatibility is important so that machines can be linked together and software shared. Also, people who operate, use or maintain the equipment become familiar with the hardware and software. Schools and colleges often standardise on certain microcomputers for the same reasons.

■ Designing the new system

The analysis phase specifies what is required of the new system. System design decides how it is to be done. It determines how data is to be input, stored and output and designs the **user interface**, ie. the way the system communicates with the user via screen displays and printed output.

Briefly, system design involves the following tasks. These are explained in more detail in Chapter 2.

- ▲ Designing codes to identify objects, such as Datapost parcels or your bank account. **Check digits** are often appended to a code to help detect input errors.
- ▲ Designing input forms, report layouts and screen displays, which must be carefully designed as they are the means of communication between people and the computer.
- ▲ Designing manual procedures, for example collecting data for input or delivering output to people.
- ▲ Deciding which processes will be done **on-line** and which will be **batch**.
- ▲ Designing **physical** data storage; this involves defining the **file structure** and deciding how each file is to be organised and how it is accessed.
- ▲ Specifying **security** and backup procedures; a **password** system and possibly **data encryption** are needed to make sure unauthorised people can't access the data. Backup copies of data files must be kept in case the data is corrupted (eg. by a disk fault or the computer breaking down).
- ▲ Specifying programs; the analysts decide what programs are needed and write **program specifications** for the programmers.

IMPLEMENTATION, TESTING AND CHANGEOVER

■ Programming

The program specifications, written in **pseudocode** or structured English, are given to the programmers who develop and test the programs. In a large project, teams of programmers work on different parts of the system and each programmer is responsible for certain program modules. Note that the design may need to be modified slightly as programming progresses in order to make the system work as efficiently as possible.

Programs are often written in a **high-level language** but in some cases a low-level language **(assembly code)** may be needed. For some applications **fourth generation languages** are used.

■ Testing

Programs are tested individually, then linked together until the complete system has been tested. The analyst is responsible for seeing that suitable test data is prepared to check that the programs work properly in all situations. Test data must contain a mixture of valid data and all types of invalid data. Also the full range of data items should be tested; for example, maximum and minimum values for numeric data items. If files are used, empty files should be tested as well as large files.

The analyst should arrange **acceptance testing**, when the users try out the system with prepared test data to detect any further problems or errors.

Modifications may be needed. When the users are satisfied with the system they formally accept it.

■ Documenting the system

Good **documentation** (a written description of the system and its programs) is very important. Poor documentation often means that people don't make best use of the system or get frustrated when things go wrong and the relevant information is not in the manual (Have you had this experience with some of the packages you've used?). If the instructions are not clear or are incorrect or even missing, it is easy for people to make mistakes.

There should be different types of documentation for different people:

- ▲ Users need to know (in non-technical language) how to use the system. For example, how to enter data, how to retrieve information, what reports are provided. This documentation can be on the computer or in a manual.
- ▲ Computer operators need instructions on how to run the system, loading disks, tapes, stationery, and what to do in the event of a breakdown.
- ▲ Programmers need technical documentation, detailing the system and all its programs. No matter how good the system, the odd error or 'bug' may occur and need fixing. Also modifications to the system in the future (**maintenance**) are difficult without proper documentation. No-one can commit the whole thing to memory and relying on the person who wrote the program is risky; they may be ill when problems arise or they may have left the company.

The systems analyst should document the analysis and design stages of the project. It is important to keep a record of this for people working on the project, both during the development and afterwards.

■ User participation and training

The users should be involved from the start. Participation is important so that users feel they are getting a computer system that suits their needs and their working environment. A new system may mean learning to use new equipment, changing jobs or even redundancies. Trade unions should be consulted at an early stage in the development process about new working practices.

Prototyping is a useful way of testing the **user interface** to make sure that it is suited to the users. This involves setting up example screens on the computer to show the users what the system will be like. This can be done early in the development process so that user feedback can be incorporated in the design.

Systems designers are becoming increasingly aware of the importance of well designed equipment, particularly for operators who spend several hours a day in front of a screen. Things like screen flicker, the angle of the screen, keyboard layouts, the chairs people sit in and the positioning of equipment all affect computer operators, sometimes causing ill health.

If users and operators are not consulted about a new system and new working practices, they may refuse to work with the system and bring it to a complete standstill. If they haven't received the right training they may not use the system properly.

■ Changeover to the new system

When the system has been thoroughly tested, the hardware installed and the initial data entered, the change can be made from the old system to the new. The best way of doing this depends on the organisation's own circumstances. It could be **direct changeover, parallel running, pilot operation** or **phased changeover**.

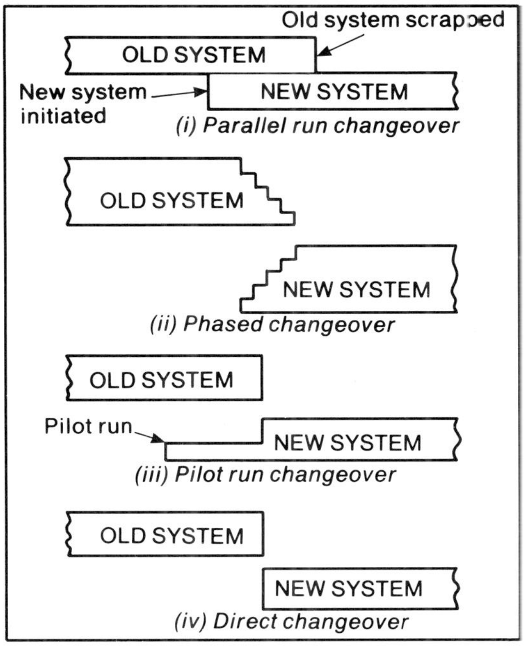

Figure 4 Changeover approaches

Direct changeover means replacing the old system with the new one all at once. This can be risky because any remaining faults in the new system could have disastrous effects. However some systems (eg. real-time ones) have to use this method because the old system can't be run at the same time as the new one.

Pilot operation (for example testing the system in one branch of a large multi-branch organisation) limits the effects of possible faults. The rest of the system is then introduced all at once or introduced in phases. The main reason for phased implementation is the size of the operation. Datapost, for example, had over 300 sites where new equipment had to be installed, users trained and the system tested. It was simply not possible to start all these up at the same time.

Parallel running means running both the old system and the new system for a certain time. It has the advantage that results from the two systems can be compared (useful for example in an accounting system) but it may not be possible as it ties up a lot of resources; it needs twice the computer time plus extra staff to run it.

■ Operation, review and maintenance

Provided that the system has been thoroughly tested and has been accepted by the users, it can go into full operation. The system should be reviewed at regular intervals to ensure that it works properly. System maintenance will be constantly required as users' needs change or legislation requires changes to the information produced. For example, if Datapost management decide they need a new report about parcels throughput, the people who developed the Datapost system would make the necessary amendments to the programs. Likewise, if tax rates are changed, all payroll systems have to be modified.

QUESTIONS

1 Look at each of the case studies and identify the stages of the systems cycle, explaining what was done at each stage. Where stages of development are not covered in the case study, say what you think would have happened.

2 Describe the work of a systems analyst during each stage of the systems cycle. Discuss the skills required for the tasks performed at each stage.

3 A car rental firm is considering installing a computer system to improve the running of the business. The firm owns a variety of cars, none more than 3 years old. Some of the cars are damaged and others are being serviced. Cars can be hired from many points within the country and need not be returned to the pick-up point.
Suppose you are a systems analyst consulted by the firm. Suggest functions which could be carried out by a suitable computer-based system and describe the necessary equipment and the staffing implications. Outline the factors which should be considered by the firm before selecting a particular system.

[COSSEC 1989]

4 Computer based systems are often introduced into a business in an attempt to improve efficiency, both in terms of staff productivity and customer services. However, unforeseen consequences, both organisational and social, can limit the effectiveness of any new system. Discuss briefly why a good technical specification alone may not be sufficient to ensure the successful implementation of a computer based system.

[ULSEB 1987]

5 (a) Suppose you have been asked to carry out a feasibility study for the manager of a local sports centre, who is considering using a computer system to help run the centre more efficiently. Explain how you would go about this task and what you would include in your feasibility report.
(b) Assume that you've developed a computer system for the sports centre. How would you test the system? What training would you give the staff and the manager? What documentation would you provide for the users?
(c) Explain why the Sports Centre system will need to be reviewed regularly. What events could necessitate maintenance of the system?

6 Your local dentist approaches you to advise on the computerisation of his records. Before providing a solution, the dentist's situation has to be investigated in some depth.
(a) Describe what factors need to be examined in such an investigation.
(b) What criteria would determine whether you recommend the adaptation of a commercially available package or the design of new software?

[COSSEC 1989] AS

CHAPTER 2

Systems Analysis and Design

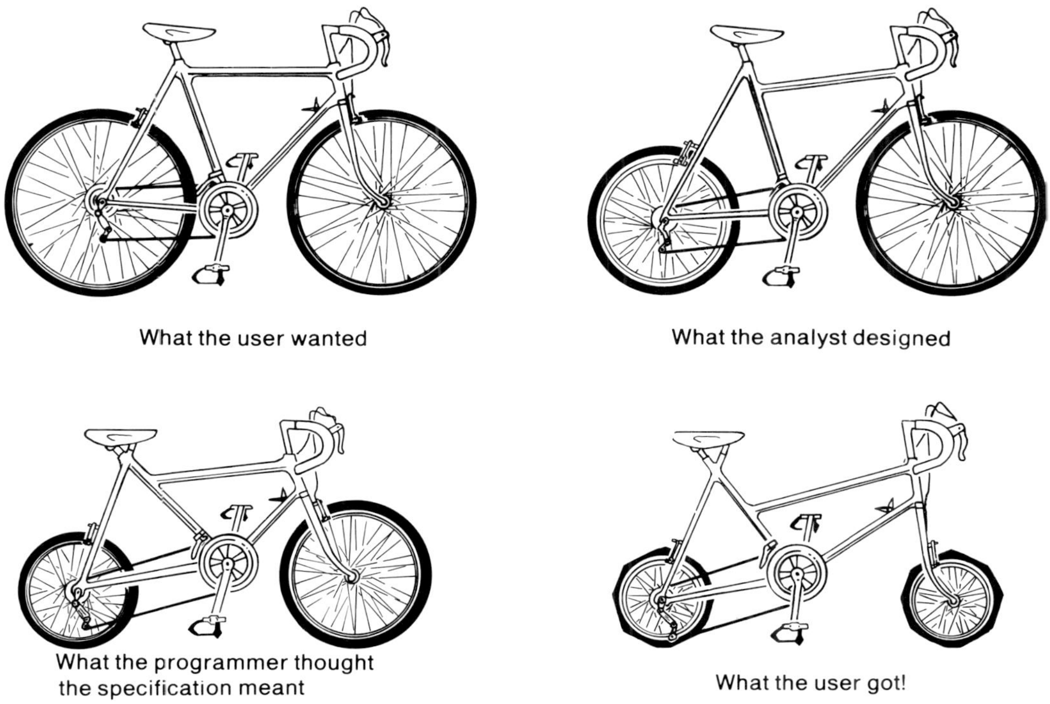

Figure 1 Possible consequences of poor analysis and design

INTRODUCTION

Chapter 1 explained the stages of development of a computerised system, from feasibility study to completion. This chapter deals with two of these stages: systems analysis and systems design. They are both very important – poor analysis and design often result in a system that is not what the users wanted, as illustrated in Fig. 1.

First, we will look at some of the methods and techniques of systems analysis; the second part of the chapter deals with the principles of systems design. There is not space within one chapter to give a very detailed account; if you need more information you are advised to refer to a book on systems analysis and design.

A HISTORICAL PERSPECTIVE

In the early days of computing, programs were written by programmers for solving specific problems. There was no systems analysis and design because each program was written as an individual task. Programs were written in **machine code** or **assembler**.

In the 1960's people started considering different methods of programming to try to improve programmer productivity and to create programs that were easier to modify. This lead to the development of **high-level** programming languages.

Figure 2 Comparing the 1960's and 1970's

In the 1970's, people realised that larger, more complex computer systems needed more planning and that analysis and design were required before doing the programming. Instead of the programmer doing everything, systems analysts were brought in to analyse requirements and design systems.

The National Computing Centre (NCC) developed methods for systems analysts and design and these methods were adopted by many organisations. This represented a big step forward in systems development. It gave systems analysts a standard way of doing things and of documenting their work. **Standards** (explained in Chapter 1) help people to communicate about the system they are working on.

Since then, people have improved on the NCC's basic methods and a number of new methods (often called **methodologies**) have been developed. The principles of analysis and design are the same, but the approaches are different and there are new tools and techniques. Fig. 3 shows some of the methods introduced since the late 1960's. Learmonth and Burchett's methods (including SSADM which was developed for the UK central government) and various Information Engineering methods are now widely used. These methods are constantly being updated and new ones introduced.

Computer people are now more aware of the importance of involving the users of a new computer system during its development. If the users

1969	Systems Analysis and Design	National Computing Centre
1975	Jackson Structured Programming	Jackson
1978	Structured Systems Analysis and Design	Yourdon & Constantine De Marco Gane & Sarson
1979	Ethics	Mumford & Weir
1981	Learmonth Structured Design Method Structured Systems Analysis & Design Method (SSADM)	Learmonth & Burchett Central Computing and Telecommunications Agency
1981	Data Analysis Information Engineering (IE)	Palmer & Rock-Evans Martin & Finkelstein
1983	Jackson Structured Design	Jackson

Figure 3 Table of methods and dates first introduced

don't get much say in it, the system may not be what they want or need and they may not be satisfied with it. Sometimes a **business analyst** is asked to help the users define what they need from the computer to help them manage their business.

New technology also changes the way things are done and the opportunities for new computer systems. For example, computers themselves can help design systems and produce programs. Many products are emerging to automate all or part of the system development process. They provide computer based tools for producing diagrams during analysis and building a **data dictionary**; for designing systems; and for automatically producing program code. People refer to **Computer Aided Systems Engineering (CASE)** tools.

An **Integrated Project Support Environment (IPSE)** is a computerised tool used for managing development projects involving large teams of analysts and programmers. For example, it helps with project planning and estimating, timing and recording planned and finished tasks, keeping track of programs and documentation. It may also include some CASE tools.

SYSTEMS ANALYSIS

■ The need for skills and techniques

First let's summarise the tasks involved in systems analysis, mentioned in Chapter 1. The **systems analyst** starts by investigating the current system and its problems; it's important to understand what people do in the organisation and how it functions. Without this knowledge the analyst is unlikely to appreciate fully the problems of the current system and the needs for a new one.

The analyst also has to find out what the managers want from the new system and what they need to help make their business more efficient or to provide a better service. Having collected all the information about the current system the analyst analyses it and produces a plan for the new system.

To perform these tasks, the analyst needs to have a variety of skills to communicate with a wide range of people and to analyse information. A logical, analytical mind and patience are required to sort out all the information collected. As well as these skills, the analyst needs to learn certain techniques for fact finding, analysing information and recording everything. If you are doing a project that involves analysis, you will need to apply some of these techniques yourself.

■ Fact-finding techniques

Fact finding involves gathering a large amount of information. The analyst uses a range of methods to do this, including:

- interviewing
- questionnaires
- observation
- reading documents about the system.

● *Interviewing*

This is a productive and useful way of fact finding. You can ask the person you are interviewing to explain things which are not clear. However, you should remember that people's opinions may be biased and what they tell you may not be totally accurate.

Here are some points to remember when interviewing:

- organise the interview in advance
- be prepared. Think about the interview and what you aim to get out of it. It's important to prepare questions to help you structure the interview and get the information you want. But also be flexible and listen to what they say – they may tell you about something you hadn't thought of or something you'd thought wasn't important
- adjust to different levels of people and ask appropriate questions. For example, ask the managing director about the business objectives and the shop floor workers about their working environment
- be polite and tactful
- take notes at the interview and write them up afterwards.

● *Questionnaires*

Questionnaires are useful if people are spread over a wide geographical area, or if answers are required from a large number of users and it would take too much time to interview them all. For example, if the people who developed the ARKS system were considering adding extra facilities or developing a new system, they might send a questionnaire to all interested zoos to find out about how they currently used ARKS, what they thought about the package's facilities and what they would like to see in a new system.

A disadvantage of questionnaires is that you can't get the respondents to explain or elaborate their answers, without interviewing them. On the other hand some people will give honest answers if the questionnaire is anonymous.

Although they save time for the analyst, questionnaires do take time to design, send out, complete and return. So they have to be planned early in the investigation so that the analyst receives the responses in time. While waiting for the responses the analyst can be doing other fact finding.

A questionnaire must be well designed if it is to provide useful and accurate information. Later in this chapter we talk about forms design; the same principles apply to questionnaires, which are a type of form.

- *Observation*

Observing people at work helps fill in some of the gaps in the picture the analyst has built up. Valuable information can be collected about people's working conditions, the use of machines and computers, interruptions, pressures of large workloads, inefficiencies, bottlenecks, supervision. For example, Datapost analysts observed parcels being recorded and recommended the repositioning of equipment to make the job easier and more efficient. These things rarely come out of an interview, or if they are mentioned they may be biased.

The problem with observation is that people often work differently when they know they are being observed and some people may even think they are being spied upon. Also observation is time consuming and therefore costly.

- *Reading about the system*

Existing records and documents about the system give the analyst a useful starting point. Reports, manuals, training aids, job descriptions all give background information. Forms and files provide examples of documents used by staff. From studying these, the analyst gains a background knowledge of the current system, which is useful when interviewing people.

■ Fact recording

If the analyst's records consist only of scribbled notes, he or she soon forgets what they mean and the notes are likely to be of little use to anyone else. The analyst will need the information to communicate with other people working on the project and for subsequent work. The facts need to be recorded systematically and promptly.

Writing a description is one way of fact recording, but the description can get longwinded and may be ambiguous. Diagrams, charts and tables are preferable. You will find a variety of these used throughout this book.

- *Describing the organisation and its employees*

An **organisation chart** shows who works for whom in a department or organisation. Fig. 4 shows an organisation chart for the computer department of an imaginary company called A1 Systems Ltd.

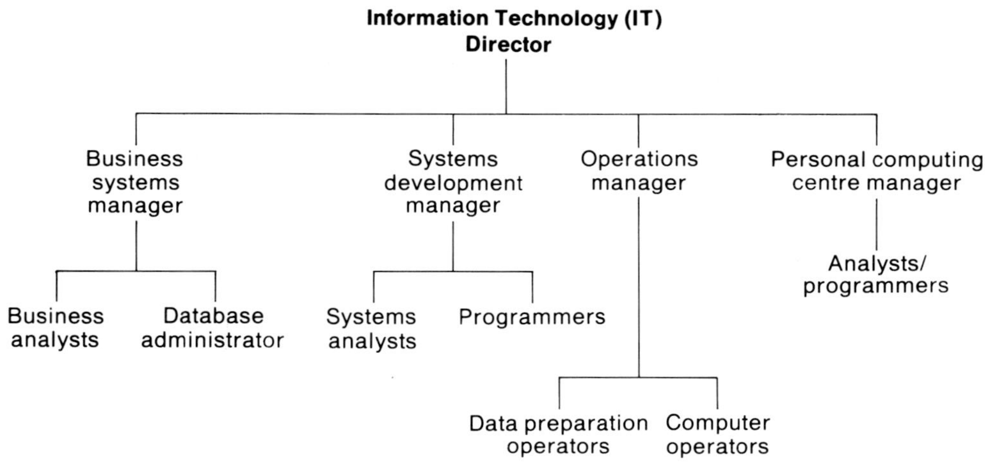

Figure 4 Organisation chart

Activity charts help the analyst to record and analyse the tasks that each employee performs and how long each task takes. The charts may show up inefficiencies or indicate that tasks could be modified or reordered. They are also useful for comparing what an employee currently does with tasks they may be given in the new system. For example, in the Special Care Baby Unit an activity chart was used to calculate the time taken for nurses' tasks, such as recording babies' data, filling in certain forms, drawing up charts and writing reports.

- *Describing the system: system flowcharts*

A **systems flowchart** gives an overall view of a data processing system, showing input and output, processes and files. There are several flowcharting methods. Fig. 5 shows some typical flowcharting symbols. A template is often used to help draw the symbols.

Fig. 6 shows the Special Care Baby Unit (SCBU) computer system. We've chosen the VDU symbol with two-way arrows for the inputs because data is entered interactively via forms on the screen; we could have used the keyboard symbol. Note the disk symbols which represent four disk files, but not four separate disks. Again the arrows are two-way because data is both written to the disk and read from the disk. The printed reports are output only.

System flowcharts are used less often nowadays; many people use **data flow diagrams** which provide more information and are better suited to systems where processes do not necessarily happen in a particular order.

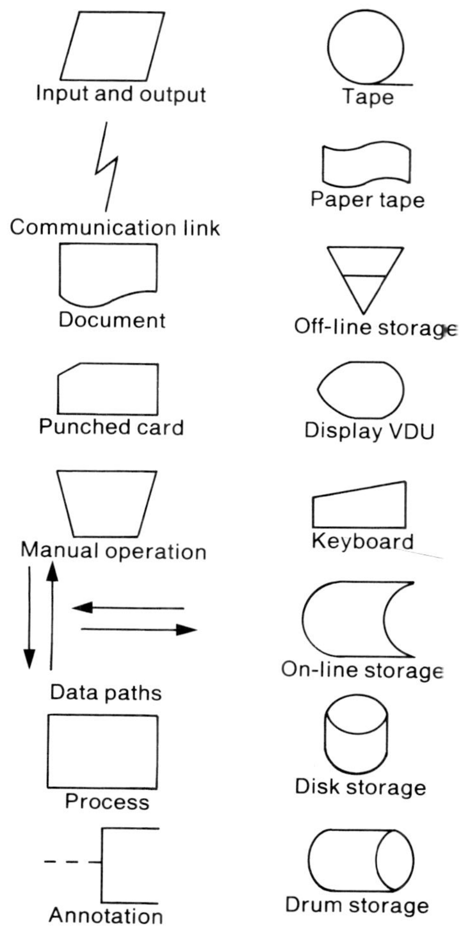

Figure 5 Flowchart symbols

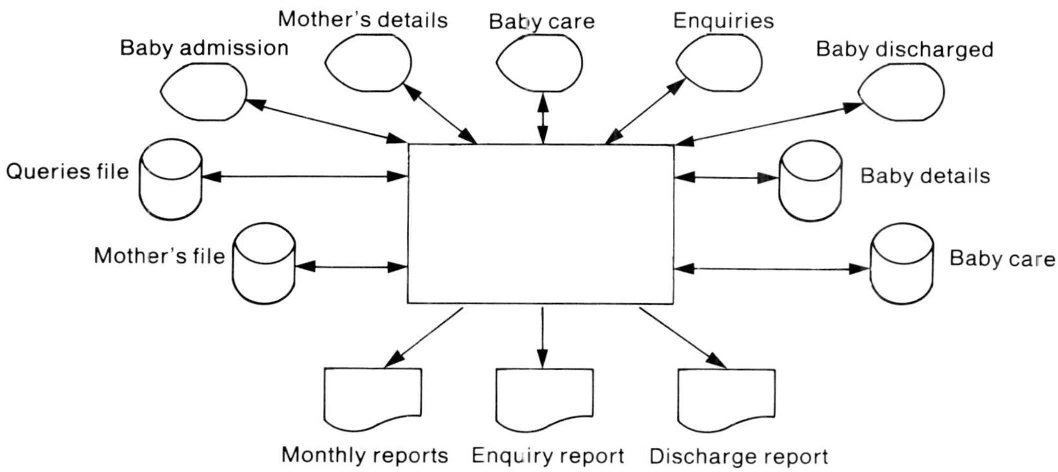

Figure 6 System flowchart for SCBU

- *Describing the system: data flow diagrams*

SSADM and some other systems analysis methods use **data flow diagrams (DFDs)** to show the processes in a system and the data which is sent from one process to another. The diagrams are used both to model the current system and to plan the new system. They provide a view of the system which is understandable to users as well as systems analysts and they are a useful basis for discussion.

An **outline flow diagram** shows the flow of documents and goods between departments within a company, suppliers and customers. An example is given in the case study on Sainsburys.

The DFDs also include functions and data stores. As an example we'll take the Special Care Baby Unit (SCBU); the systems analyst drew some data flow diagrams to help her understand how the manual system of recording data worked. Fig. 7 shows a level 1 data flow diagram, with two main functions. The baby may be admitted from the post-natal ward, the labour suite or operating theatre or the emergency area. Case notes accompany the baby and from these, plus the consultant's initial diagnosis, the nurses prepare an initial case notes folder. This is updated as the baby is treated and cared for. The hospital laboratory performs any tests required.

Fig. 8 shows the meanings of the symbols used. The data flows should all be named with the data or information that they carry (never use a verb on a data flow). A process or function box describes the main action(s) involved and notes the person responsible. Data stores may be manual (pieces of paper, forms, folders, card files, books) or computer files. Each data store is labelled with M for manual or C for computer and is given a number.

SSADM symbols

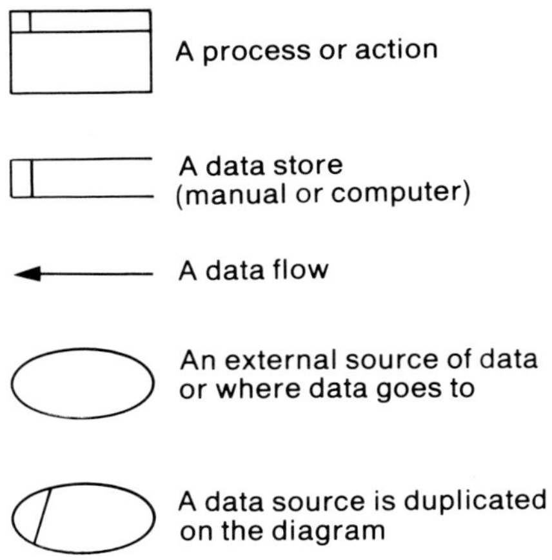

Figure 8 Dataflow symbols

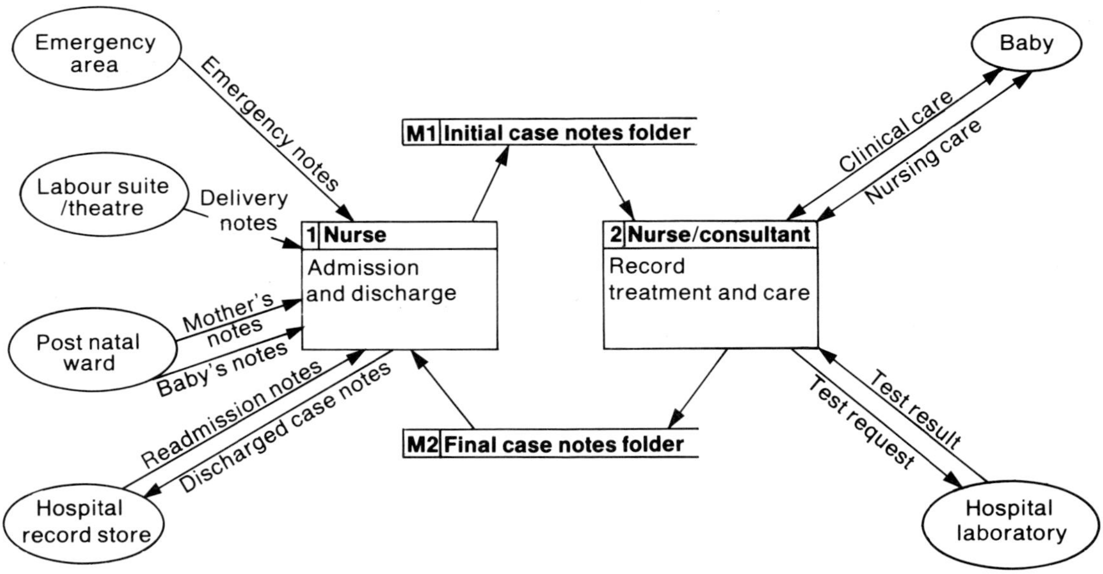

Figure 7 Dataflow diagram for SCBU Level 1

Each of the two main functions can be further decomposed by 'zooming in' on what that function does. We call these level 2 diagrams. Fig. 9 shows the level 2 data flow diagram for function 1, admission and discharge. Note that there are four more data stores in this diagram. The admission book contains the date of admission, the baby's hospital number and a few basic details about the baby. The all babies book is used to classify babies by birthweight, etc.

The principle of decomposition shown here is important, particularly in a large system. A system is much easier to understand if it's split up into manageable parts. The example only has two levels but a large system can have several levels. The same principle applies to computer programming (Chapter 4).

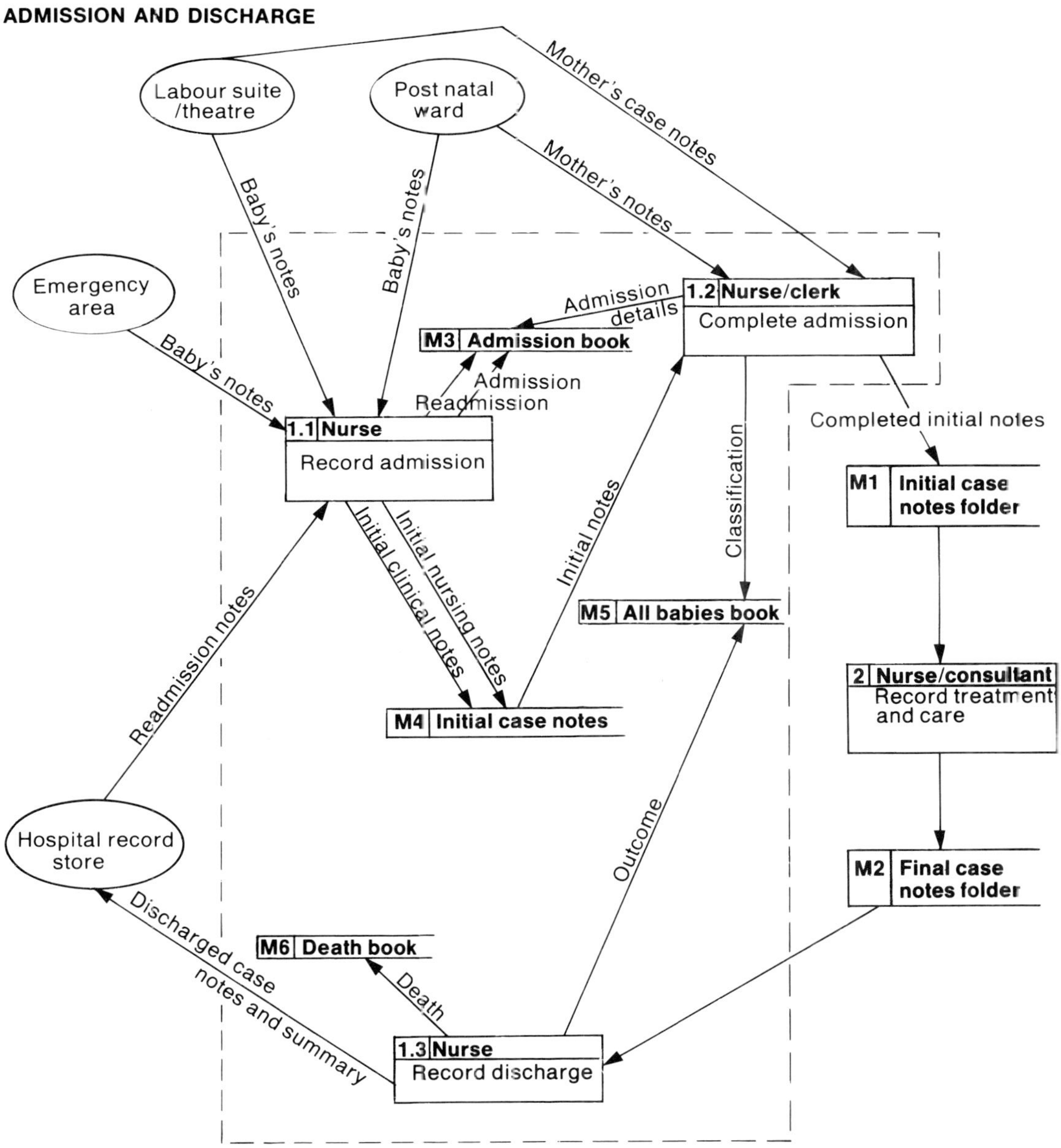

Figure 9 Dataflow diagram for SCBU Level 2

- *Describing procedures*

A **procedure flowchart** describes the detailed logic of a process or procedure, such as sorting and checking customers' orders, sending students their exam results, admitting a baby to hospital. Fig. 10 shows a flowchart for the old manual SCBU admissions procedure. The symbols used are for manual procedures; they are different from the ones used for computer routines.

Compare this flowchart with the data flow diagram in Fig. 9. Similar functions are shown, but the flowchart orders the tasks. This particular procedure is not very suitable for flowcharting because the tasks are not always done in a particular order. In general, a flowchart is useful for describing a small, ordered procedure but becomes unmanageable as it gets larger. With structured programming techniques, large flowcharts are now seldom used. **Pseudocode** or

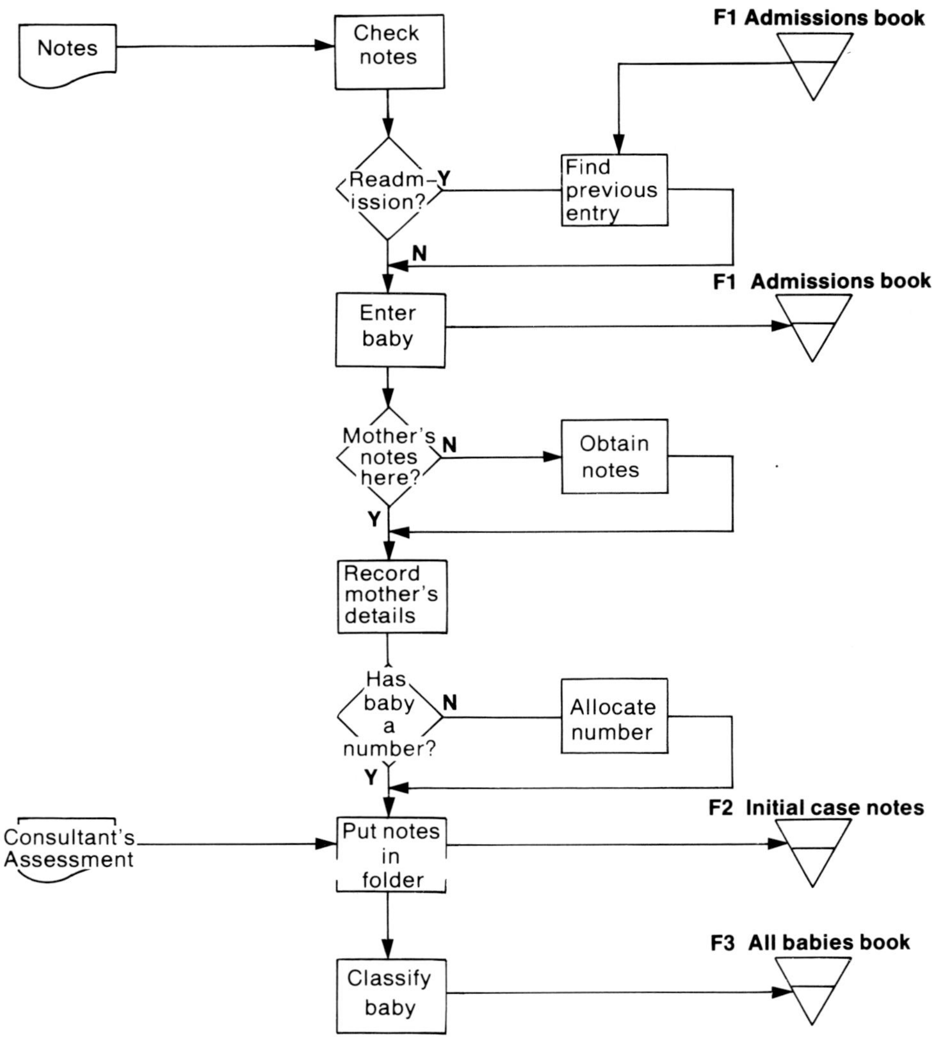

Figure 10 Admissions procedure

		Rules							
Conditions	Readmission	Y	Y	Y	Y	N	N	N	N
	Mother's notes available	Y	Y	N	N	Y	Y	N	N
	Hospital no. allocated	Y	N	N	Y	Y	N	Y	N
Actions	Find previous admission entry	X	X	X	X				
	Obtain mother's notes			X	X			X	X
	Allocate hospital no.		X	X			X		X

Figure 11 Decision tables for SCBU admissions

		Rules							
Conditions	Red	Y	Y	Y	Y	N	N	N	N
	Amber	Y	Y	N	N	Y	Y	N	N
	Green	Y	N	Y	N	Y	N	Y	N
Actions	Go							X	
	Stop	X	X	X	X	X	X		X
	Call Police	X		X		X			X

Figure 12 Decision tables for traffic lights

structured English is used to describe procedures.

- *Decision tables*

These are useful for recording the logic behind sometimes complicated processes. Computer programs can be produced directly from decision table input and there are a number of packages available for this purpose. Fig. 11 shows a **decision table** for the SCBU admissions process, which can be compared with the procedure flowchart above. This is not a particularly good example, however, because the three conditions are not interdependant. In Fig. 12 the action does depend on the combination of conditions.

■ Data analysis

- *Logical and physical data*

A system can only produce the information people want if the necessary data is collected and if the data is organised properly.

Data is often described in two ways, as **logical data** or **physical data**. Logical refers to the type and structure of the data and the relationships between different data items. Physical data refers to the way the data is stored in files on disk (or other storage) and the way the files are organised and accessed. This section on data analysis is about logical data. Physical data is covered in Chapter 3.

- *Data models*

When the systems analysts investigate the old system and the requirements for the new one, they draw up a list of the items of data that need to be stored in the computer. The objects about which data are stored are called **entities** and the details of each entity are called **attributes**. For example, in the Datapost system, the main entity is a parcel and its attributes are destination, sender, date of posting, etc. The entities in ARKS are animals, the cages they live in, etc.

Fig. 13 shows a **data model** or **entity model** for the ARKS system. It's important to note that there is rarely one correct model; it isn't like a mathematical problem with one correct solution. Different people may view the data structure in different ways and come up with different models. That doesn't matter, in fact it may be useful for promoting a discussion about the data.

Entities have **relationships** between them. In Fig. 13, a species (eg. gorilla) can include many animals (there are several gorillas in the zoo). This is called a one-to-many relationship and is shown by the symbol which looks like a crow's foot. Similarly, one animal can have many transactions, for example, it can be loaned to several zoos (at different times).

The attributes are listed on an entity description form as shown in Fig. 15 opposite.

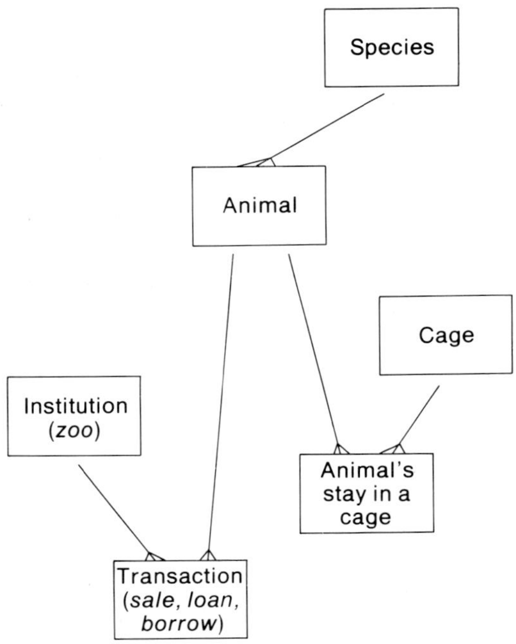

Figure 13 ARKS entity model

- *Data dictionaries*

A **data dictionary** (like any other dictionary) records the names and definitions of data items. The dictionary may be created manually or on a computer. Each definition includes a description of the data item and information such as its length and format, its relationships with other items, other names it is known by, the processes it is used in, and its security level (ie. whether a special password is required to access it).

SYSTEMS DESIGN

■ The design process

Design is very important in computing, just as it is in designing things to make in CDT, designing a building, a car, etc. Designing something is a creative process, but at the same time the capabilities of the people (users), together with the suitability of materials and equipment involved, have to be taken into account. It is no use designing something which looks good but is not usable or something which performs its task well but is difficult to use. This applies to computer systems as it does to anything else.

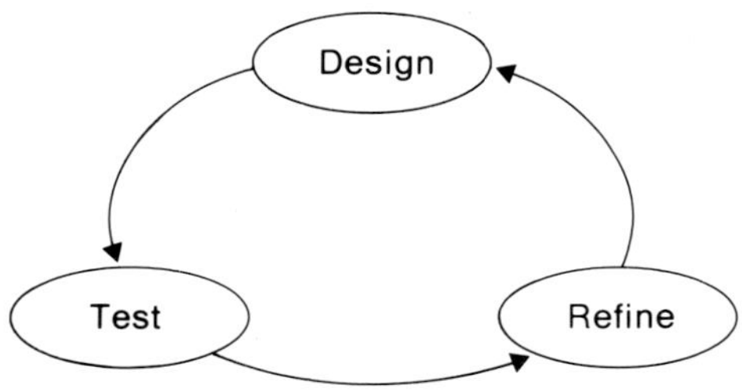

Figure 14 The iterative design process

Design starts from a **requirements specification**. Imagine you are designing a mountain bicycle – the requirements might be that the bike should:

- be able to cope with rough ground
- be able to go up steep hills
- have an attractive appearance
- be available in certain sizes
- cost a certain amount
- be easy to handle and not too heavy.

SYSTEM: ARKS

Entity ID & Name: Animal Volume: Average 50 Max 100

Entity Description:

Key	Data Items	Format	Length	Comments
✓	id code	C	6	
	species	C	35	Latin name
	name	C	25	Zoo name
	date of birth	D	8	
	date of arrival	D	8	
	date of leaving	D	8	
	hybrid	L	1	True or False
	sex	N	1	M, F or U (unknown)
	mother's id	C	6	
	mother's zoo	C	9	
	father's id	C	6	
	father's zoo	C	9	
	birth type	C	1	Captive or wild
	birth location	C	11	
	current enclosure	C	8	
		Total size	142	

Figure 15 An entity description

In computing systems the requirements specification follows the same principle, ie. it details what the system should be able to do and certain important criteria such as cost. The designer specifies how the system will satisfy the requirements and how it will communicate with users. In reality, design is an iterative process – the designer works at increasingly detailed levels, going back and making changes until the design is complete.

With any but very small systems, it is common for a **project team** to work on the design. In a very large system there may be several teams involved. Coordination and cooperation are very important; frequent meetings between all the contributing team members are required to discuss progress and to make sure that the different parts of the design fit together.

The objectives of good design are:

- practicality (the system must fulfil the requirements)
- usability (it must be easy to use and have appropriate interfaces for users at different levels)
- efficiency (it must make best use of people and equipment; it must be accurate and sufficiently fast)
- flexibility (it must be responsive to different users' needs; it must be easy to modify; it should be, if possible, easily adapted to run on other machines ie. it should be portable)
- reliability (the hardware should be reliable and there should be emergency procedures in case of breakdown or fire; the software should be robust and should not fail)
- security (the risk of fraud and abuse should be minimised)
- safety.

The main steps involved in the design process are:

design of data codes

input design

output design

process design and program specification

security and privacy considerations

file structures and organisation.

■ Design of data codes

• *Design features*

It is often necessary to use an **identification code** to identify something uniquely. (Identification is often shortened to 'id' and we'll refer to id codes). For example, in ARKS, each animal has an id code; the name can't be used because two animals might have the same name. Id codes are given to bank accounts, library books, students, parcels, foods, etc.

Codes are also useful to categorise things, for example, the ARKS animals also have an ISIS number which categorises them according to their species; it is an internationally used number. A standardised coding system of this type is necessary where data is exchanged between systems. Another good example is the use of bar codes to identify foods and other goods.

Codes may be numerical or alphanumeric (letters mixed with numbers). They can hold information themselves in addition to identifying something. Codes help to save storage space and to speed up data entry when the code is used instead of a more lengthy name or description.

Here are some hints for good code design:

- the code should be meaningful to people who use it
- a long code (more than six digits) is difficult to remember and error prone. So, break up a long code with gaps or symbols (eg. 3128/12). This makes the code easier to recognise. The code needn't be stored this way in the computer but will appear like this on the screen and on printouts
- avoid letters which can be confusing when handwritten, eg. I, O, Q, S, G; also avoid ones that sound similar when spoken
- allow scope for adding more codes later, in case the system expands.

An existing system may already use some codes. There are advantages in keeping these codes, because people are used to them. However, it may be necessary to change the codes and introduce some new ones for an efficient system. Careful planning is needed to ensure that all the codes used throughout the organisation are consistent and sensibly designed. For example, problems may arise if the production department of a company uses codes for goods they produce which are different codes from those used by the sales department when selling the goods.

• *Coding methods*

Here are some examples of coding methods.

► **1** Simple numerical sequence. For example, each patient admitted to the hospital (including babies admitted to the SCBU) is allocated the next number. This is the simplest coding method, but it holds no real information about the patient.

► **2** A block of codes could be assigned to each ward in the hospital. For example, if there were 15 wards, you could allocate 0001–0999 for Ward 1 (a large ward), 1000–1499 for Ward 2 (a smaller ward), etc. The patient's number would then tell us the ward of admission.

However, there are a number of problems: What happens when the numbers for a particular ward are all used? If a patient is transferred to another ward the number would need changing.

► **3** Mnemonic code. Meaningful letters are used to make the codes easier to read and understand. For example, Datapost codes start with DP, standing for Datapost, and finish with GB for Great Britain. This helps people to identify parcels when they go abroad.

► **4** Derived codes are formed from the original name or description of the person or item. One example is to start with the first letter, then remove all vowels, W's, H's and Y's from the name. Then, numerically code the next three consonants as follows:

1 (for B, F, P, V)
2 (for C, G, J, K, Q, S, X, Z)
3 (for D, T)
4 (for L)
5 (for M, N)
6 (for R).

Try this on your surname – you should get a code made up of a letter followed by three numbers, unless your name is very short.

► **5** A decimal or hierarchical code. One example is the international disease code used in the SCBU, and in hospitals generally. The first set of digits indicates the name of the disease and each following digit specifies the disease in more and more detail.

For example:

774 jaundice
774.6 neonatal jaundice
774.62 baby under 24 hours old
774.63 baby between 24 and 48 hours
774.64 baby more than 48 hours old.

The advantage of this coding method is that it is easily extended when new diseases are catalogued. The varying length of the code can sometimes be a disadvantage in a computer system.

► **6** Faceted codes – each digit (or group of digits) represents some characteristic or facet of the item. An advantage is that they can be changed and extended easily. Also people using the codes get used to their meaning.

For example, if you were a company making screws, bolts and washers of various sizes and materials you could use a three-digit code as follows:

First digit for the object
(1 = screw, 2 = bolt, 3 = washer)

Second digit for the material
(1 = steel, 2 = brass, 3 = copper)

Third digit for the length
(1 = 1 cm, 2 = 1.5 cm, 3 = 2 cm).

So for example, the code for a 2 cm brass screw is 123. When dealing with metric lengths in the example above we might use the length in millimetres as part of the code. So 1225 would represent a 25 mm brass screw. Alternatively SB25 might be easier to recognise.

In practice, combinations of these types of codes are often used. For example flight codes combine the mnemonic for the destination with a sequence number for the actual flight (265NYK to New York, 112LON to London). Datapost parcel bar codes combine mnemonics with an 8-digit serial number.

■ Input design

● *The need for design*

A computer system needs data to process and that data has to be input in some way. It is important to choose the best method of input and to design the **data entry** system well. Data entry is a costly process.

When specifying the input the systems analyst has to consider:

exactly what data needs to be input

how often data is entered and how much data there is

which input device is to be used.

He/she has to design:

input validation procedures

error procedures

forms for people to fill in

screens for data entry.

● *Specifying the input*

There are many different processes in a system and each requires some input data. The data either **updates** the data already in the system or is an **enquiry**, requesting information from the system. Updating methods are discussed in Chapter 3.

Briefly, there are three types of update:

- creating a new piece of data (eg. an animal arrives at London Zoo, a new baby is born or a parcel is accepted by Datapost)
- modifying or adding to some existing data (eg. an animal moves to another cage a baby is given medicines or a parcel arrives somewhere)
- deleting or archiving data (eg. an animal is sold, a baby leaves the hospital or a parcel is delivered).

An enquiry involves input of some key data by which the information can be retrieved. For example, giving a parcel's id number to find out where the parcel is; specifying a type of animal and asking for a list of those animals; finding all the babies who have had a certain illness.

- *Selecting an input device*

There are a whole range of **hardware** devices for entering data. Data can be input directly from barcodes, tags, magnetic stripe cards, etc. or from machine readable documents. Data which can't be entered directly is typed in. Chapter 8 describes the hardware used for data input and explains when and why different methods are used.

To help select the right input method, the designer needs to estimate how much data there is likely to be and when it needs to be entered (at regular intervals or as it's available). Peak times have to be considered. For example, Sainsburys rely on quick throughput at the point-of-sale till to give the customer a more efficient service. Both the data input devices and the computer system must be able to cope in the busiest periods. The volume of data also needs to be measured to estimate the number of tills that are required.

■ Validation and verification

Stories about someone receiving a bill for £1 000 000 or for £0.00 are often used to illustrate the old saying 'Garbage in – garbage out'. People are quick to blame the computer for errors, but in fact almost all errors are made by people at one stage or another. Typing errors are easily made and the **source document** (ie. the form someone has filled in with the data) may be difficult to read if handwritten. Alternatively, the form might have been filled in incorrectly.

It is up to the system designers to avoid output errors by making sure that input data is properly checked by the computer system. Many errors can be detected as the data is input or before it is processed. However, not all errors can be detected; for example, if you enter Mart instead of Mary or 12 June instead of 21 June, the computer system has no way of knowing that these are wrong because they are valid.

Checks fall into two categories: **verification** and **validation**. Verification is carried out by a second person who enters the same data as the first person. Any discrepancies in the data input are detected by the computer system, the operator is notified and mistakes are then corrected. The following are some methods of validating data.

- *Allowable entries*

Some data items have certain allowed entries. For example, a baby's sex is restricted to M for male or F for female. Codes, such as the ISIS numbers used in the ARKS system and the international disease classifications used in the Special Care Baby Unit, are stored in a list and when data is entered it is compared with the list. This process checks the validity of the input but it is still possible to enter the code for a different animal or disease by mistake.

- *Range checking*

This is used where the upper and lower limits of a data item are known. For example, a date being within a certain time span; a baby's birth weight being between sensible limits. Dates can be checked to make sure the day number matches the month (eg. to reject 31 April).

- *Type checking*

Individual characters can be checked to make sure they are the right type, for example a baby's birthweight must be numeric, but the surname must be alphabetic. A postcode has a special format, so M15 2LP is accepted, but 15M 2LP is rejected.

- *Hash and control totals*

These provide a method of checking a batch of numerical data. The values on an input form are added up and written down. When they are entered into the computer, it checks the written total with the actual total. If they disagree, either the data entry operator has made a mistake or the person who filled in the form has added up the totals incorrectly. In both cases the error is detected and can be corrected.

When the values that are added together have some real meaning (amounts of money on order forms, for example) they are called **control totals**. Values that are meaningless and just used for error checking (for example, the sum of code numbers) are called **hash totals**. If the form in Fig. 16 is entered, the computer should detect two errors. What are they and how would the operator find out what should have been written on the form?

Order no:	27568			
Customer:	J. Black PLC 29 London Ave Newtown N1 2QP			
Item code	Quantity	Unit price	Price	Description
2675	2	0.75	1.50	Glasses
0423	5	2.50	5.00	Teapots
4289	20	1.00	2.00	Teatowels
1614	1	32.00	32.00	Tablecloth
9061	28	36.25	40.50	

Figure 16 Order form

- *Check digits*

A check digit is added to a numerical code, such as a bank account number or a barcode to form a 'self-checking number'. This helps detect **transcription errors** (characters which look similar) and **transposition errors** (characters in wrong order, eg. 2465 instead of 2456). The check digit is calculated when the code is first input and becomes part of the code. Then when the full code is entered it is checked by calculating what the check digit should be and comparing it with the input.

For example, if the code is 513, we could form a check digit by simply adding the numbers together (5+1+3 = **9**) thus giving the code 513**9**. If we enter 519**3** the code will fail the test because 5+1+9 = 15 and not **3**. However, if we enter an incorrect code of 1539, it passes the test because the numbers add up correctly.

Simply adding the digits is not a very useful error detection method. Most systems use weights (each digit is multiplied by a weight) and a modulus (the number the sum is divided by). For example, a commonly used method is called weighted modulus eleven. Suppose we have a five-digit code 26350.

- Multiply digits by weights

Digit	2	6	3	5	0
Weight	6	5	4	3	2
Product	12	30	12	15	0

- Add the products 69
- Divide by 11 and take remainder
  69/11 = 6 remainder 3
- Subtract remainder from modulus
  11−3 = 8

  The new code is therefore 263508.

■ Designing forms

Forms that people fill in are often **source documents** for entry into a computer. You are probably familiar with mail order forms, cash withdrawal forms for bank or building society, TV licence forms, questionnaires, etc. It is very important to design forms that are easy to fill in. Forms that look complicated can put people off and people may fill them in wrongly if they aren't clear.

A form might have a title, a reference number, the name of the organisation or company, headings for different sections, questions for people to answer and space for office use. The form should be well laid out, with appropriate spaces for people to write in; often forms don't provide enough space to write in. Boxes to tick, options to circle or delete as appropriate are useful, they save writing and limit the response to certain options.

The wording must be polite, clear and precise, with no jargon. The questions must not be ambiguous or ask too much at once. The order of the form should be logical and clear. Presentation affects the appearance of the form and its ease of use. Different colours, fonts and sizes of print, capital letters and underlining can be used. Consistency of presentation of questions and of answer method is important. Inconsistency leads to confusion and the form takes longer to fill in.

Instructions for filling in the form should be clear and if necessary there can be explanatory notes. These need to be positioned carefully otherwise they clutter up the form and make it look complicated. It is often better to put them separately at the start or end. Forms should be tested out ('piloted') on the sort of people who will have to use them before they are put into circulation. This aims to show up any faults in the form and instructions or questions that aren't clear.

The designer also has to consider what sort of paper and printing method should be used. Paper comes in different colours, sizes, thicknesses and may be multipart. Printing may be done on different types of machine. The choice depends on the number of copies required, the cost of producing copies and the printing facilities available.

A form should also be clear for the data entry operator, to avoid mistakes. It's a good idea to match the design of the form with what appears on the screen.

■ Output design

The items to be output from each process must be specified. If the output is a printed **report** its layout is designed. Fig. 17 shows a print layout form used in the design of the SCBU system. Most of what we've said about designing forms also applies to reports. They need to be well presented with the required information and clear headings.

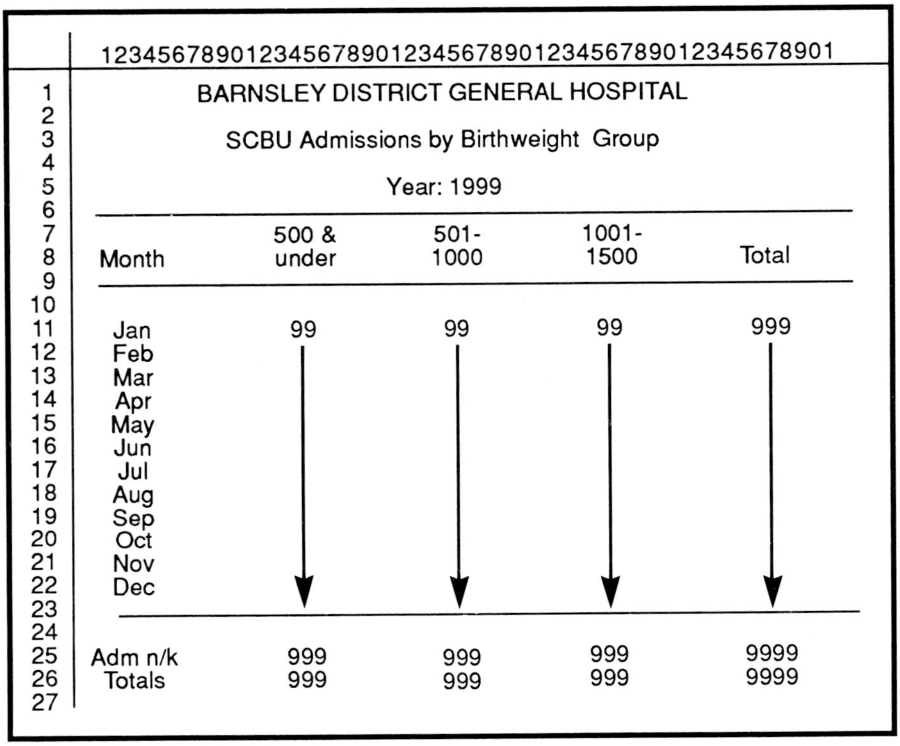

Figure 17 SCBU form

■ The user interface

● *Catering for the users*

The **user interface** is the part of the system that communicates with the user, usually via a screen. All the user sees is what's on this screen, not what is happening inside the computer. Therefore, if screens are poorly presented or instructions are not clear, the user will not feel happy using the system, however good the data processing might be. As well as an efficient system, users want one that is easy to use, understandable and well presented.

It is important to consult users about the interface. **Prototyping**, where screens are created for users to try out and comment on, is useful. Users can decide whether the design is understandable, acceptable and can check for omissions and inconsistencies. A simple example is entry of the date, which could be in one of many formats (eg. 25/07/89 or 25th July 1989 or 07/25/89). It is better to stick to what users are used to, providing it does not impair the system operation.

Most systems have a variety of users, from experienced data entry operators at one end of the scale, who need to enter data very quickly, to the occasional user (for example, a member of the public using a tourist information system). It is vital that the system designer considers the different users and caters for their needs.

- *Designing screens*

Much of what has been said about form design applies to **screen design** as well; presentation, layout and wording affect the appearance of the screen and thus the user's attitude towards it. The difference is that a screen is limited in size and one's attention tends to focus on the centre of the screen rather than reading a printed document from top to bottom. Also, colour and special effects can be used on a screen, though it is not a good idea to overdo them! Use them to highlight important items.

Because there are many screens in a system, consistency is important. Headings, layout and positioning of error and help messages should be standardised and the way the user responds to the system should be consistent. Consistent use of colours can help to distinguish certain types of items.

- *Input screens*

Form filling is used widely as a means of data input. The form is presented on the screen with headings and instructions as appropriate. After entering one data item, the cursor jumps to the next position for entry. Often you can go backwards or forwards on the screen to enter or amend data. A particular key may be used (eg. the control key with S) to save the screenful of data. Alternatively, when the last data item on the screen has been entered a question appears (eg. 'save screen?') and you reply yes or no.

Form filling enables an experienced user to enter data quickly. For example, when you order goods from a mail order company you write your order on a form which you send to the company. Data entry operators then enter your order into the computer system, by filling in a similar form on the screen.

Fig. 18 shows a screen design for the Special Care Baby Unit admission. A standard screen layout form has been used. The alternative is to design screens on the computer, if there is a facility for doing this.

An alternative to form filling is to present the user with a question or instruction and await the answer or response before continuing. For example, a cash card machine might say:

> 'Please enter your personal identification number' *1234*
> 'Please enter the amount in pence' *5000*

This conversational approach appears friendly and easy and is suitable for the occasional user. However, it is slow if a lot of input is involved. For example, it would not be suitable for entering a baby's details, nor for entering mail order forms.

AUTHOR: DIANNA   DATE: 9/5/88   SCREEN LAYOUT: Admission   PAGE: 22

	5 10 15 20 25 30 35 40		45 50 55 60 65 70 75 80	
1	Date: ..-..-..		PROCESS SCBU ADMISSION	
2	Time: ..-..			
3				
4	BABY		MOTHER	
5				
6	Unit No:	....	Unit No:	......
7				
8	Forename:	......	Forename:	....
9	Surname:	....	Surname:	....
10				
11	Date of Birth:	..-..-..	Date of Birth:	..-..-..
12	Time of Birth:	..-..		
13				
14	Birthweight:	....		
15				
16	Date of Admission:	..-..-..		
17	Time:	..-..		
18				
19	Admitted for:	.		
20	Reason:	.		
21	Consultant:	.		
22				
23				
24				

Figure 18   SCBU screen design

- *Moving around the system*

A **menu** displays a list of options and the user selects one, either by moving the cursor up and down the list and pressing a particular key (often RETURN) to select, or by entering a number or letter corresponding to their choice. Menus are easiest for inexperienced users as there is no need to remember what the options are. However, they can become tedious if you have to go through several levels to get to the part of the system you want. Also getting back may be tedious, depending on how the designer has organised the routing. Some systems use the ESCAPE key to go back to the previous level.

An example of a **hierarchical menu-driven system** is the SCBU system. Whilst being easy to use for new staff, it has features which allow the more experienced staff to bypass the menus by typing in commands. It also allows them to go backwards through the menus as well as forwards, and has a special key to take them back to the start menu.

Menus are used extensively nowadays. Most people are familiar with Viewdata and Teletext systems (eg. Prestel, Ceefax) which are based on menus. Cash dispensers also use menus and some provide special keys or buttons alongside the options for withdrawing cash, getting a statement, etc.

Pull-down menu

Pull-down (or pop-up) menus, normally used with a **mouse**, provide an easy to use menu system and are available on most machines (see photo). Often referred to as **WIMPS**, they provide: windows which may overlap; icons which are tiny pictures representing objects for selection; the mouse for pointing and selecting.

A **command-driven system** is suitable for the more experienced user who is familiar with the system and uses it frequently enough to remember what's available and what the commands do. The system displays a prompt (often one character) to indicate it is ready to receive a command from the user. The command input may be a word or an abbreviation or a combination of commands. It is usually quicker than going through menus and less frustrating for experienced users. An example of a command system is a personal computer running the MS-DOS operating system, as shown in Fig. 19.

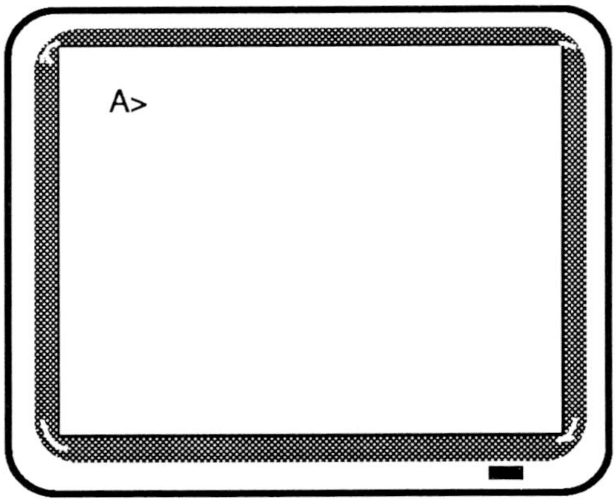

Figure 19 A command-driven system

- *Help systems*

Different users need different amounts and types of help. A good **help system** is particularly important for the new user. The help may consist of additional messages, prompts and menus which appear as the user works through the system. It may provide a complete online manual which can be referenced much as you might look at a manual on paper. Or it may be 'context relevant' help; for example, how to alter the margins if you are using a wordprocessor and have just pressed the key for margins.

Some systems allow you to specify the help level you require. Wordstar does this – as you change level you get progressively less information on the menus and at the lowest level you get no help (though you can always go back and change the level if you need help). Some systems allow you to turn the help level on or off. Other systems have a help key which allows you to display help and, when you've finished, to go back to where you were.

Where a limited choice of answers is available, a list of these may be presented to the user for them to select one. An example is the SCBU where a list of diseases is available on request, useful when the user is new or has forgotten the available responses. It is better than guessing at the response and getting lots of error messages.

There are different views on whether all help should be online or whether manuals should be provided – some people like to have a printed manual to refer to. Context relevant help is useful when you suddenly need to know what to do, but a manual may be preferred for browsing through information about the system facilities.

- *Error messages*

Nothing is more frustrating to a user than to get a message that simply says 'error', with no explanation of why the error has occurred or what the user should do to correct it. Therefore error messages should be carefully designed to be as meaningful and helpful as possible, without being too long (see Fig. 20).

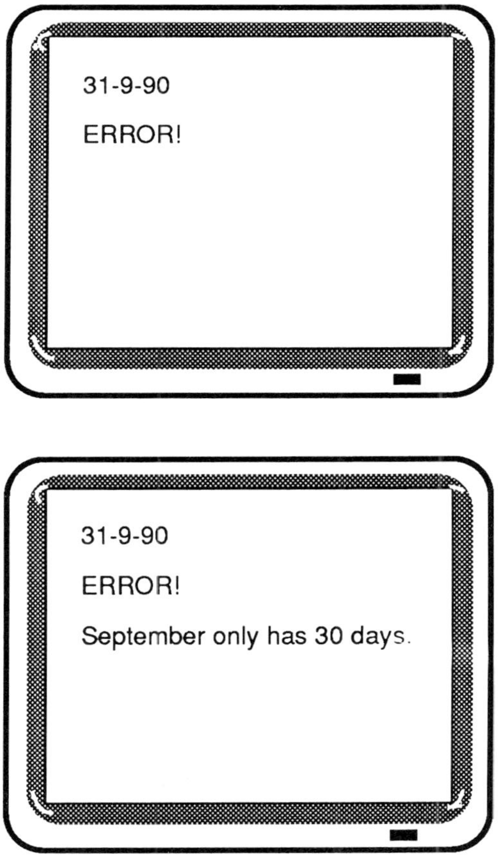

Figure 20 Error message

File structures and organisation

Data analysis decides what data items are needed and produces a data model. Now the analyst must decide how that data should be stored on the computer, in files or in a database. If separate files are used, the analyst decides how each file should be **organised** and **accessed**.

Sequential files are suitable for processing a large number of records in a batch, for example when processing a payroll. **Random files** can be accessed very quickly to find a particular record, for example for an urgent enquiry. **Indexed sequential files** are a compromise; for example a file of electricity customer accounts is processed sequentially to send out all the bills but it is accessed directly to find out when Mrs. Jones last paid her account. Chapter 3 describes these types of files in more detail and explains how they can be accessed.

Planning should take account of a file's future size and its rate of growth. The choice of file organisation and access method is affected by its likely **activity** or **hit rate**, ie. the percentage of records processed on average in a day. Also the **volatility** of the file, ie. the rate at which new records are added and old ones deleted, is important.

Process design and specifying programs

The analyst uses **pseudocode** or structured English to describe each process (each box on the data flow diagram). **Program specifications**, consisting of the process descriptions, screen designs and file structures, are given to the programmer.

Note that in most systems there are manual processes as well as computer ones. They involve things like collecting and batching forms for data entry, sending computer output to people and dealing with enquiries or orders over the phone. The analyst needs to specify how these processes are to be done.

The analyst must specify which computer processes are **online interactive** and which are **batch**. An online interactive process is required to respond almost immediately. Batch processes are done periodically (eg. daily, weekly or monthly) or when enough data is collected; input data is assembled and fed into the computer in batches.

An example of a **batch** system is a payroll system, where every week the hours each employee has worked are input and the payslips are produced. There would be no point in doing this online – the person entering the data would have to wait after each employee for the computer to do the calculations, update the employee's record and print the payslip. It is far more sensible to enter all the data offline (**key-to-disk** probably) and then send it to the computer in batches to be processed, probably overnight when the computer is less busy.

A **real-time** system, such as Kew Gardens uses, needs to react immediately to a signal. Imagine if its input data were processed in batch mode, it would be opening the windows hours after the sun had warmed the greenhouse! Airline bookings systems are another example of a real-time system. If you book the last seat on a flight, for example, the system needs to know immediately so that the next person wanting a seat is told that the flight is full.

Most systems involve some online processes and some batch ones. For example, the NOAH system is updated monthly with batches of ARKS data from all the zoos. However, it is accessed online by users who retrieve information from the database. When people need quick access to information, it has to be online.

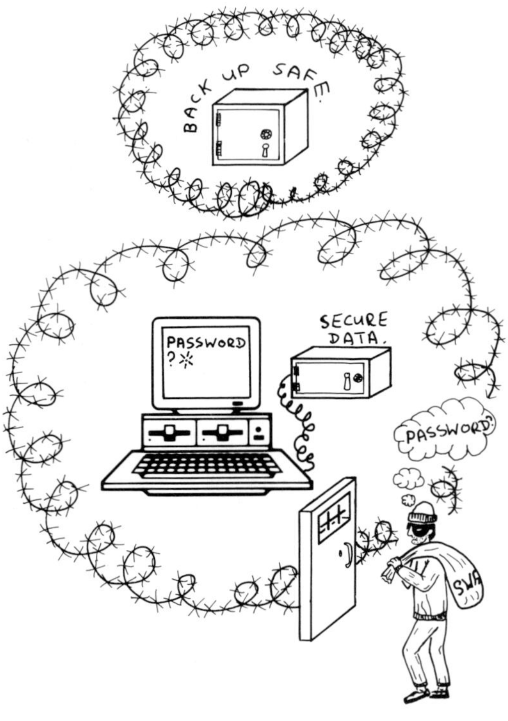

Figure 21 Data is valuable. Protect it!

■ Security

Part of the systems analyst's job is to consider the security of the system and to design access paths and **backup** and **recovery** procedures. Imagine that you use a computer system to run your business. What happens if there is an equipment breakdown, a power cut or a fire? How do you prevent unauthorised people from tampering with your system (intentionally or by accident)? What controls do you need on your system to satisfy the auditor?

• *Computer failure*

Organisations which rely on their computer systems for the day to day running of their business often have a standby system which can take over from the system which has broken down. For example, each Sainsburys branch has two computers, both storing the same data; if one fails, the other takes over. Some companies duplicate only parts of the system. Duplicating hardware is expensive and a balance must be reached between the cost and the likely losses incurred as a result of computer failure.

Most systems will suffer from 'down' time when routine maintenance is carried out or equipment is replaced. This should be considered when designing the system.

• *Backup of software and data*

Data and programs may be lost or corrupted if:

- a disk drive breaks down or the disk 'crashes' because the head has touched the disk surface
- someone deletes files by mistake
- there is a fire.

Taking regular **backups** is important. Many large systems automatically **dump** all their programs and data to backing storage every few hours. Copies of transactions are kept in a **transaction log** file. If a problem occurs, the data is reinstated from the backup and the lost transactions are put through the system again. Backups should be kept somewhere safe and many companies use fireproof safes to protect their data.

On a microcomputer it is generally the user who has to remember to take backup copies of software and data files on floppy disk. It's a good idea to get into the habit of saving your work and taking regular backup copies. Otherwise it's easy to forget and regret it later!

- *Preventing unauthorised access*

Most systems are used by more than one person. Problems can be caused by:

a person who doesn't understand the system and deletes or alters data by accident

a **hacker** who gets into the system for kicks and who may leave a **virus** in the system

a person who knowingly commits fraud, for example altering the system to pay money into his own bank account.

To prevent unauthorised access many computer systems have **user ids** and **passwords**. These are mentioned in some of the case studies; they only allow access to people who have been authorised to use the system. Passwords are also used for protecting users' data; each user is allocated a separate area on the disk for storing programs and data. Most systems have several different levels of access. Some people are only allowed to view data, some people can change data. The system manager has the highest level of access.

Large computer systems usually have restricted physical access as well. People need a special id card or badge to enter the computer rooms. Often the card is inserted in a special machine on the door to open it. In places where the public may gain access, for example a doctor's surgery, a key for the hardware could be used.

- *Audit controls*

The auditor is a qualified person who checks the 'truth and fairness' of a company's financial statements. A **computer auditor** is specially trained to check the controls in the company's computer system. The controls should pick up errors and should be able to detect fraud. It's more difficult to follow an **audit trail** on a computer than it is on manual records; because data is not visible, it's harder to spot errors or deliberate alterations to the records.

The computer system should log transactions so that checks can be made. It should also log user access, so that any unauthorised access can be spotted. Regular printouts of certain data help the auditor to make checks. **Control totals** and **input validation** help prevent data entry errors.

Some of the techniques used by the auditor are:

follow through a transaction from entry through processing (audit trail)

enter wrong data and check that it is detected and rejected by the system

get a printout of exceptional items (eg. very large amounts of money) and check these.

The term **data integrity** means ensuring that data is accurate. The controls and validation mentioned help to do this. Large database systems often have additional integrity checks that are run to check all the links in the database.

- *Encryption*

Cryptography (literally 'secret writing') is an ancient art. Julius Caesar used a simple substitution method where each letter is displaced a constant number of places. You have probably used secret codes yourself. Any private information which is communicated through telephone, radio, satellite links needs to be coded so that other people can't understand it. (One of the first uses of computers was for code breaking during the Second World War.)

Many different methods are available for coding or encrypting data and researchers are always looking for new ones, which are harder to break. Powerful computers are good at encrypting data but their processing speed can also be harnessed to break codes.

■ Privacy and the Data Protection Act

Computers are in use throughout society and much of the information they hold concerns people. Personal data is subject to the **Data Protection Act** 1984, which gives rights to individuals about whom information is stored (**data subjects**) and places obligations on those who record and use personal data (**data users**).

Data users have to register and give details of the personal data they store, the purposes for which they use it, the sources from which it is obtained and who has access to it. Registered users must comply with the eight principles laid down in the Data Protection Act (see Fig. 22).

Exemptions from the Act include: data held by an individual for personal or recreational affairs; members' clubs (provided no member objects); data which is made public anyway, such as the electoral register; data to safeguard national security.

You can inspect the register at major public libraries. You are entitled to request from a data user a copy of personal data held about you. Complaints may be made if personal data is inaccurate and, in certain cases, compensation may be claimed.

B.4 COMPLIANCE WITH THE DATA PROTECTION PRINCIPLES *(Act—Schedule 1)*

The Data Protection Principles are based upon the requirements of the Council of Europe Convention for the Protection of Individuals with Regard to Automatic Processing of Personal Data. Compliance with the principles is central to the purpose of the Act. It will be immediately apparent that they are mainly concerned with aspects of good data processing practice.

One of the Registrar's main functions is to promote observance of the eight Data Protection Principles. His powers to enforce compliance with the principles will come into full effect two years after the start of the registration process.

All eight principles apply to Data Users, only the eighth applies to Computer Bureaux.

The Data Protection Principles are as follows:

"1. The information to be contained in personal data shall be obtained, and personal data shall be processed, fairly and lawfully."

In considering whether information is obtained fairly the Registrar will consider whether any person has been deceived or misled as to the purpose for which it is to be held, used or disclosed.

"2. Personal data shall be held only for one or more specified and lawful purposes."

Specified purposes are those described on the Register.

"3. Personal data held for any purpose or purposes shall not be used or disclosed in any manner incompatible with that purpose or those purposes."

Incompatible use or disclosure means otherwise than as described on the Register.

"4. Personal data held for any purpose or purposes shall be adequate, relevant and not excessive in relation to that purpose or those purposes."

"5. Personal data shall be accurate and, where necessary, kept up to date."

"Accurate" means correct and not misleading as to any matter of fact.

You may be unable to ensure the accuracy of data received from the Data Subject or a third party. There are provisions in the Act whereby by marking and processing such data appropriately you will not be considered to be in breach of this principle. Such marking or processing will also absolve you from any liability to pay compensation for damage caused by the inaccuracy of the data (see *B.5—Individuals' Rights).*

Data should be kept up to date except where the purpose for which it is held does not require it to be.

"6. Personal data held for any purpose or purposes shall not be kept for longer than is necessary for that purpose or those purposes."

"7. An individual shall be entitled:

(a) at reasonable intervals and without undue delay or expense:—

(i) to be informed by any Data User whether he holds personal data of which that individual is the Subject, and

(ii) to access to any such data held by a Data User; and

(b) where appropriate, to have such data corrected or erased."

This principle introduces the right of subject access which is fully described in Section 21 of the Act (and it is considered again in *B.5—Individuals' Rights*).

"Reasonable intervals" will vary with the nature of the data, the nature and frequency of processing, etc. and is not defined.

The Act stipulates that subject access requests shall be met in 40 days after receipt or determination of additional necessary information (see *B.5—Individuals' Rights*).

The Secretary of State will make an Order fixing the maximum fee which may be charged for subject access, thus ensuring that no "undue expense" is incurred by Data Subjects.

"8. Appropriate security measures shall be taken against unauthorised access to, or alteration, disclosure or destruction of, personal data and against accidental loss or destruction of personal data."

In considering whether security measures are appropriate regard should be had to the nature of the personal data and the potential harm which could result from unauthorised access, etc. It will be necessary also to consider the place where data are stored, security measures programmed into the equipment and measures taken for ensuring the reliability of staff having access to the data.

This eighth principle applies to Computer Bureaux as well as Data Users.

There are special dispensations for data held for historical and research purposes, where their use is such that it does not cause, or is not likely to cause, damage or distress to any Data Subject. Such data shall not be regarded as unfairly obtained merely because the historical or research purpose was not declared when it was obtained, and it may be kept indefinitely without breaching the sixth principle.

Where a breach of any principle comes to the Registrar's attention he may serve a notice requiring you to take steps to comply with the principle or principles in question. Failure to comply with the terms of such a notice will be an offence (see *B.7—Enforcement and Appeal Provisions*).

Figure 22 Data Protection Act

QUESTIONS

1 (a) Draw an organisation chart for your school/college.
(b) Time yourself over a day's activities and make up an activity chart.

2 Suppose you are given the job of designing a computer system to store records of all the people (staff and students) in your school/college. What would be the main entities and their attributes? Draw a data model showing the relationships between the entities.

3 (a) Describe a standard coding system that is used nationally (or internationally). Why is a standard code necessary?
(b) Find out how the Dewey Decimal code for library books works.
(c) Find out about driving licence codes, TV licence codes and any others you come across in everyday use. Discuss the reasons for the design of each code.

4 Collect some forms (eg. from the Post Office) and discuss them. Discuss how easy they are to understand and to fill in. Suggest how they might be improved.

5 By means of a suitable application in each case, explain what is meant by
(a) a menu selection dialogue
(b) a command dialogue with a help list
(c) a forms dialogue.

[*ULSEB 1989*] *Specimen paper*

6 A word processing package is to be designed for a machine with coloured screen capabilities. State, with reasons, *three* ways of making use of colour on the screen, which are relevant to this application.

[*JMB 1988*]

7 Consider the following problem: an expressline coach company wishes to program a reservation system. The data to be stored in the computer will include:

(i) All tours for the next 60 days, stored by tour number and date.
(ii) The names of all passengers holding reservations on those tours, together with a variable length character string of data about each passenger.
(iii) Details of the types of unreserved seats on each tour. (This data will be continuously changing as seats are sold or cancelled and as information changes.)

Produce an outline design for the user environment required to accomplish this task. This might include the use of windows, icons, menus and pointers. You should include in your design a suitable screen display(s) showing the information required to enable queries to be answered and bookings to be made, changed or cancelled;
and also indicate how the user would:

(a) move through the separate records
(b) find an individual record (via tour number or date or passenger name)
(c) change a record
(d) enter/delete a record
(e) display a passenger list for a given tour in sorted order.

Also explain the kind of facility needed within the program to update the number and class of reserved seats.

[*Oxford 1989*]

8 A company is engaged in the manufacture and marketing of buttons of various designs. Included in its activities are the following:

(i) ordering and maintaining a stock of raw materials;
(ii) scheduling production according to known requirements and forecasts for orders, existing stock of buttons, and the availability of materials, labour and machinery;
(iii) marketing the company's products, receiving orders, and making sales forecasts;
(iv) maintaining a stock of buttons and fulfilling orders for them;
(v) handling all of the company's financial transactions;
(vi) providing overall management of the company and planning for the future.

These six fields of activity are broadly the responsibility of six departments in the company, respectively known as Raw materials (R), Production scheduling (P), Sales and marketing (S), Button dispatch (B), Accounts (A) and Management (M).

Describe, by means of an outline flow diagram with notes, the flow of data between these departments within the company.
Identify the activities in which a computer system might be involved, and in each case explain how it would be used.

[*COSSEC 1989*] *AS Specimen paper*

9 When files of data are stored on a computer system there are problems of:

(i) users accessing the system and corrupting the data accidentally
(ii) unauthorised users deliberately corrupting the data.

Describe briefly how each of these problems can be minimised.

[*ULSEB 1989*]

10 Your local video shop manager asks you to design a computerised system for running the video hire business. Specify the requirements and design a suitable system. You will need to consider: the manual processes; the data which will need to be stored; the data flows; the computer processes; input and output design; manual document design.

11 State *three* duties which the Data Protection Act imposes on data users.

[*JMB 1987*]

12 The following is part of a newspaper article.

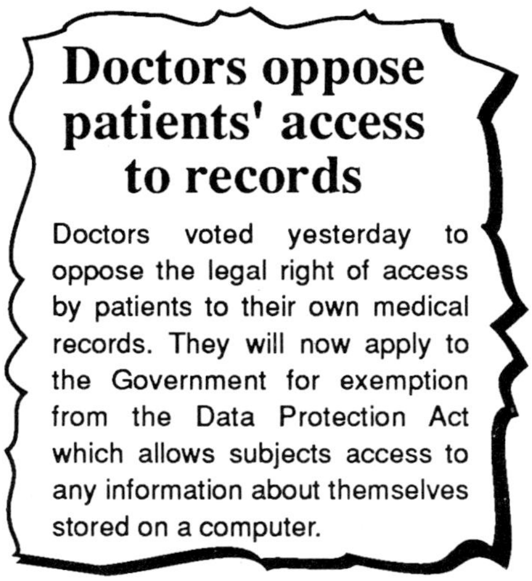

Doctors oppose patients' access to records

Doctors voted yesterday to oppose the legal right of access by patients to their own medical records. They will now apply to the Government for exemption from the Data Protection Act which allows subjects access to any information about themselves stored on a computer.

Outline the arguments for and against patients having legal right of access to their own medical records.

[*SCE Higher 1990*]

Reader Tailored to fit

IN SYSTEMS development nothing is more fundamental than assessing user requirements. If you don't know what the system is required to do; you don't know anything.

But many system developers are unable to assess requirements properly. They seem to think that you can ask a businessman what his requirements are and get an answer that amounts to a draft system specification. A doctor doesn't ask his patient what treatment to prescribe. The patient can explain only what the problem is. It is the doctor that provides the remedy.

If you ask a user what sort of system he wants you will be met with a blank look. A user may have a deep knowledge of business problems, but knowing little about computers, has no idea how they should be tackled. Yet, analysts are heard asking time and again, "Tell me what you want. We've gone away from the days of systems imposed by the data processing department, this is going to be a system for the users."

But of course the users don't know what they want, so they end up getting another duff system.

An effective analyst provides the same service to the business as the doctor provides to the patient. He finds out what the needs of the business are, and prescribes the cure. The user tells the analyst what the problems are, and the analyst decides, at least in broad terms, what the user requires.

But the analyst has one great advantage over the doctor. Once the user becomes familiar with the proposed system, helpful comments come thick and fast. "Oh, this will be of great help in ordering raw materials, but sometimes we get part deliveries, could we have an extra facility to deal with those? And what about orders not delivered on time? If we could list those we'd have advance warning of shortage problems on the assembly lines two months before they occur. Now that would be a great leap forward."

Unfortunately you cannot reach this stage until you have developed a prototype system. And you can't develop a prototype system because the users haven't got a clue what they want. Most of them are probably muttering, "I'm too busy to get involved in this sort of thing. What's wrong with the old system anyway?"

The only way to develop a prototype is for the analyst to get inside the head of the user and, thinking like a user, decide what sort of system is required. Of course, the initial system will not be perfect. The analyst cannot hope to understand the business as well in a few weeks as the user does after many years. But once the user sees the system, channels of communication will open. Instead of persuading the user to specify requirements, the analyst will be driven by the user to meet key needs.

Good system development goes through two distinct phases. Initially the analyst does all the work, leading the user towards a system he thinks is right for the business. But once the user sees the potential of the system, a change in attitude takes place. The process becomes demand driven by the user. The analyst is then forced on the defensive, explaining why new features cannot be included because they are technically difficult or prohibitively expensive.

Traditionally, systems were validated by users agreeing functional specifications. In theory, validation meant that the user had read the specification, imagined how the system would work in practice, and agreed the design.

It was only when using a "test" version of the system (available just before the planned implementation date) that difficulties would come to light, and a host of change requests be issued.

The advent of fourth generation languages (4GLs) has made system development much easier. With a 4GL an initial prototype can be put together quickly. This means feedback is obtained early in the development process, and the system can grow around the user's requirements.

Crucial to the development process is the relationship built up between the analyst and the user. The best systems arise when both have a deep understanding of each other's jobs.

Many developers use business analysts to ensure that the development team maintain a proper focus on business requirements. But this can be counter-productive, as it cuts off communication between the systems analyst and the user. Too much specialisation is bad for systems development; it feeds the temptation to get engrossed in technical difficulties and forget about the underlying business needs.

If you should stroll into a pub and meet an analyst and a user talking about work, and you cannot tell one from the other, they have probably developed a successful system together.

QUESTIONS

1 Explain, in your words, what prototyping is and why it is important.

2 How might you go about prototyping your video shop system? (Chapter 2, Question 10.)

3 What is a fourth generation language and why have these languages made system development much easier?

CHAPTER 3

Files and Database Systems

Introduction

Part of the systems design process is deciding how the data we want to store should be structured and organised. Most data is stored in **files**, a useful data structure for large amounts of data and for data of mixed types. (Chapter 4 discusses data types.)

There is normally not enough space in **main memory** for very large amounts of data. So data files are kept on backing store (**magnetic disk** or **tape**) and data is passed to and from **file buffers** in main memory when it is required. This can slow things down because, when the user needs to access some data to view it or to change it, the data has to be found and transferred. If the data is changed it also has to be put back.

The time taken to find a piece of data depends on how the data file is structured and organised. In this chapter we explain different ways of organising data in files and ways of accessing that data. The advantages and disadvantages are also referred to in Chapter 2, and Chapter 8 describes how data is stored physically on the hardware. The final section of this chapter looks briefly at databases and their structure.

Fields, records and files

Each piece of data is stored in a **field**. A **record** is a set of fields of data about one person, animal or object, etc. For example, each animal at London Zoo has a record, the layout of which is shown below (Fig. 2). A **file** is a set of records.

Note that often a file is just one of many files in a **database**. For example the ARKS database does not only contain a file of the animals known, it also has files of data about loans to other zoos, animals' stays in different cages and descriptions of animal species. We will discuss this in more detail later.

A file usually contains data about one **entity** and each field contains an **attribute** of that entity. In Fig. 2 the entity is animal and the attributes are id, species, name, etc.

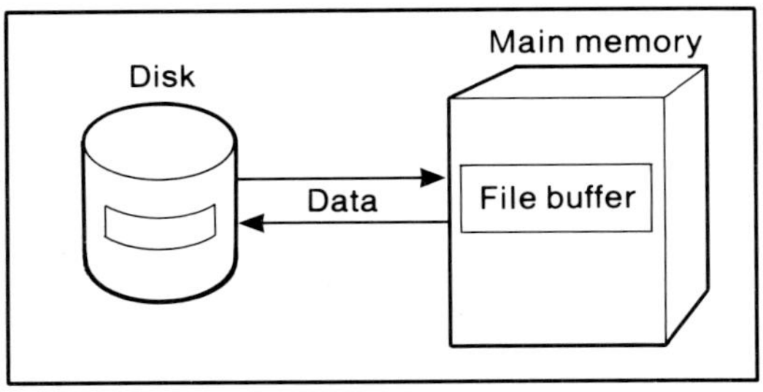

Figure 1 Transfer of data

A1	Gorilla	Salome	16/7/76	
Id	Species	Name	Birth	Other data
↑ *Field 1*	↑ *Field 2*			

Figure 2 Animal record

■ Keys

A **key** field identifies a record in some way, so that records can be retrieved or sorted into order. Any field could be a key field. Usually there is one field which uniquely identifies each record; this is called the **primary key**. In the animal record, the primary key is the animal's identification code. No two animals are given the same code number. Note that the name could not be used as the primary key because two animals could have the same name. Similarly, the primary key for the babies in the SCBU is their unit number.

	Species	
A401	Aardvark	
	.	
A80	Goat	
A1	Gorilla	
A2	Gorilla	
A3	Gorilla	
A4	Gorilla	
A46	Gorilla	
	.	
A6	Kangaroo	
	.	
A5	Lion	

Figure 3 Animal file sorted into species order

Any other field can act as a **secondary key**. For example, if we wanted to retrieve all the records about gorillas, we would use the species field as a secondary key. Also we could sort the file into species order alphabetically, as shown in Fig. 3.

Sometimes there is no single field which uniquely identifies each record. Suppose the animals were not given an id code. The name alone is not enough to identify the record as there may be several Salomes in the zoo. The species, possibly the date of birth as well, is needed to identify each animal. This is called a **compound key**.

■ File formats

● *Field type and length*

Every file has its own **format** or **record structure**. Its records have a certain number of fields each of a particular **type** and **length**. For example, the animal records shown above might be specified as shown in Fig. 5 below.

The format must be chosen carefully, bearing in mind which fields are likely to be needed for retrieving data. Fields containing letters and possibly numbers as well are character fields. Any fields used in calculations must be specified as numeric. Dates are a special case. A date may be stored as three separate numeric values for day, month and year or as a single character string (see Fig. 4). Many packages have a special date type; internally the date is stored as a number (for example Lotus 1-2-3 stores the number of days from 1/1/1900) but the date is displayed as a character string.

(a) Day : numeric 25
Month : numeric 01
Year : numeric 90

(b) Date : character
25/01/90

(c) Date : the date
Internal 32898
Display 25/01/90

Figure 4 Storing dates

Fieldname	*Description*	*Type*	*Maximum length*
Id	Animal identification	Character	6
Species	Latin name	Character	35
Name	Zoo name	Character	25
Birth	Date of Birth	Date	8
Arrival	Arrival at zoo	Date	8
Leaving	Final leaving	Date	8
Hybrid	Yes or No	Logical	1
Sex	Male, Female, Unknown	Numeric	1

Figure 5 Part of an animal record structure

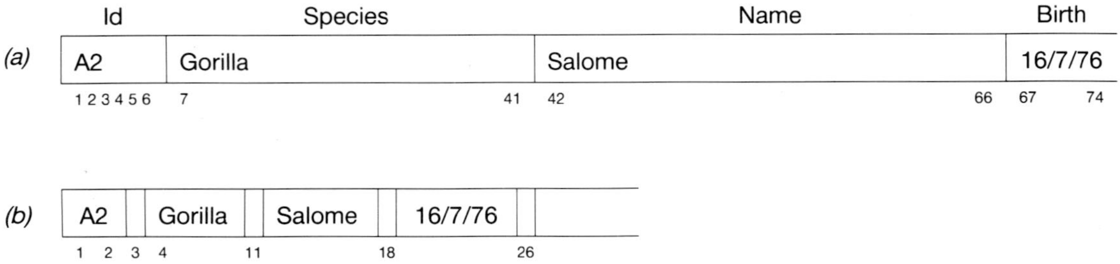

Figure 6 (a) Fixed and (b) variable length records

- *Fixed and variable length fields*

Fig. 6 shows the animal record stored in two different ways:

(a) with all its fields of a **fixed length** (the maximum length) and
(b) with **variable length** fields.

Fixed length fields make processing easier because the computer can calculate the exact position of a field within a record; for example, the id always starts at the 36th character of the record. However, space is wasted when a name in a particular field is short.

Variable length fields only use as much space as the data requires; there is no wasted space. A special character is needed to separate the fields. Processing is different; to find the animal's sex, for example, the computer has to read through all the characters in the record, counting the separators until it reaches the seventh field.

- *Fixed and variable length records*

If all fields in a record are fixed length, the record itself is fixed length. Therefore it is easy to calculate a record's position within the file. For example, the above record has 142 characters. So the 12th record in the file will start at character position 1563. This is useful if you want to access the 12th record directly.

If, on the other hand, a record has one or more variable fields, it is variable length. The position of the 12th record can't be calculated and the computer has to read through the other records to find it.

FILE ORGANISATION

■ Serial file

This is a simple file where the records follow each other in no particular order. A new record is simply appended to the end of the file.

■ Sequential file

This is a serial file, but the records are held in some sequence. For example, ARKS animal records are stored in identification code sequence.

■ Indexed sequential files

If you wanted to find this chapter in this book the contents page at the front would help you find it more quickly by telling you which page this chapter starts on. **Indexed sequential** files are similar; the records are stored sequentially and there is an index which is used to help locate the record required. The use of an index speeds up the retrieval process considerably.

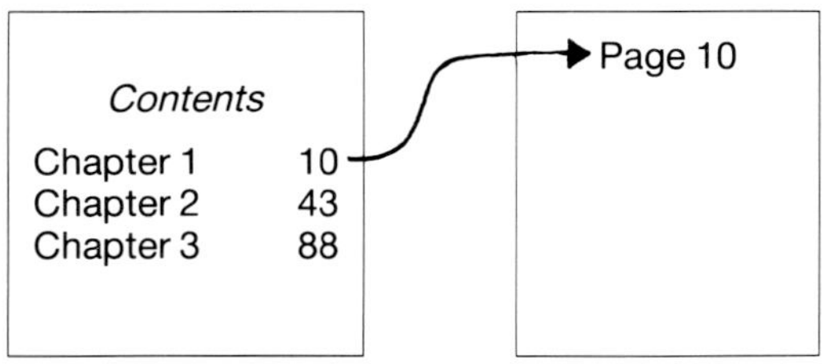

Figure 7 The concept of indexing

■ Random files

Random files are stored on disk. As the name suggests, records do not occur one after the other and they are not stored in any particular order. However, when a record is put on the disk, it can't just be put anywhere; we need some means of knowing where to find it again without searching the whole disk.

This is done by using a formula or **hashing algorithm** which is applied to the record's **primary key** to calculate its disk address. There are a number of different algorithms used; a simple example is prime number division.

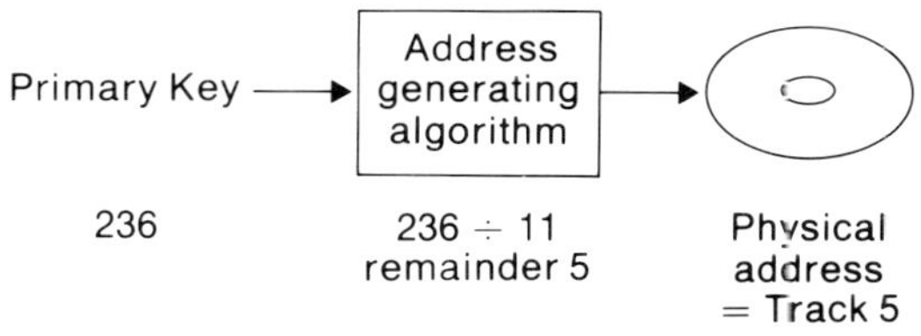

Figure 8 Address generation

- *Prime number division*

The key is divided by the largest prime number below the available number of **tracks** or **blocks**. A block is the basic unit of data that is transferred to and from the file buffer in memory. A block usually contains several records and its size depends on the computer; some computers allow the programmer to set the block size. The remainder of the division gives the track/block number. The **cylinder** number is worked out from this. Chapter 8 explains cylinders and tracks.

For example, suppose that an area of 12 tracks on a disk is used for a small file. The records have three-digit keys. Record with key 236 is put on track 5. (236/11 gives remainder 5.) Record 316 is put on track 8 and record 555 will be on track 5, with record 236.

- *Overflow*

The aim of using certain algorithms is to get an even spread of records. The example above shows that a number of records will share the same track. Problems occur when the track becomes full because records then have to be put into a special **overflow** area. In our example, only 11 tracks are used (tracks 0 to 10) and the extra track (track 11) could be used for overflow. Suppose that track 5 becomes full and record 247 has to be stored in track 11. When we want to access this record the division calculates that it's on track 5; it searches track 5 but doesn't find the record and searches the overflow track to find it.

Alternative overflow methods use pointers to lead to the records not stored at their 'home' address. However, overflow slows down the process of storing and retrieving records and should be avoided as far as possible by planning ahead and allowing plenty of space for the file to grow. When the file does get too large it has to be reorganised.

FILE ACCESS AND PROCESSING

It is no use storing data in a file if individual records can't be found again. So methods of **accessing** records are needed. Files can be accessed serially, sequentially, directly or by means of an index.

■ Serial access

Any file can be accessed serially; the computer simply reads every record until it reaches the one required.

■ Sequential access

This is similar to serial access, though the records are in order. If only one record needs to be accessed it is slow, but if most or all records in the file are to be processed, it is an efficient method of access.

■ Direct access

When files are stored on disk, it is possible to go directly to a record, without having to pass through all the preceding records. This is called **direct access**. However, to do this, there must be some way of knowing where the record is on the disk. Both indexed sequential files and random files can be accessed directly.

- *Indexed sequential files*

In an ordinary telephone directory, the first entry on each page is used as a heading to help you find the page you need and from there the name you are looking for. Fig. 9 shows a page from a directory and what the index might look like.

Indexing of a computer file follows the same principle. The index directs the computer to the appropriate area of the disk and this area is searched for the record required. This is called **partial indexing** because the index does not include every single record. This method is frequently used for files on large **disk packs** on **mainframe** computers. Methods vary according to the computer system, here we explain the principles.

A single level index (Fig. 10(a)) contains the first key in each block. A large file usually has a **multiple level** (hierarchical) **index** because a single level index would be large and would take longer to search. Suppose we have a small animals file of 60 records, organised indexed sequentially. Fig. 10(b) shows how a two-level index might look and how the record A53 would be accessed.

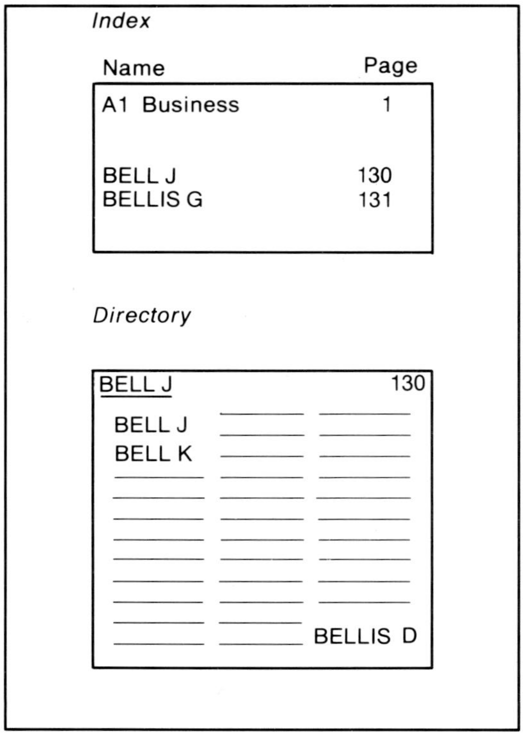

Figure 9 Index and directory

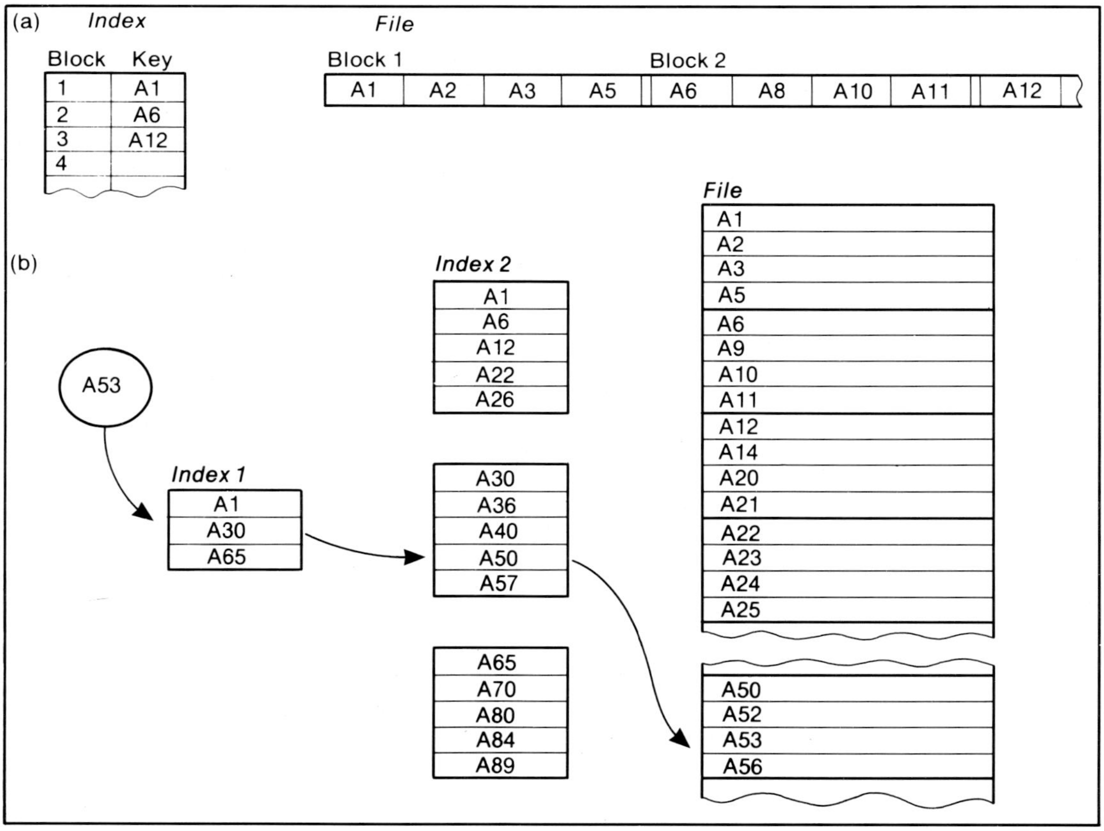

Figure 10 Single and two-level indexes

In practice, the two-level index comprises a **cylinder** index and a **track** or **block** index. The cylinder index is searched to find the relevant cylinder (Fig. 11). On this cylinder there is a track index which is searched to find the track. The track is searched to find the record. A large file may spread over several disks, requiring a three-level index: disk, cylinder and track/block. Some methods store the highest key in each area, rather than the first (lowest) key.

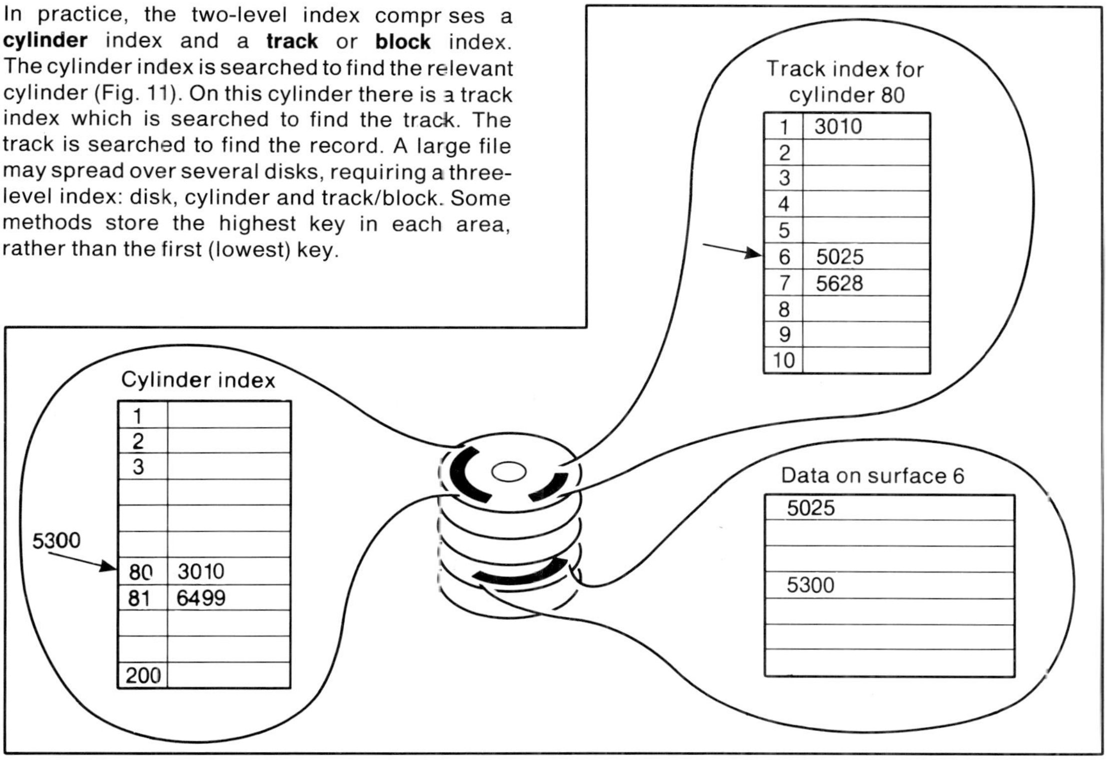

Figure 11 Indexed sequential file on disk

- *Random files*

These are accessed directly using an algorithm as described earlier. Random files can only be accessed sequentially if you have a list of all the record keys (in sequence).

■ Indexes

- *Primary and secondary key full indexes*

Any file, whether it is sequenced or not, can have a full index on its primary key; the index contains the keys of all records in the file. The index is used to quickly access individual records. Fig. 12 shows the ARKS file (unsequenced) with an animal id index.

As mentioned in the section on keys, we may also need to access the data using a secondary key. For example, suppose we want to access the animal file by species, to find all the gorillas. The simplest way is to search through the whole file picking out any gorilla records but this is very slow. Another way is to sort the whole file into species order (Fig. 3) and keep the sorted file on disk as well as the original file. This method speeds up access, because the gorilla records are grouped together, but it duplicates the data and takes up a lot of space.

Primary index

Id	Position
A1	1
A2	2
A3	26
A5	9

Secondary index

Species	Position
Aardvark	3
.	
.	
.	
Gorilla	1
Gorilla	2
Gorilla	26

File

	Id	Species	Other fields
1	A1	Gorilla	
2	A2	Gorilla	
3	A80	Aardvark	
4	A12	Kangaroo	
5	A13	Lion	
6	A14	Tiger	
7	A25	Kangaroo	
8	A68	Lion	
9	A5	Lion	

Figure 12 Primary and Secondary indexes

A better method is to create a species index to the file (Fig. 12). The index can either store the position of each record in the file (as shown) or its disk address.

- *Inverted lists*

An **inverted list** is a form of **secondary index**. The inverted species list, for example, contains each species name with the primary keys of all the animals of that species (Fig. 13). A fully inverted file has lists for all its attributes.

Species inverted list

Aardvark	A401
.	
.	
Gorilla	A1, A2, A3, A4, A212
.	
.	
Kangaroo	A6, A24, A128
.	
.	
Lion	A5, A56, A200, A201, A202
.	
.	

Figure 13 Inverted list of species

■ Searching an index

Any index can be searched serially, by simply reading through the entries until the required one is reached. However, if the index is organised sequentially, there are quicker methods of searching for a particular entry. On average, a serial search of an index of 600 entries requires 300 probes, whereas a **block search** takes 24 and a **binary chop search** takes 8.

- *Binary chop search*

This method goes to the middle of the list and compares the key with the one wanted. This identifies which half of the list contains the wanted key. The process is repeated until the key is found.

Suppose we are searching the list in Fig. 14 for the key 48. There are 15 entries so the middle one is the eighth, which is 54. 48 is lower than this so we limit our search to the lower half of the list. The middle of these is the fourth entry, which is 35. 48 is higher than 35, so the search is narrowed down to the fourth to eighth entries. The middle of these is the sixth, which is 48, the one we are looking for.

- *Block searching*

This method looks at a chunk or block of the index at a time. The size of the block is the square root of the index size. In the above example, there are 15 entries so it looks at every fourth one. If we are again searching for key 48, it stops at the second block. Then it searches backwards to find key 48.

- *Hash tables*

A hash table (where values are stored in a table, using a hashing algorithm to calculate each value's address within the table) may be used as an index. The record key and the record's disc address are stored in the index. Searching the index involves applying the algorithm to the record key to directly locate the relevant record address.

1	2	3	4	5	6	7	8	9	10	11	12	13	14	15
15	22	31	35	44	48	50	54	61	66	68	69	72	83	98
			↑ 2		↑ 3		↑ 1							

Figure 14 Binary chop search

1	2	3	4	5	6	7	8	9	10	11	12	13	14	15
15	22	31	35	44	48	50	54	61	66	68	69	72	83	98
			↑ 1		↑ 4	↑ 3	↑ 2							

Figure 15 Block search

■ Sorting files

Often a file needs to be **sorted** into some sequence. This can be done using any one field or a combination of fields as a **sort key**. For example, Fig. 3 showed the animals file sorted in species order. It could be further sorted into order of birth date within species. There are a number of methods of sorting files, including the bubble sort and the exchange sort.

■ Merging files

The data from two or more files can be **merged**, providing that the files are of the same format, have the same key and are in the same order. Fig. 16 shows a simple example.

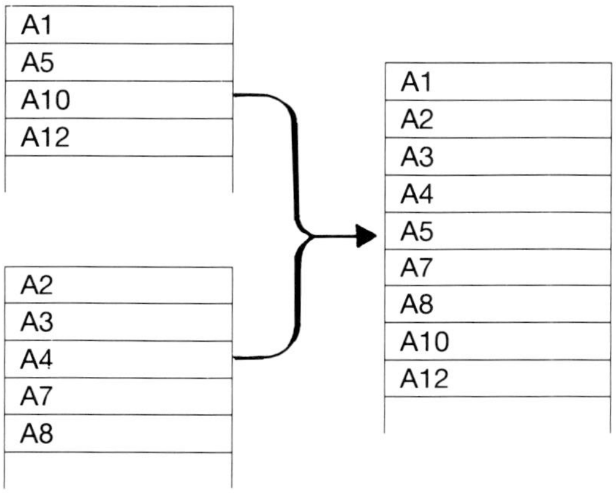

Figure 16 Merging two animal files

■ Information retrieval

Handling enquiries and producing reports involve searching files, retrieving data and putting the results together to supply the required information. For example, an ARKS enquiry may want details of all the institutions which have loaned gorillas to the zoo. This involves extracting data from three files, the animals file, the loans file and the institutions file of names and addresses.

■ Updating

A record goes through three main **update** processes: it is input (for example when an animal arrives at the zoo); it may be modified a number of times (when the animal is loaned to another zoo or when it moves to another enclosure) and eventually it will be deleted or **archived** (when the animal is sold or dies). Archiving means filing the record away (on magnetic tape or perhaps CD-ROM); no more updates are done but it can be accessed for reference purposes.

■ Updating a serial file

Adding records is simple; they are appended to the end of the file. But changing or deleting a record requires a search of the file. If there are several changes or deletions to make, the process is very slow because each one needs a search of the whole file. A sequential file is quicker to update.

■ Updating a sequential file

We will take the animals file as an example. Suppose the file is in sequential order on animal id, which is its primary key, and we want to insert a new animal record with id A5. One way is to append the record to the end of the file and then re-sort the file; this is time consuming. Another way is to copy the file into a new file, inserting A5. Fig. 17 shows the insertion process. The original file is called the **master file** and the A5 record is a **transaction**.

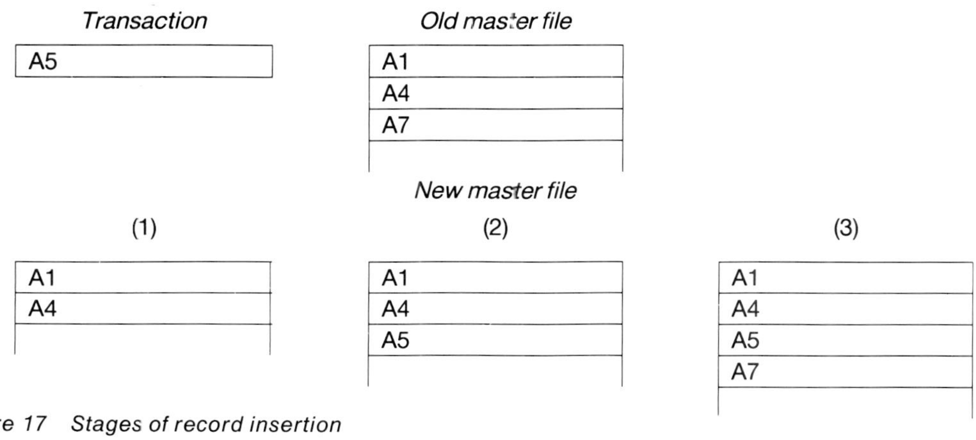

Figure 17 Stages of record insertion

■ Batch update

Batch update is used with magnetic tape files, because of the way they are accessed. But it can also be used with sequential disk files in the same way.

Transactions are processed in a **batch**. Insertions, changes and deletions, each with a code to say which type of transaction it is, are entered and stored in a **transaction file**. The file is put through a **validation** program to check for any errors and afterwards an error list is printed. The valid transactions are carried forward to update the master file. The invalid ones have to be corrected and sent through the whole process again.

The systems flowchart in Fig. 18 shows the processes and files involved. Note that the transaction file is sorted before the update process. This is necessary so that both files are in the same order and the update only reads the files once. The new master file is often called the son, the old master file the father and the previous master file the grandfather. Usually these three files are kept for **backup**.

To illustrate the update process, take our previous example a stage further. Fig. 19 shows six transactions for updating the master file.

The update program compares the keys of the first transaction and first master (A4 and A1). A1 is lower than A4 so A1 is put into the new master file and the next master record is read (A2). This continues until A6 is read. A4 is lower than A6 and is inserted in the new file. A8 is the next transaction read. A6 being the lower, it is put into the new file and A8 is read from the master file. Now we have two equal keys. Changes are made to A8's record and it is put in the new master. The next transaction and old master records are read.

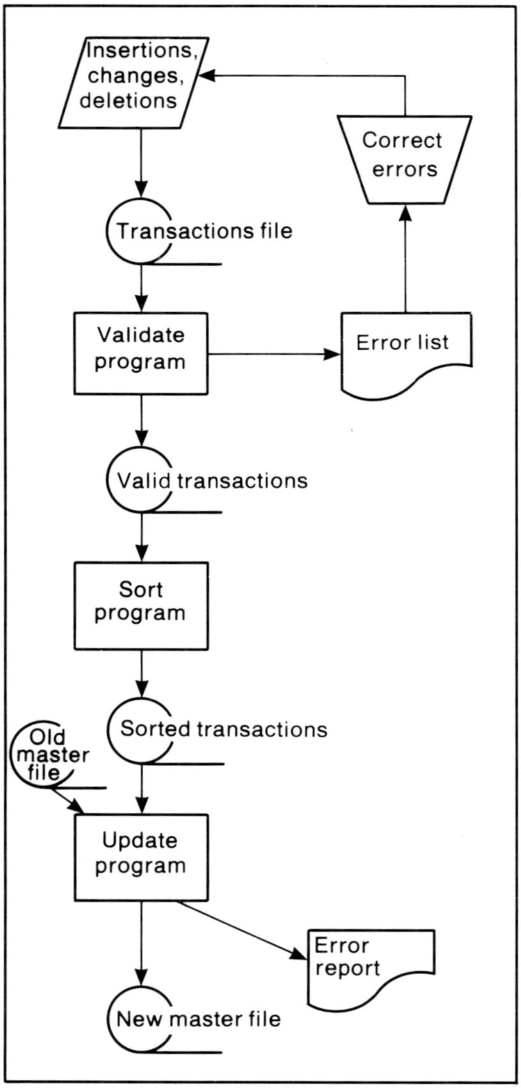

Figure 18 System flowchart for batch update

Transaction File

I	A4
C	A8
C	A11
D	A12
I	A17
I	A20

Old Master

A1
A2
A3
A6
A8
A10
A11
A12
A18

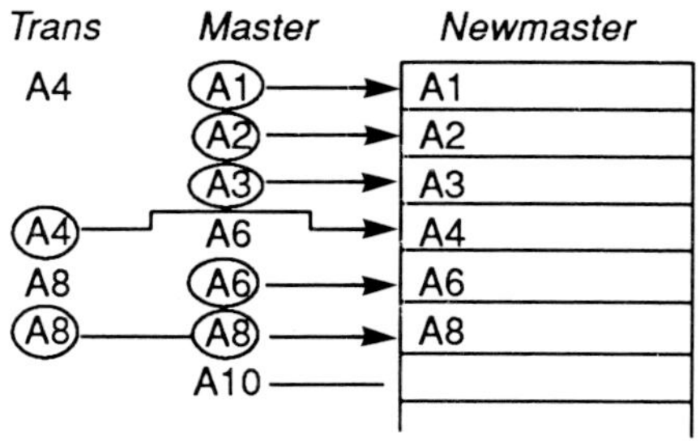

Figure 19 Stages of batch update. Note: A8 is limited to A8 because the information on the transaction and the information on the master are combined to make the new master record

The process continues in this way. Once a record has been dealt with, the next record is read from that file. The program always has one transaction and one master record to compare keys. Occasionally a transaction is invalid (inserting a record that's already there, deleting or changing a record that is not there). In the example, one of the transactions was entered wrongly. The validation program does not pick up this error; it can only check that the data is the right type. The update program detects the error.

To keep the example simple, there was only one transaction per master record but in practice there may be more. For example, if an animal was moved to a new cage and was almost immediately loaned out, it would have two transaction records.

■ Updating an indexed sequential file

Since the file is organised sequentially, a batch update as above can be used; both the file and its index are rewritten. Alternatively, if there are only a few transactions these could be processed individually. When new records are added the file must either be reshuffled or the new records must be placed in a separate location (an **overflow** area). The disadvantage is that it takes longer to find these records. Periodically the overflow area becomes full and the file is reorganised and the index reconstructed. One way to lessen the need for overflows is to leave empty record positions throughout the file.

■ Random file update

● *Batch update*

A batch of transactions can be used to update a random file. The transaction file can be in any order. Each record's address is generated and the record is inserted, altered or deleted. The system flowchart in Fig. 20 shows one method. Note that the validate and update programs could be combined in which case the second transaction file is not needed.

● *Online update*

In an **interactive** or a **real-time** system, each transaction must be dealt with when it is received by the computer. Examples are flight bookings and monitoring data for the control system at Kew Gardens. Fig. 21 overleaf shows the update process. First the transaction is validated and any errors are immediately reported to the user for correction. If the transaction is a flight booking, for example, the operator might type an

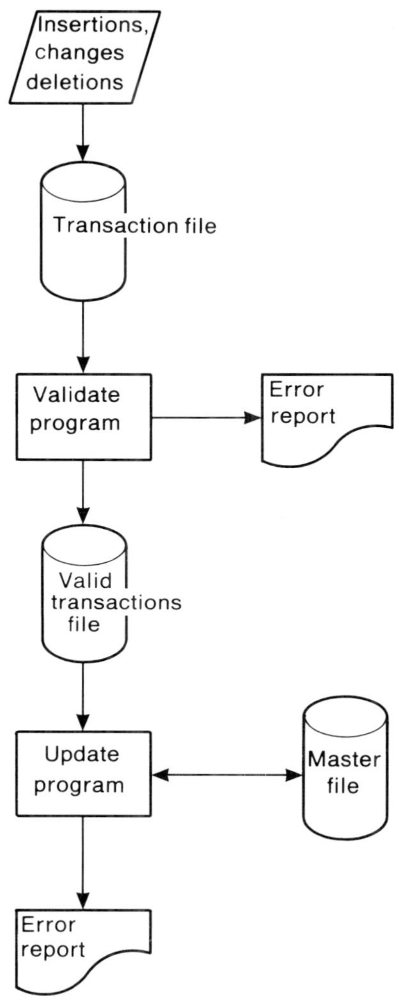

Figure 20 Batch update of random file

invalid flight number and an error message would be displayed. On the Kew control system the error could be from a faulty sensor.

Once accepted, the transaction is processed. If it's a flight booking, the seat is booked (or a message is displayed to say the flight is full). If the transaction is data from the sensors at Kew, the data is inserted in the file and appropriate action is taken (for example if it's too hot the windows are opened). In both cases, the master file is updated with the new data.

If the system is **multi-user**, **security** is needed in case two people try to access the same record at the same time. The record must be **locked out** to the second user until the first user has finished with that record.

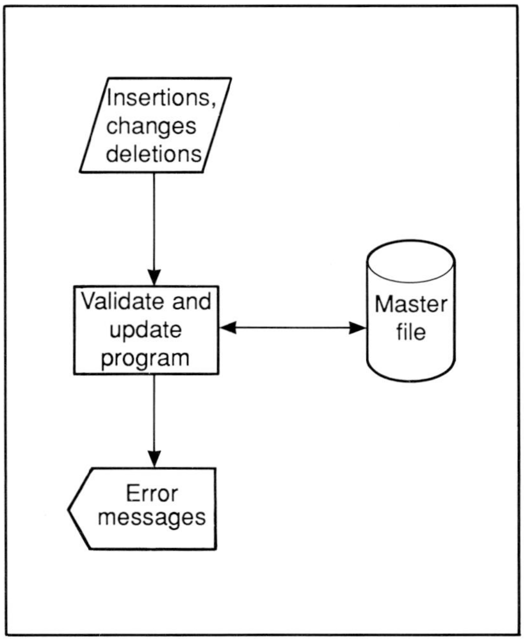

Figure 21 System flowchart for online update

Database systems

■ From file management to database systems

When organisations first started to use computers they began by computerising one application at a time. For example, they started with the accounts, then computerised stock control, and so on. They produced what were essentially **file management systems**. The systems were all separate and data was often transferred from one department to another on paper and the same data was typed in again. Connecting the systems was not an easy task as they were all separately designed.

Database systems changed things; they made it possible to integrate the data from several departments in one database. The data can be accessed by anyone (with the right access password of course) and data from different files and different departments can be shared.

The database itself is a collection of files, which are linked together to serve multiple applications. The database is not much use on its own; it needs a **database management system** (DBMS) to organise and sort data and to allow users to create files, to enter and edit data and to retrieve information.

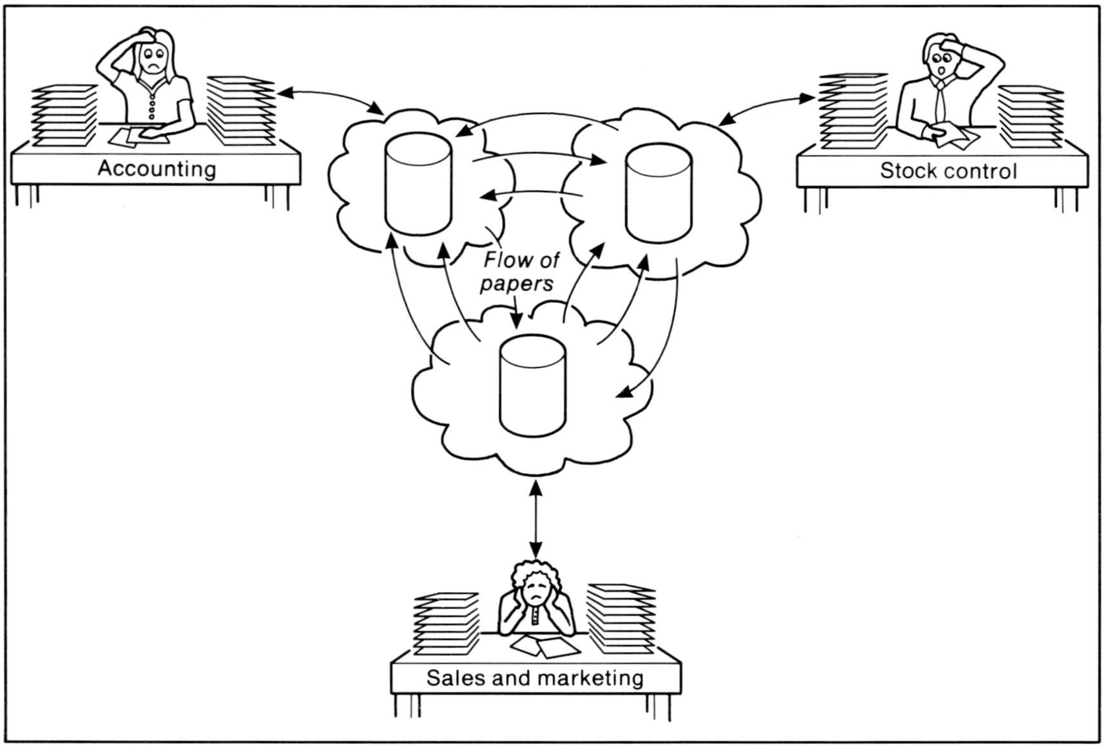

Figure 22 Separate systems (chaos)

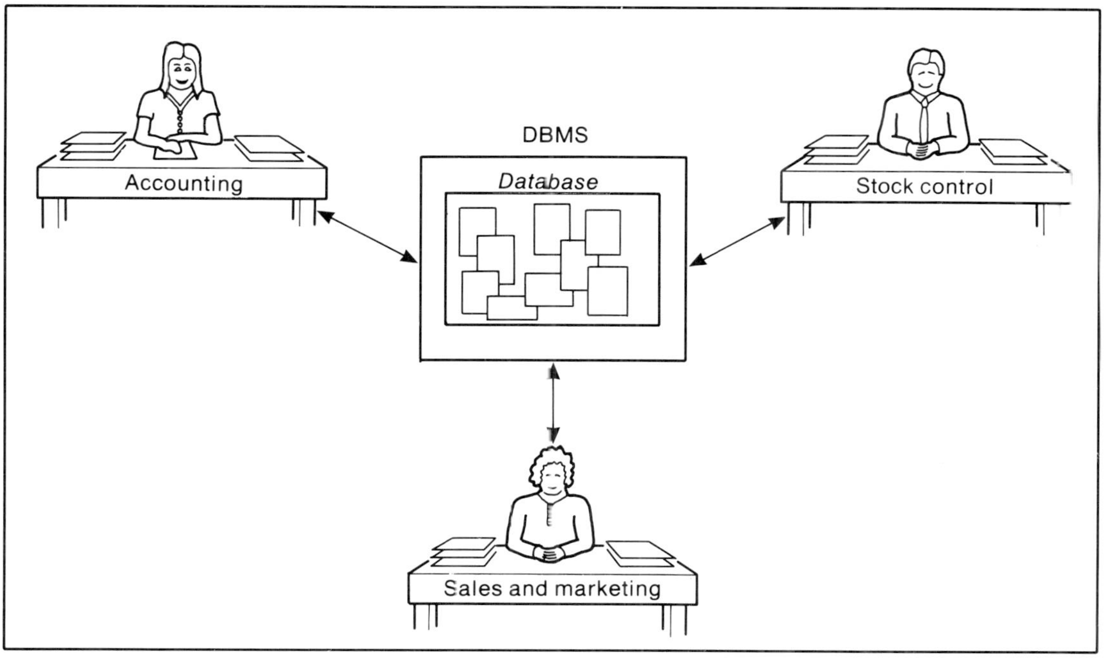

Figure 23 Separate systems (under control)

■ Database management systems

A DBMS provides a company with centralised control of its operational data. The aims are to minimise duplication of data and to ensure consistency of data. In the older systems described above an item of data may be duplicated in several files. Apart from the waste of storage space, this can lead to inconsistencies if the item is altered in one file and not in the other. In a database system, data normally appears once; if duplication is necessary, the database keeps track of each item and makes sure that alterations are consistent.

Because data from different applications is integrated and shared, it must be controlled. The **database administrator** is a person who designs the central data model for the database (called the **schema**), defines **security** and **integrity** checks, monitors the performance of the database and responds to the changing requirements of users. The DBMS provides tools and utility programs to help the administrator, including the **data dictionary** which keeps track of all the data items.

Each user (end-user, programmer, analyst, database administrator) has a different **view** of the data model. Most users only need to see and use a subset of the database. Different users' subsets will naturally overlap (for example, the stock department and the sales department both need descriptions of the products sold) but their views of that data may differ at a detailed level.

The database administrator needs to have the freedom to change the way data is physically stored and accessed in response to changing requirements, for example as the database grows in size. Similarly, programmers need to be able to add new applications without affecting existing ones. There are three independent levels within the DBMS as shown in Fig. 24. The DBMS handles the mapping between the levels

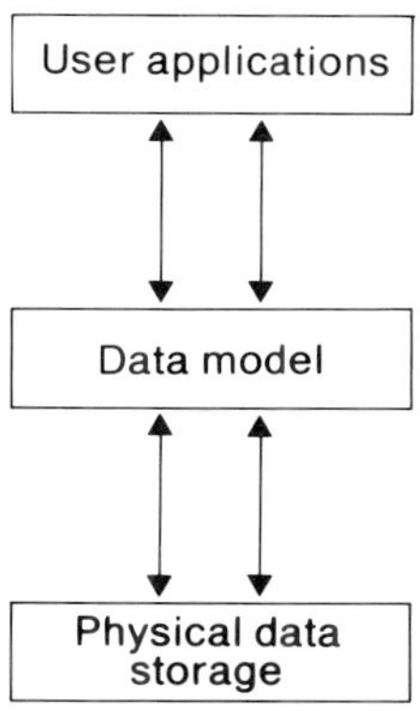

Figure 24 Database levels

Baby **X**	Admission	T	T	T		Admission	T	T	T	T	
details	**1**	**1**	**2**	**3**		**2**	**1**	**2**	**3**	**4**	

Figure 25 Data stored in one file

■ Database structures

Files are linked together via their keys, but this can be done in different ways. Different database packages have different ways of structuring their files. They fall into three categories, **hierarchical**, **network** and **relational**.

Take the Special Care Baby Unit as an example. One possibility is to store all related data in one huge file (Fig. 25). But accessing items of data and adding data requires searching through the record to find the appropriate place. Inserting, say, another treatment record is a problem because the rest of the data has to be shifted to make space.

■ Hierarchical model

The hierarchical model suits some applications and not others. The SCBU baby data is a good example of a hierarchical tree structure. The baby's details, admission details and treatments are stored in separate records, linked by **pointers**. (A pointer is an extra field of a record, giving the address of the record to which it is linked.) For example, the details record for baby X has two pointers, linking baby X with two admission records (baby X was admitted twice). Each admission record points to the treatments the baby was given. The records have to be linked otherwise we wouldn't know which baby had which treatment.

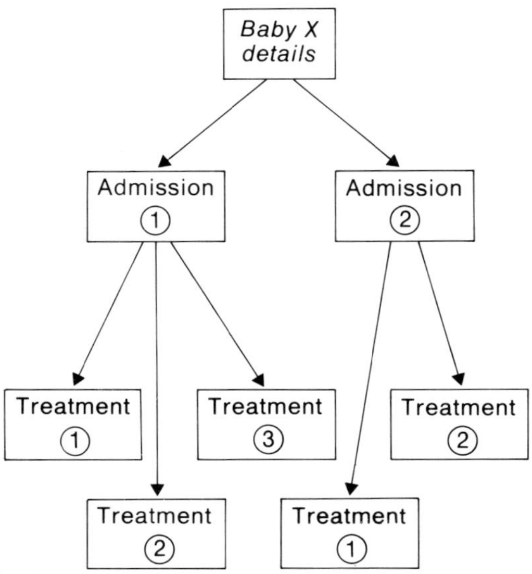

Figure 26 Hierarchical structure

Using the pointers, the database can quickly access the details for a particular baby. Adding a treatment for the baby is also straightforward; a new treatment record is added to the treatments file and it is linked to the admission and baby records with pointers. However, finding all the babies who have been given a particular treatment is slower; it requires a search of all the treatment records. Then each treatment record found is traced back up the tree to the baby who was given that treatment.

■ Network model

The network model is really an extension of the hierarchical. Network database systems provide good performance but they are very complex. This time pointers link records of the same type to each other and to their 'owner'. Fig. 27 shows how this works. Each set of pointers forms a ring.

This structure allows us to add records describing types of treatment and linking each of these to the babies' treatment records. It is now easy to find out which babies have had a particular treatment; simply find the type of treatment and follow the pointers. For example, both babies have had treatment type A. Only Baby John has had treatment B and he has had it twice.

■ Relational model

Relational databases are simpler in structure and now widely used. The data is perceived by the user as **tables**. Each table represents an **entity**; it contains a set of records with a unique key. For example, the ARKS system is relational and each table is stored in a file. Fig. 28 shows some of the tables.

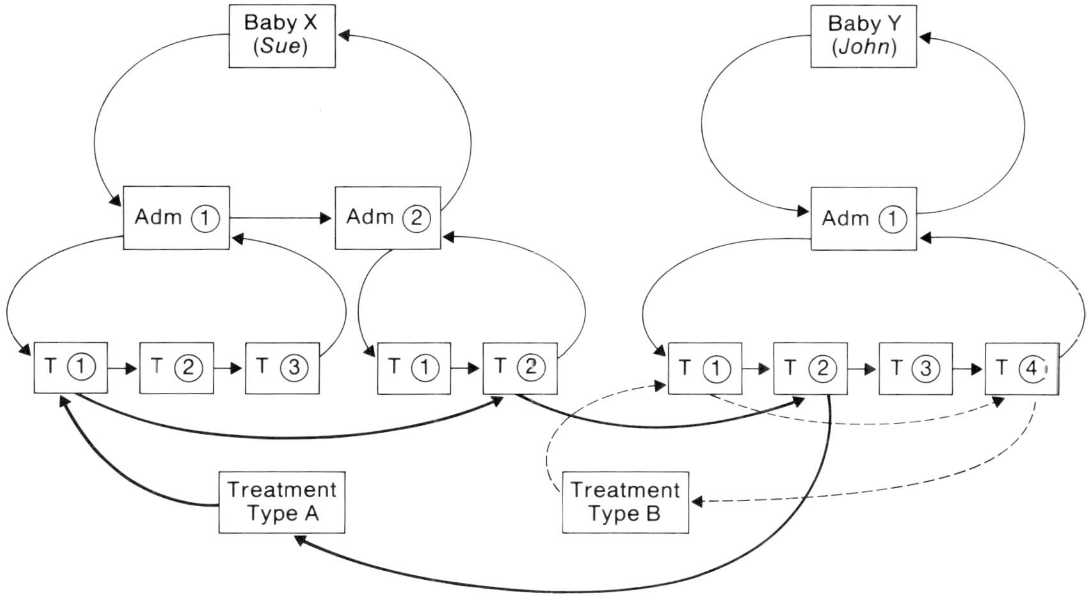

Figure 27 Network structure

Animals table

Id	Species	Name	Birth	Other
A1	Gorilla	Salome	16/7/76	
A2	Gorilla	Kumba	11/6/68	
A3	Gorilla	Zaire	23/10/74	
A4	Gorilla	Kamili	31/5/87	
A5	Lion	Henry	2/2/87	
A6	Kangaroo	Freda	12/5/87	

Transactions table

Id	Transaction	Institution	Date
A2	Loan in	Ches	7/6/84
A2	Loan out	Jers	26/7/84
A2	Loan out	Jers	22/3/88
A3	Loan in	Jers	26/7/84
A5	Sold	Canb	5/9/88
A6	Loan out	Ches	3/3/89
A6	Loan out	Ches	2/5/90
A4	Loan out	New York	24/9/90

Institutions table

Inst. id	Name	Address	Phone
Canb	Canberra Zoo	15 Park Ave, Canberra, Australia	21460872
Ches	Chessington Zoo	Chessington Park, Surrey	02498372
Jers	Jersey Wildlife Park	Lake Road, Newtown, Jersey	062749318

Figure 28 Relational model

Notice how the data has been split up. It would be possible to store the data in one huge table (Fig. 30 overleaf) with a record for each animal transaction; however there would be much duplication of data. Also, if Chessington Zoo changes its telephone number, for example, changes have to be made to all records involving that zoo.

The model in Fig. 28 makes it easy to alter the zoo's telephone number; it only occurs once. The only data duplicated are the key fields which provide links between the tables.

Id	*Species*	*Name*	*Birth*	*Other details*	*Trans*	*Inst name*	*Address*	*Phone*	*Date*
A2	Gorilla	Kumba	11/6/68		Loan in	Chessington Zoo/Park	Chessington Park, Surrey	02498372	7/6/84
A2	Gorilla	Kumba	11/6/68		Loan out	Jersey Wildlife Park	Lake Road	062749318	21/1/86
A2	Gorilla	Kumba	11/6/68		Loan out	Jersey Wildlife Park	Lake Road	062749318	22/3/88
A3	Gorilla	Zaire	23/10/74		Loan in	Jersey Wildlife Park	Lake Road	062749318	26/7/84
A5	Lion	Henry	2/2/87		Sold	Canberra Zoo Park	15 Park Ave, Canberra	21460872	5/9/88
A6	Kangaroo	Freda	12/5/87		Loan out	Chessington Zoo/Park	Chessington Park, Surrey	02498372	3/3/89
A6	Kangaroo	Freda	12/5/87		Loan out	Chessington Zoo/Park	Chessington Park, Surrey	02498372	2/5/90

Figure 29 A single file

• *Structured Query Language (SQL)*

A **query language** enables the user to access and update the database. The name 'query language' is really a misnomer because it is not only used for answering queries; most query languages include creation of tables, updating, deletion and many other facilities. **SQL** is the language supported by IBM database systems and is also used by many other vendors.

Suppose that we have already used the CREATE command to create the tables shown in Fig. 28. Two basic operations are available to retrieve data from tables. Firstly, records can be selected from a table.

For example, to get a list of all the gorillas (their id, name and date of birth):

```
SELECT ID, NAME, BIRTH
  FROM ANIMALS
  WHERE SPECIES = 'Gorilla'
```

To find the animals which left the zoo on loan or were sold during 1990 (their id, where they went and when):

```
SELECT ID, INSTITUTION, DATE
  FROM TRANSACTIONS
  WHERE (TRANSACTION = 'loan out'
    OR TRANSACTION = 'sold')
    AND YEAR (DATE) = 90
```

Secondly, tables can be joined together or merged, by matching the contents of one field. For example, if we want to find out which species of animal have been out on loan we need data from two tables, animals and transactions. SQL picks out rows from the two tables where the animal's id matches the transaction's id and where the transaction type is a loan out.

Note that we have to specify ANIMALS . ID (not just ID) because id appears in two tables.

```
SELECT ANIMALS . ID, ANIMALS . SPECIES
  FROM ANIMALS, TRANSACTIONS
  WHERE ANIMALS . ID =
      TRANSACTIONS . ID
    AND TRANSACTION = 'Loan out'
```

The result from the data shown in Fig. 28 would be: A6 kangaroo, A6 kangaroo, A4 gorilla.

■ Mainframe and microcomputer database packages

Early database systems were of hierarchical or network structure. The relational model was an important development and was based on theories of relational calculus. Most recent database systems are relational. Mainframe systems include DB2 (IBM), ORACLE and INGRES. Scaled down versions of ORACLE and INGRES are available on the more powerful microcomputers.

Some of the very simple schools packages (for example those used in primary schools) only work on one file at a time; they are therefore only suitable for simple applications. Microcomputer packages such as dBase are used commercially as well as in education and are more sophisticated. dBase is based on the relational model; it stores data in tables and the user can select from and join tables. It also has a programming language that can be used to develop applications.

ORACLE is a **command-driven** system, whereas dBase IV has a menu selection system which is designed to be easy to use, though SQL commands can be used.

A database system has many advantages, but the effort and expense required to develop the system should not be underestimated. Good design is crucial to the success of the system. In particular, **security** and **integrity** of data (see Chapter 2) are very important because the data is shared between so many users.

A large database management system takes regular **backups** automatically and monitors people's access of the system. It also checks the files and keeps the indexes up to date. Most microcomputer packages do not have these facilities; it is left to the user to remember to take backups and to re-index files.

QUESTIONS

1 (a) Work through the batch update example shown in Fig. 19. Identify the invalid transaction and explain why it is invalid.
(b) Write an algorithm for the batch update described. Test your algorithm with the files shown in the example. Make up some more data of your own and use that to test the algorithm. Can your algorithm find invalid transactions?

2 Investigate the file structures of a database package that you are familiar with. How does it organise its files (serial/sequential/random)? How does it access the files? Can it sort files? Does it have a facility for creating indexes to a file that has been set up? Can it deal with more than one file at once?

3 Investigate a programming language you are familiar with. How does it store character strings? How are records stored (fixed/variable length, etc.)?

4 Find out about different methods of sorting a file (eg. bubble sort, exchange sort, quick sort). Write an algorithm for each method. Explain the difference between an internal and an external sort. When is each sort used?

5 A large indexed sequential file contains records of a company's customers. The file is updated online by operators as details of new customers or changes are received. The computer keeps a serial transaction log of all updates. At the end of the day, a backup of the customer file is made.
(a) Describe the structure of the indexed sequential file.
(b) What data items would you expect to find in the log?
(c) Suppose the file is corrupted. Suggest a suitable recovery procedure.

6 A large area of disused railway land has been divided into plots for local people to grow fruit and vegetables. The manager of these allotments, Mr. Hacker, is a computer enthusiast and wishes to use a computer to store data about each allotment. This will include:

the identification number of the allotment
the name and address of the user
the size of the plot (in m^2)
the annual rent
the date when the next rent is due
a list of the types of fruit and vegetable currently grown.

The data will need to be modified, for example when rent is paid, when the crops being grown are changed, or when the allotment is transferred to another user.

(a) Design a suitable way of organising the data for storage in a file(s).
(b) Describe how your design allows for the data to be modified easily.
(c) Mr. Hacker has been alerted to an outbreak of potato blight and needs urgently to get in touch with all of the allotment users who are growing potatoes. If your data organisation allows him to discover quickly who these users are, explain how it does so, otherwise describe what changes would be necessary to allow it.

[*UCLES 1989*]

7 A newsagent in a thriving city suburb has acquired a computer system which enables her to successfully manage a number of shops in the city. The newsagent delivers newspapers and periodicals within the area using paperboys and girls. From time to time customers change their orders. Delivery has to be suspended for a day or more when customers are away for trips or holidays. The newsagent wishes to anticipate any complaints and handle queries in an efficient manner. In order to achieve this she requires rapid access to up-to-date information regarding her customers, orders and her delivery personnel.

(a) Design computer records suitable for the newsagent's use and suggest, with reasons, an efficient type of file structure that she should adopt in order to achieve the above requirement.
(b) What benefits do you think such a system would offer to the newsagent and her customers?

[*Welsh Joint Education Committee 1988*]

CHAPTER 4

Computer Programming

Introduction

This chapter does not aim to teach you a computer **programming language**. The only real way to learn programming is to use a language to produce programs of your own, to test them and to convince yourself that they work. Programming can be great fun. Getting a program to work for the first time is a very satisfying experience. Programming can also be very frustrating. When a program doesn't work, and it is rare that a program works first time, it can be difficult to find the reason why. However, finding the '**bug**', correcting it and then finding that the program works is all part of the challenge.

What this chapter does aim to do is to show that there are good programming techniques and, conversely, bad ways to program. Using good programming technique helps to reduce the incidence of errors in code and increases the chances of achieving a correctly functioning program. Well written programs are also easier to understand, making them easier to **maintain**. ie. to modify and possibly correct errors which become known through using the program.

Algorithms, Data and Programs

One definition of a computer program is as follows:

ALGORITHMS + DATA STRUCTURES = PROGRAM

This means that a program is a combination of a correctly defined description of the logic of the program (**algorithm**) plus a well chosen **data structure** to solve the stated problem.

This chapter is, therefore, divided into two main parts. Part 1 deals with an approach to defining an algorithm using 'Structured Top Down Design'. Part 2 considers data, and data structures and their application. But first it is worth making some comments about programming languages themselves.

There are many different types of programming languages, the following is a list of some of them and some examples of each, in brackets:

- Imperative (Pascal, BASIC, COBOL, FORTRAN)
- Logic (Prolog)
- Functional (Lisp, Hope, Logo)
- Concurrent (Occam)
- High-level (Pascal, BASIC)
- Low-level (Assembly level)
- Fourth generation (dBase)
- Third generation (Pascal, BASIC)

Each of these types has different characteristics which makes them more suited to solving particular types of problems. However, the same comments concerning good practice applies to whichever type of language is being used.

As you can see from the above list some languages appear in more than one classification. The languages which are probably most familiar to you are BASIC, COBOL, FORTRAN and Pascal. These are generally classed as **third generation, high-level, imperative** languages. If you would like to know more about the other types of languages then you could consult an introductory text about a particular language. If you can get access to a **compiler**, **assembler** or **interpreter** for the language, then you could try some practical programming with the language.

Part 1 Program Design

■ Algorithms

An algorithm is a precisely defined statement of what the program is to do. This could be stated in straightforward English, but could become imprecise, ambiguous and difficult to follow.

A more effective approach is to use simple English statements of the actions to be carried out, but to define the relationship between these actions using a small set of '**structuring**' definitions.

■ Structured English (Pseudocode)

There are several different approaches to defining the structure of a program. Amongst these are flowcharts, Structured English, Nassi–Schneiderman diagrams and Jackson Structured Programming. Here, we describe **Structured English** as the means of defining an algorithm. This is often called **pseudocode** because of its similarity to program code. At some points in the description of pseudocode, equivalent flowcharts are shown to contrast the two approaches. In pseudocode, the individual actions to be carried out by the program are stated in simple English statements, the structures used are defined as being of three types:

Sequence

Selection

Repetition.

• *Sequence*

Sequence is the simple definition of a sequence of actions. For example,

```
read a number
read a number
add the numbers together
print the sum
```

In a flowchart, this would simply be:

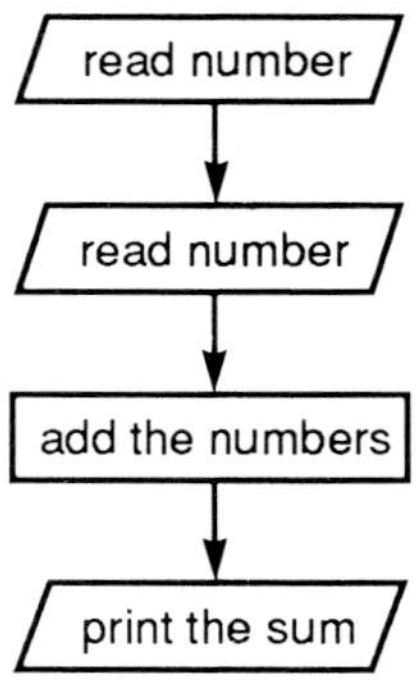

• *Selection*

Selection allows for a choice to be made between two or more options. The choice is made by testing if a 'logical condition' is TRUE or FALSE. The test is made within a standard type of statement as follows:

```
IF {logical condition test}
   THEN {action}
   ELSE {alternative action}
```

{action} is carried out if the result of the test is TRUE
{alternative action} takes place if the result is FALSE.

For example: If we wanted to print the larger of the two numbers input in the previous example under 'sequence' we could define the algorithm as follows:

```
read a number
read a number
IF first number > second number
   THEN print first number
   ELSE print second number
add the numbers together
print the sum
```

The flowchart for this would be as follows:

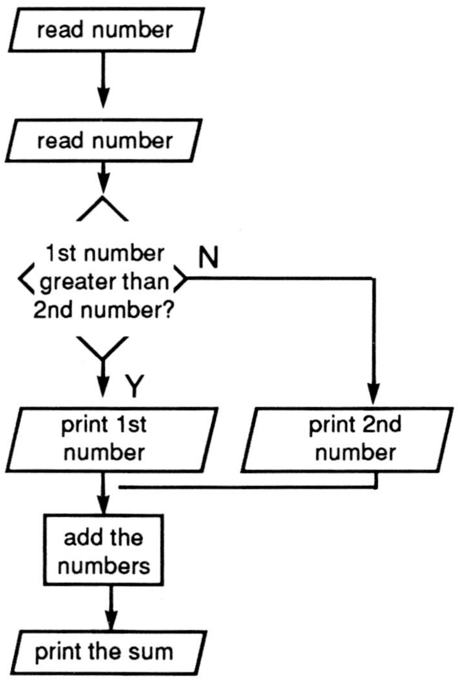

• *Repetition*

If we now wanted to extend our solution to process a series of pairs of numbers in the same way, a solution could look like this:

```
WHILE there are more numbers DO
   read a number
   read a number
   IF first number > second number
      THEN print first number
      ELSE print second number
   add the numbers together
   print the sum
ENDWHILE
```

Alternatively:

```
REPEAT
   read a number
   read a number
   IF first number > second number
      THEN print first number
      ELSE print second number
   add the numbers together
   print the sum
UNTIL there are no more numbers
```

There is another repetition structure which is used if the repetition is for a known number of times. In the examples used above the repetition is until a condition changes, ie. the repetition stops when there are no more numbers. If however, we knew how many numbers to expect then we could use the FOR . . . DO loop construct.

For example: if we know that there are always ten pairs of numbers we could use the following structure:

```
FOR I = 1 TO 10 DO
   read a number
   read a number
   IF first number > second number
      THEN print first number
      ELSE print second number
   add the numbers together
   print the sum
ENDFOR
```

The examples show that there is an important difference between the WHILE . . . DO and REPEAT . . . UNTIL structures and the FOR . . . DO structure. The first two test for a condition to change before terminating the loop, the other 'counts' the number of repetitions and terminates when so many have been counted. But what are the differences between the WHILE and the REPEAT structures?

- *Use of repetition structures*

If you look closely at the operation of the WHILE . . . DO structure you will notice that the condition is tested before entering the statements within the repetition. In the REPEAT . . . UNTIL structure the condition is not tested until after the statements have been executed. This means that the statements in a WHILE . . . DO structure will not be executed at all if the condition test result is FALSE at the first test in the repetition. In a REPEAT . . . UNTIL structure the statements will always be executed at least once, no matter what the result of the first condition test is.

Both these structures should be used in cases where it is required to carry out some action until a condition changes. If there is a chance that the condition being tested might be FALSE before entering the **loop** then the WHILE . . DO structure should be used. The following example pieces of code illustrate the difference this can make to the running of a program. In the examples, the number 999 is being used to 'stop' the loop.

set total to zero	set total to zero
read a number	REPEAT
WHILE number <> 999 DO	read a number
add number to total	add number to total
read a number	UNTIL number = 999
ENDWHILE	print the total

Try these with a set of numbers, for example 4, 6, 3, 8, 999.

The total produced should be 21, but in the case of the REPEAT loop the value 999 gets added before it has been tested, giving an answer of 1020! Of course we could add an extra line to subtract 999 before printing the total:

eg. . . .
. . .
UNTIL number = 999
subtract 999 from total
print total

But there are often circumstances where it is essential to have discovered the condition change before processing spurious data.

A final point on the WHILE structure. Notice that it was necessary to 'read a number' before entering the loop. This is because the program needs to have read a number before it can test it. This also means that the 'read' and 'add' instructions are reversed inside the loop.

■ Building up complete programs – step-wise refinement

When writing a project report or essay or book it is easier to write and to read if it is broken down into subsections or chapters. The same applies to algorithms. An algorithm is a description of the logic of a program. It too is easier to write and understand if it is broken down into smaller sections. This is done by breaking the algorithm down into **blocks**. The start of a block is defined with the word BEGIN, the end of a block by the word END. If this is done with the example used under the **Repetition** section above, we could get:

```
WHILE there are more numbers DO
  BEGIN
    read a number
    read a number
    IF first number > second number
      THEN print first number
      ELSE print second number
    add the numbers
    print the sum
  END
ENDWHILE
```

The part within the BEGIN ... END is equivalent to a subsection within the WHILE ... DO loop. Notice that the statements inside the block are all indented. This helps to make clearer where the block begins and ends, again making the pseudocode easier to read and understand.

BEGIN and END and indentation can be used to 'block' up associated, complex pieces of pseudocode anywhere in an algorithm. Doing this properly makes an algorithm a lot easier to follow. Another use of the approach is to give a block a name so that it may be referred to elsewhere in the algorithm by that name. Here is the example used earlier with some blocking and naming introduced.

```
WHILE there are more numbers DO

  READTESTADD

ENDWHILE

READTESTADD

BEGIN
  read a number
  read a number
  IF first number > second number
    THEN print first number
    ELSE print second number
  add the numbers
  print the sum
END
```

The main reading, testing, adding and printing operations have been grouped together in a block called **READTESTADD**. Writing an algorithm in this way has other advantages, in addition to making it easier to read. For instance, if the algorithm required the same logic elsewhere it could be referred to by using the name again; the detail needs describing only once. It also has the advantage that the detail may be written at some other time or even by someone else! Large programs may be developed by a team of programmers, each member of the team working on separate blocks. These named blocks of code are referred to as **procedures, subroutines** or **functions**.

A function is used in a slightly different way to procedures and subroutines. Functions may only **return** one value to the calling procedure or function. Procedures may return any number of values. Functions are usually **called** within **expressions. Procedure calls** are complete **statements**.

For example, Pascal contains a function called SQR, which calculates the square root of a number. It may be used as follows:

```
X := 16;
Root := SQR(X) + 4;
```

SQR(X) is the call to the function SQR with the value 16 in the variable X. The square root of 16 is calculated and then 4 is added to it, giving the answer 8 in the variable root.

■ Procedures, subroutines and functions

Using procedures or subroutines to define the logic of a program makes the definition of the program clearer. The relationship between procedures may be shown by a 'structure chart' of the program. Fig. 1 gives an example of such a chart.

The structure is generally a **tree**, with the **root** at the top, branching downwards. The 'root' is the main program, each **leaf** in the tree is a **procedure**. The 'branches' show that the procedure or **main program** 'calls' the procedure at the lower end of the branch.

For example: In the chart in Fig. 1 'MAIN' calls 'READTESTADD'.

Using this approach provides a very simple picture of the overall structure of the program. The detailed logic of the individual procedures is described using pseudocode.

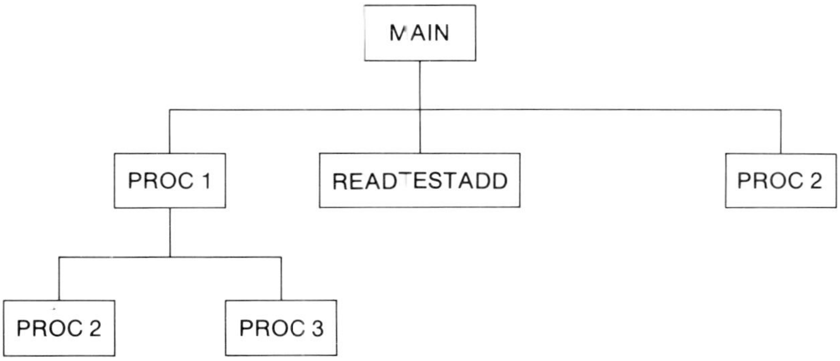

Figure 1 Structure chart

To illustrate the use of this technique, the outline algorithm and structure diagram for the package described in the case study on Audiocalc (the speaking spreadsheet) is given in Fig. 2.

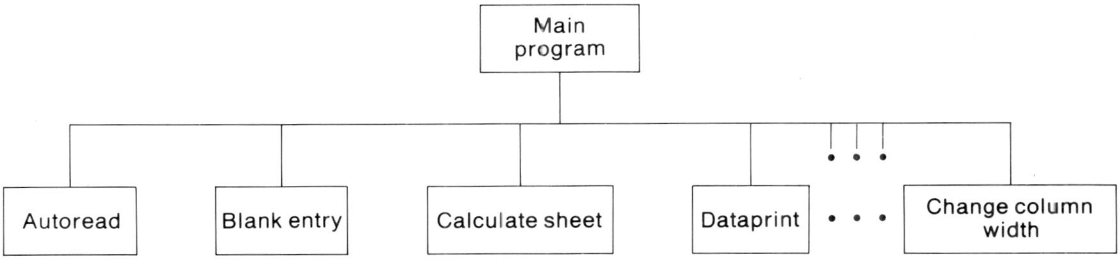

Audiocalc Algorithm:

```
BEGIN
  Output 'System Ready' message to speech synthesiser;
  Display Main Screen;
  Accept Command;
  WHILE Command not = 'Quit' Do
  BEGIN
    If Control key pressed THEN Process control function
    ELSE
    IF Command = 'A' THEN Autoread
    ELSE
    IF Command = 'B' THEN Blank entry
    ELSE
    IF Command = 'C' THEN Calculate sheet
    ELSE
    If Command = 'D' THEN Dataprint
    .
    ELSE
    IF Command = 'W' THEN Change column width
    ELSE Output error message to synthesiser
  END {while};
    Output 'Audiocalc finished' message to synthesiser;
 END:
```

Autoread

```
BEGIN
  .
  .
  . Define autoread;
  .
  .
  END:
```

Blank entry

```
  .
  .
  .
  etc.
```

Figure 2 Audiocalc structure diagram and algorithm

■ Recursion

As we have seen above, a procedure, subroutine or function can **call** other procedures etc. In some languages, Pascal and Logo for example, a procedure or function may call itself. This is known as **recursion**.

It sometimes happens that, after making some progress towards solving a problem, we arrive at a simplified version of the same problem. When a procedure or function arrives at this point, it can call itself to solve a simplified version of the original problem. Such a call is said to be **recursive**.

Recursion is a form of **repetition**. Each recursive call makes another recursive call, until some condition changes, causing the calling sequence to **terminate**. However, like repetition, recursion can fail to terminate. The recursive function or procedure could continue to call itself without ever making progress towards solving the original problem. For a sequence of recursive calls to terminate successfully, two conditions must hold. These are:

- ► 1 The function or procedure must always call itself to solve a **simplified** version of the original problem.
- ► 2 Repeated simplification must lead to a trivial version of the problem, which can be solved without further recursive calls.

● *A recursive factorial function*

Here is an example to illustrate recursion:

The **factorial** of a value N is the product of all the integers from 1 through the value of N. For example, the factorial of 4 is 1×2×3×4, which equals 24. Factorial N is often written as N! For example 4! = 24.

The following code is a recursive function (written in Pascal) which calculates a factorial:

```
FUNCTION Factorial (N: integer);
BEGIN
  IF N = 1
  THEN
  Factorial := 1
  ELSE
  Factorial: = N*Factorial (N-1)
END;
:
:
N = 4                        {Set N to 4}
Answer = Factorial (N);      {Call Factorial}
:                            {Put the result}
:                            {in Answer}
```

In the brackets after the function name, N is declared as a **parameter**. Parameters are described in more detail in the next section. In this example we can see that whatever the initial value of N is, its value will be reduced by one, each time Factorial is called after the initial call. Eventually, N will become equal to 1, and this will terminate the calling sequence because when N = 1, Factorial is not called. The recursive function will return the factorial of the original value of N.

To investigate recursion more fully you should experiment with it, using a language that supports it. Logo is an excellent language for this, because it is easy to write recursive functions which draw pictures, illustrating the effect. Go ahead, TRY IT!

PART 2
DATA AND DATA STRUCTURES IN PROGRAMS

■ Data in programs

All programs process **data**. Data may be numbers, words, patterns or signals. In programming languages such as Pascal or BASIC, data is processed via **variables** defined within the program. In Pascal, variables are defined in **VAR** statements. In Pascal the **TYPE** of data which may be held in the variables has to be declared along with the variable's name.

```
eg.  Var    Height  :  Integer;
```

In this example, we have introduced a variable called 'Height' and have stated that it should only hold **Integer** values. That is, whole numbers. The **compiler** can check that the code which uses this variable assigns only integer values to it, and flag an error if the ruie is broken.

```
eg.  Height  :=  10;     is O.K.
     Height  :=  3.75;   is an error.
```

If the variable is one which receives data from the keyboard when the program runs, the checking may take place as the program runs.

```
eg.  Read (Height);   —input 10     O.K.
                      —input 3.75   error.
```

Typing of variables gives extra checking in programs and helps to reduce possible errors by the programmer.

Some languages, especially newer ones, require that all variables are declared and typed before they are used in the program's logic.

The BASIC programming language has variable typing of the following form:

Height ... is type real
Height% ... is type integer
Name$ ... is text

The data typing is **implicit** in the variable name used, rather than having a **type declaration**.

■ Global data, local data and sharing data

● *Global data*

We have already said that data is processed in programs by the use of variables. What is a **variable**? Take a look at Fig. 3.

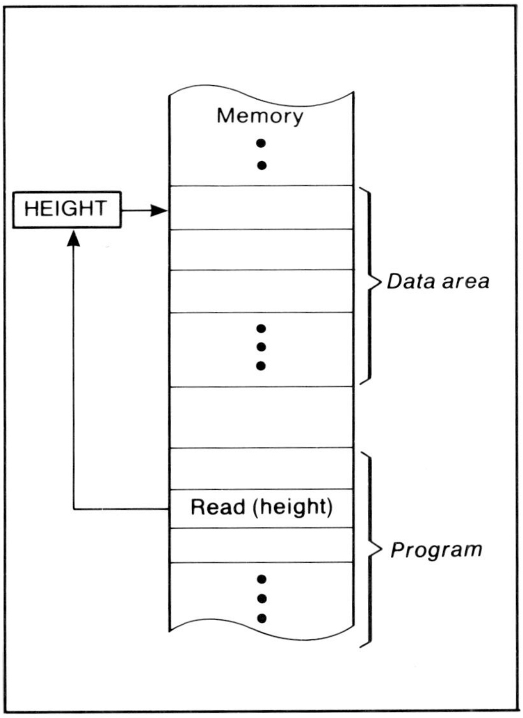

Figure 3 Accessing a variable

The diagram represents a program and its data area stored in **computer memory**. If the program refers to a variable called 'Height', for instance, then what this means is that the programmer has given a **memory location** the name 'Height'. This is more convenient than referring to a memory location by number. The variable, or memory location, is then used to **store** and manipulate values.

eg. READ (Height); –
[takes a value from the keyboard and stores it in the location called Height.]
Area := Height × Width; –
[takes the values in the locations named 'Height' and 'Width', multiplies them together and puts the result in the location named Area.]

Any program spends most of its running time doing this sort of thing, manipulating memory via variables. The memory space defined with variables is available to all instructions in the logic. It is said to be **global data**. This implies that the program could use the 'Height' variable in any of its instructions, there are no restrictions on the access to that memory location. This gives the programmer great flexibility because any variable or memory location may be used in any part of the program. However it can also cause problems.

In the earlier part of this chapter it was said that breaking down a program into smaller chunks such as procedures or subroutines is good practice. Each part of the program can be defined as a separate unit. The **structure diagram** shows you how each procedure relates to the others. If global data is used, each part of the program may refer to any variable. Procedures may be written at different times and maybe by different people. If global data is used, the names of all the variables used need to be defined once at the beginning of the program. This means that if two or more procedures use the variable 'Height', the writer or writers must spell 'Height' the same and perhaps know what the writers of other procedures are doing with 'Height'. The contents of 'Height' may be changed in one procedure, causing the failure of another procedure using the same variable name.

Thus, it can be seen that using global memory to hold variables when using procedures creates disadvantages which reduce and maybe outweigh the advantages gained.

The answer is to use **local data**.

● *Local data*

The problems caused by using global data with procedures or subroutines can be solved by the use of local data.

If you look at Fig. 4 opposite you will see that the data space defined for the program has now been split up. Each procedure or subroutine now has its own data space instead of one global space available to all. This means that each procedure has now become a little 'program', defining some specific part of the larger program's logic. The writers of the separate procedures can ignore how the writers of the other procedures use particular variables.

It means, for instance, that two or more procedures may use the same variable name. But the name now refers to two or more separate memory locations. Fig. 5 illustrates this.

When a procedure is written, the programmer declares the variables required in that procedure without the need to consider if other procedures use the same name.

But, there is still a problem. What if a procedure needs to **pass** data to another?

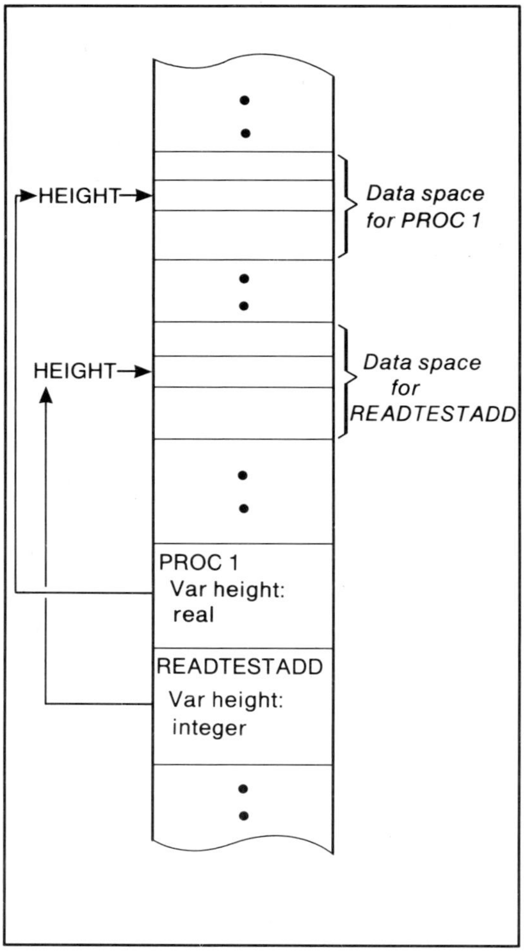

Figure 5 Different procedures may use the same variable name

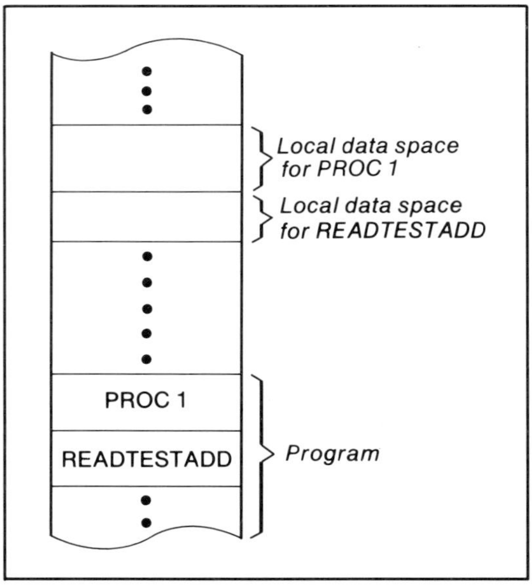

Figure 4 Local data spaces

- *Sharing data by global memory*

Using local data allows for less error prone programming. But we still need the ability to share data between different parts of the same program. For example, it may be required to do some processing on 'Height' in one procedure and also in another.

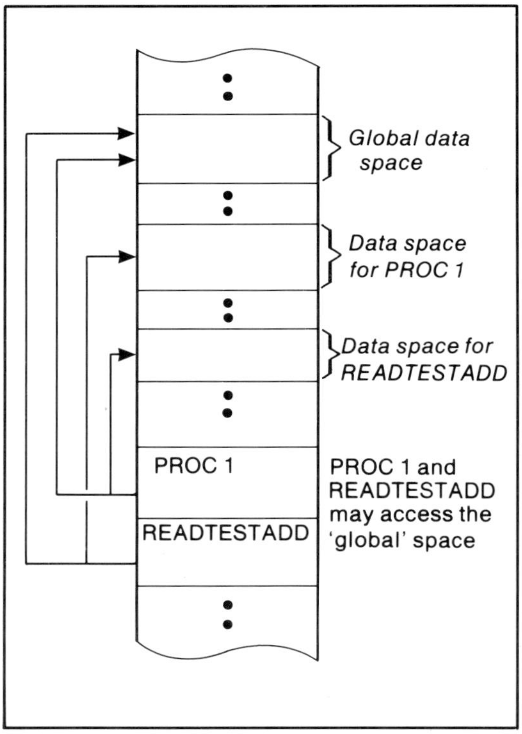

Figure 6 Global and local data spaces

One way of allowing for this would be to keep some global memory, to hold variables to be shared, and to define local memory for all non-shared variables. Fig. 6 illustrates this approach.

In this way, the global memory is kept to a minimum. But it still means that all users of the global memory need to know the exact names of global variables.

A better way of solving the sharing data problem is by using **parameter passing**.

- *Sharing data by parameter passing*

Using parameters with procedures gives the most flexible and safest method of sharing data between different parts of a program.

The principle of parameter passing is that each procedure has its **local data area** defined as above. Additionally, those variables which are to be shared or **passed** to other procedures are also defined. These variables often take the special name of **parameters**. Parameters are **passed** between procedures. Only those variables which need to be passed to other procedures are defined as parameters. The following is an example piece of Pascal code, illustrating how local data and parameters are defined.

The code shows two procedures, each one processing a value for height. In procedure A the value is processed in a local variable 'Height'.

In procedure B the value is processed in a variable called 'Ht.' Don't worry if you don't fully understand the code shown here. The important points to note are highlighted in the diagram. Notice that no global data is defined, only local data. The variable that needs to pass from A to B is defined in the brackets following 'Procedure A', which defines the detail of A and 'A' inside Procedure B, which shows where A is used. This is also illustrated in Fig. 7.

Now we've discussed the importance of variables and their use in programs let's look back at the definition of a program given at the beginning of the chapter. That is:

ALGORITHM + DATA STRUCTURES = PROGRAM

Having read the previous sections on **procedures, local data** and **data sharing**, you may be beginning to realise that the use of **variables** in a program is as important as the definition of the **logic** of the processing. But why does the definition given here refer to DATA STRUCTURES?

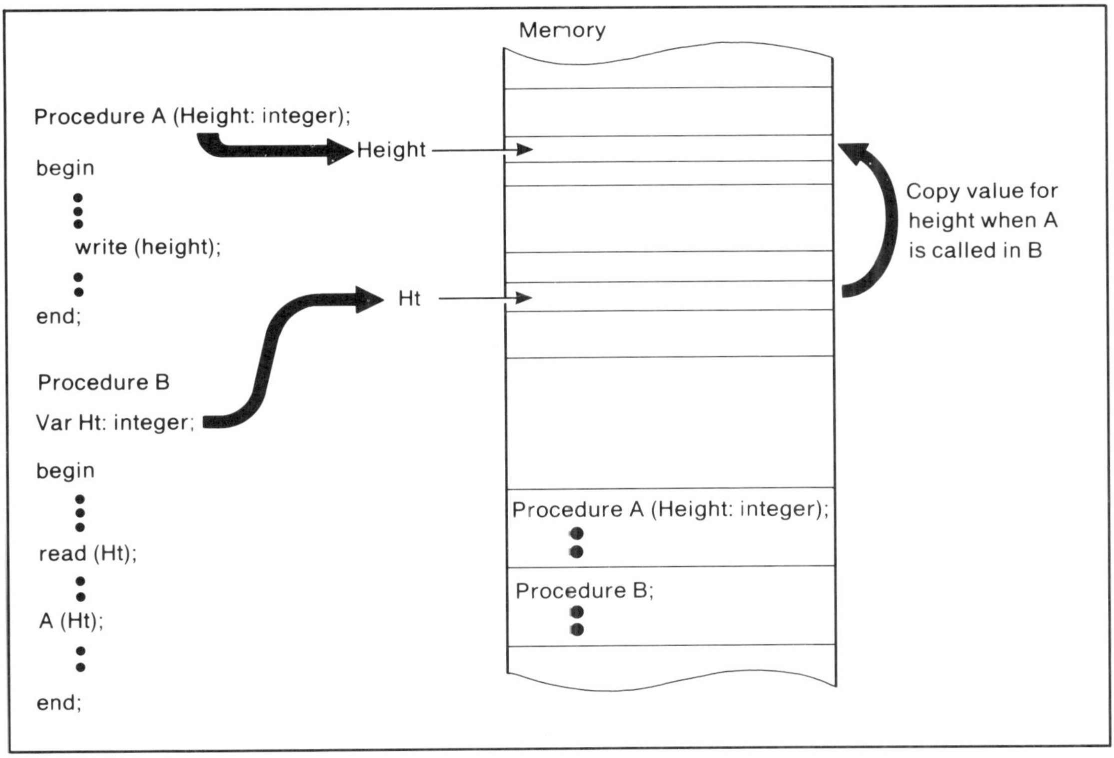

Figure 7 Passing data via parameters

■ Data structures

• *Variables*

In the above description of programming, **variables** were used to hold data items. In each example the variable refers to a single memory location eg. the variable 'Height' refers to a single memory location which we would expect to hold a value representing some height. But what if the program was required to process a set of say ten heights, and that each of these heights should be held in memory at the same time?

Let's consider a program required to process these heights. For example, a program which reads a series of heights and outputs a number of '*'s equivalent to each height, giving a simple graph of heights.

```
ie.  Input    3, 9, 4, 6, 2, 8, 11, 7, 13, 4
     Output
              ***
              *********
              ****
              ******
              **
              ********
              ***********
              *******
              *************
              ****
```

One way of doing this would be to read a value and print the number of stars equivalent to the value. The problem with this approach is that the input values become mixed with the output graph because the screen is being used to prompt for the input and for the output. The result would be something like this:

```
Please input number:  3
***
Please input number:  9
*********
etc.
```

To get the graph output without the input prompts requires all the input before any output. This requires that the **input** values are stored prior to **output**. Therefore, a variable is required for each value. Remember, each variable refers to a separate memory location and must have a unique name.

This could be achieved as follows:

```
var height1, height2, . . . height10: integer;
```

That is, a separate variable for each value. However, the logic of the program is as follows:

```
For i := 1 to 10 do
  Read a height
End for
For i := 1 to 10 do
  For j := 1 to height do
    Print '*'
  End for
End for
```

Having a different variable name for each height would mean that 'height' in the 'Read a height' and 'For j := 1 to height' lines would actually be height1, height2 ... etc. for each separate value. This would mean that the **For ... Do loops** couldn't be used. The program would look more like this:

```
Read height1
Read height2
:
Read height10
For i := 1 to height1 do
  Print a star
End for
For i := 1 to height2 do
  Print a star
End for
:
:
For i := 1 to height10 do
  Print a star
End for
```

To allow the simpler first version to be used a **data structure** called **array** is required.

• *Arrays*

An array is the definition of a group of memory locations. The group of locations is given a single name. Each **element** of the array may then be referenced by the group name and a **subscript**.

The example is now shown using an array of heights.

```
For i := 1 to 10 do
  Read height (i)
End for
For i := 1 to 10 do
  For j := to height (i) do
      Print '*'
  End for
    Print a new line
End for
```

Height										
	1	2	3	4	5	6	7	8	9	10

Figure 8 An array called "height"

Height	3	9	4	6	2	8	11	7	13	4
	1	2	3	4	5	6	7	8	9	10

Figure 9 The same array with values stored in it

Notice that when height is used it is followed by brackets containing a variable (i). Fig. 8 shows how the memory is allocated for the array 'Height'.

To declare this in Pascal the following code is used.

```
var Height: Array [1 . . . 10] of Integer;
```

This declaration means 'allocate ten memory locations of type integer and name them height'. The subscript value may only be in the range 1 to 10. If its value is 1 the first element in the array is accessed; if the value is 2, the second, and so on.

If you examine the code in the example above you will see that the 'For i := 1 to 10 Do' loops vary the value of i from 1 to 10.

The first loop reads in the values and stores them in the array. The second loop prints the number of stars according to the contents of each element of the array; the heights.

Fig. 9 shows the array with the values stored in it. Note the difference between the **contents** of an **array element** and its subscript (the position of the element in the array).

All the elements are **integers**. They could be of any **type**, for example we could have an array of **characters**. However, the subscript for an array is always an integer in the **range** defined for the array.

Considering arrays has introduced the idea that a programmer can create relationships between data items to make programming a solution to a problem easier. We shall now take a look at some other useful data structures which may be used when programming.

- *Records*

An array is a group of data items which are all the same type. A **record** is a group of data items which may be of different types. For example, the personal details for a person might consist of:

Name
Age
Sex
Date of Birth

Name and Sex are alphabetic. Age and Date of Birth are numeric. However, since they all refer to one person it is convenient to group them together in a RECORD data structure.

Data is often held on **backing store** in **files** of **records**. Each of the data items is referred to as a **field**. You will find more detailed description and discussion of this in Chapters 1, 2 and 3 and the Arks and Noah, Sainsburys and Datapost case studies. It is sufficient to realise here that, for a programming language to be useful for **data processing** it must be able to handle a data structure of this type.

Name (1)	Name (2)	. .	. .
Age (1)	Age (2)	. .	. .
Sex (1)	Sex (2)	. .	. .
Date of birth (1)	Date of birth (2)	. .	. .
1	2	3	4

Figure 10 An array of records

Take a look at Fig. 10. You can see that it illustrates an array, but that each element of the array is a record. In other words, an element of an array does not have to be a simple data type. It can be any other, more complex data type. It could be another array. Fig. 11 illustrates this. A structure of this sort is often called a **two-dimensional array**.

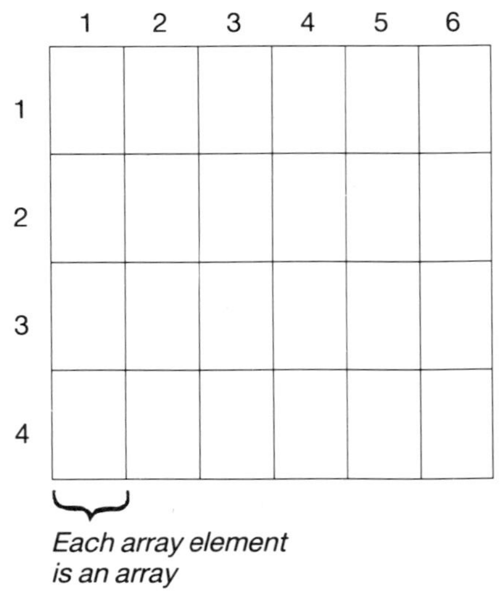

Figure 11 A two-dimensional array – an array of arrays

A record structure can also contain an array.

The ability to process such data structures depends on the programming language being used. It is usual for a language to allow for the definition of arrays and records. It is up to the programmer to choose the most effective structure to solve the given problem.

Arrays and records are data structures which describe a relationship between data items. Having these structures available also allows for easier **data handling** in algorithms. These structures don't, however, imply anything about how they should be processed. They can be used in any way that the programmer thinks best or easiest. An array is just a list of data items. A record is just a convenient way of grouping certain data items together.

A data structure can be made slightly more complex and more useful for some purposes by defining the **order** of processing of elements in the data structure. Two common examples of this are **stacks** and **queues**.

- *Stacks and queues*

A stack is a list in which all insertions and deletions are made at one end. It may also be called a **Pushdown** or **Last In First Out list (LIFO)**, like a stack of trays in a cafeteria.

A queue is a list in which insertions are made at one end and deletions are made at the other. It may also be called a **First In First Out list (FIFO)** like an (orderly) bus queue. A variation of the queue is the **deque** (double ended queue), which allows insertions and deletions at both ends.

Fig. 12 shows how items are added to and removed from a **stack** and a **queue**.

Notice that the list is stored exactly as for an array. The only difference is in that by saying the structure is a stack or a queue, we are saying how the structure should be **processed.**

- *Applications of stacks and queues*

The stack is a very widely used data structure. Its **LIFO** characteristic makes it useful for **backtracking**.

For example: Consider a program which makes a series of **calls** to **subroutines** as in Fig. 13. You can see that Program A calls routine B, which calls routine C, which calls routine D.

Figure 12 Adding to and removing from a stack and queue

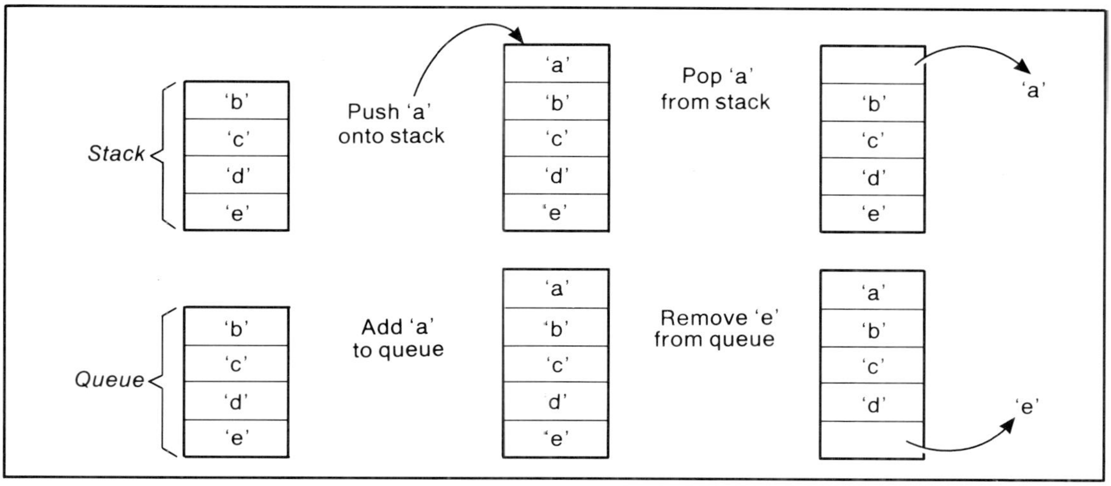

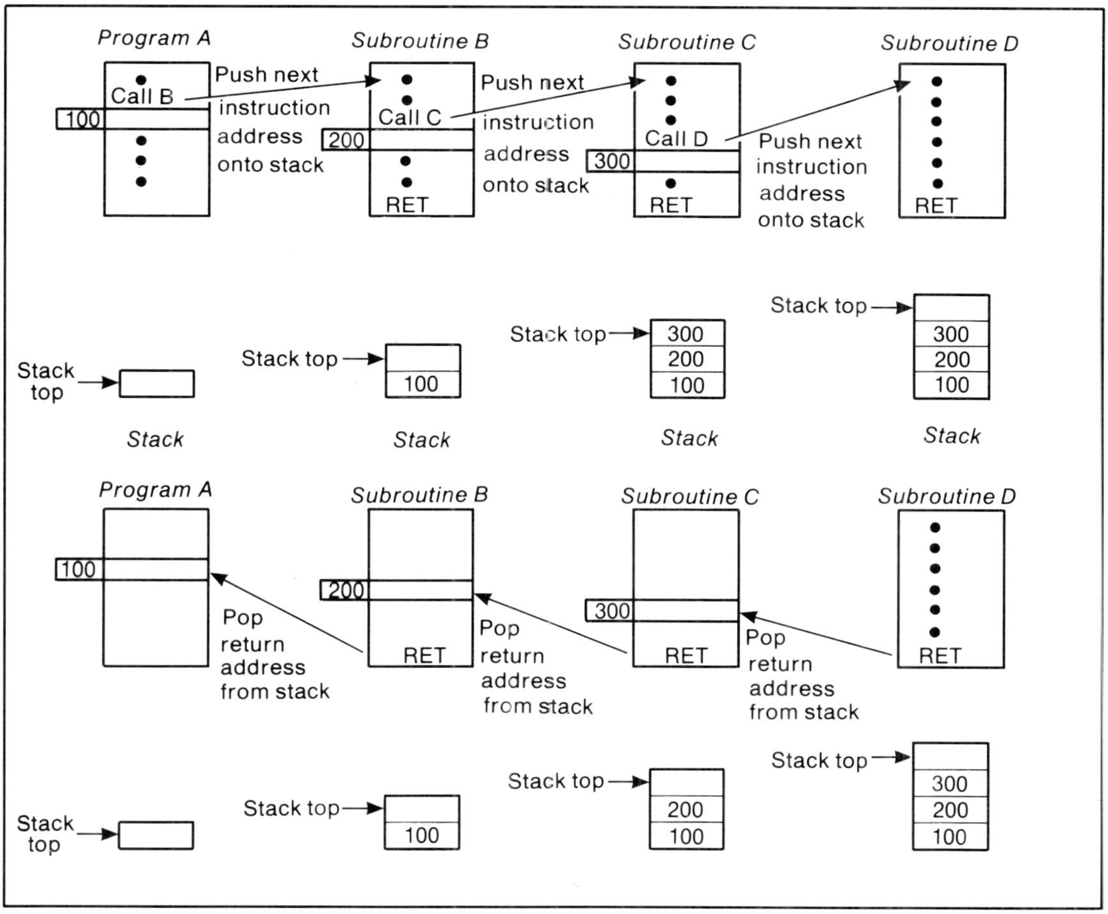

Figure 13 Use of a stack

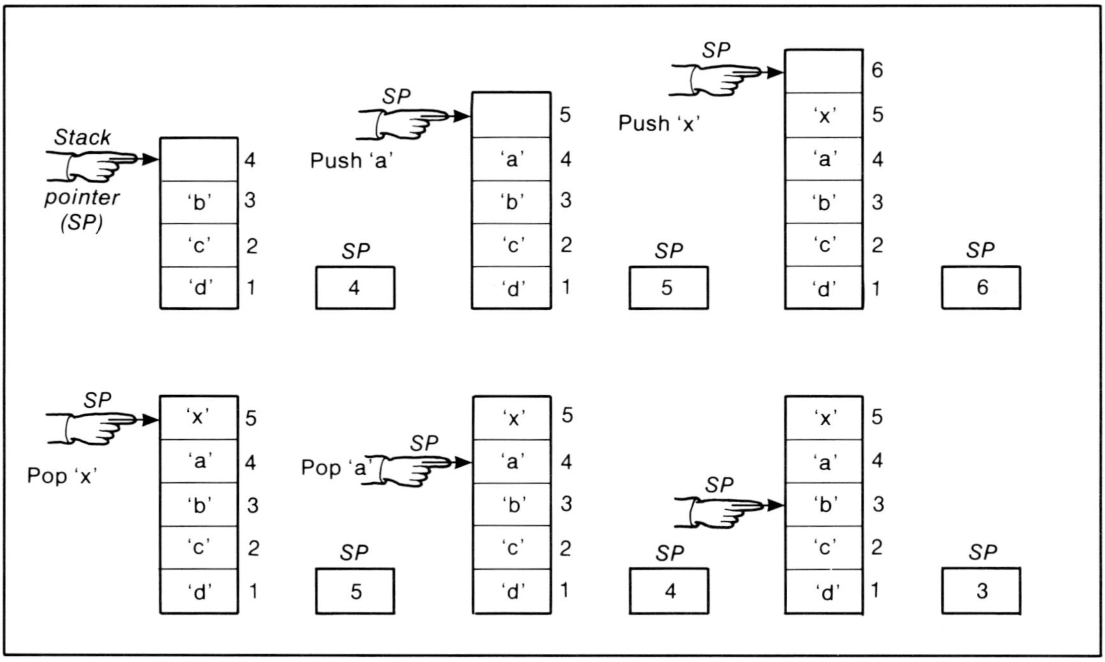

Figure 14 The stack pointer changes value for each push or pop

Each subroutine must return to the program location from where it was called. Thus routine D should return to routine C. Routine C to B, and so on.

To achieve this, the return addresses are **pushed** onto a stack as the routines are called so that when routine D is being executed, the return address in C is at the top of the stack. When routine D completes its processing the return address is **popped** from the top of the stack. When C completes, the address to return to, B, is popped from the stack, and so on.

The example introduces the operations **push** and **pop**. Some languages include these as instructions for processing a stack data structure. All they really do is to move a **pointer** up or down the list and add or remove an item. Fig. 14 shows how the pointer moves.

The pointer is the address of a memory location. In a **high-level language** it may be an **array subscript**. In a **low-level** or **assembler-level language** it may be a **memory address reference**.

Another common application of a stack is in the conversion and evaluation of **arithmetic expressions** in computer programs by the **compiler** or **interpreter**.

It is usual for us to write arithmetic expressions as follows:

$$A \times (B + C)$$

This notation is known as **infix**, the **operators** ($\times$, $+$, $-$) come between the **operands** (A, B, C). There are '**precedence rules**' which govern the order in which operators are evaluated, eg. $\times$ before $+$. The parentheses are used to change the order of evaluation.

An alternative notation is **postfix** or **reverse Polish** (named after the Polish logician J. Lukasiewicz, 1958). The above expression in postfix is as follows:

$$ABC + \times$$

Note that the parentheses have disappeared and the operators appear **after** the operands. Postfix notation has several advantages over infix. These are:

▲ Any formula can be evaluated without using parentheses.

▲ Precedence rules for operators are not required.

▲ Expressions in postfix form are easier to evaluate using a **stack** on a computer.

Here is an algorithm for evaluating the postfix form of the expression above. Note that the algorithm uses a **stack** as its main **data structure**.

```
Read next item in the expression
WHILE expression not finished DO
BEGIN
  IF current input item is a number
  THEN push it onto the stack
  ELSE   (the current item is an operator)
  BEGIN
    pop top two items off the stack
    compute these two items using the current
      operator
    push the result onto the stack
  END;  {If}
  read next item in the expression
END;  {While}
the final result is left at the top of the stack
```

This algorithm evaluates the expressions, which are already in postfix form. Most programming languages allow the program writer to use the infix form for expressions when writing code. An algorithm is also needed to convert the original expression from infix to postfix form before evaluation. The compiler or interpreter will carry out the conversion and evaluate the expression using the infix form.

► ***Exercise:*** Invent some values for A, B and C in the above expression and calculate the result using the postfix form and the algorithm. Calculate the result using the infix form. Check that you get the same result from both forms.

► ***Exercise:*** Write an algorithm, and maybe a program, which inputs a list of numbers and prints them out in reverse order.

The **queue** structure is more specialised in its uses. Its main uses are in:

simulation programs

operating systems

process control programs.

A simulation program may be one which is being used to investigate the behaviour of a system in which queues arise. For example, a supermarket checkout, a petrol filling station or air traffic control at an airport.

In multi-user operating systems (see Chapter 5) there are often **multiple requests** for resources. These requests are often dealt with in **FIFO** sequence. The operating system will manipulate a **queue data structure** to handle these requests.

Process control programs are similar to operating systems in that they manage resources used in a **process**. As objects from around the system, being controlled by the computer, request resources, queues may form which may be indicated in the **control program**.

● *Linked lists*

In all the data structures discussed so far it has been assumed that all the data items are stored in **consecutive** memory locations. Another way of storing the lists is by **linking** the elements so that they may be stored anywhere in the computer memory.

Take a look at Fig. 15. It illustrates a list of letters which are not in alphabetic sequence.

To get them into alphabetic sequence we could move them around. With a small number of items this wouldn't be a great problem. But what if there were thousands of items? What if each item was a **record** rather than a simple single data item? In this case the process of actually moving the items around in the computer memory would become very time consuming.

A more effective way to organise the data is shown in Fig. 16.

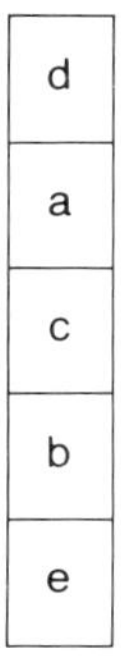

Figure 15 List of letters in non-alphabetical sequence

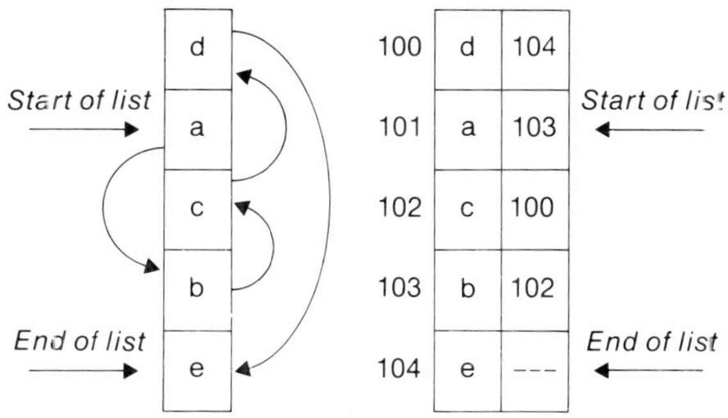

Figure 16 List of letters with "links"

Fig. 17 illustrates the effect of some of the different operations on linked lists.

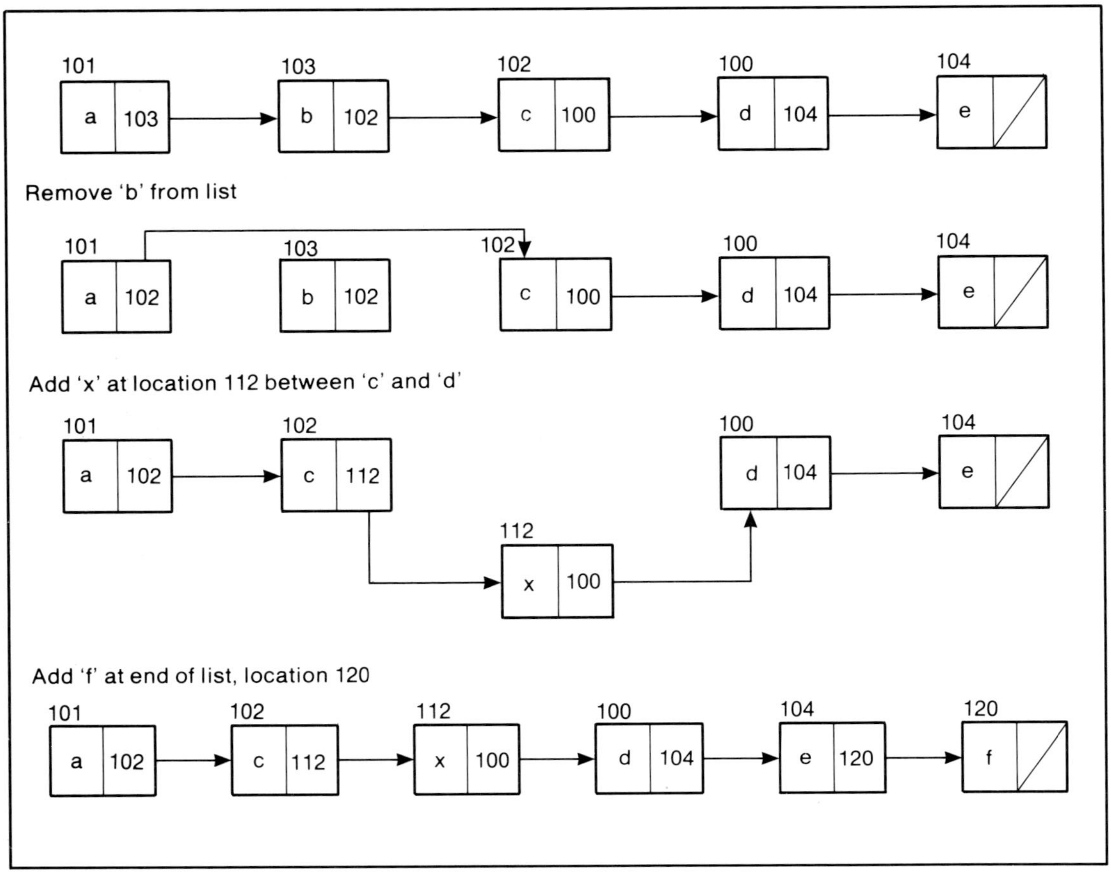

Figure 17 Some possible operations on a linked list

- *Linked lists and memory allocation*

One advantage of **linked lists** is as stated above. They allow for data manipulation, eg. **sorting**, without the need to move data around in memory. Another advantage is that the memory required for a data structure does not necessarily have to be allocated when the program is loaded. Some explanation of this is required.

Consider a program which is required to hold and process up to 1000 elements. The key phrase here is up to. One thousand is the maximum number of elements it has to process at any time. But it may be that most times it runs it only has to process 10, 15 or a 100 or so elements.

If a normal array is used in the program it would have to be **declared** to be of size 1000.

```
eg. VAR     HEIGHTS : ARRAY [1 . . . 1000]
                 OF INTEGER;
```

The memory required for this array would be allocated every time the program was loaded. Most of the times the program is run, much of the space would be wasted. In **multi-user** systems this would be a waste of memory which could be used by other programs running at the same time and sharing the memory. If the program was ever required to hold more than 1000 elements it would fail.

Linked lists, however, allow for the space to be allocated (and freed) as the program runs. To do this, some form of **dynamic memory allocation** is required. That is, space for **nodes** to be added to a **list** can be created as required. The space left by **deleting** items from a list may be made available for use elsewhere.

We can see that by manipulating pointers linked lists may grow and shrink as required. They will use only the memory required at any given time.

Here is a list of some advantages and disadvantages of linked lists.

Advantages:

▲ No need for moving large amounts of data around in memory when inserting, deleting or sorting.

▲ An item may be in more than one list at the same time.

▲ Possible to have complex lists with sublists.

▲ Don't have to allocate a fixed amount of memory for the list, it may be allocated as the program runs.

Disdavantages:

▲ Each node in the list has to be larger to hold the pointer to the next node.

▲ To get to any particular node, the pointers must be followed. **Random access** to any one node is not possible.

● *Backward pointers and multiple pointers*

In all the examples shown so far the nodes contain just one **pointer**. This '**points**' to the next item in the list. Each node could also contain another pointer pointing to the previous node in the list. Fig. 18 illustrates this.

This allows for **traversal** of the list in either direction. In fact, there is no reason why a list should not contain any number of pointers, allowing different sequences and/or relationships to be shown. Fig. 19 shows how a simple dictionary and thesaurus (list of words with similar meanings) may be stored.

Each letter of the alphabet is associated with the start of a list of words starting with that letter. The words are stored in a linked list with pointers pointing to the next word in the alphabetic list. Another set of pointers link those words in different alphabetic lists having similar meanings.

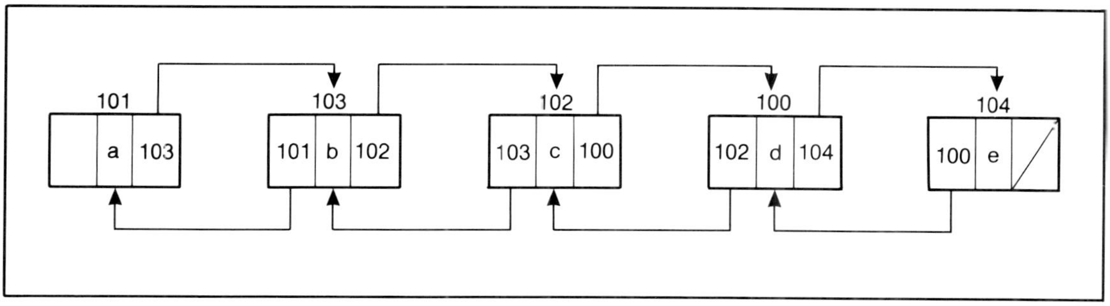

Figure 18 A linked list with forward and backward pointers

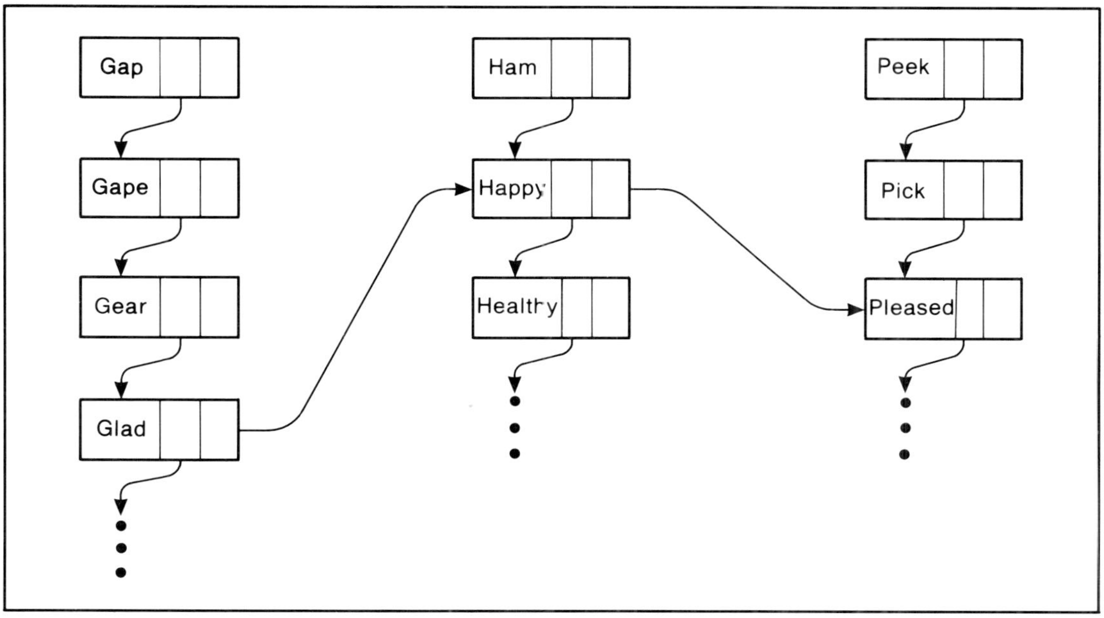

Figure 19 Simple dictionary and thesaurus storage and links

Having looked at the principles and some uses of linked lists, pointers and so on, let's look at a special type of structure called the tree.

- *Trees, branches and leaves*

No, we've not suddenly changed from studying computing to woodland. The **tree** is a fundamental structure in computing as in many other sciences. It is used to describe the relationship between elements in systems. The tree is often drawn upside-down with the **root** at the top and **branches** growing downwards. Trees are used to describe **hierarchies**. That is, with the starting, most fundamental or controlling element at the top and sub-elements represented as **leaves** or **nodes** at the ends of branches growing down from the top. Nodes at higher levels are said to be the **parents** of nodes at lower levels, the **children**. Fig. 20 opposite gives some example **tree structures**.

- *Representing and processing trees in programs*

Because the tree structure is so important, it is useful to consider how it may be represented in memory. Fig. 21 shows a tree structure, with names held at each leaf in the tree. This tree structure can be held in memory as shown in Fig. 22.

In this example, the number of branches at each node varies. In some cases there are three branches, in others two and in others four. You can see that a pointer is required for each branch from a leaf or node.

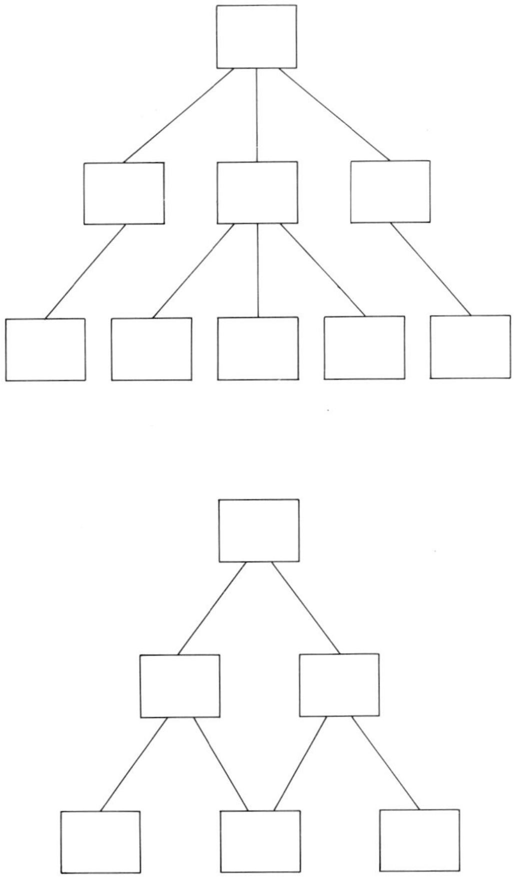

Figure 20 Some examples of tree structures

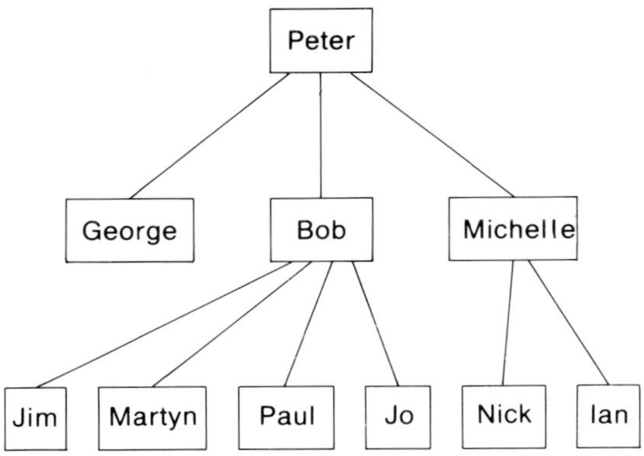

Figure 21 A tree structure of names

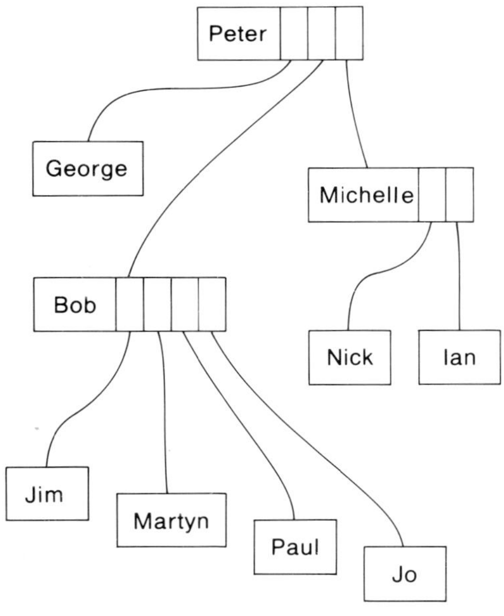

Figure 22 A tree structure of names with pointers

- *Binary trees*

Having a variable number of branches at each node is a waste of space. The storage required for each node would have to be enough to allow for the maximum number of branches. Also, when **traversing** the tree (following the branches) the algorithm would have to check how many pointers there were and test for which one to follow. This all becomes simpler and less wasteful if the tree is a **binary** tree. A binary tree is one in which each node or leaf always has two branches. Fig. 23 shows a binary tree.

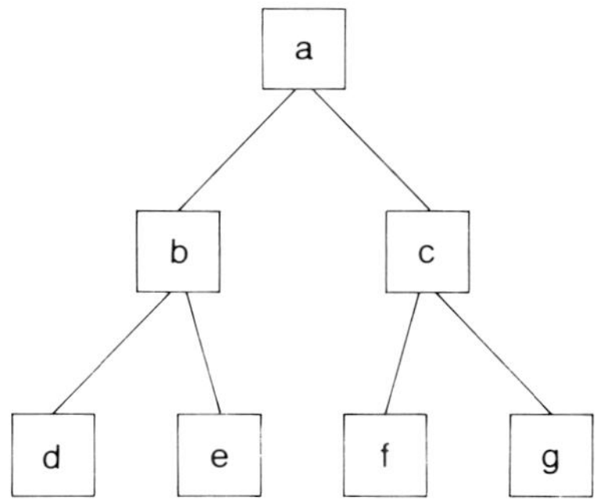

Figure 23 A binary tree

All trees can be converted to binary trees as follows:

▲ Remove all the branches except from a **parent** to its leftmost **child**.

▲ Link together all of a parent's children.

This is illustrated in Fig. 24.

Processing a binary tree is simplified because the processing will involve selecting the right or the left link at a given node. So, what are trees used for?

Here is a list of some of the applications of trees.

▲ Analysing arithmetic expressions.

▲ Sorting.

▲ Table lookup.

▲ Compilation of programs.

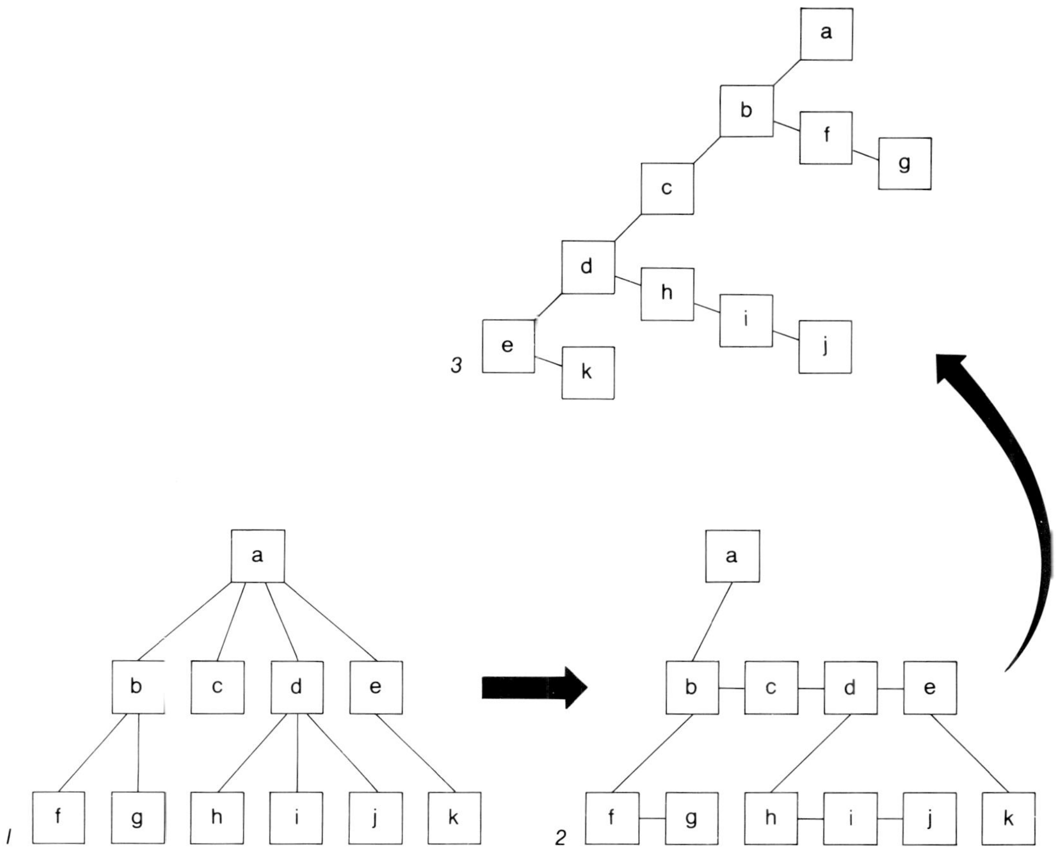

Figure 24 Converting a tree to a binary tree

DEFINING A PROGRAMMING LANGUAGE

Any language, English, French, Urdu etc. is written according to a set of rules, known as the **grammar** of the language. The grammar rules of a language give the language its **structure** and help us to understand it.

Programming languages are much simpler than languages used for communication between people, containing very few words and symbols. However, rules of grammar are still needed. The main elements of grammar are **syntax** and **semantics**.

These may be defined in simple terms as follows:

- ▲ Syntax rules define the basic elements of a language. The correct words, signs, symbols, etc., and the sequence in which they should appear.
- ▲ Semantic rules define the meaning of individual or groups of words, symbols etc.

Before a compiler or interpreter can be written for a language these rules must be strictly defined. The algorithm for the compiler or interpreter program must be designed according to the grammatical rules of the language.

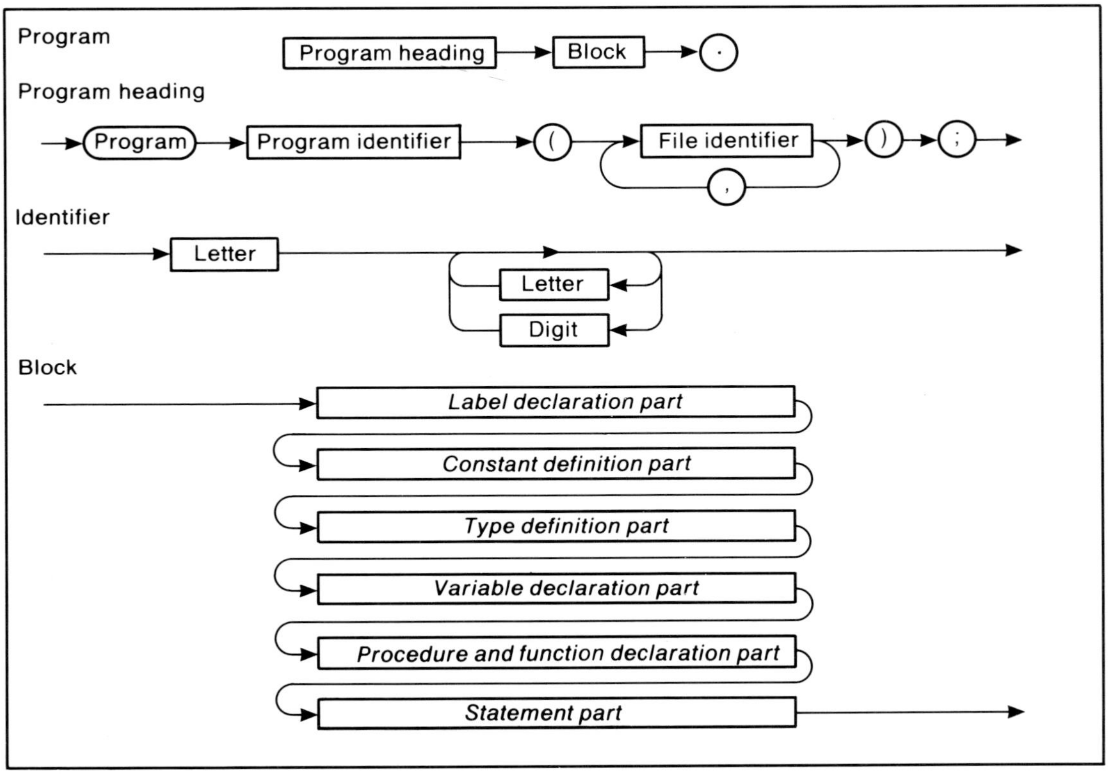

Figure 25 Example of a syntax diagram for PASCAL

⟨digit⟩	::= 0|1|2|3|4|5|6|7|8|9
⟨unsigned integer⟩	::= ⟨digit⟩ | ⟨unsigned integer⟩⟨digit⟩
⟨integer⟩	::= ⟨unsigned integer⟩ | +⟨unsigned integer⟩ | −⟨unsigned integer⟩
⟨decimal fraction⟩	::= .⟨unsigned integer⟩
⟨exponent part⟩	::= 10⟨integer⟩ *
⟨decimal number⟩	::= ⟨unsigned integer⟩ | ⟨decimal fraction⟩ | ⟨unsigned integer⟩⟨decimal fraction⟩
⟨unsigned number⟩	::= ⟨decimal number⟩ | ⟨exponent part⟩ | ⟨decimal number⟩⟨exponent part⟩
⟨number⟩	::= ⟨unsigned number⟩ | +⟨unsigned number⟩ | −⟨unsigned number⟩

* this ⟨integer⟩ is a superscript

Figure 26 Example of a BNF definition of numbers allowed in a language

- *Syntax diagrams*

Syntax diagrams are one way of defining the syntax rules for a language. The **Pascal programming language** is defined using syntax diagrams. Fig. 25 illustrates some of the syntax diagrams for the language. Most books on Pascal will include the complete set of syntax diagrams for the language. Anyone writing a Pascal compiler writes the algorithms to translate Pascal code according to the rules defined in the syntax diagrams.

- *Backus-Naur Form (BNF)*

This form of defining the syntax rules for a language is as shown in the example in Fig. 26. It was first used to define the ALGOL-60 programming language. All the valid elements of a language are defined in terms of lower level or simpler elements. The lowest level of definition is known as a '**terminal**'.

For example:

<u>BASIC variable name</u>

```
⟨variable⟩ ::= ⟨letter⟩|⟨letter⟩⟨digit⟩
⟨letter⟩   ::= a|b|c|d|e|f|g|h|i|j|k|l|m|n|o|p|q|r|s|t|u|v|w|x|y|z
⟨digit⟩    ::= 0|1 2|3|4|5|6|7|8|9
```

::= means 'is made of'
| means 'or'
⟨ ⟩ surround non-terminals

Both **syntax diagrams** and **BNF** can be used to determine whether an expression in a program is valid, ie. syntactically correct. The algorithm for the compiler or interpreter, written according to the rules defined by the syntax diagrams or BNF carries out **syntax analysis** before attempting to convert the code to **machine code**.

SUMMARY

The development of computer programs or **software** is a combination of developing the correct algorithm and choosing the most effective data structure. This chapter has set out to show how **structured programming** produces better programs. Some of the most commonly used **data structures** have been described, along with some uses for them.

Programming language definition techniques were introduced, with some explanation about how **formal language definition** is used when designing a compiler or interpreter.

As stated earlier in the chapter, learning to program is best done by practise, not reading. However, knowing about good design, types of data structures and programming language definition will help you to become a better programmer!

QUESTIONS

1 (a) Explain why many programming languages have both FOR and WHILE constructs to program loops. Under what circumstances would each be used? Show how the FOR construct may be programmed using a WHILE loop.
(b) Give *two* reasons why an incorrectly programmed loop may never terminate. How would the TRACE facility of a debugging system be used to ensure a WHILE loop iterates the correct number of times?
(c) Two integers may be multiplied by repeated addition. Using a WHILE loop, give an algorithm for such a multiplication. Explain how you would dry run this algorithm. Carry out such a dry run for the two values 4 and 6.

[*JMB 1988*]

2 (a) By drawing annotated diagrams show what is meant by:
(i) a stack,
(ii) a queue.
(b) How can a stack be implemented using an array? Describe carefully the stack operations of adding and removing items using this representation.
(c) The three words 'red', 'amber', 'green' can be written in six different orders. Given the input sequence 'red', 'amber', 'green', show how five of these sequences can be generated using only the stack described above.

[*WJEC 1988*]

3 (a) Write down the reverse Polish form for the following expression.

x := (a + b) * (c + d)

(b) Why do compilers often convert infix expressions into reverse Polish?

[*ULSEB 1989*]

4 Explain what is meant by the *scope* of a variable in a block structured language. Explain how a variable may not be in scope throughout the whole of the procedure in which it is defined.

[*AEB 1989*]

5 'In the design and implementation of computer programs, modularisation is generally considered to be a valuable technique.'
State and justify *three* arguments in support of this claim.

[*AEB 1989*]

6 The syntax of ⟨number⟩ is expressed in BNF notation using the following rules.

1. ⟨number⟩ ::=
⟨unsigned number⟩|+⟨unsigned number⟩|
−⟨unsigned number⟩
2. ⟨unsigned number⟩ ::=
⟨decimal number⟩|⟨exponent part⟩|
⟨decimal number⟩ ⟨exponent part⟩
3. ⟨decimal number⟩ ::=
⟨unsigned integer⟩|⟨decimal fraction⟩|
⟨unsigned integer⟩ ⟨decimal fraction⟩
4. ⟨exponent part⟩ ::= E ⟨integer⟩
5. ⟨decimal fraction⟩ ::= . ⟨unsigned integer⟩
6. ⟨integer⟩ ::=
⟨unsigned integer⟩|+⟨unsigned integer⟩|
−⟨unsigned integer⟩
7. ⟨unsigned integer⟩ ::=
⟨digit⟩|⟨unsigned integer⟩ ⟨digit⟩
8. ⟨digit⟩ ::= 0|1|2|3|4|5|6|7|8|9

(a) Show how you would use the above definitions to test whether the following are valid numbers.
(i) +23.45
(ii) 27
(iii) +E+7

(b) The above definitions place no restrictions on the sizes of numbers. In practical computer implementations, such restrictions will exist.
(i) Explain why this is so.
(ii) Integer values are held in two's complement form in a single 32-bit word.
What approximate range of values can be stored?
(iii) Real values are held as
a 24-bit two's complement fraction,
and
an eight-bit two's complement binary exponent.
What approximate range of values can be stored?

Express your answers to parts (ii) and (iii) using powers of two. (See also Chapter 6.)

[*UCLES 1988*]

7 (a) Describe, with the aid of diagrams, how names may be stored in alphabetical order in a linked list structure by using arrays. Use the names Rachel, Majid, Siân, Mary, Jonathan as example data.
(b) Show how the free space can be managed so that items can be easily added to or deleted from the linked list. Use as examples
(i) adding the name Henry to the list;
(ii) deleting the name Majid from the list.

[*UCLES 1989*]

8 The competitors' names and match results of a completed knock-out competition (eg. a tennis tournament) are to be stored in such a way that it is possible to output the details of all the matches played by the winner of the competition in the reverse order in which they were played.
(i) Suggest a suitable data structure for storing each competitor's name and match score, and explain how the data structure could be represented in a computer's main memory.
(ii) Derive an algorithm, or other appropriate method, to extract from the data structure the results of the matches played by the winner.
(iii) Explain how, with the use of an additional data structure, it would be possible to efficiently locate the results of the matches played by any player in the competition.

[*JMB 1987*]

9 A game consists of a quantity of blue and yellow pieces, one colour for each player, and a vertical frame of seven adjacent columns into each of which up to seven pieces may be placed.
The columns are initially empty. Each player in turn places one of his or her pieces in a column which is not already full up, and the piece falls to the bottom of the column or to rest on top of one or more other pieces previously placed in that column. A player wins the game by placing the pieces so as to achieve an unbroken straight line of four of his or her pieces, horizontally, vertically or diagonally. If all seven columns become full up before such a line is formed by either player, the game is drawn.
Develop an algorithm which would be suitable for a computer program to recommend, at each stage of the game, in which column the player should place a piece.

[*UCLES 1988*]

CHAPTER 5

Operating Systems and Systems Software

INTRODUCTION

The operating system has the job of making **computer hardware** usable. Without an operating system every program would have to be written in **machine code**. It would have to be put into the machine by setting hardware switches and even the simplest output would be extremely time-consuming and tedious.

EARLY DAYS: 1950–1960

In the earliest days of electronic computing, operating systems didn't exist and the only way to get programs to run was as described above. Programmers soon realised that most programs contained some code which was commonly required. For example, most programs would **input** some data and **output** some results. The code for inputting to and outputting from a **device** was always the same. This code was put into a routine and made available in a **library**. When a programmer wanted a program to input or output, the required routine could be **called** with a one line instruction instead of the programmer having to write the detail code every time. This approach had another attraction, the code was known to work! Rewriting the same code brings with it the problem of possible errors.

■ Software libraries and utilities

There were very few computers used at this time, and the variety of **peripherals**, eg. paper-tape readers and punches, card-readers, tele-types, was very limited. However, the availability of a **library** of routines was very time saving and made programs more reliable.

At the same time **higher-level programming languages** were being developed. A **compiler** and **editor** are required for the creation of every high-level program. It is obviously convenient to save these in a library. The programmer can take a **routine** from the library and use it in a program. The **compiler** or **assembler** can also be taken from the library when required.

Although these early computers were large in size, occupying a large air-conditioned room, they could only run one program at once. The **computer operator** would load the program into the computer and press 'GO'. The program would then run. If it required input data this would be loaded into the card-reader or paper-tape reader by the operator when required. The output would be sent to a teletype, paper-tape punch, card punch or printer.

But the fundamentals of operating systems had been established. These were:

- ▲ To provide the **interface** code for input and output devices in a standard form.
- ▲ To provide a library of **software routines** or **utilities** used by many or all programs.

BATCH PROCESSING

With the single job approach to computing, the computer was spending most of its time doing nothing. It was doing very short bursts of work in between relatively lengthy periods of waiting for the next job. Remember, these were very expensive machines requiring specialist operators. To have the computer doing nothing for most of the time was regarded as expensive inactivity A way of getting more computing done in the time available had to be found. The solution was to group or **batch** programs together.

Magnetic disk and **tape storage** was becoming more readily available. This allowed for programs and data to be stored on disk or tape and quickly read into the computer when required.

The idea with **batch processing** was to give the computer instructions about which program to load and run and which data **files** to make available. The instructions about which program to run were input on punched cards or paper-tape. The desired program could be loaded from magnetic disk or tape. If the operator knew the sequence of programs to be run, a series of cards could be input. This reduced the need for operator intervention between each program run. The computer could go straight to the next program as instructed by the next card.

Thus, two more major advances in the development of operating systems had taken place. These were:

- ▲ Storing programs and data on **backing store** to be loaded and used when required ie. **offline storage**.
- ▲ The use of a **Job Command Language (JCL)**, instructing the computer about which program to run and when to run it.

MULTI-PROGRAMMING SYSTEMS

Although using a **JCL** and reducing operator intervention saves a lot of wasted time, the machines could be made even more efficient. If a program is doing a lot of reading or writing of data, the CPU is spending most of the time doing nothing. A CPU can execute a lot of instructions in the time taken to read or write an item of data from a peripheral device. It was thought useful to use that wasted time doing other work.

The simplest way to achieve this is to run two programs at the same time. As one program stops using the CPU to do input or output, the other starts to use it. This works as shown below.

Program A (request for i/o ↓; i/o finished ↓)
RUNNING ⟶ DOING I/O ⟶ RUNNING

Program B (request for i/o ↓)
IDLE ⟶ RUNNING ⟶ DOING I/O

Both program A and Program B are loaded into memory.

Program A starts to run. Program B is doing nothing.

Eventually, Program A requests to do i/o.

Program B starts to run.

Program A finishes i/o, Program B starts i/o.

We can see that the advantage gained is that the **processor** is kept occupied for more of the available time. The assumption is made that the i/o device, eg. the disk drive, has its own **controller** to manage the actual i/o.

However, there are still problems here. The relationship between Program A and Program B may not be as simple as the diagram suggests. It is very unlikely that one program would 'start i/o' just as the other program 'stops i/o'. It is far more likely that these times do not coincide. For instance, it is likely that both A and B would either be using or waiting for the i/o device. The answer to this problem is to add more **jobs** into the scheme, so that there is always at least one job ready to use the CPU when it is released. This leads to the principle of **multi-programming**. Let's look at some of the principles involved in multi-programming systems.

■ Managing a multi-programming system

A multi-programming system contains the following major elements:

- ▲ It has several programs which appear to be running at the same time.
- ▲ These programs share the use of the computer's facilities eg. the CPU, memory and i/o devices.
- ▲ The programs must not 'interfere' with each other ie. corrupt each other's instructions or data areas.
- ▲ The programs must be capable of being stopped and started again at the point where they were stopped.

MULTI-USER SYSTEMS

Batch processing still depended on the user providing the operator with the running instructions. However, a new piece of computer hardware was now being introduced which was to change the way people used computers dramatically. This was the **computer terminal**. Linking terminals directly to the computer meant that for the first time users had **direct access** to the machine's facilities. They no longer needed to communicate through the operator. This meant that a new set of demands was put upon the operating system.

■ Online processing

The initial use of the terminal was to provide a means of requesting the computer to run a program or a series of programs directly. This was exactly as it had previously been done using little packs of cards. The requests used the same JCL instructions, the responses from the computer were displayed on the screen. Basically, however, the computer was operating in the same general way as it had done before. But, now there could be several users trying to communicate with the computer at the same time. Previously, only the computer operator would be communicating. Machines were not only **multi-programming** machines, they had also become **multi-user** or **multi-access** machines.

■ Interactive processing

Having got their terminals people began to require more control over what the machine was actually doing, and when it did it. **Online** processing provided the user with **direct access** to the machine, but it still ran programs when its **scheduler** allowed it to (see more on scheduling below). The computer still acted as if it received its instruction on cards.

The answer was to provide for more **interaction** with the computer; allowing the user to run a program when it is required and to see what the results of that program are straight away. As described in the sections below, this has had a great impact on the requirements of the operating system.

■ Real-time processing

For **interactive processing** the computer is required to respond in a reasonable time, say two seconds maximum, for each **user** on the system.

In systems where the computer is providing the control mechanism the response may be required more immediately. The computer is expected to respond according to external time requirements. The case study on the Royal Botanical Gardens at Kew illustrates a **real-time control** system. The section on **interrupts** in Chapter 6 is also worth reading on this subject.

■ Programs and processes

When referring to programs running in multi-programming systems it is more usual to refer to them as **processes**. This is because a program may be split into smaller parts by the operating system to make it more efficient to manage. Note that you should avoid confusion here with the term **multi-processing** operating systems. A multi-processing operating system is one which manages a computer with several CPUs. Of course, an operating system may be both **multi-programming** and **multi-processing**. To make things easier for ourselves, we'll assume that our multi-programming system has only one CPU but has separate **controllers** for **i/o devices**.

• *Process states and state transitions*

A multi-programming operating system manages a set of processes. While a process is in the system it may be in one of a number of **states**. At various times a process will make a **state transition**. That is, it will make a change from one state to another. The possible states and state transitions are shown below:

▲ Process states

RUNNING (the process is using the CPU)

READY (the process could use the CPU)

BLOCKED (the process cannot use the CPU because it is waiting for some event to occur)

These process states are described as follows:

RUNNING The instructions contained within the process are actually being executed on the CPU. Note that this involves the instructions and data being taken from the memory for processing.

READY The process is waiting to use the CPU. It can't use the CPU until the process which is currently RUNNING relinquishes it. There may be several processes waiting to use the CPU. The operating system will select which process should run next. See the section on **scheduling** below.

BLOCKED A process is BLOCKED when it is waiting for some activity external to the CPU to finish. This is usually input/output, although it could be that some error condition has occurred.

Note that only one process may be running, but there may be several processes READY or BLOCKED.

The possible state transitions are as follows:

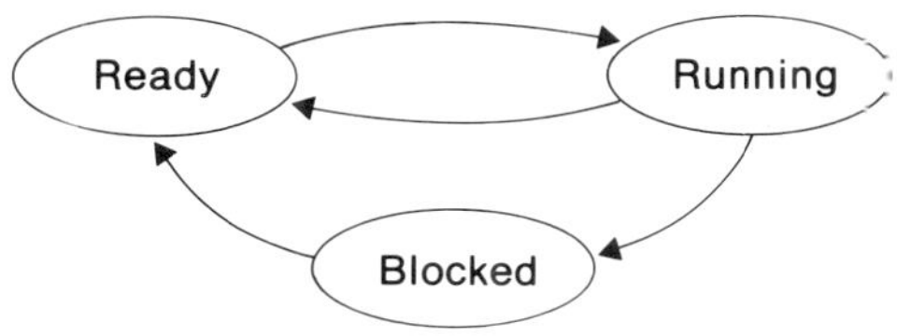

The arrows show the possible state changes. A process may make the following state transitions:

READY	⟶	RUNNING
RUNNING	⟶	READY
RUNNING	⟶	BLOCKED
BLOCKED	⟶	READY

Let's take a look at how the operating system manages these state transitions.

- *Keeping track of processes – the process control block*

During the time that a process is being managed by the operating system it may change states hundreds, even thousands of times. This means that the process is being stopped and started over and over again. Each time a process is re-started, it must resume at the **instruction** immediately following the last one executed. There are usually only one or two sets of **general purpose registers** and a **program counter** for the CPU (see Chapter 6). If these are to be shared, their contents must be stored in memory when the process is BLOCKED or READY. They will be **reset** from the store when that process is made RUNNING.

This information, along with other relevant facts are stored in an area known as the **Process Control Block (PCB)**. Each process has a PCB created for it when it first enters the system. The exact contents of the PCBs will vary according to the actual operating system.

Pointer	Process State
Process number	
Program counter	
Registers	
Memory limits	
List of open files	
. . . .	

Figure 1 Contents of the PCB for a UNIX process

The diagram above illustrates the contents of the PCB for processes managed by the **UNIX operating system**.

Each process has a unique **Process Identification Number** assigned to it. The example PCB shown in the diagram also contains the '**Priority**' and '**Memory location**'. We shall look in more detail under the headings 'Process scheduling' and 'Managing the memory' later in this section.

The PCB is very important in a multiprogramming system, it is the means by which the operating system keeps track of what is happening with the processes it is managing. The PCBs are usually kept in memory with very fast **access** times, eg. **cache memory** (see Chapter 6) or in a special set of **registers** close to the CPU.

■ Process scheduling

Earlier, we saw that several processes may be READY and that the operating system must choose one of these to change to RUNNING. How does it decide which to choose? The decision is taken according to rules in the **scheduler**.

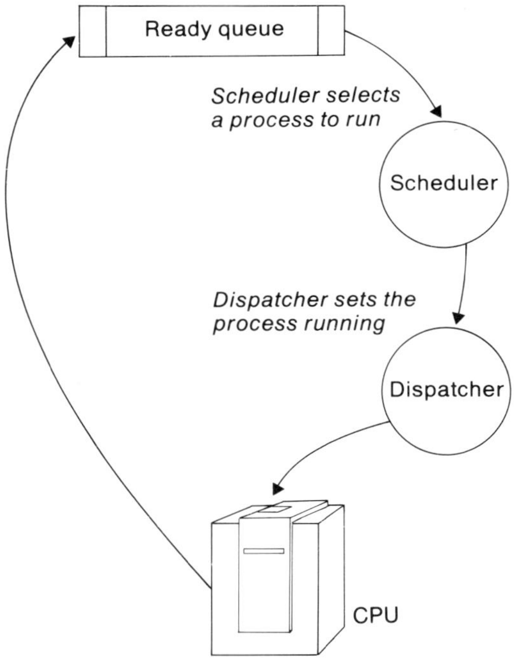

Figure 2 The scheduler and dispatcher select a process and set it running

The scheduler is an **algorithm** (see Chapter 4) which is designed to select a particular process according to the rules decided upon by the **designers** of the operating system. It selects the process to be run, the **dispatcher** then sets the chosen process running. The program counter and the general registers are reset with the

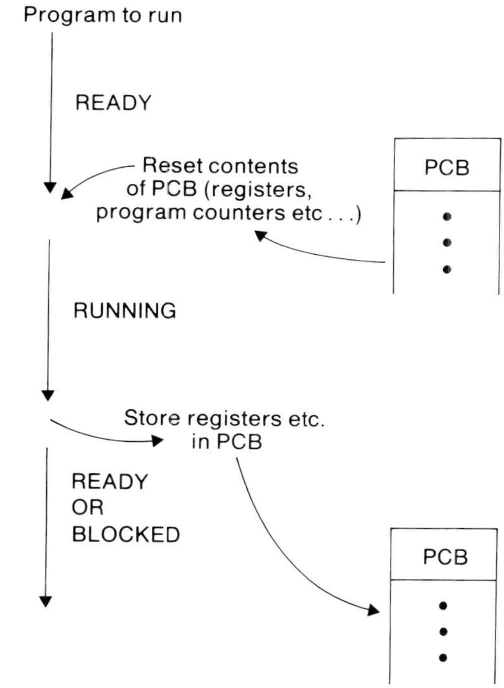

Figure 3 The PCB is used to save and restore

values from that process's PCB and the process starts to run from the **location** indicated by the reset program counter.

- *Scheduling algorithms – priorities*

There are many different sorts of rules applied in scheduling algorithms. The rules used vary according to the requirements of the users of the system.

Here is a short list of possible requirements:

- ▲ A maximum response time for a number of users of less than one second.
- ▲ Maximum utilisation of the computer's CPU.
- ▲ Maximum job throughput.
- ▲ Minimised waiting times.

The computer system may be one which is providing an **interactive** working environment at the same time as providing a **batch processing** service. The exact requirements of users and the type of service the computer is expected to provide have a major impact on the design of the scheduler. Following is a brief description of some of the major types of scheduling algorithms.

- ▲ First Come First Served: The first process to be put into the ready list (ie. the one that has been in the list the longest) is the next one to be run.
- ▲ Shortest Job First: The process with the shortest estimated time to run is run next.
- ▲ Highest Priority First: Each process has a priority rating associated with it. This might be set according to the type of work it is, eg. program development or an application. The process with the highest priority in the list is chosen to be run next. Information about priority and time to run may be held in the PCB.

- *Round-robin scheduling*

In interactive systems with several users using the system at the same time, it is important that each user is given a quick response rate. If each process started to run and then ran to completion, all the waiting processes would have a long wait, which would be unacceptable, To avoid this problem a **round-robin** scheme of scheduling is employed. Each process in the system is allowed to run for a short period of time and is then stopped. This period of time is known as a **quantum** or **time-slice**. The next process from the ready list is set running for a quantum, and so on.

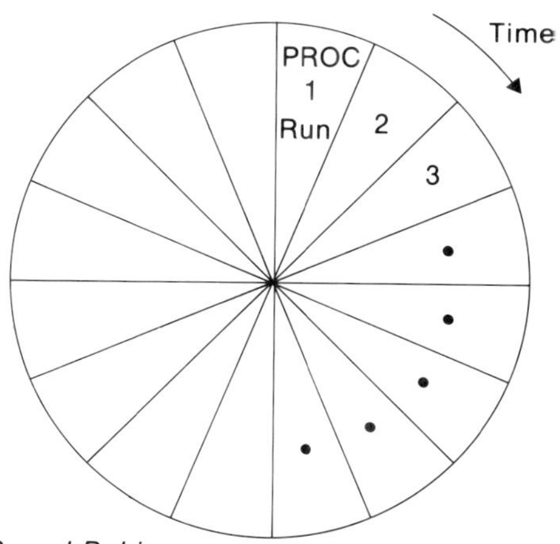

Round-Robin

Figure 4 Each process (PROC) is given a slice, or a quantum of time, in a cyclic manner

If a process executes an **i/o operation** in its quantum period and is blocked as described earlier, it is temporarily removed from the round-robin. In this way, each user appears to be receiving continuous service from the computer.

Here is an example of how one scheduling requirement of a computer system works against another. Among the possible aims of scheduling algorithms listed earlier are the following two items:

short response times and

maximum utilisation of the CPU.

With the round-robin approach to process scheduling a short response time is achieved but at the expense of CPU utilisation. Each time a process is taken off the CPU to be replaced by another, the CPU is required to do the processing required to handle the swap. The contents of the PCB have to be set/reset, and the scheduler and dispatcher run. This takes time, and it is not productive work. So, although a short response time is achieved, the CPU is not being utilised fully for productive work.

Memory management

Every running process requires space in the **main memory**, since this is where the **instructions** and **data** are held while the process is running. If the process is to be started, stopped and restarted, its memory space must be preserved when it is not running. To allow for this, the operating system must manage the memory space so that the running processes do not corrupt each other's memory space.

There are many different approaches to the organisation of **shared memory**. Fig. 5 illustrates the evolution of the types of **storage systems**. These are then described on the following pages.

Real	*Real*		*Virtual*		
Single user dedicated systems	Real storage multiprogramming systems		Virtual storage multiprogramming systems		
	Fixed partition multiprogramming	Variable partition multiprogramming	Pure paging	Pure segmentation	Combine paging and segmentation
	Absolute / Relocatable				

Figure 5 Types of memory management

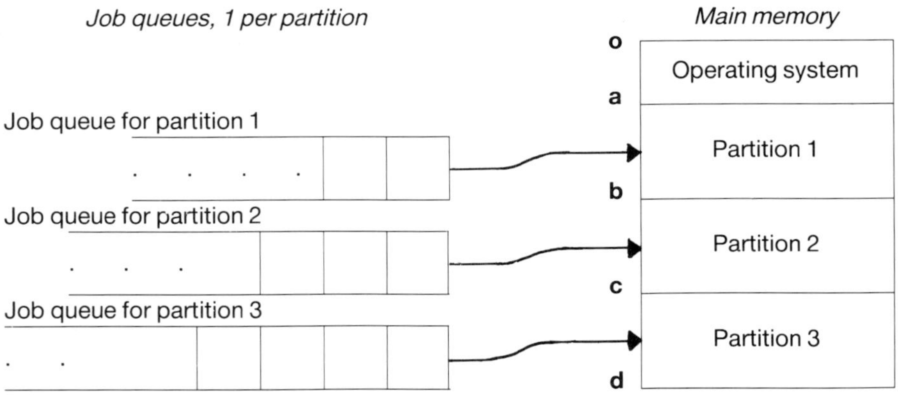

Figure 6 Fixed partition multi-programming

■ Fixed partition multi-programming

Here, the memory is divided into fixed sized **partitions** and separate **job queues** are maintained for each partition. The partitions may be of different fixed sizes. At **compile** time programs may be generated with their **addresses** set relative to the start address of the partition in which they are to be run. Alternatively, the program loader may '**relocate**' the program for the required partition at **run-time**. (See Fig. 7.)

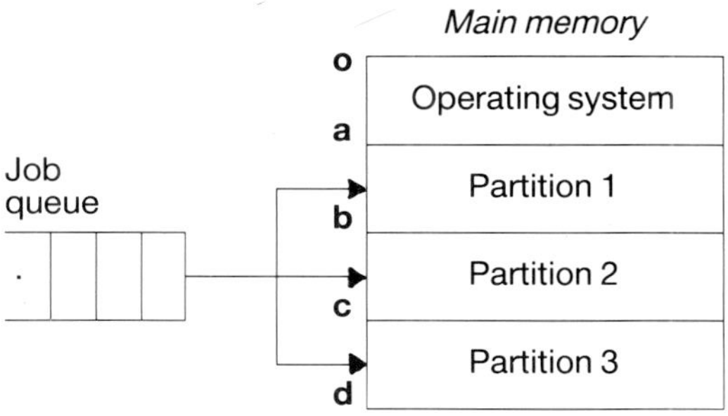

Figure 7 Fixed partition multi-programming with relocation. The operating system chooses the partition when the program runs

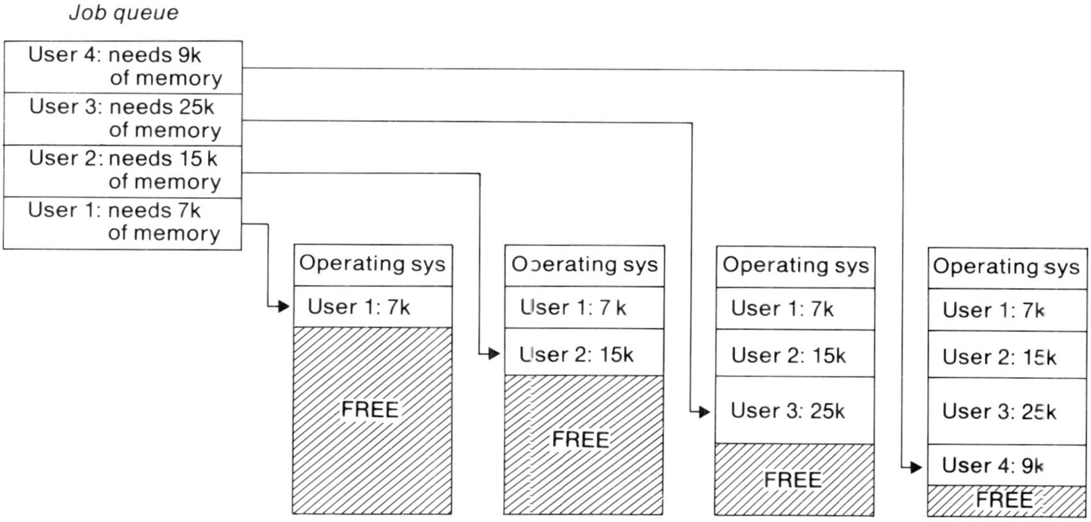

Figure 8 Variable partitioning – initial memory allocations

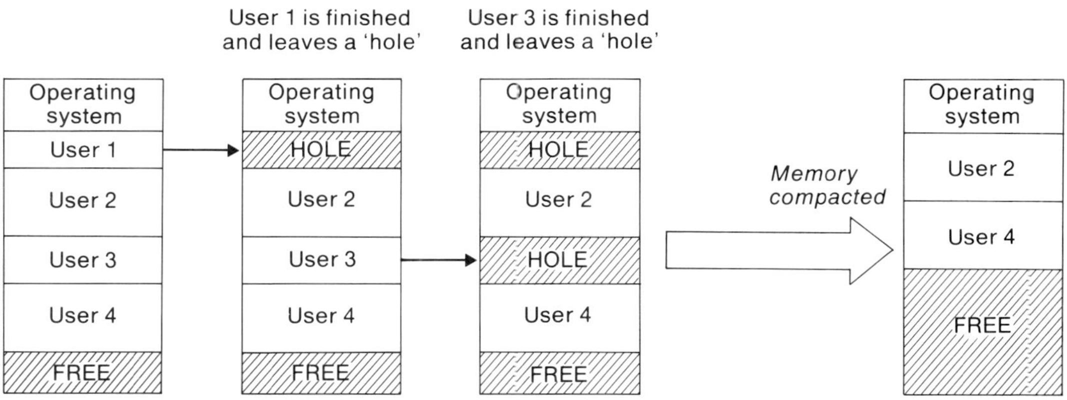

As each job is finished, 'holes' are left.
These may be removed by using memory 'compacting'

Figure 9 Hole creation and compacting

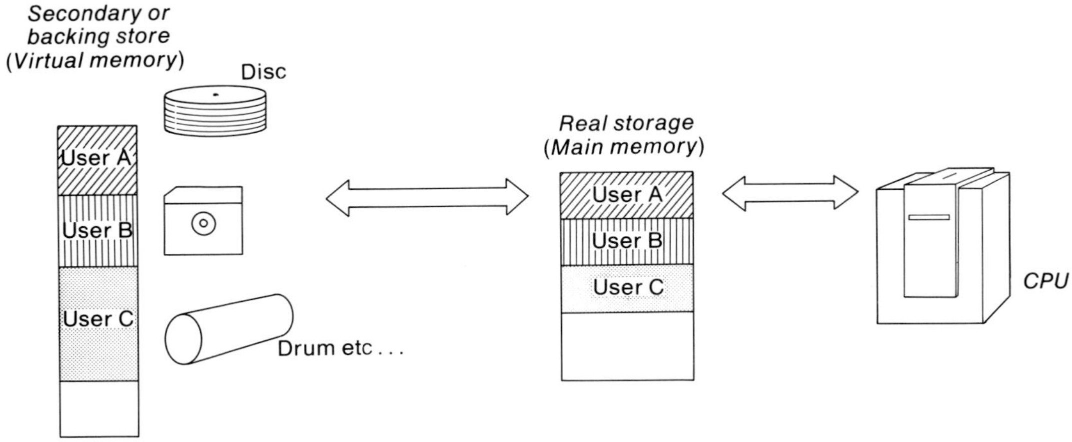

Figure 10 Virtual memory – the main memory is extended

■ Variable partition multi-programming

With this approach, a process is given the amount of memory space it needs. Although this initially makes more efficient use of the overall memory space than fixed partition memory, the problems start to occur as processes finish and their memory space is relinquished. (See Fig. 8.)

'Holes' of varying sizes are left. It may be that waiting jobs require more or less space than is left by the completed job. If less space is required, space is wasted. If more space is required, the waiting jobs can't run until more space is released. This problem may be partially solved by occasionally 'compacting' the memory. That is, moving all the occupied memory to one **contiguous** area. This then leaves one larger free memory space, which may be easier for waiting processes to use. (See Fig. 9.)

■ Virtual memory

The underlying principle of **virtual memory systems** is that the memory space available in the computer's main storage is extended into **secondary** or **backing storage**. A **virtual address** is one which may be in the main store or in the backing store. When a process is running it must occupy the main memory. The operating system converts or **maps** the virtual memory addresses on to the main memory as **real** addresses. This means that the computer can appear to have a very large main memory space available.

When reference is made to an address which is actually in the backing store, the operating system will transfer that memory space to the main memory. The user of the system is not aware that this is happening. The object of providing virtual memory is to give user programs effective access to a very large memory space.

■ Block mapping in virtual memory

The transfer of a process's memory space between main and backing store is done in blocks, since it would be very inefficient to map every single address separately. When a reference is made to an address in a running program it is converted to a block displacement address as shown in the diagram below.

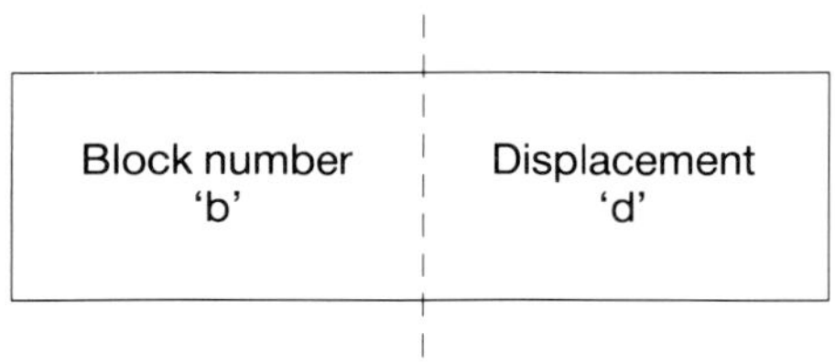

Virtual address = block, displacement

Figure 11 Virtual address

■ Paged virtual memory

In **paged virtual memory**, the blocks are of a fixed size. A virtual address is made up of the page number and the displacement within the page. The main memory is divided into fixed size pages called **page frames**. Pages may be moved between the backing store and the page frames. A process may occupy several page frames in the main memory, some may be in the backing store. The operating system maintains a **page map table**.

The **address translation** procedure takes place for each memory reference. This is known as **dynamic address translation**.

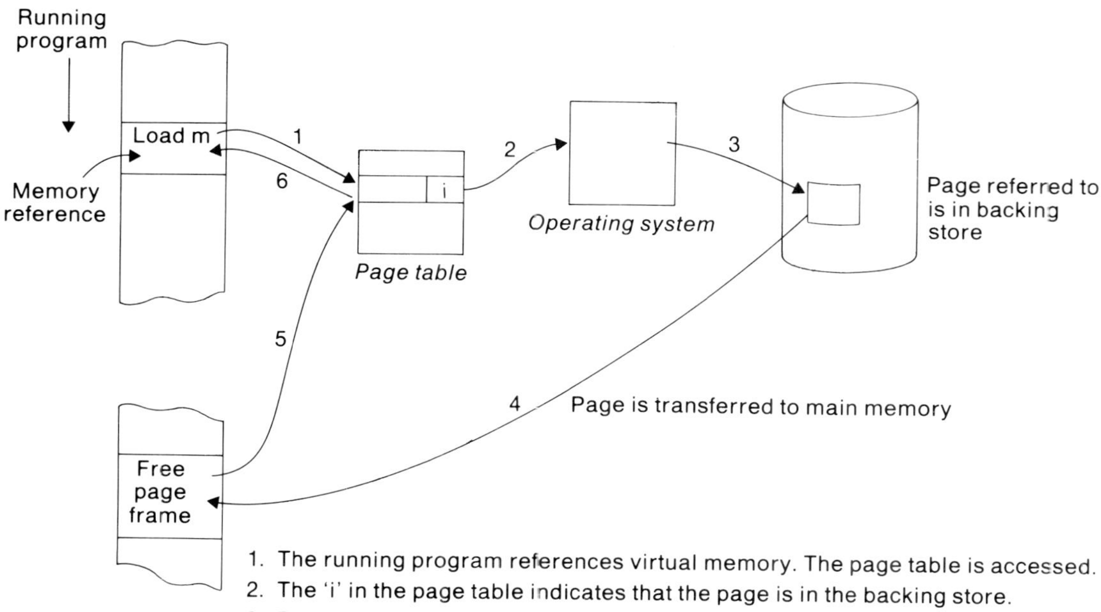

1. The running program references virtual memory. The page table is accessed.
2. The 'i' in the page table indicates that the page is in the backing store.
3. The operating system accesses the backing store for the required page.
4. The page is transferred to the main memory.
5. The page table is updated with the address of the page in memory.
6. The original program restarts.

Figure 12 Dynamic address translation

The process for dynamic address translation is as follows:

- ▲ A running process references a virtual storage address.
- ▲ A page mapping mechanism looks up the page in the page map table to find which page frame the page occupies.
- ▲ The real address then becomes the displacement within the page frame.

It may be that the required page is not in the main memory, the page map entry indicates this. If this is so then the required page must be transferred from the backing store to the main memory into an available page frame. However, the main memory will usually be full. A page must be removed and stored in the backing store to make space for the incoming page. Thus, a process of **swapping** takes place, the pages are swapped between main store and backing store. Once the required page is in main store, the **real address** may then be calculated.

A variation in virtual memory management is to allow for variable size pages, known as **segments**.

As you may well imagine, the work involved for the operating system in managing the operation of a virtual memory is considerable. It is also potentially very time consuming. The designers of such systems have considered this problem and provide for extremely fast processing of address translation. A great deal of research has also gone into devising means of reducing the number of times such systems have to transfer pages between backing and main store. However, despite all these problems, manufacturers of large multi-programming systems consider the availability of virtual memory to be very important.

THE RISE OF THE MICRO: BACK TO BASICS?

All the information about scheduling, memory management etc. presented above relates to the operation of **multi-programming systems**. You may be wondering what this has to do with someone who is merely **wordprocessing** or space-invading on a **personal microcomputer**. After all, only one person can use the microcomputer at the same time.

It may be said that someone using a microcomputer is using the computer in the same way that those early users of the first computers in the 1940's and 50's were doing. The basic requirements of the operating systems for such machines are the same as they were for those early machines. That is, to provide easy access to **utilities** and **software libraries**, to run user programs and to provide easy access to the machine's **peripherals**. The differences are that now the computer costs maybe a few hundred pounds, sits on a desk or lap top, and uses a keyboard and screen.

Another major difference between those early single-user systems and today's single user systems is this: whereas there were only a small number of those early expensive machines, there are now millions of microcomputers. Producers of operating systems for these machines realise that if they can persuade computer manufacturers to use their operating system, the market for their product will be larger. An operating system which will run on a range of machines allows for **applications software** to be run on that range of machines. This creates a larger market for the software manufacturers, which in turn increases the attractiveness of the machine, both to software writers and computer buyers.

Operating systems are now available for all types of computing requirements. On some very large mainframe computers the operating system is often required to allow for various types of usage at the same time. That is, to allow for **batch processing** and **interactive working** for many users all at the same time. Computers are often linked together via **networks** (see Chapter 7). The operating system is required to provide the **interface** with the **networking mechanisms**.

As computer hardware and usage develops, then so will operating systems. Remember, computer hardware is virtually useless without its operating system software.

A COMPARISON OF TWO OPERATING SYSTEMS – UNIX AND MS-DOS

■ Introduction

This comparison summarises the main characteristics of UNIX, a very popular **multi-user** system, and MS-DOS the **single-user** system used on the IBM-PC and many other microcomputers. It illustrates the major differences between a multi- and single-user system. It also shows that in some ways the two systems are similar.

■ The UNIX operating system

UNIX is a **multi-programming**, **multi-user**, **time-sharing** operating system. It is designed to be portable between different makes of computers. This is achieved by having the bulk of its code written in a **high-level programming language**, the language 'C'. At the core of the system is a small 'kernel' which is written in the **assembler language** of the machine on which it is to run. Each **concurrent** user of the system is allocated an 'image'. This provides the user with the impression that they alone are using the machine. Each user **logged on** to the system has the impression that they have their own computer, with memory, screen, keyboard, printer and disk files.

UNIX includes a **scheduler** which 'shares' the central processor between users. This is done so that each user gets fair access to the **central processor**. Since the system is **interactive**, the scheduler aims to give each user a reasonable response rate at the keyboard.

The system operates a system of **virtual memory**, swapping **segments** of user's memory allocation between **main memory** and **backing store** as required. This allows for many users all having large memory allocations, without being restricted by the size of the main memory.

All users of a UNIX system have access to a **tree-structured hierarchical directory** of files on backing store. This allows for flexible management of backing store for a large number of users. The directory structure includes the facility for users to assign their own **access rights** to each of their own files. The **user interface** to UNIX is provided by the 'shell' (see Fig. 13). The shell includes a large number of **utility programs** designed for use in the development of **applications software** and many other features which make the running of programs simpler.

UNIX has proved to be a very popular and successful operating system, especially with institutions of higher education. Because UNIX is available on many machines, users may transfer their knowledge between machines. The system has the effect of 'standardising' computers.

One major criticism of UNIX, however, is that the file directory structure is not **secure** enough for a lot of commercial applications. Critics say that it is too easy for **illegal access** to be made to confidential files. In other words, one of the features which make it attractive to programmers, who usually like to share files, makes it unattractive to, say, bankers who don't like to share files.

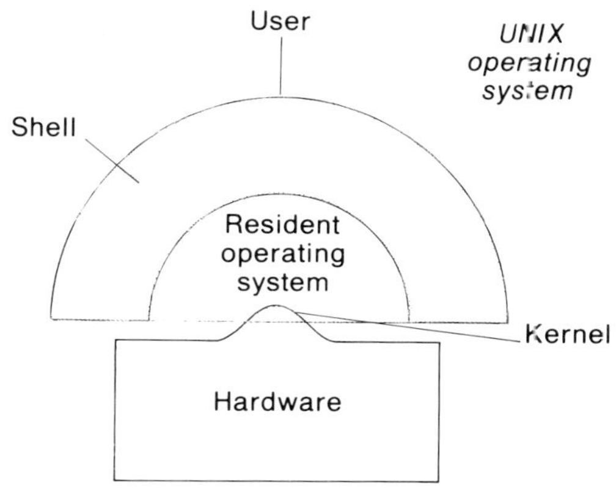

Figure 13 UNIX users communicate with the operating system through the shell. Hardware-dependent software is contained in the kernel

■ The MS-DOS operating system

A Disc Operating System (DOS) such as MS-DOS or, in the case of the IBM-PC, PC-DOS, is designed to provide the following functions on a personal computer. It:

- makes it possible to use **application software**
- allows for the creation and management of **files** on **backing store**
- provides **access** to devices such as printers, floppy disks, hard disks etc.

The system is designed for **single-user** use.

It provides the user with a set of **commands** which allow common **functions** allowing him or her to FORMAT disks, COPY files, COMPare, TYPE the contents of a file, RENAME files, ERASE files, list the names of files stored on disk (DIR), amongst others (the capitals are the command names). It can provide the user with information, such as how much space is available on disk or in main store.

Its main functions are provided by entering simple commands in response to the operating system **prompt**. If the computer has more than one disk drive the system prompt indicates which disk drive is currently being accessed.

eg. A〉
The system prompt, A〉
indicates the drive currently being accessed is the 'A' drive.

B〉
indicates the 'B' drive, and so on.

A user may run an **application program** by simply typing the program name in response to the prompt. The program must be stored on the drive currently being accessed. The commands entered are read by the **command line interpreter**. This reads the command, accesses the relevant program from main memory or backing store and sets it running.

As with UNIX, the disk storage is organised as a **tree-structured hierarchical directory**. However, since the system is **single-user**, no provision is made for assigning **access rights**.

A short description of tree-structured directories follows.

■ Storing and accessing files in directories

Both UNIX and MS-DOS provide the user with a means of creating and using **directories** of files. The directories are organised as **hierarchical trees**. It is easier to think of the tree as being 'upside down', that is with the **root** at the top and the **branches** growing down. Fig. 14 illustrates this concept. At the very top of the tree is a **root directory**.

A user may create as many **sub-directories** below this as are required. In this way a user can organise their work in a **structured** way.

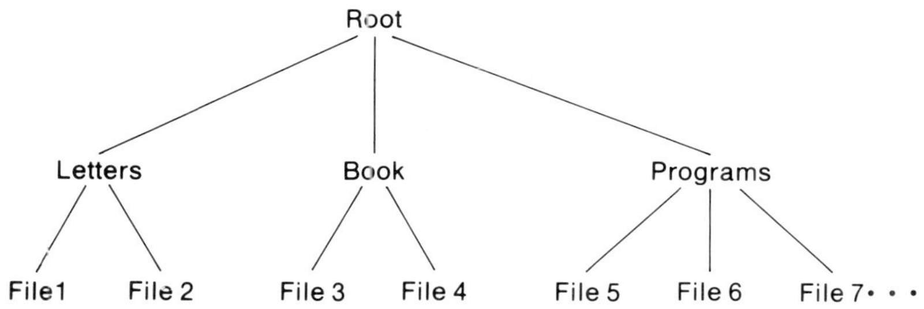

Figure 14 The directory is tree-structured with the root at the top. "Letters", "book" and "programs" are sub-directaries to the root. Files 1–7 contain different types of information

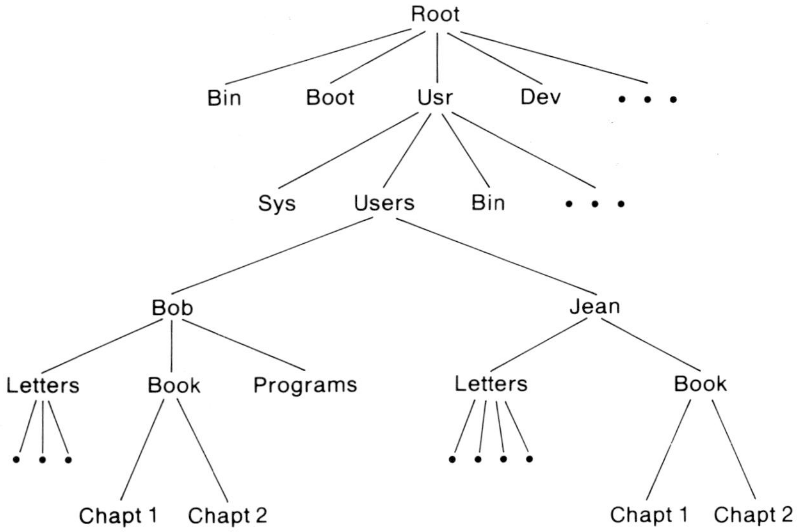

Figure 15 In this directory structure Bob and Jean both have files with the same name ie. "Chapt 1" and "Chapt 2". However, they have different pathnames and are, therefore, unique

Fig. 15 shows a directory structure for a user 'Bob' who has three **sub-directories**, 'letters', 'book' and 'programs'. The book sub-directory contains three files, 'chapt1', 'chapt2', and 'chapt3'.

Note that although MS-DOS is single-user, the disc storage may be being used by several people using the machine at different times. Each user may create their own directory to hold their files.

■ Pathnames

A full filename is a **pathname**. The pathname for a file defines the route the system has to take through the **tree structure** to get to the required file. This specifies the names of all the directories and sub-directories on the route. In the diagram (Fig. 15) you can see that user 'Jean' also owns a sub-directory called 'book' containing a file called 'chapt1'. The pathname for 'chapt1' belonging to 'Bob' is:

/usr/user/bob/book/chapt1

For Jean's chapt1 the pathname is:

/usr/user/jean/book/chapt1

In this way a unique file name is created for each of the two users.

These names are obviously very long, and if the user is currently working in their own directory, it is not necessary to specify the whole pathname. For example if Jean was working in her directory, she would only need to specify book/chapt1 to get at the chapt1 file.

■ Conclusion

Both UNIX and MS-DOS provide the essential requirements of operating systems. That is, they make the computer hardware usable by providing the user with a means of entering commands and controlling the machine's **resources**. They are each designed for very different computing environments but have the common characteristic of being available on a wide range of computers. This factor helps computer users to use different machines without having to re-learn everything they know about how to use them.

QUESTIONS

1 Study the user guide for any operating system you have used or know of and describe the function and execution of a set of commands.

2 Distinguish between **multi-programming** and **multi-access**. Outline methods by which each is achieved by an operating system and indicate the effects on the user.

[*COSSEC 1988*] *Specimen paper*

3 Explain why **virtual memory** may be a desirable feature in **multi-programming** systems.

4 A computer system has been installed an an intensive care unit of a hospital to monitor continuously each patient's temperature, heart rate and blood pressure, and to report any significant changes in the patient's condition to the nursing staff. Describe the hardware and software features that you would expect such a system to have, and explain how they would be used.

Explain how it may be possible to use the same computer system to carry out other tasks within the hospital, such as routine hospital administration, while still performing the same patient monitoring tasks as before. (You may wish to tackle the second part only of this question.)

[*COSSEC 1988*] *Specimen paper*

5 Describe the function of **software libraries** and why it is useful for the operating system to provide these.

6 (a) Explain the main tasks required of a typical **single-user** operating system. You may illustrate your answer by referring to an operating system with which you are familiar.
(b) Explain the additional requirements of an operating system in a **multi-tasking** environment.

[*SCE Higher 1990*] *Specimen paper*

7 Describe *three* file **utility** programs you would expect to find in a large computer installation.

[*JMB 1987*] *175 Advanced*

8 In a typical large **multi-access** system served by a single computer there are normally many programs of various sizes present in the system at any one time. Some of these programs are potentially active; a potentially active program can make immediate use of the processor when the processor is allocated to it. Other programs are dormant because they cannot proceed until some peripheral action has been completed. At frequent intervals, programs finish and are removed from the system or new programs are required and are loaded. Some programs, such as an editor, an interpreter or an application program, are directly interacting with users, while others are batch jobs. There are also several programs which form the operating system and are always present in the system and intermittently active.

There is usually only enough main store to hold a small proportion of these programs at once, and the other programs are held temporarily on disk backing storage. An operating system program has the task of managing this swapping of complete programs between main store and backing store and also of organising the use of main store and backing store for this purpose.

(a) Discuss ways in which the use of main store and backing store can be organised to make the swapping system efficient.

In a system which has **paged virtual storage**, the main store and all programs are divided up into pages of equal size, for example 1K bytes each. A program which is running need only have in main store those pages containing words which are currently being used. If a word is needed from a page which is not at present in main store, that page is first loaded from backing store, and if a page ceases to be used it can be removed from main store. Pages can be placed anywhere that is free in main store, and a complex system of **address mapping** provides a very rapid conversion between **program addresses** and the **relevant main store addresses.**

(b) Explain how a **paged virtual storage** system makes the task of the **swapping system** much simpler and why users should expect to receive a faster service, both in response to individual commands and in overall processing.

[*UCLES 1988*] *9345/0*

9 Study the short article 'Still a Pain in the Neck' overleaf.
Make notes on the following questions:
(a) What factors in computer development does the author state are forcing operating systems to change?
(b) What reasons are given by the author for UNIX not being a truly standard Operating System?
(c) What is the author's major criticism of IBM's 370 operating system?

Reader Still a pain in the neck

The decision by IBM to take personal computing in a different direction with Operating System 2 shows how crucial operating systems have become to the industry. When operating systems were the proprietary property of individual manufacturers and only worked on their own machines, the rest of the industry could breeze along in blissful ignorance of the workings of operating systems.

This had the disadvantage of tying customers to a specific hardware supplier and it was inevitable that a change would come. The software industry too wanted a shift away from hardware independence and a common operating system is an attractive way of expanding potential markets.

As a result in the last couple of years operating systems have moved to the centre of the computing stage. In addition to IBM's introduction of OS2, an event which has still to permeate through to the computer user, a plethora of other alternatives to the aging MS-DOS emerged as potential challengers to OS2.

And earlier this year Unix, which has long suffered from over-marketing, took its first tentative steps towards international standardisation. Unix has also become an important issue at IBM and other mainframe manufacturers, with the long-term possibility of it replacing many proprietary operating systems.

This activity has taken place against a background of change in the role of operating systems. They are no longer the province of the systems programmer. They have become an issue for everyone from hardware builders, through technical DP staff, to the end user.

An important development is the move to make a Unix-like operating system an international standard under the auspices of the Institute of Electrical and Electronics Engineering (IEEE). Under the name of Posix, this is the first time that an attempt has been made to standardise an operating system and this has stimulated a wide debate on what an operating system is.

Traditionally, operating systems have played a limited role in computing. They have been required to control resources and provide facilities to access peripherals at a low level.

Most operating systems have been developed by manufacturers with special reference to the idiosyncrasies of their proprietary hardware.

IBM's range of mainframe operating systems for the 370 architecture is the most notorious example of this.

But the spread of personal computers has helped change attitudes to operating systems. For the first time, users have been in daily contact with powerful computers and have had to learn to cope with operating system commands.

At the same time, manufacturers recognised that they stood a better chance of selling their product if it offered a more pleasant environment for end users.

Apple's success with the Macintosh, contrary to early forecasts, proved the personal computer user's desire to seek alternatives to the terseness of the IBM personal computer's MS-DOS command set.

The later success of Microsoft's Windows environment, which brought a Macintosh-like interface to the PC, confirms this.

While any technology which improves the usability of operating systems must be applauded, the use of graphics-based interfaces like those in the Macintosh and Windows raises important questions for operating system developers.

Operating systems must now take account of complex graphics-processing standards, in addition to everything else.

It is not only at the interface with the outside world where operating systems face change. There is a trend towards including more and more functions in operating systems, with the result that database interfaces and communications interfaces are now considered an important part of operating systems design.

The importance of database interfaces was highlighted last year when, following IBM's announcement that it would build an SQL interface into OS2, leading database supplier Ashton-Tate came under pressure.

SQL has already grown into a de facto standard in large computer systems and is acknowledged by third party database suppliers as the way to go. By including SQL in its plans for OS2, IBM threatens Ashton-Tate's position as the leading supplier of database software to the personal computer market.

Investment analysts argued that it would make life very difficult for Ashton-Tate, if key parts of the database management system were already included in OS2.

Similarly, there is a trend towards incorporating communications interfaces into operating systems. Again, this has been driven by user demand. The most notable example where communications have become central to operating systems is in the so-called workstation computing sector based on the Unix operating system.

The original design of Unix did not anticipate the development of networks of computers which are the basis of these systems. AT&T was slow to produce appropriate communications interfaces and was beaten to the punch by Soft Microsystem's Networked File System (NFS), a communications component which allows Unix board systems to share files over a network.

These developments have stirred up the world of operating systems and led developers to find ways of extending operating systems to cope with them.

They have also led to a desire for manufacturer-independent operating systems which can be used as a vehicle for moving applications software from one type of hardware to another.

Running against this trend, hardware has grown more complex and placed more demands on operating systems. The emergence of reduced instruction-set computers (Risc) from IBM and Hewlett-Packard among others has stimulated the growth of a new layer of software which sits between the hardware and the operating systems.

This layer, usually some form of "virtual" interface, allows hardware manufacturers to continue to offer common operating system interfaces like those intended for Unix, while still allowing proprietary hardware architectures.

IBM's AIX is a good example of this strategy. AIX cannot work without this extra layer, the virtual resource manager.

It will probably take many years for a set of truly common operating system interfaces to emerge. Meanwhile application developers and users will have to tolerate a wide range of differing standards.

CHAPTER 6

Computer Architecture

INTRODUCTION

Just as most car drivers don't need to know much about how the car's engine works, most computer users don't need to know about the detailed workings of their computer. However, knowing a little about the internal workings of a computer gives a better understanding about computers, programming and computerised systems.

This chapter describes the internal design and workings of a **digital** computer – that is, **computer architecture**.

BINARY REPRESENTATION

The electronic circuits of a computer can only be in two different states. The two digits '1' and '0' are used to stand for these two states. For this reason all the data inside a computer has to be represented by patterns of 1's and 0's. These are called **binary patterns**. The representation of data by 1's and 0's is called **binary representation**.

What sort of data will these binary patterns need to represent? Binary patterns are needed to stand for:

- ▲ Numbers: small ones and large ones, positive and negative whole numbers and fractions.
- ▲ Letters: all the letters of our alphabet (including capitals), punctuation marks, addition and subtraction, brackets, special signs and so on.
- ▲ Control codes: to clear the screen, move the cursor on the VDU etc.
- ▲ Program instructions.
- ▲ Addresses: of memory locations which hold data and instructions.

All these items have to be represented by their own unique pattern of 1's and 0's. The methods used to do this are explained in this chapter.

- *Bit patterns*

Using just the binary digits 1 and 0, four different patterns may be formed:

0 0   0 1   1 0   1 1

With three bits eight binary patterns may be formed:

0 0 0   0 0 1
0 1 0   0 1 1
1 0 0   1 0 1
1 1 0   1 1 1

For example, each of the seven colours of the rainbow could be given its own binary code by using three bits as shown in the table.

Colour	Binary code
Red	0 0 1
Orange	0 1 0
Yellow	0 1 1
Green	1 0 0
Blue	1 0 1
Indigo	1 1 0
Violet	1 1 1

But to represent 15 different colurs, four bits are needed to make enough patterns so that each colour has its own unique code. With four bits there can be 2^4 or 16 distinct patterns; with five bits, 32 patterns; with six bits, 64 patterns and so on (have a look at the 'Powers of 2' table, Fig. 1).

THE POWERS OF 2										
2^{10}	2^9	2^8	2^7	2^6	2^5	2^4	2^3	2^2	2^1	2^0
1024	512	256	128	64	32	16	8	4	2	1

Figure 1 "Powers of 2" table

● *Bytes*

A group of bits arranged in a binary pattern is called a byte. Usually eight bits are used. With eight bits, 256 or 2^8 patterns may be formed. Each one of these patterns can be used to stand for a different number, letter of the alphabet, or symbol. For example:

0 1 0 0   0 0 1 1

could be used to stand for the character 'C'

0 0 1 1   0 0 1 1

could be used to stand for the character '3'

0 0 1 0   0 0 0 1

could be used to stand for the character '!'

Note that a byte is usually equivalent to a character. Each pattern of 1's and 0's is called a **code**. Letters, numbers and symbols (like !, %, ;) are called **characters**. Different computers use different codes for characters. The section after the next will show you some of these **character codes.**

● *Words*

These codes are used inside the computer. They are stored in the computer's main memory and used in processing instructions (see later). In the memory, the codes are stored in individual **memory locations**. The collection of 1's and 0's inside the location is called a **binary word.**

These words are often eight bits long, ie. the same length as a byte, but the large, mainframe computers use word lengths of 16, 24, 32 or even 48 bits (multiples of bytes).

● *Character codes*

Characters are the things you see on the keyboard of a microcomputer. They may be letters of the alphabet (alphabetic characters) or numbers from 0 to 9 (numeric characters). Data which contains a mixture of these characters is called **alphanumeric** data. Characters may be symbols like %, ;, £ or $ – these are called **special characters**. Pressing the keys on the keyboard causes the required patterns of 1's and 0's to be transferred to the memory of the computer. Each character must have its own pattern or code.

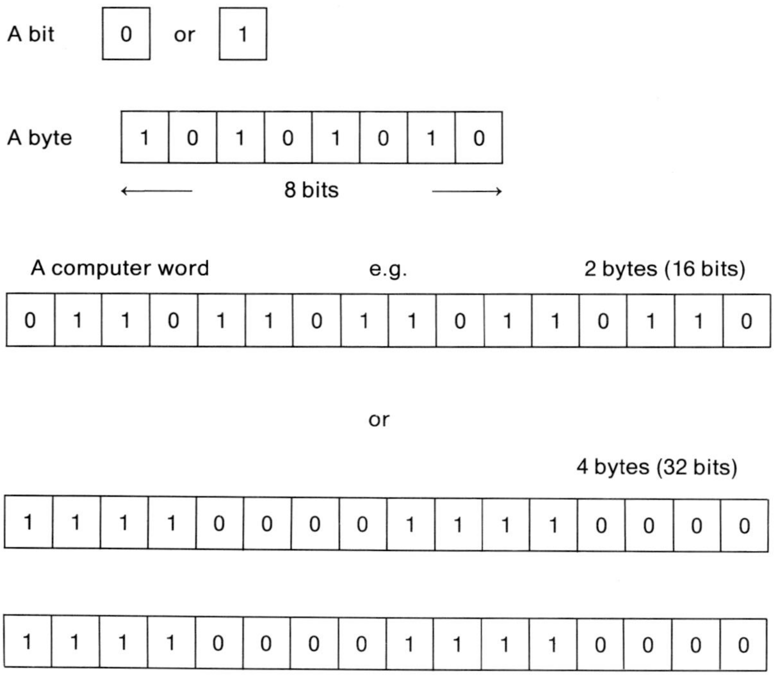

Figure 2   A bit, a byte and a computer word

Character	ASCII code	Character	ASCII code
@	100 0000	0	011 0000
A	100 0001	1	011 0001
B	100 0010	2	011 0010
C	100 0011	3	011 0011
D	100 0100	4	011 0100
E	100 0101	5	011 0101
F	100 0110	6	011 0110
G	100 0111	7	011 0111
H	100 1000	8	011 1000
I	100 1001	9	011 1001
J	100 1010	:	011 1010
K	100 1011	;	011 1011
L	100 1100	<	011 1100
M	100 1101	+	011 1101
N	100 1110	>	011 1110
O	100 1111	?	011 1111
P	101 0000	Space	010 0000
Q	101 0001	!	010 0001
R	101 0010	“	010 0010
S	101 0011	#	010 0011
T	101 0100	$	010 0100
U	101 0101	%	010 0101
V	101 0110	&	010 0110
W	101 0111	’	010 0111
X	101 1000	(	010 1000
Y	101 1001	)	010 1001
Z	101 1010	*	010 1010
[	101 1011	+	010 1011
\	101 1100	,	010 1100
]	101 1101	—	010 1101
↑	101 1110	.	010 1110
—	101 1111	/	010 1111

Figure 3 American standard code for information interchange (ASCII)

You could make up your own code for characters, but in practice it is convenient if everyone uses the same codes. One widely used character code ‘standard’ was accepted internationally in 1968. It is called the **ASCII code** and uses seven bits to represent the codes for computer character sets. Look at Fig. 2 and find the codes for A, B and C. You can see that the code for B is a larger number than for A while C is larger than B, and so on. This is used when a computer **sorts** letters and words into alphabetical order.

- *Parity bits*

An eighth bit is added to the left-hand end of the **ASCII code** to make the total number of 1's even. For example:

Parity bit
↓
A–0 1 0 0   0 0 0 1 (a zero added)

C–1 1 0 0   0 0 1 1 (a one added)

M–0 1 0 0   1 1 0 1 (a zero added)

Z–0 1 0 1   1 0 1 0 (a zero added)

You can see that the code for each letter of the alphabet has an even number of 1's in it (eg. A has two 1's, Z has four 1's). The extra bit is called a **parity check bit**. The eight bits stay together all through the processing inside a computer. (However, when the code is stored in memory the parity bit is ignored.) When data is moved around, the number of 1's in each character code is checked by the system. If the number of 1's is even, processing continues. If the number is odd, an error message is sent out and processing stops.

This system is called **even parity**, where the total number of 1's in the pattern has to be even. Sometimes, **odd parity** is used, where the number of 1's should then be an odd number.

■ Instructions and addresses

A computer is a data processor. It needs to store data and **instructions** telling it what to do with the data. Instructions are given by means of a **program**. Chapter 4 explains some principles of **programming** and **data structures**. This is described for programming in **high-level** programming languages ie. languages that we can understand (if we learn them!). These programs need to be converted into a language the machine can use: **machine code**.

Machine code is **binary** code. Machine code essentially consists of two elements:

the address of the data to be processed

what to do with the data.

Before going on to look at machine code instructions in detail, we shall look at binary **numbers** and **computer logic**.

■ Representing whole numbers

• *Binary to decimal and back again*

Today most people use decimal or **denary** numbers. These are base-10 numbers. They use the digits 0, 1, 2, 3, 4, 5, 6, 7, 8 and 9. As you count past 9 you go on to 10, 11, 12 . . . and so on. We use this number system partly because we have ten fingers (some ancient civilizations used other bases for their numbers). The Babylonians used base 60 for counting. Others have used base 20, (perhaps using fingers and toes!).

Look at the decimal number 3267 and the binary number 1110. To show that one is a base-10 number and that the other is a base-2 number, we write them as:

$$3267_{10} \quad \text{and} \quad 1110_2$$

Reading a decimal number from right to left, the first digit tells you the number of units, the second the number of tens, the third the hundreds, the fourth the thousands, and so on.

1000	100	10	1
3	2	6	7

The 'column headings' 1, 10, 100, 1000, . . . are called **place values**.

With base-2, or binary, numbers the first digit on the right tells you the number of 'units', the next digit tells you the number of 'twos', the next the 'fours', the next the 'eights', and so on. We write this as:

8	4	2	1
1	1	1	0

Binary numbers have place values of 1, 2, 4, 8, 16, 32, . . . and so on.

Only two digits can be used in binary: 1 or 0, while ten digits are used in denary: 0, 1, 2 . . . 9. The highest digit in a number system is always one less than the base (9 in denary, 1 in binary).

Information given to a computer is usually in decimal numbers, but data in the central processing unit can only be handled in binary form. So a computer system must be able to convert numbers from one base to another and back again.

• *Converting binary to decimal*

Any binary number can be converted to denary by multiplying each digit by its place value and then finding the sum of the products. For example:

$$\begin{aligned} 1110_2 &\rightarrow (1\times8)+(1\times4)+(1\times2)+(0\times1) \\ &= 8+4+2+0 \\ &= 14 \end{aligned}$$

ie. $1110_2 \rightarrow 14_{10}$

Take another example: Convert 1101011_2 into denary.

Step 1: Work out the place values for each of the digits:

64	32	16	8	4	2	1
1	1	0	1	0	1	1

Step 2: Add up the numbers which have a '1' underneath them:

$$64+32+8+2+1 = 107$$

ie. $1101011_2 \rightarrow 107_{10}$

• *Converting decimal to binary*

Converting this way round takes slightly longer, but there are two methods you can use. (Note: It's worth checking the result by converting it back to denary.)

Convert 83_{10} to binary.

<u>Method 1</u>

Step 1: Find the highest binary place value that can be subtracted from the decimal (83). In this case it is 64.

$$83-64 = 19$$

Place a 1 in the 64's column as shown:

64	32	16	8	4	2	1
1						

Step 2: Find the next highest value that can be subtracted from the remainder (19). In this case it is 16.

$$19 - 16 = 3$$

Place a 1 in the 16's column.

Step 3: Find the next highest place value that can be subtracted from the remainder (3). In this case it is 2.

$$3 - 2 = 1$$

Place a 1 in the 2's column.

Step 4: Keep going until the remainder is a 1 or 0 and place it in the units column. In our example a 1 goes in the units column.

Step 5: Fill the remaining empty columns with zeros,

64	32	16	8	4	2	1
1	0	1	0	0	1	1

and the binary representation of 83 can be read off:

$$83_{10} \rightarrow 1010011_2$$

This method can be quite lengthy and slow. Method 2 is quicker.

Method 2

Step 1: Divide the decimal number over and over again by 2 until you reach zero. After each division the remainder is written down – it will be either 1 or 0.

83 ÷ 2 = 41 remainder 1
41 ÷ 2 = 20 remainder 1
20 ÷ 2 = 10 remainder 0
10 ÷ 2 = 5 remainder 0
5 ÷ 2 = 2 remainder 1
2 ÷ 2 = 1 remainder 0
1 ÷ 2 = 0 remainder 1

Step 2: The last remainder is your first binary digit. Write down all the remainders, from the bottom upwards, to give your binary number. In this case it is 1010011.

ie. $83_{10} \rightarrow 1010011_2$

(the same result as Method 1).

The next section shows you how whole positive numbers are represented in binary form in a computer.

● *Pure binary representation*

A whole number is called an integer. One way of using 1's and 0's to stand for an integer inside the computer is by converting the integer directly into binary. For example:

6 → 1 1 0
9 → 1 0 0 1

With large numbers, more bits are needed. For example:

235 → 1 1 1 0 1 0 1 1

Here, eight bits are needed. If these bits are stored in a location inside the computer, the location then contains the number 235.

This is called **pure binary representation**. One location in the computer is needed to hold one number. The problem is this: the size of the number that the computer can represent is limited by the number of bits in a location, eg. with eight bits in a location the highest number would be 255.

Another way of storing numbers is by **Binary Coded Decimal (BCD)**.

● *Binary coded decimal*

To change a decimal number to a binary coded decimal you take one decimal digit at a time, and convert it to binary. Each digit from 0 to 9 can be converted to binary using only four bits.

Decimal digit	Binary code
0	0 0 0 0
1	0 0 0 1
2	0 0 1 0
3	0 0 1 1
4	0 1 0 0
5	0 1 0 1
6	0 1 1 0
7	0 1 1 1
8	1 0 0 0
9	1 0 0 1

To convert the decimal number 23 to BCD you first convert the 3, then the 2:

2	3	denary number becomes
0 0 1 0	0 0 1 1	binary coded decimal

This needs eight bits. Using eight bits, numbers as high as 99 can be represented:

9	9
1 0 0 1	1 0 0 1

With twelve bits you can go up to 999:

9	9	9
1 0 0 1	1 0 0 1	1 0 0 1

Sixteen bits will represent numbers as high as 9999, and so on.

In some computers, processing BCD is useful and efficient, for example where numeric data is being processed but not used in calculations. This is because only four bits are needed for each character. However, BCD is normally less efficient than pure binary representation; 16 bits in BCD can only represent numbers up to 9999, compared to 65535 in pure binary.

- *Shorthand for binary code*

A long string of 1's and 0's can be very difficult for human beings to remember. Imagine remembering a binary code made up of 16 bits like 1011010110101110. A long binary code also takes a long time to write. For these reasons a shorthand version is often used to help people, for example when a machine-code computer program is being checked.

- *Hexadecimal (hex)*

Many microprocessors have a word length of eight bits. These words can be split into two groups of four bits, eg. 0011 1101. Each of these four-bit groups can be arranged in 16 different combinations.

Binary codes (using 4 bits)	Hexadecimal shorthand
0 0 0 0	0
0 0 0 1	1
0 0 1 0	2
0 0 1 1	3
0 1 0 0	4
0 1 0 1	5
0 1 1 0	6
0 1 1 1	7
1 0 0 0	8
1 0 0 1	9
1 0 1 0	A
1 0 1 1	B
1 1 0 0	C
1 1 0 1	D
1 1 1 0	E
1 1 1 1	F

Hexadecimal, or **base-16 numbers**, can be used as shorthand to stand for these bits because the hexadecimal system uses 16 different digits. The hex system uses the letters A, B, C, D, E and F to stand for the decimal numbers 10, 11, 12, 13, 14 and 15.

Binary codes can easily be converted into hex (by first making groups of four bits) and hexadecimal numbers can easily be changed into binary.

Binary to hex

0 1 1 0 1 1 1 1 1 0 1 0 ⇒ 6FA
1 1 0 1 0 0 1 0 0 0 1 1 ⇒ D23

Hex to binary

BF2 ⇒ 1 0 1 1 1 1 1 1 0 0 1 0
7AE ⇒ 0 1 1 1 1 0 1 0 1 1 1 0

Hexadecimal codes are widely used with microcomputers as shorthand for eight-bit and 16-bit binary codes. Another type of shorthand is sometimes used with 12- and 24-bit word length computers (eg. minicomputers). This is the **octal** system.

- *Octal*

A binary code of 12 bits breaks down easily into groups of three. Each group of three bits can be arranged in eight different patterns. The octal base-8, number system has a digit for each of these binary patterns (see table).

Binary codes (using 3 bits)	Octal shorthand
0 0 0	0
0 0 1	1
0 1 0	2
0 1 1	3
1 0 0	4
1 0 1	5
1 1 0	6
1 1 1	7

The octal number system uses only eight digits: 0, 1, 2, 3, 4, 5, 6 and 7.

Binary numbers can easily be changed into octal by first putting them in groups of three bits.

eg. 1 1 0 1 1 1 → 67 in octal.

ie. $110111_2 = 67_8$

Here are two more examples:

Binary to octal	Octal to binary
0 0 1 1 0 1_2	6 2_8
3 5_8	1 1 0 0 1 0_2

Negative numbers in binary

Sign-and-magnitude representation

A positive number like +9 can be written down in binary as +1001. On a piece of paper we can write −9 as −1001. But how can this be represented inside a computer? A computer has no way of storing a + sign or a − sign.

So a binary digit must be used. This bit is used simply to show whether a number is positive or negative. It is called a **sign bit**. A sign bit of **1** shows a negative number, **0** indicates a positive number.

Using sign-and-magnitude coding the left-hand bit of the binary pattern stands for the sign of the number. This is called the **most significant bit**. The other bits stand for the size or magnitude of the number for example:

Binary	Denary
0 1 0 =	+2
1 1 0 =	−2
1 1 0 0 0 =	−8
0 1 0 0 0 =	+8

(The sign bit is in bold type.)

Using an eight-bit word you can represent numbers ranging from:

0 1 1 1 1 1 1 1 = +127

1 1 1 1 1 1 1 1 = −127

The main disadvantage with this way of coding is that there are two zeros!

Half way between +127 and −127 there:

0 0 0 0 0 0 0 0

and also **1** 0 0 0 0 0 0 0

Both stand for zero. This can cause problems, so a different method is used in modern computers.

Two's-complement representation

Suppose you wanted to do this sum:

$$5-3$$

This sum is the same as:

$$5+(-3)$$

In other words, subtracting a number is the same as adding the negative of that number. For example:

$$7-2 = 7+(-2)$$
$$12-9 = 12+(-9)$$
$$11-8 = 11+(-8)$$

This is how most computers subtract numbers – by making the number negative then adding it. The number is made negative by the **two's-complement method**. Using this method, the bit on the far left of a binary number actually carries a negative value instead of a positive one. The place values for a three-bit, two's-complement number are, for example:

```
−4 2 1
 1 1 0 = −4+2+0 = −2
```

The bit on the far left, the most significant bit, stands for a negative quantity. Here is an example with six bits:

```
−32 16 8 4 2 1
  1  0 1 1 1 0 = −32+8+4+2
               = −18
```

Fig. 4 shows the two's complement of some simple numbers using only three bits. Follow the numbers on this diagram from +3 round to −4. It is rather like turning the clock back.

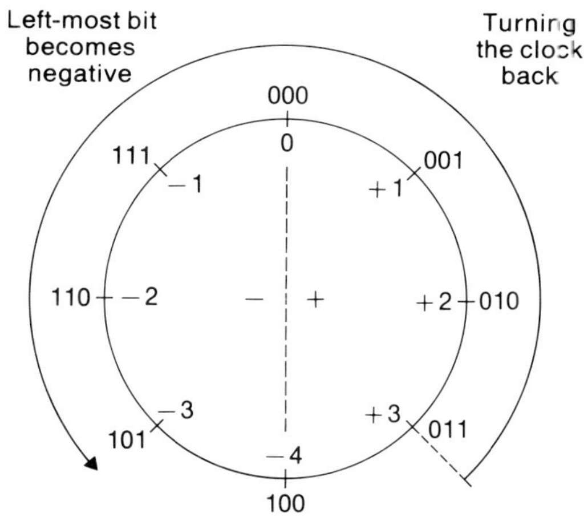

Using 3 bits you can represent −4 to +3

For example: −4 +2 +1
1 1 1 = −1

Figure 4 Two's complement representation using three bits

Try adding +3 to −3. You can see that the result is zero (as it should be).

```
     0 1 1   (+3)
     1 0 1   (−3)
   ___________
 (1) 0 0 0   Zero, using three bits only.
```

The left-hand bit, which must be ignored, is called the **overflow bit**. Fig. 5 shows you two's-complement representation using four bits. Try adding +6 to −6:

```
     0 1 1 0   (+6)
     1 0 1 0   (−6)
   ____________
 (1) 0 0 0 0   Zero, using four bits only.
```

Again the result is zero. (Notice that there is only one representation of zero with this method.)

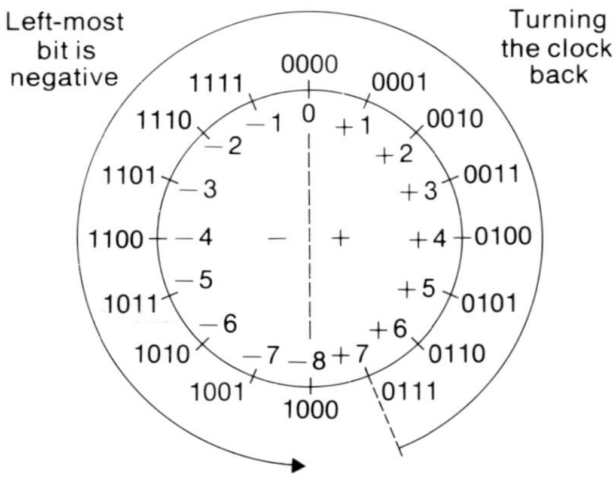

Using 4 bits −8 to +7 can be represented

For example: −8 +4 +2 +1
1 1 1 1 = −1

Figure 5 Two's complement representation using four bits

The more bits used, the wider the range of numbers that can be represented. Eight bits can be used to represent numbers from −128 up to +127. Try adding +127 to −127. What result do you get?

Eight bits		Denary number
0 1 1 1	1 1 1 1	+127
...		.
...		.

Positive numbers

....		
0 0 0 0	1 0 0 0	+8
0 0 0 0	0 1 1 1	+7
0 0 0 0	0 1 1 0	+6
0 0 0 0	0 1 0 1	+5
0 0 0 0	0 1 0 0	+4
0 0 0 0	0 0 1 1	+3
0 0 0 0	0 0 1 0	+2
0 0 0 0	0 0 0 1	+1
0 0 0 0	0 0 0 0	0

Negative numbers

1 1 1 1	1 1 1 1	−1
1 1 1 1	1 1 1 0	−2
1 1 1 1	1 1 0 1	−3
1 1 1 1	1 1 0 0	−4
1 1 1 1	1 0 1 1	−5
1 1 1 1	1 0 1 0	−6
1 1 1 1	1 0 0 1	−7
1 1 1 1	1 0 0 0	−8
....		.
....		.
1 0 0 0	0 0 0 0	−128

The table below shows you the ranges of numbers that can be represented with more and more bits.

Number of bits	Ranges of numbers that can be represented
3	−4 to +3
4	−8 to +7
8	−128 to +127
16	−32768 to +32767
24	−838608 to +8388607

- *Forming the two's complement of a number*

There are two methods that may be followed for changing a positive binary number into its two's complement.

Example 1: Convert +11 into its two's complement using six bits.

Method 1

Step 1: Convert +11 to pure binary.

+11 ⇒ 0 0 1 0 1 1

Step 2: Change every 0 to a 1 and every 1 to a 0

1 1 0 1 0 0

Step 3: Add 1

1 1 0 1 0 1

Step 4: Check your answer.

$$-32+16+4+1=-11$$

Example 2: Change +22 into its two's complement using six bits.

Method 2

Step 1: Convert +22 into pure binary.

$+22 \Rightarrow$ 0 1 0 1 1 0

Step 2: Copy down each digit from the right until you reach the first 1. Copy the first 1 but after that change every 1 to a 0 and every 0 to a 1

1 0 1 0 1 0

Step 3: Check your answer.

$$-32+8+2=-22$$

Both methods give the same result. Try them out on some simple examples.

Checking

There are three ways of checking that you have the right answer:

▲ All even numbers end in 0. All odd numbers end in 1.

▲ All positive numbers start with 0. All negative numbers start with 1.

▲ Try adding the negative number to its corresponding positive number eg. $+22+(-22)$. With a fixed number of bits the result should be zero.

Example 3: Show how the subtraction $^{+}25-8$ is done using two's-complement binary representation.

Step 1: Convert +125 to pure binary.

$+125 \Rightarrow$ 1 1 1 1 1 0 1

Step 2: Add a leading zero to indicate a positive number.

0 1 1 1   1 1 0 1 (= 125)

Step 3: Convert +8 to pure binary.

$+8 \Rightarrow$ 1 0 0 0

Step 4: Add four leading zeros to make the same number of bits.

0 0 0 0   1 0 0 0 (+8)

Step 5: Form the two's complement of +8

1 1 1 1   1 0 0 0 (−8)

Step 6: Add the result of Step 5 to the result of Step 2.

```
    0 1 1 1   1 1 0 1  (+125)
    1 1 1 1   1 0 0 0  (−8)
---------------------
(1) 0 1 1 1   0 1 0 1
```

Step 7: Ignore the leading 1. The final answer is:

0 1 1 1   0 1 0 1 (+117)

Step 8: Check your answer!

■ Representing fractions and real numbers

● *Using 1's and 0's to represent fractions*

A computer must be able to represent fractions as well as whole numbers. The table below shows the fractions that are easy to represent in binary.

Fraction	Power of 2	Binary fraction	Decimal
1	2^0	1	1
$\frac{1}{2}$	2^{-1}	0.1	0.5
$\frac{1}{4}$	2^{-2}	0.01	0.25
$\frac{1}{8}$	2^{-3}	0.001	0.125
$\frac{1}{16}$	2^{-4}	0.0001	0.0625
$\frac{1}{32}$	2^{-5}	0.00001	—
$\frac{1}{64}$	2^{-6}	0.000001	—

Fractions, and whole numbers followed by a fraction, are easy to represent in binary if they are made up from fractions in this table. For example:

$$\tfrac{3}{4} = 0.1 + 0.01 = 0.11$$
$$7\tfrac{1}{4} = 111 + 0.01 = 111.01$$
$$\tfrac{7}{8} = 0.11 + 0.001 = 0.111$$
$$4\tfrac{3}{16} = 100 + 0.001 + 0.0001 = 100.0011$$

● *Errors*

Some fractions are much harder to change into binary. One example is $\frac{4}{5}$. Using six bits you get:

$$\tfrac{4}{5} \rightarrow \begin{matrix} \frac{1}{2} & \frac{1}{4} & \frac{1}{8} & \frac{1}{16} & \frac{1}{32} & \frac{1}{64} \\ 1 & 1 & 0 & 0 & 1 & 1 \end{matrix}$$

But $\frac{1}{2}+\frac{1}{4}+\frac{1}{32}+\frac{1}{64} = \frac{32}{64}+\frac{16}{64}+\frac{2}{64}+\frac{1}{64}$
$= \frac{51}{64}$
$= 0.7969$

In fact $\frac{4}{5} = 0.8000$

So this binary fraction is not exactly equal to $\frac{4}{5}$. More and more bits are needed to bring it closer and closer to the true value. There is a similar problem when changing some fractions to to decimals. For example: $\frac{2}{3} = 0.6666666666\ldots$ and so on, forever. The fraction has to be cut off or **truncated** after a certain number of decimal places, eg. $\frac{2}{3} = 0.6666$. Because the two are not exactly equal this is called a **truncation error**. In binary: $\frac{2}{3} \rightarrow 0.101010$, if only six bits are available ($= 0.65625$ in decimal).

● *Rounding*

Fractions are often 'rounded off' for, example $\frac{2}{3}$ is rounded off to 0.6667 in decimal. The last 6 is changed to a 7. Binary fractions can be rounded too. For example $\frac{2}{3} = 0.101011$, rounded to six binary places. The rule is: the last 0 is changed to a 1 if the next figure would have been a 1. The binary representation is still not exact, but the error, called a **rounding error**, is not as bad as a truncation error. These errors are present in all computer arithmetic.

● *Fixed-point representation*

Numbers which are not whole numbers (integers) are called real numbers, eg. $2\frac{1}{2}$, $6\frac{3}{4}$, $7\frac{1}{16}$. These can be stored inside an eight-bit location by changing them to binary and assuming that the decimal point (sometimes called the **bicimal point**) is fixed in a certain position.

For example:

$7\frac{1}{16}$ → 0 1 1 1 ↑ 0 0 0 1
(↑ Sign bit under the first 0; ↑ Bicimal point before 0 0 0 1)

$2\frac{1}{2}$ → 0 0 0 1 0 ↑ 1 0 0
(↑ Bicimal point)

$6\frac{3}{4}$ → 0 0 1 1 0 ↑ 1 1 0
(↑ Bicimal point)

The bicimal point is assumed to lie in a certain fixed position inside the word in a particular machine. This is called **fixed-point representation**. The three examples above are easy ones. They fit nicely into an 8-bit word, but what about a larger number like 105.125? Change this to binary and it becomes: 1101001.001. This needs 10 bits. If you try to put it into an 8-bit location it fills it up then 'overflows'. This is one type of **overflow error**. A way of avoiding this is to use a 'floating' bicimal point.

● *Floating-point representation*

The speed of light is 300 000 000 metres per second. To save writing these eight noughts all the time you can just write

$$3 \times 10^8$$

The earth is 150 million kilometres from the sun. This number can be written as 1.5×10^8 km. To change back you must move the decimal point eight places to the right:

$$1.5 \times 10^8 = 150\,000\,000.0$$

A similar method is used to store binary numbers in a computer. The first part of the word tells you the number itself. The second part tells you how far the bicimal point must be moved to the right. For example:

Mantissa	Exponent
1 1 0 1	1 0 0
↑ Bicimal point	

The first part (the number) is called the **mantissa**. The second part, telling you where to put the bicimal point, is called the **exponent**. The bicimal point always starts at the far left of the mantissa – the exponent then tell you where to move it. In this example the exponent is 100 (binary), or 4 (decimal). So you move the bicimal point four places to the right. The number, or mantissa, then becomes 1101, or 13. This way of coding number is called **floating-point representation** because the bicimal point starts off by 'floating' to the far left of the mantissa.

Two more bits are needed before every number can be represented with this method:

▲ A sign bit is needed for the mantissa to show whether the number is negative or positive.

▲ A sign bit is needed for the exponent to show whether the bicimal point must be moved right (to represent numbers bigger than 1) or left (to represent numbers smaller than 1).

A complete representation using a floating bicimal point might then be:

Mantissa	Exponent
0 1 1 0	0 0 1 1
↑↑ Bicimal point	↑
Sign bit	Sign bit

Looking at the exponent you see that the point needs to move three places to the right, because the sign bit is 0. So the binary number is 110, and it is positive. (Notice that the bicimal point starts off just to the right of the sign bit.)

- *Representing negative numbers*

A positive number has the same exponent as a negative number, but its mantissa will be different. For example:

	Mantissa	Exponent
+67 ⇒	0 1 0 0 0 0 1 1	0 1 1 1
	↑	
	Mantissa	Exponent
−67 ⇒	1 0 1 1 1 1 0 1	0 1 1 1
	↑	

As can be seen, the exponents of +67 and −67 are the same. But the mantissa of −67 is the two's complement of +67.

- *Representing fractions*

With every fraction the exponent has to be negative. The negative exponent is usually represented in two's complement form. For example:

$\frac{1}{8} \rightarrow$ 0.001 (fixed point)
0 1 1 0
↑ ↑ Exponent of −2

The exponent of −2 (10 in two's complement form) shows that the bicimal point must be moved two places to the left.

This worked example gives you step-by-step instructions for changing decimal numbers into floating-point representation.

- *Storing real numbers*

Computers may use one, two or even four **words** to store a floating-point number. Often, 23 bits will be used for the mantissa and nine bits for the exponent. This could be stored in a 32-bit word, or two 16-bit words. The larger the exponent, the larger the number that can be stored. Floating point representation may be used for a wide range of sizes and types of number inside the computer; it is used for integers, real numbers, negative numbers and fractions.

Computer Logic

- *Logic gates: what are they?*

Binary bits are represented inside the computer by electrical pulses. These pulses are passed around the computer's electronic circuits through switches or **logic gates**. A gate may 'open' to pass on a pulse, or 'closed' to stop it. (But note that logic gates have no moving parts.) Using these gates, pulses can be routed along different paths inside a computer.

Electrical pulses can also be combined according to certain logical rules. This is another job done by logic gates. A certain combination of binary pulses into a logic gate gives a certain combination of binary pulses out. This combining of inputs to provide certain outputs is called **computer logic**.

- *Three common logic gates*

The NOT gate. A very simple logic gate is called the 'NOT gate'. If it receives an input pulse (a '1'), its output is no pulse (a '0').

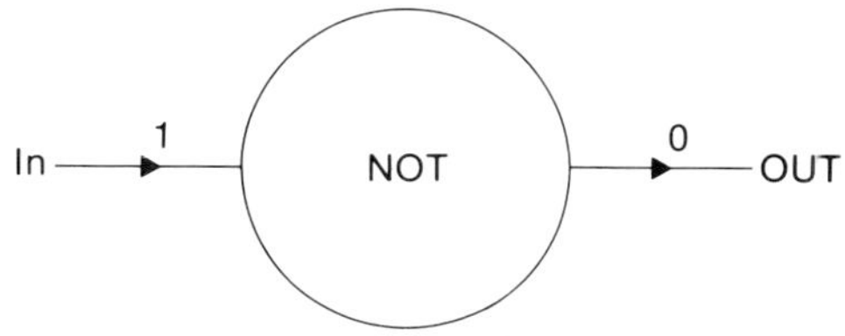

Figure 6 The NOT gate with a "1" input

If it receives no pulse (a '0'), its output is a pulse (a '1').

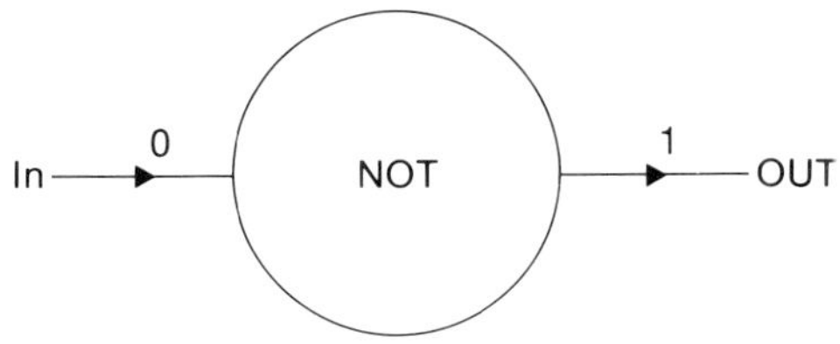

Figure 7 The NOT gate with a "0" input

The signal put in is always reversed. This may be shown with a simple table.

Input	Output
1	0
0	1

This is called a **truth table** or an **operation table**.

The AND gate. The next simplest gate has two inputs and one output. When both the inputs are 1 the output is 1.

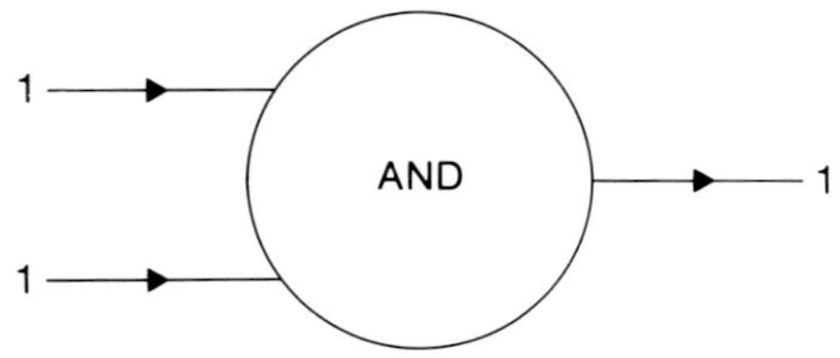

Figure 8 The AND gate with two "1"s input

This is called an 'AND gate'. If either of the inputs is 0, then the output is 0.

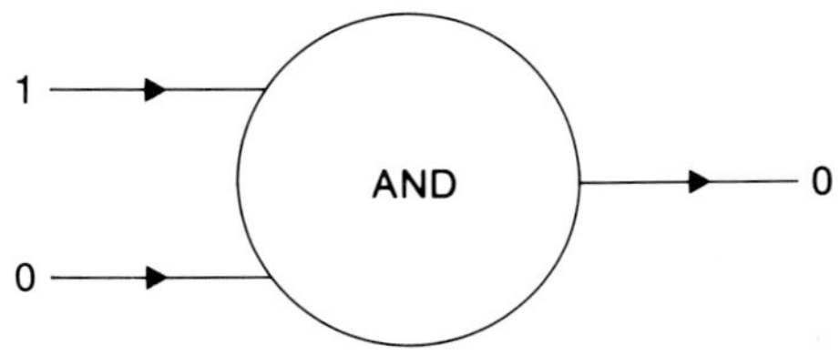

Figure 9 The AND gate with "1" and "0" input

The different combinations of 1's and 0's can be shown in a truth table. Call the two inputs A and B, and the output C. The table here shows four possible combinations of inputs A and B.

Input A	Input B	Output C = A and B
0	0	0
0	1	0
1	0	0
1	1	1

The output C is 1 only if A and B are both 1. For all the other combinations of A and B the output C is 0.

An AND gate can have more than two inputs. If three inputs were used the same rule would apply – the output is only 1 if all the inputs are 1.

The OR gate. Like the AND gate, an OR gate can have two, or more, inputs and has one output.

This gate produces an output pulse C if either of the input pulses is 1 or if both inputs are 1.

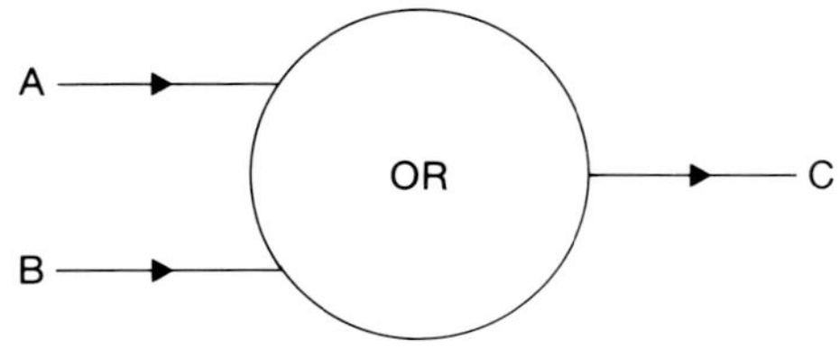

Figure 10 The OR gate

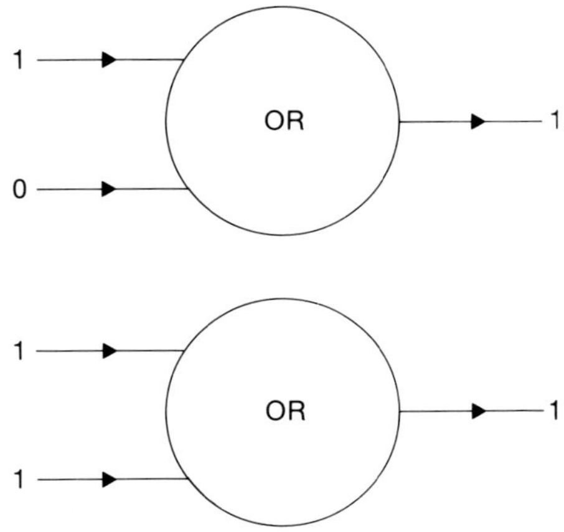

Figure 11 The OR gate with different inputs

The output is 0 only if both inputs are 0.

The different combinations for an OR gate can be shown by a truth table.

Inputs A	Inputs B	Output C
0	0	0
0	1	1
1	0	1
1	1	1

The three logic gates described above (AND, OR and NOT) can be put together to make **logic circuits**.

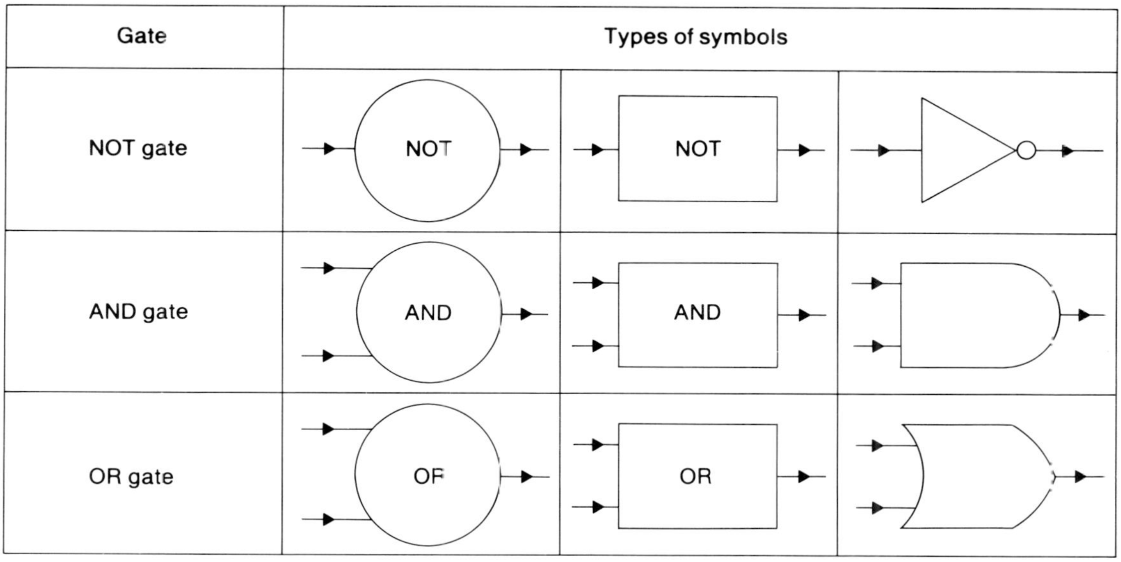

Figure 12 Table of symbols

- *Using logic gates to make logic circuits*

A logic circuit or **logic network** is a combination of logic gates joined together. All computer logic circuits can be built up from the three basic gates already described: AND, OR and NOT. A simple example of a logic network using these three gates is shown in Fig. 13. The three inputs are A, B and C. The output from the AND gate is called X. This output will be 1 only if A and B are both 1. The NOT gate then reverses X, giving output Y. Finally, the two pulses Y and C meet at the OR gate. The output from this gate is called Z. This output, Z, will be 0 only if the input pulses Y and C are both 0. The complete truth table for this logic network is also shown.

More complicated logic circuits can be built up from the three basic AND, OR and NOT gates. In fact, all computer logic circuits can be built up using only these gates.

- *Jobs done by logic circuits*

Here is an outline of some of the uses of logic circuits:

for comparing binary words

for transferring data from one place to another

for decoding instructions, eg. recognising certain binary patterns

for calculating, eg. adding two binary numbers

for storing data, eg. by the use of 'flip-flops' (two-state memory devices).

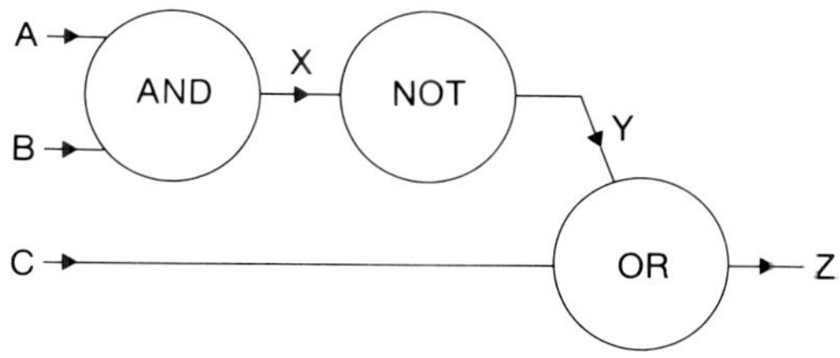

Three inputs			A and B	Not X	Final output (Y or C)
A	B	C	X	Y	Z
0	0	0	0	1	1
0	0	1	0	1	1
0	1	0	0	1	1
0	1	1	0	1	1
1	0	0	0	1	1
1	0	1	0	1	1
1	1	0	1	0	0
1	1	1	1	0	1

Figure 13 A simple logic network and its corresponding truth table

The next section describes two logic circuits for adding numbers. These circuits are called the **half-adder** and the **full-adder**.

- *Adding with logic circuits*

Adding two binary digits. Look back at the unit on binary numbers. There are four rules for adding two binary digits.

They are:

Digit		Carry	Sum
0+0	=	0	0
0+1	=	0	1
1+0	=	0	1
1+1	=	1	0

A logic network is needed to do these simple additions inside a computer. It must have a **truth table** exactly corresponding to these four rules of addition.

Two inputs		Outputs	
A	B	Carry	Sum
0	0	0	0
0	1	0	1
1	0	0	1
1	1	1	0

Compare this table with the four rules of addition above. There is no simple logic gate which has this truth table so a logic network has to be made up with two outputs called a **sum** and a **carry**. The network is shown in Fig. 14. It is called a **half-adder**.

Check this half-adder for yourself. Trace the different inputs (starting with A = 0 and B = 0) through the network to see that it produces the right sum and carry for each combination.

Adding three binary digits. The half-adder works perfectly for two bits. But it is often necessary to add three bits – one bit from each of the numbers to be added and the carry bit from the previous addition. A more complex circuit is needed for adding three binary digits. This is the **full-adder**.

For three digits there are eight different rules:

Digit	Carry	Sum
0+0+0 =	0	0
0+0+1 =	0	1
0+1+0 =	0	1
1+0+0 =	0	1
0+1+1 =	1	0
1+0+1 =	1	0
1+1+0 =	1	0
1+1+1 =	1	1

The logic network for adding three digits must have a truth table exactly corresponding to these eight rules of addition. Compare the table below carefully with the eight rules of addition above.

Three inputs			Outputs	
A	B	C	CARRY	SUM
0	0	0	0	0
0	0	1	0	1
0	1	0	0	1
1	0	0	0	1
0	1	1	1	0
1	0	1	1	0
1	1	0	1	0
1	1	1	1	1

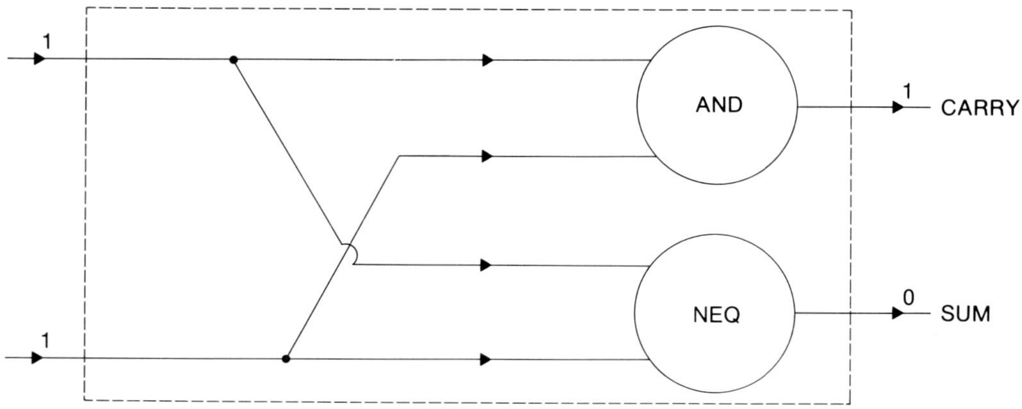

Figure 14 A half-adder made from an AND and a NEQ gate

The logic network for adding three digits, ie. a full-adder, is made by joining two half-adders. A full adder which produces the correct sum and carry is shown in Fig. 15. Check this for yourself. Trace the different inputs through the network for each of the eight combinations.

Notice that a half-adder is shown in Fig. 15 in the units column. But in practice a full-adder is placed there so that the same circuit can be employed for subtraction using the two's-complement method. The complete circuit is called a **parallel adder**. A special register in the CPU is used to signal whether overflow has occurred at the final full-adder, ie. if the last carry is a 1. This is called a **flag register**.

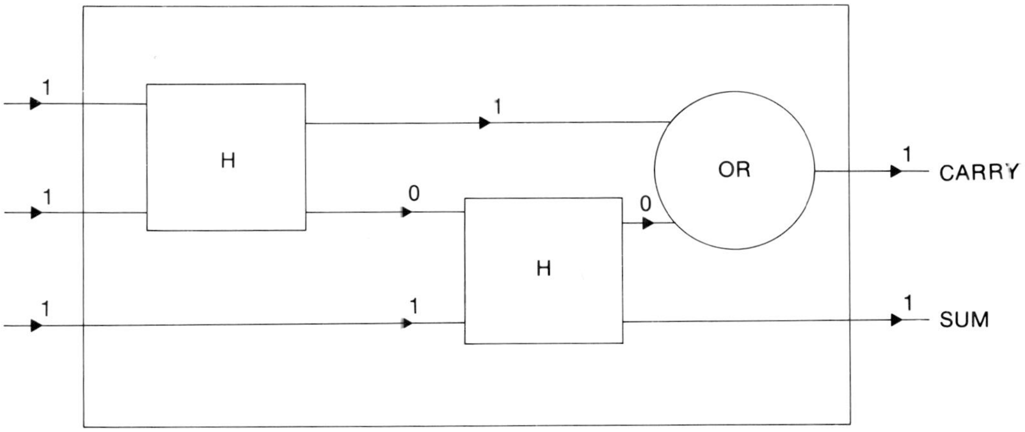

The symbol for a full adder is:

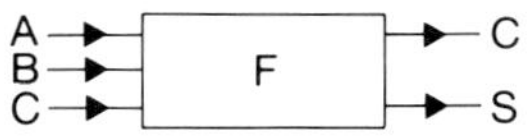

Figure 15 A full-adder

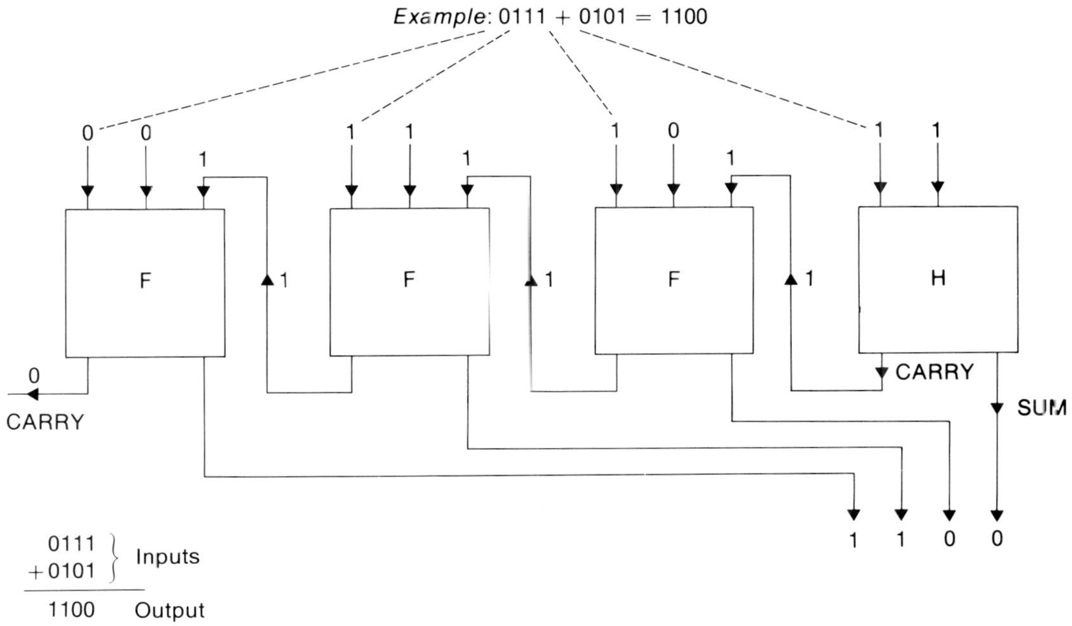

Figure 16 Adding two four-bit numbers with a parallel adder

• *How computers do their sums*

Computers can do all kinds of arithmetic: adding, subtracting, multiplying and dividing. Computer calculations are complicated but, in fact, the basic operation is addition. For example, one number can be subtracted from another by making it negative then adding it:

$$6-3=6+(-3)=3$$

Many computers subtract numbers in this way. The negative number is found by the two's-complement method already explained. It is then added.

Multiplication can be done by adding numbers over and over again, for example:

$$6\times 2=2+2+2+2+2+2$$

Division can be done by repeated subtraction.

The logic circuits rarely go wrong but they can sometimes give unexpected results when they do a calculation. One reason is that certain fractions cannot be represented exactly in binary form, or decimal form (eg. $\frac{1}{3}=0.333333\ldots$). The number has to be truncated to fit it into a binary word.

Another problem is overflow. The result of a calculation may contain too many bits to fit into a storage location.

• *Errors in computer arithmetic*

Errors in computer arithmetic are unavoidable. An **error** is the difference between the true value and the value stored in the computer. Errors result from trying to store numbers in a binary word of fixed length. Normally, the shorter the word length the greater the probability of error. The table below gives a summary of errors in computer arithmetic.

Computers which carry out huge, complex calculations have been designed to reduce these errors to a minimum.

Type of error	Meaning	Example
Overflow	The result of a calculation is too large to fit into the storage location intended for it (the computer word)	The answer to a multiplication is outside the range of numbers a computer can represent – an error message is output
Truncation	A fraction is cut off (truncated) after a certain number of binary or decimal places	$\frac{2}{3}=0.101010_2$ $\frac{2}{3}=0.6666_{10}$ to four places
Rounding	Binary fractions are rounded by raising the last figure to 1 if the next figure would have been a 1 Decimal fractions are rounded by raising the last figure by 1 if the next figure would have been above 5	$\frac{2}{3}=0.101011_2$ $\frac{2}{3}=0.6667_{10}$
Underflow	The result of a calculation is too small to be held in the computer word	A result of 0.000000001 becomes 0.00000000 in 8 bits

● *Other logic gates*

AND, OR and NOT are not the only logic gates. This section explains three others: **NAND, NOR** and **EXCLUSIVE-OR**.

The NAND gate. A NAND gate is made by putting a NOT gate after an AND gate.

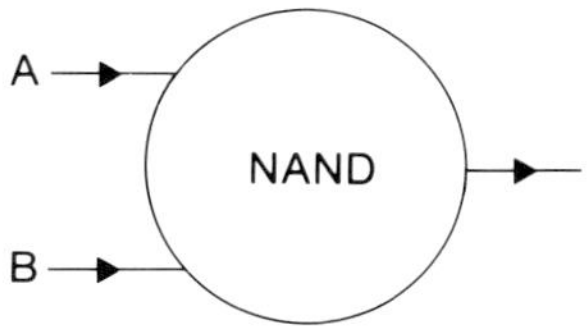

is the same as:

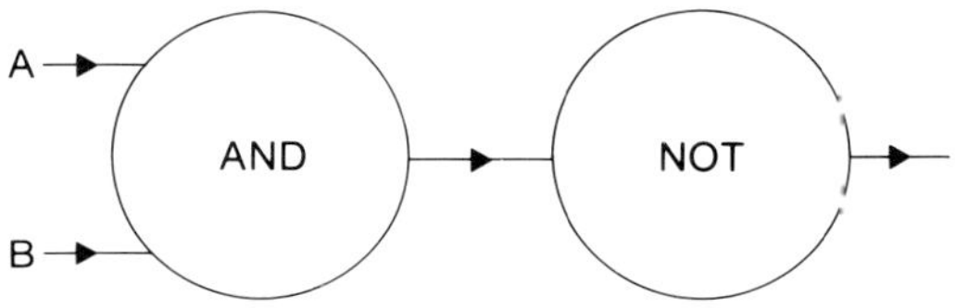

Figure 17 The NAND gate

NAND is short for NOT-AND. Its truth table is the exact reverse of the AND gate.

A	B	NAND
0	0	1
0	1	1
1	0	1
1	1	0

The NOR gate. This is made by putting a NOT gate after an OR gate.

NOR is short for NOT-OR. Its truth table is the exact reverse of the OR gate.

A	B	NOR
0	0	1
0	1	0
1	0	0
1	1	0

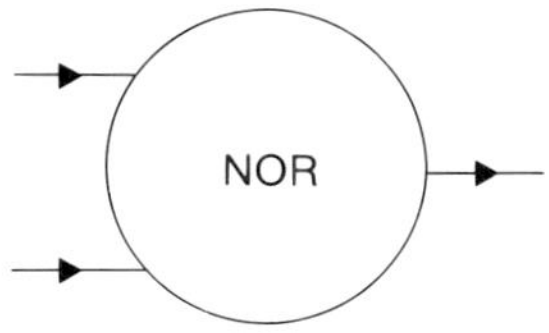

is the same as:

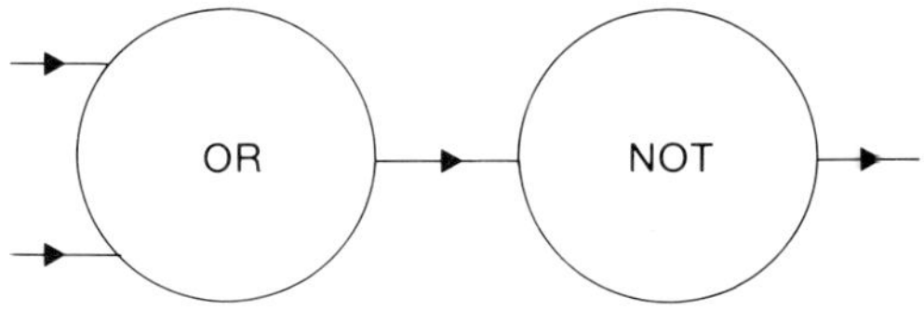

Figure 18 The NOR gate

Every computer logic circuit can be built from NAND gates only or from NOR gates only. In fact, all the other logic gates can be built by combining NAND gates in the right patterns.

The EXCLUSIVE-OR gate. This final gate gives an output of 0 when both the inputs are the same, ie. when both inputs are equivalent. It is sometimes called the **NOT-EQUIVALENT** gate.

A	B	XOR
0	0	0
0	1	1
1	0	1
1	1	0

More than one symbol is used to show an EXCLUSIVE-OR (XOR) gate.

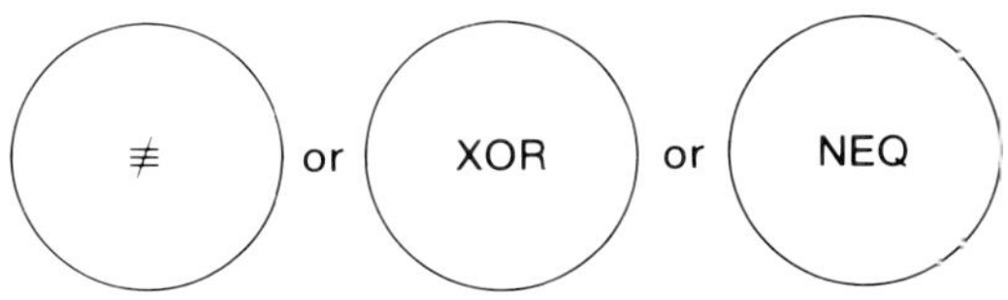

Figure 19 Symbols for the EXCLUSIVE – OR/NOT EQUIVALENT gate

This gate actually means: 'Either A or B but not both'. You can see from the truth table that this gate gives the sum of two binary digits, eg. 1+0 = 1. So it can be used as part of the logic circuit for a half-adder, as Fig. 14 shows. Check this circuit with different patterns of 1's and 0's to see that it works.

This section has explained the job that different logic gates do. You do not need to know how these logic gates are made, or what goes on inside them. This is the concern of the electronic engineer.

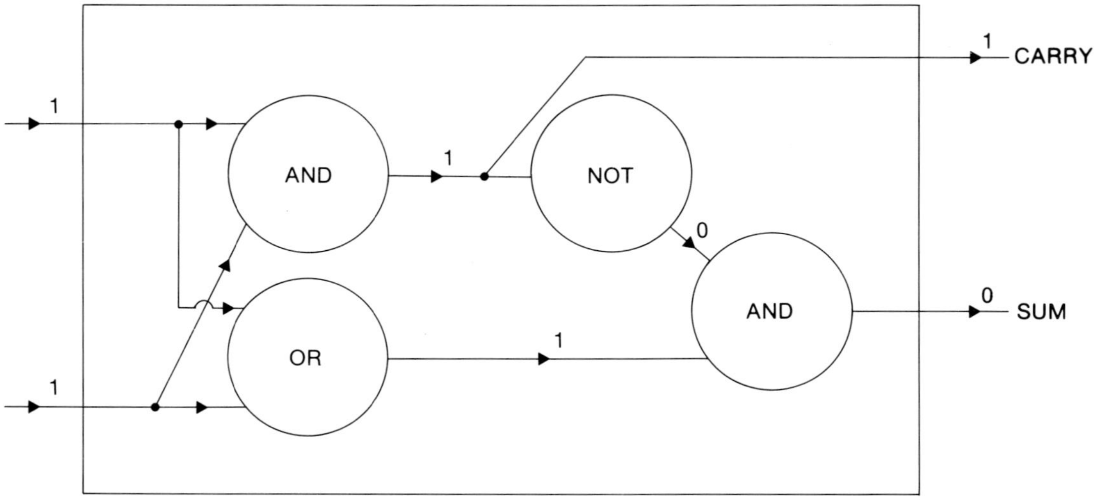

The symbol for the half-adder is:

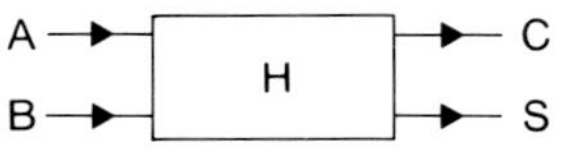

Figure 20 A half-adder using a NAND gate

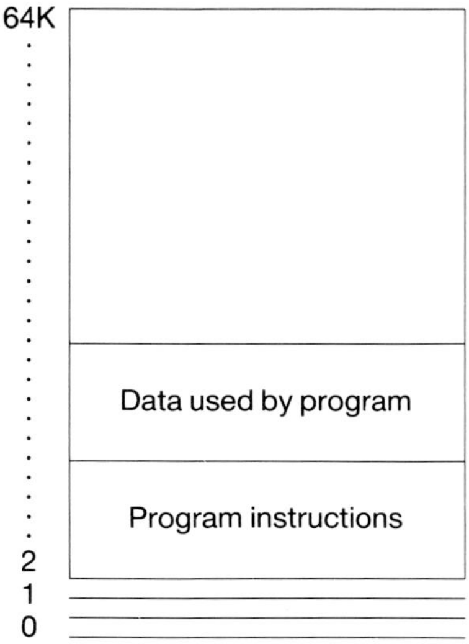

Figure 21 Main memory

MACHINE ARCHITECTURE

The design of most modern computer architectures is based on the model shown in Fig. 21. It was first proposed by John Von Neumann in the 1940's. The principle of the model is that the computer has a memory containing a set of **locations**, each location having an **address**. **Programs** and **data** are stored in the memory.

The memory is often called the '**main memory**' to distinguish it from auxiliary memory or **backing store**. Auxiliary memory is usually external to the computer and is stored on magnetic disk or tape, optical disk etc.

The main memory is connected to the **Central Processing Unit (CPU)**. The CPU takes **instructions** from the program stored in the main memory and executes them ie. it carries out the instructions. The instructions use the data which is also stored in the memory.

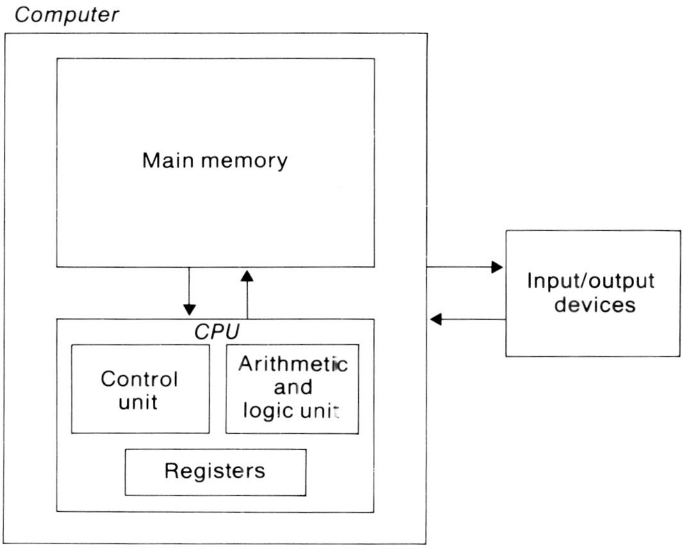

Figure 22 *General layout of the CPU and memory*

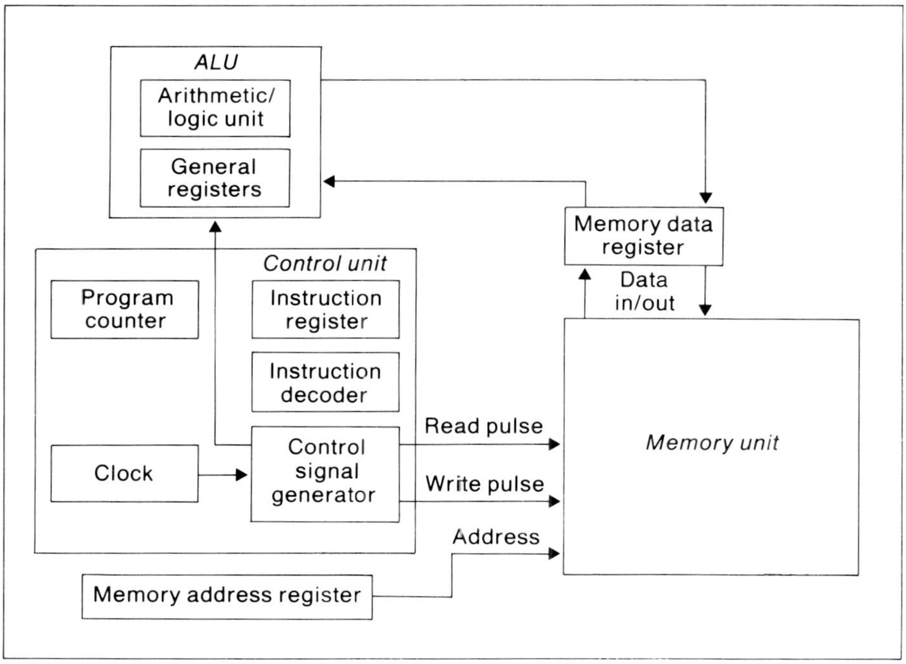

Figure 23 *The CPU showing flow of information and control lines*

Size of memory (bytes)	Addresses	Number of bits required
2^{11} = 2K = 2048	0–2047	11
2^{12} = 4K = 4096	0–4095	12
2^{13} = 8K = 8192	0–8191	13
2^{14} = 16K = 16384	0–16383	14
2^{15} = 32K = 32768	0–32767	15
2^{16} = 64K = 65536	0–65535	16
2^{17} = 128K = 131072	0–131071	17
2^{18} = 256K = 262144	0–262143	18

Figure 24 Number of bits needed to address various sizes of memory

- *Addresses*

Some instructions take data from or store data in the memory. To do this they must be given the address of the location containing the data. The number of bits needed to specify an address depends on how many locations there are altogether in the memory. The lowest address is always zero.

If the memory has 4 kilobytes (ie. 4096 bytes) then the number of bits needed for an address is 12. This is because the addresses range from 0 to 4095. The binary value for 4095 is 1111 1111 1111, ie. 12 bits set to 1. The table below shows the number of bits needed to address all the locations in different sizes of memory.

Control unit. The control unit is the part of the CPU which is responsible for executing instructions. It retrieves the next instruction in the program from the main memory. It decodes this instruction and sets the circuits of the computer ready to carry out the instruction. For instructions which use data it also obtains the data from the correct memory address.

Arithmetic unit. A lot of program instructions carry out arithmetic on data, eg. adding two numbers, multiplying, etc. These operations are carried out by the arithmetic unit under control of the control unit.

Special registers. These are storage locations similar to those in the main memory. But they can be accessed more quickly than main memory locations because they are physically closer to the control unit and the arithmetic unit. Also, each register has a name and does not have to be accessed by an address.

Some registers are used for temporarily holding data during calculations. These are often called **general registers** or **accumulators**. Other registers have a special purpose.

Some examples are listed below:

- ▲ Instruction Register (IR)
- ▲ Memory Address Register (MAR)
- ▲ Memory Buffer Register (MBR) or Memory Data Register (MDR)
- ▲ Program Counter (PC) or Sequence Control Register (SCR).

These registers are used in the execution of an instruction.

Instructions. The instructions executed by the CPU are in **machine code**. Remember, these are held as strings of **binary digits**. A computer is designed to execute a given **instruction set**. This means that the circuits within the CPU are capable of executing a particular set of instructions. Instruction sets vary from computer to computer. For instance, the instruction set for an ICL 2900 is very different to those set for an IBM 370. A Zilog Z80 CPU chip has a different instruction set to a MOS technology 6502 chip, and so on.

An instruction is identified by an **operation code**. A computer may have a hundred or more operation codes in its instruction set. Each of these is represented as a different **binary pattern**.

There are four main types of instructions. These are:

data transfer

arithmetic and logic

test and branch

input and output.

If the instruction is one which operates on data in the main store, it will also include an address as a binary number.

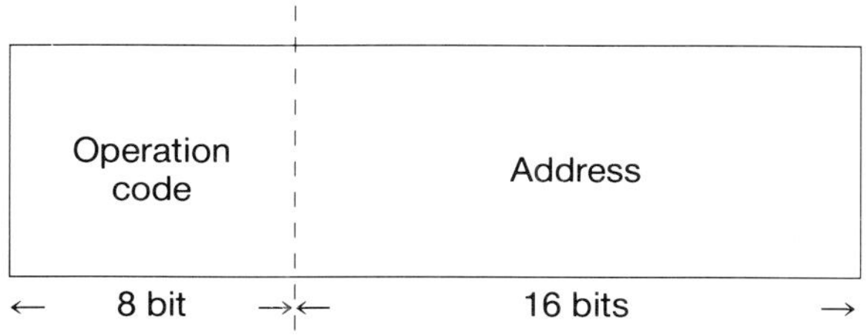

Figure 25 A typical instruction

The diagram above shows the layout of an instruction which contains an address. The operation code uses eight bits, the address uses 16 bits. This means that the maximum number of different instructions is 255 and the highest possible address is 65535 with this layout.

The program in the example shown here loads two values from memory, adds them and puts the answer back in the memory. The machine code shown is for a Z80 CPU. The comments explain what the code is doing. The code is also shown in **assembler level code** (see Chapter 4). Notice how the LD B, A and ADD A, B instructions use one byte but that the others use three. This is because a Z80 can address up to 64 kilobytes. An instruction needs 16 bits (or 2 bytes) for an address. Some CPUs (eg. Z80) can use bytes for operation codes, thereby increasing the number of available instructions.

Example: A machine code program to add two numbers is shown below.

The memory locations contain (after execution) are listed here:

Location	Contents (binary)		Contents (hex)
100	0 0 1 1	1 0 1 0	3A
101	0 0 0 0	0 0 0 0	00
102	0 0 1 0	0 0 0 0	20
103	0 1 0 0	0 1 1 1	47
104	0 0 1 1	1 0 1 0	3A
105	0 0 0 0	0 0 0 1	01
106	0 0 1 0	0 0 0 0	20
107	1 0 0 0	0 0 0 0	80
108	0 0 1 1	0 0 1 0	32
109	0 0 0 0	0 0 1 0	02
10A	0 0 1 0	0 0 0 0	20
10B	0 1 1 1	0 1 1 0	76
2000	0 0 0 0	0 1 0 0	04
2001	0 0 0 0	1 0 0 0	08
2002	0 0 0 0	1 1 0 0	0C

Comments	Memory location (hex)	Mnemonic	Machine code (hex)
Load contents of address 2000H into A	100	LD A, (2000H)	3A0020
Load A into B	103	LD B, A	47
Load content of address 2001H into A	104	LD A, (2001H)	3A0120
Add B to A	107	ADD A, B	80
Load A into address 2002H	108	LD (2002H), A	320220
Halt the program	10B	HALT	76
First number	2000	DEFB 4	04
Second number	2001	DEFB 8	08
Space for result	2002	DEFB 0	00

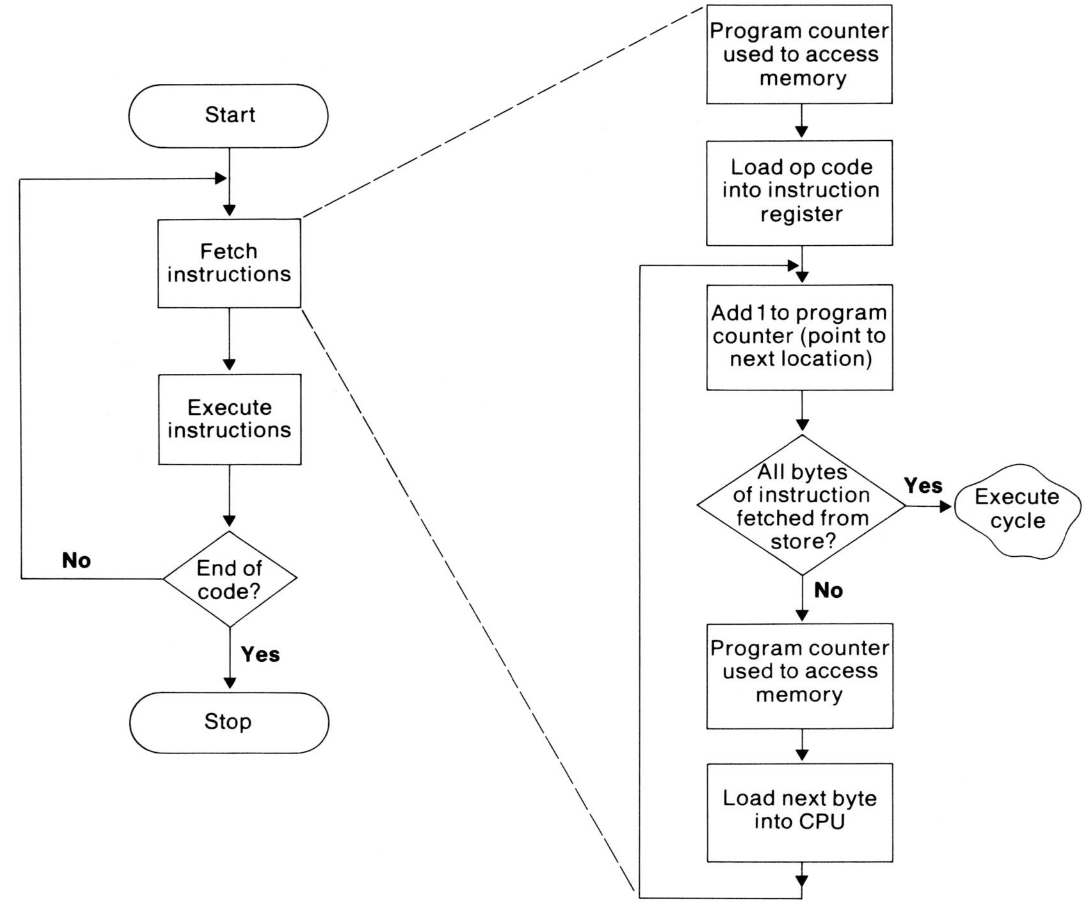

Figure 26 The fetch-execute cycle for a program

The execute cycle is as follows.

- **1** The instruction is in the instruction register (IR). The instruction decoder (ID) sets the control signal generator to send out the correct control signals.
- **2** If the instruction requires data from memory eg. LD A, (ADDR) a read pulse is generated. This takes the contents of the location whose address is in the memory address register (MAR). This is set in the fetch cycle. The contents of the location are put in the memory data register (MDR).
- **3** The data can now be taken from the MDR and put into the arithmetic and logic unit (ALU). The control unit generates the signal for this and the signals for the operation to be performed (eg. ADD).
- **4** If the instruction is one which places data in memory eg. LD (ADDR), A, then the control unit generates signals to transfer data from the ALU into the MDR.
- **5** Once in the MDR, the data may then be transferred to memory. This is done by the control unit generating a WRITE pulse. The address of the location to be used is again in the MAR.

Notice that the steps required are different for loading data into the CPU from memory and storing data into memory from the CPU.

In the example shown earlier the instructions LD A, (ADDR) follow steps **1**, **2** and **3**. The instruction LD (2002H), A follows steps **1**, **4** and **5**. The LD B, A and ADD A, B instructions do not access memory. The control signals for these would be to the ALU only.

■ Machine codes and memory addressing techniques

Earlier, we said that any processor has an instruction set. We can classify the instructions in a machine's instruction set as follows:

▲ Memory reference instructions – these operate on data stored in the memory.

▲ Non-memory reference instructions – these require no data and can operate on data stored in the general purpose registers.

▲ Input/output instructions – these allow transfer of data to and from **peripherals** connected to the computer eg. printers, disk drives.

Let's take a look at some memory referencing operations.

In the example program (p. 169) three instructions refer to memory – LD A, (2000H, LD A, (2001H) and LD (2002H), A. These instructions take values from specified memory locations and store a value in a specified memory location. Most instruction sets also allow the following operations on memory locations:

add the contents of a memory location to a register

subtract the contents of a memory location from a register

compare the contents of a register with a memory location

increment (add one to) the contents of a memory location

combine the contents of a memory location with those of a register by **logically** operating on corresponding **bits** – ANDing, ORing, exclusive ORing (XOR) bit values together

shift the contents left or right, bit by bit, losing bits as they are shifted out of a location; or shifting the bits into the other end of the location in a circular fashion.

All these operations are associated with the data stored in memory. Another type of memory addressing instruction is the **BRANCH** instruction, which causes a jump to a specified location address. BRANCH instructions may be of the following types:

▲ Unconditional – these execute the instruction stored at the specified address, rather than the next instruction in sequence.

▲ Conditional – these execute the instruction stored at the specified address, if the **condition** specified is TRUE.

▲ Subroutine call – these jump to the specified address and execute a sequence of instructions starting at that address. The sequence of instructions will be terminated by an instruction which causes a jump back to the instruction following the subroutine call.

Fig. 27 illustrates these forms of branching.

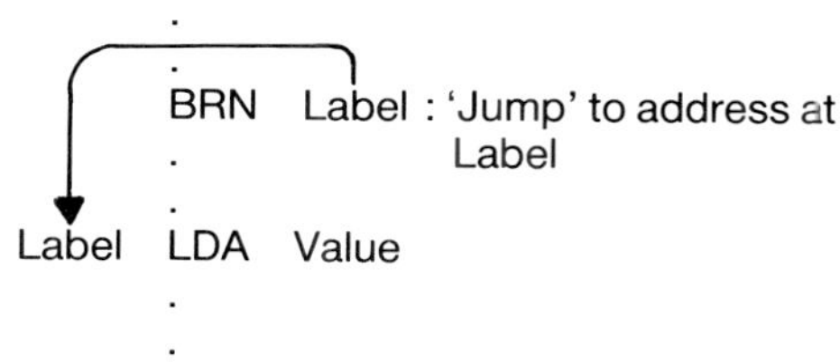

Figure 27 (a) Unconditional branch

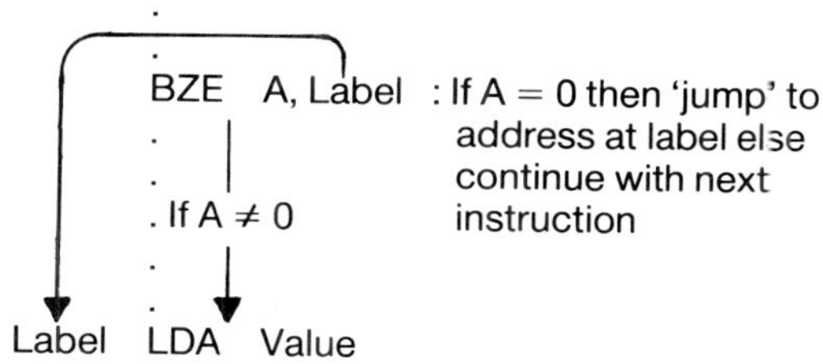

Figure 27 (b) Conditional branch

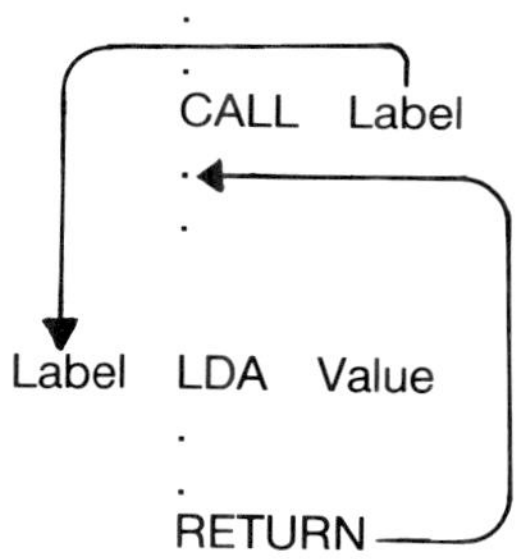

Figure 27 (c) Subroutine call

■ **Types of memory addressing**

● *Direct addressing*

All the instructions looked at so far specify the **absolute address** to be referenced. That is, the address required is stored in the instruction. This is known as **direct addressing**. The range of locations which may be addressed in this way is limited to the number of bits allowed in the instruction (see page 168).

- *Indirect addressing*

In this method the address required is stored in a register, or pair of registers, rather than in the instruction itself. The instruction refers to the register or registers; the register(s) contains the required address. The advantage of this arrangement is that all the register or registers can be used for the address. This allows for larger values to be used, since in direct addressing many bits are used for the operation code. Fig. 28 illustrates this principle.

```
    .
    .
LD   HL, Address  : Store large address in
    .               register pair H and L
LDA  HL           : Load value at address
    .               stored in HL into A
    .
```

Figure 28 Indirect addressing

- *Index addressing*

In this method the instruction contains an address and an index:

eg. LD A, LIST(IX)

The effective address of the location required is obtained by adding the contents of the IX (index) register to the address LIST. The contents of that location are then transferred to the A register. Fig. 29 illustrates this.

```
         .
         .
      LDI   IX, I0        : Set index reg=10
Loop  LDA   Address (IX)  : Load value at
         .                  address +IX in A
      ADD   Total, A      : Add to total
      DEC   IX            : Subtract 1 from
         .                  index register
      BNZ   Loop          : If index register=0,
                            loop
```

Figure 29 Index addressing

This allows for easier processing of lists of data, ie. accessing consecutive locations in sequence by setting IX equal to zero initially and incrementing it by 1 in a loop of instructions to carry out the same operations on a sequence of memory locations. In this way a computer may carry out the processing required for handling arrays (see Chapter 4) in **higher-level languages**.

■ More on memories

There may be more than one memory **unit** in the computer with its own MAR and MDR. In this case, the units are connected to the CPU via a **memory bus**, linking all the units together. Fig. 30 illustrates this.

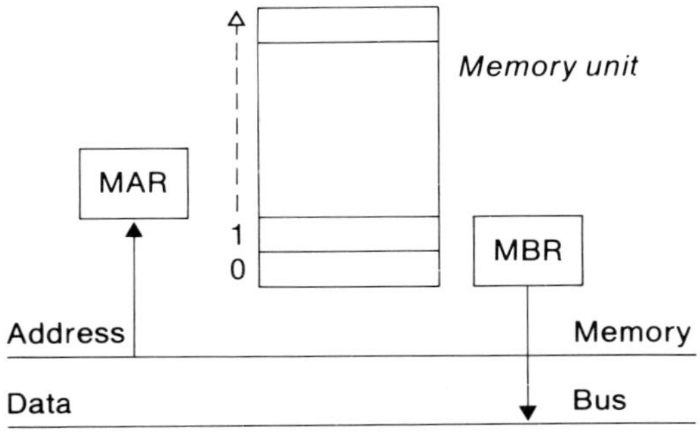

Figure 30 Memory bus

Each memory unit communicates with the CPU via its MAR and MDR registers and the memory bus. The bus is similar to a highway, along which all data and memory references travel.

This approach leads to two main difficulties. These are:

- ▲ Only one memory location may be accessed at one time, limiting processing speeds.
- ▲ There is no physical separation between data and programs. If the program is in error, it may attempt to execute a data item as if it were an instruction.

The **execution speed** of the example program above would be greatly increased if locations 2000H and 2001H could be referenced at the same time. However, the basic Von Neumann model insists that the sequence specified for executing instructions is followed.

To try and improve speed, various new approaches to design have been developed. Some of these approaches are summarised below.

- *Associative memories*

These memories allow for the processing of many locations in **parallel**, based on the **content** of the location and not its address. The executing program does not have to address a location directly. A special mechanism matches an **interrogate register** with a range of memory cells, and produces an output in a **data-out register** if the required data is present. A 'no match flag' is set if the required value is not present.

- *Interleaved memories*

In interleaved memories the memory is divided into **banks** of locations, each with its own MAR and MDR. The banks are connected directly to a processing unit, rather than via a **common bus**. Therefore, it is possible to access a word from all banks of the memory at the same time. The sequence of program instructions may be divided up between the banks of memory so that several instructions from the program, and the required data, may be accessed at the same time.

In addition to the development of approaches to faster memory accessing there have also been the development of **parallel processing** machines.

■ Parallel computing

Parallel processing means executing different parts of the same program at the same time. Following is a summary of some of the approaches to providing computers which do their processing in parallel rather than in sequence.

- *Look ahead or pipeline processors*

Pipeline processing means that as the processor is executing a particular instruction as described in the **fetch-execute cycle** above, the next instruction in sequence is being fetched from the memory ready for execution. Thus, the processing of instructions is overlapped.

Fig. 31 illustrates this.

The fetch cycle for the next instruction is overlapped with the current instruction's execute cycle.

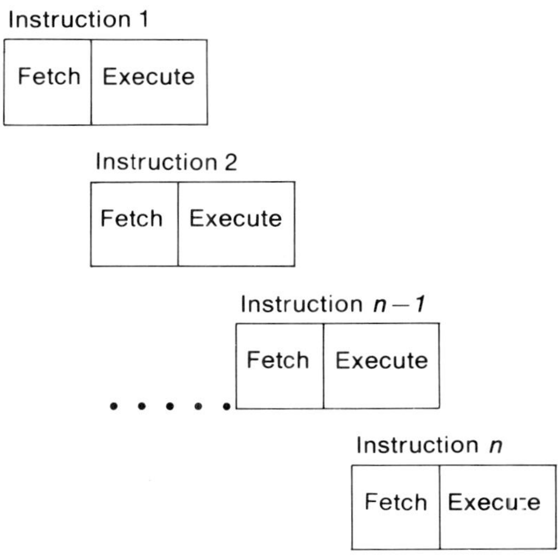

Figure 31 Pipeline processing

- *Array processors*

In array processing machines there are a number of processing units. Each processing unit may operate on different parts of the memory at the same time. The data to be processed is divided up and stored in the separate memory units. The program is designed to allow for the processing of the different memory areas at the same time. Some large scale and time-consuming applications such as weather forecasting benefit from this approach. Example machines are the ICL DAP and CRAY machines.

- *Dataflow machines*

Dataflow machines are based on the principle that an instruction will execute when its data is available. There is no fixed sequence of control. If there are several instructions with their data available, they can execute. This means that there must be a processor available for each instruction which is ready to execute.

Fig. 32 illustrates how a dataflow computer may execute a program.

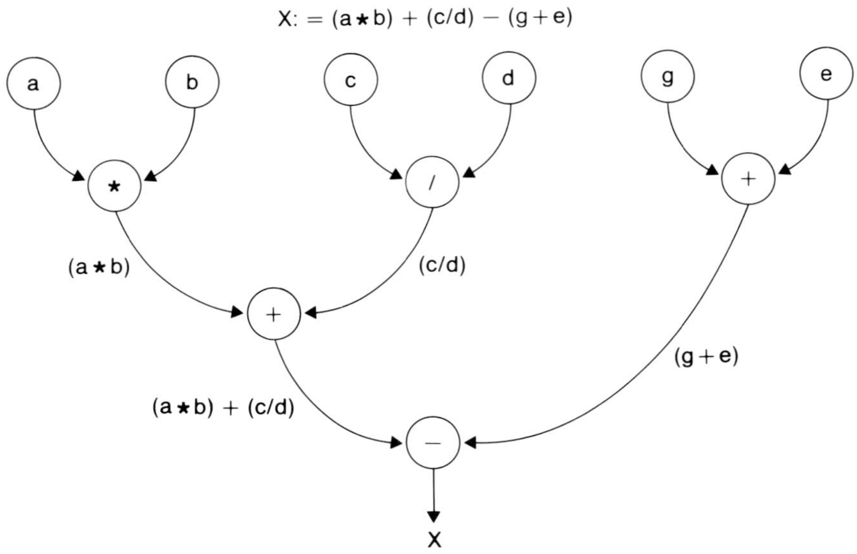

Figure 32 The dataflow model – each operator may execute a program when it has all its inputs

- *The transputer*

The transputer is essentially a computer on a **chip**. It consists of a processor, memory, registers and input-output channels – all on one chip. It may be used as a conventional single-processor computer. It may also be connected with other transputers. Each transputer may be executing a different part of the same program at the same time. If data needs to be transferred from one transputer to another, it may be passed over **point-to-point connections** ie. directly from one transputer to another.

The transputer has been designed along with its own parallel programming language, **Occam**. (See the reader: **The Transputer – Main Concepts** for further information.)

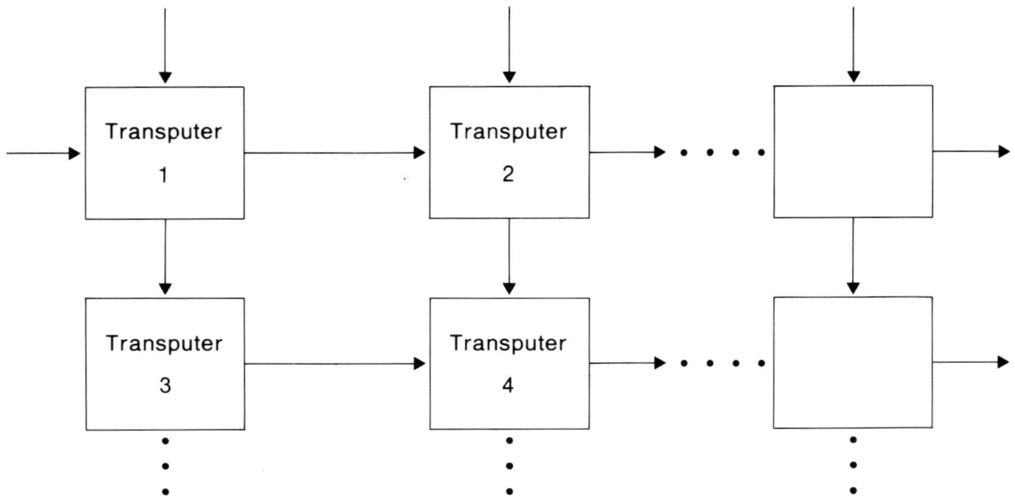

Figure 33 Any number of transputers may be linked together with direct links – providing many computers

■ Summary

The basic design of most computers is based on a **global** memory and a processor. The processor executes instructions from a program stored in the memory in a strict sequence, controlled by the program counter. The data required by the program is also stored in the memory, and is taken from and put into the memory according to instructions in the program. This approach to computer design was first proposed and developed by John Von Neumann.

There are various techniques available for **addressing** the memory and these are provided for in the processor's **instruction set**.

The approach of a single instruction execution and accessing the memory has long been recognised as an obstacle to increasing computing speeds. Various developments in the design of memories and ways of accessing the memory have aimed to reduce these delays (often called the Von Neumann bottleneck!).

Parallel processing is regarded as providing the solution to the problem of how to make computing faster. The **transputer**, along with its programming language, Occam, is regarded as one of the major breakthroughs in parallel computer design.

■ Interrupts

During the execution of a program many situations can arise which require prompt attention, either to utilise the whole computer system efficiently or to prevent a serious mishap occurring. In order to ensure that such situations are dealt with as quickly as necessary, the execution of the current program is **interrupted**. The computer is then able to execute a special program which determines the cause of the interrupt and deals with it accordingly. After this interruption has been dealt with, the original program can be resumed at the point of interruption, unless it was a computer error or programming error which caused the interrupt.

Interrupts may occur for a variety of reasons. These are:

hardware faults

program errors

input/output.

● *Hardware faults*

The circuits in a computer carry out various checks for any malfunctions. Two examples of these are power failure and memory **parity checks**.

To maintain correct functioning a computer requires a steady, uninterrupted electricity supply. If the power fails or voltage begins to fluctuate the contents of **registers** and **memory** may be lost or become corrupted. If such a problem occurs it is necessary to suspend processing until the problem is rectified. The computer may detect a voltage drop and assume that the power is beginning to fail. This will cause the generation of an interrupt to stop the processing, and store the contents of the registers in a **non-volatile** memory. When the power is restored, the contents of the registers may be reset and the program resumed from the point at which it was stopped.

● *Program errors*

Running programs may accidently contain errors which may cause the generation of interrupts. Example of these errors are as follows:

▲ **Overflow errors:** The earlier section on Representing fractions and real numbers describes how **overflow errors** may occur. When these errors occur, an interrupt is generated. A message will be output, signalling the error and maybe stopping the program in which the error occurred.

▲ **Memory protection violation:** A running program may inadvertantly try to change the contents of a memory location which ies outside the range allowed. An example is an address which is occupied by the **operating system**. The operating system is **protected** from such illegal operations. If this occurs, an interrupt is generated and the program causing the error is suspended.

● *Input/output*

The CPU executes instructions at very high speed. Peripherals operate much more slowly. While data is being transferred to or from a peripheral, the CPU may be doing other processing. To make full use of the CPU, it continues to run a program whilst data is being transferred to and from the peripheral device. When the device has finished transferring data, it generates an interrupt to the CPU to indicate it is ready to resume running the program which executed the i/o instruction.

• *Handling interrupts*

Here is a list of the steps involved in handling interrupts.

1 The main program receives an interrupt signal.
2 The execution of the main program stops.
3 The contents of the general registers and the program counter are stored.
4 The computer jumps to the start of the **interrupt service routine**.
5 The interrupt service routine runs.
6 At the end of the interrupt service routine the contents of the registers and program counter are reset.
7 The interrupted program resumes from the point just after it was interrupted.

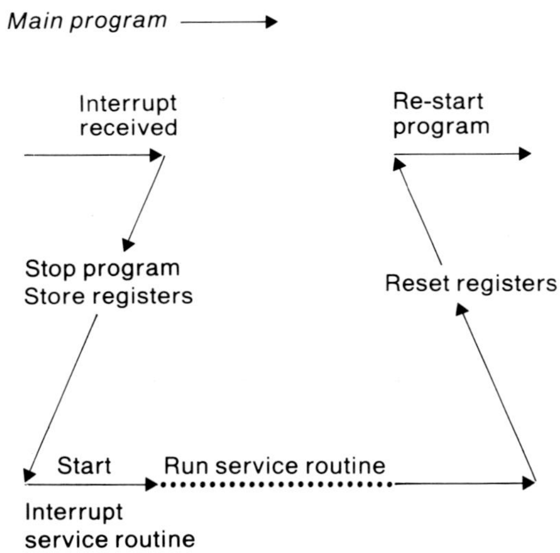

Figure 34 Interrupt service routine sequence

If the computer is running a **multi-programming** system (see Chapter 5), it could be running another program whilst the interrupted program is suspended.

• *Identifying interrupt sources*

A computer may receive interrupts from different sources – from different peripherals, memory faults and so on. Each type of interrupt will have a different interrupt service routine. To know which one to run, the interrupt source must be identified. This may be done by software or hardware.

• *Software identification of interrupts*

When a device signals an interrupt request, the hardware causes control to transfer to a service routine as described above. In that description it was assumed that this would be the device service routine. If, however, there can be a number of devices attached to this line, the routine will be an **interrupt service routine** whose task is to identify the device requesting the interrupt and then to transfer control to its **device service routine**.

In order to determine which device is requesting the interrupt, the routine will examine all the devices on that line, one at a time. This is known as **software polling**. A common technique is to make use of a special **skip** instruction which allows examination of a particular peripheral device **interface**.

On a peripheral device interface there is often a **flag bit** which is set to one when an interrupt request is generated and back to zero when the interrupt has been dealt with. One of the set of input-output instructions examines this flag and skips the next instruction when it is set to 0.

An example of a software polling interrupt service is shown in Fig. 35 opposite. It assumes that four devices are attached to the same **interrupt request line**, that memory location 0 is used to store the **program counter**, and that the program was executing the instruction at location 4000 when it was interrupted.

• *Hardware identification of interrupts*

Identification by software is relatively slow, especially for the last device to be **polled**. An alternative approach is to provide special hardware to identify and respond to interrupts.

In this case the CPU responds to an interrupt by sending out, on a separate line, an **interrupt acknowledge signal (INTA)** to each device, Only the device that generated the original interrupt signal will respond. It does this by supplying the CPU with the starting address of its service routine.

• *Interrupt priorities*

Often the computer will receive an interrupt whilst a previous one is still being serviced. This interrupt may have a higher or lower **priority** than the one currently being serviced.

Address	Mnemonic/contents	
0	4001	Location for saving program counter for returning to the main program.
1000	SKDEV1	Skip next instruction if device is not requesting an interrupt.
1001	BRN2000	Jump to location 2000 (start of interrupt service routine for device 1).
1002	SKDEV2	As for device 1.
1003	BRN2575	2575 is start address for device 2.
1006	SKDEV4	
1007	BRN4450	
2000		Start address of service routine for device 1.
2574	BR 0	Jump to location stored in 0 – the address of the next instruction in the main program.
2575		Start of service routine for device 2.
⋮	⋮	etc.

Figure 35 Software polling interrupt service sequence

If an interrupt with a higher priority is received, the current service routine must be suspended. The service routine for the higher priority interrupt will start to run. When completed, the original service routine will be resumed. The interrupts are said to be **nested**. The second interrupt routine may itself be interrupted by a yet higher priority interrupt, and so on. Each interrupted routine will resume at the point of suspension as the higher priority routine completes. Eventually, the program which was running when the original interrupt was received will be resumed. Fig. 36 illustrates the 'nesting' of interrupts.

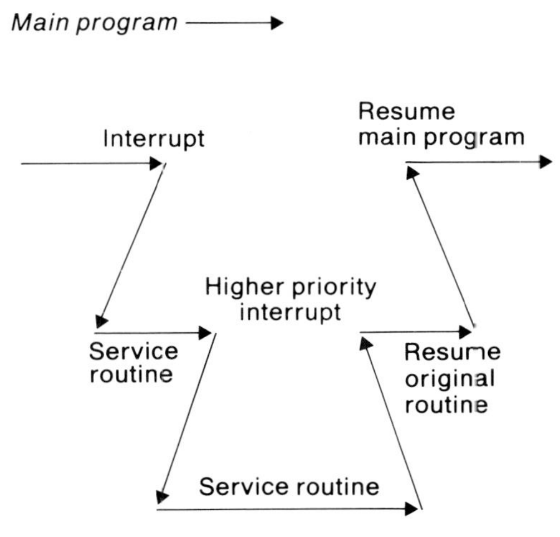

Figure 36 "Nested" interrupts

■ Summary

In many computer applications it is necessary to be able to interrupt the normal execution of programs in order to service higher priority requests that need urgent attention. Most computers have a mechanism for dealing with these requests. The complexity of the facilities provided for handling such interrupts varies from computer to computer.

Using hardware rather than software to handle interrupts is faster. The falling cost of hardware means that more and more machines use hardware to do the work required.

QUESTIONS

1 The contents of a particular register can be written in hexadecimal format as E6.

(a) If this bit pattern were to represent in turn

(i) an unsigned integer

(ii) an integer in two's complement form,

what would be the decimal value of each representation?

(b) Write down the contents of this register, in hexadecimal format, after it has been subjected to an arithmetic shift of one place to the right.

[ULSEB 1989] Specimen paper 105

2 (a) Describe, with the aid of examples, the fixed-point and floating-point representations of numbers. Explain why both forms are needed and show how positive and negative numbers can be catered for in each representation.

(b) Choose appropriate fixed-point and floating-point representations to store the numbers

$$-256 \text{ and } 512.875$$

using a 24-bit word. Express each number in your representation in octal and hexadecimal notation. What are the largest numbers that can be stored in your representation and what is the accuracy that can be achieved in each case?

(c) Summarise the processes that are involved when a computer performs floating-point arithmetic. How do these differ from those used in fixed-point arithmetic?

[WJEC 1988] Computer Science A2

3 (a) Summarise the elements of Boolean Algebra and explain how they can be used in the design of a simple logical device. Write down truth tables to describe the

(i) AND gate,

(ii) OR gate,

(iii) NAND gate,

and show how the AND and OR gates can be expressed in terms of NAND gates.

(b) A company selling burglar alarms for houses and offices uses a computer to control the alarm. Sensors are placed in the rooms at the entry points, one at each window and external door. A firm contacts the burglar alarm company with a view to having an alarm installed in one of its offices.

The office has four external doors, five rear windows and four front windows. Each evening the office windows and doors are shut securely and checked by a security guard. The managing director of the firm wishes to install a display panel, at head office, with indicator lights to show whether any window or door has been opened by an intruder. The alarm company proposes three such lights, E, R and F where:

E indicates at least one external door is open;

R indicates at least one rear window is open;

F indicates at least one front window is open.

Each of the 13 sensors, four on the doors, nine on the windows, is given a unique number from 1–15. If any one of the windows or doors is opened then the corresponding number, in binary, is used to set to 1 the appropriate bits A, B, C, D of a control register.

(i) Assuming that the doors are numbered 12, 13, 14 and 15 assign suitable numbers to each of the windows.

(ii) Write down a truth table linking the indicators E, R and F to the four bits A, B, C and D.

(iii) Devise minimal logical expressions for E, R and F in terms of A, B, C and D for your assignments of numbers.

[WJEC 1988] Computer Science A1

4 For 30 years, Colonel Wythington-Smythe has drunk a special brew of tea prepared for him by his butler. Unfortunately, the butler has recently passed on, but, being an amateur chemist, has left detailed notes concerning the unique brew. Having become something of a recluse, the colonel has ordered that an automatic, computer-controlled, teamaker be constructed to provide him with the drink to which he has become accustomed.

Design an appropriate system for the colonel. The device should ensure that the water is really boiling as it is added to the pot and should be able to withdraw a bag of tea leaves from the pot when the brew is at a predetermined strength. The device should not fill the colonel's cup too full either!

[UCLES 1989] AS 8420/1

5 Illustrate diagrammatically and explain the relationship between the components of a computer system comprising: Central Processing Unit (CPU); main memory; backing store; input/output devices; data, address and control buses.

[*SCE Higher 1990*] *Specimen paper*

6 (a) Describe what is meant by the fetch-execute cycle. Explain carefully the use of internal registers in the fetch process.
(b) What is an **interrupt**? How do interrupts influence the fetch-execute cycle?

[*ULSEB 1989*] *Specimen paper 105*

7 (a) Explain what happens when a peripheral device requiring attention sends an **interrupt** to the processor.
(b) Why do interrupts from different peripheral devices normally have various levels of **priority**?

[*WJEC 1989*]

8 What are the limitations of a conventional processor? Why is there such interest in overcoming these limitations? Outline a technique that may be used to overcome these limitations.

[*ULSEB 1989*] *Specimen paper 105*

Reader The transputer—main concepts

Conventional approaches to hardware developments have led to bottlenecks in **memory accessing**. Adding extra processing elements to systems and connecting them via **communications busses** has also led to problems of **contention** on the communication paths. So, despite tremendous increases in the computing power available on modern processing **chips** a fundamental restriction to achieving significant increases in power is apparent.

Requirements for '5th generation' computing are predicted to be of the order of **10 mips**. Thus a shortfall of computing power is expected to be a major obstacle to the future development of advanced systems.

Transputer system throughput

The transputer approach is to greatly increase **concurrency** available in a given system. This is to be achieved by building systems from a number of individual units, each one of these units consists of a processor and local memory. Each of these units is a **transputer**. The transputer is a processor with its own memory (transputer derives from 'trans'istor/com'puter'). A single transputer may carry out concurrent processing because it is provided with the capability for **timeslicing** ie. processing with apparent concurrency. But the transputer is designed as a building block to be used to build larger systems. Such systems can thus provide actual **parallelism**. Any number of transputers may be linked together and run in parallel to achieve a high degree of true parallelism. Each transputer is also provided with the means of handling 'simple' **communication channels**.

The y-axis of the graph indicates the instruction processing rates of a **transputer** system (million instructions per second) and the **data transmission rates** (million bytes per second) over the communications channels. In other words the processing rates and communication rates increase in direct proportion. Additionally, the

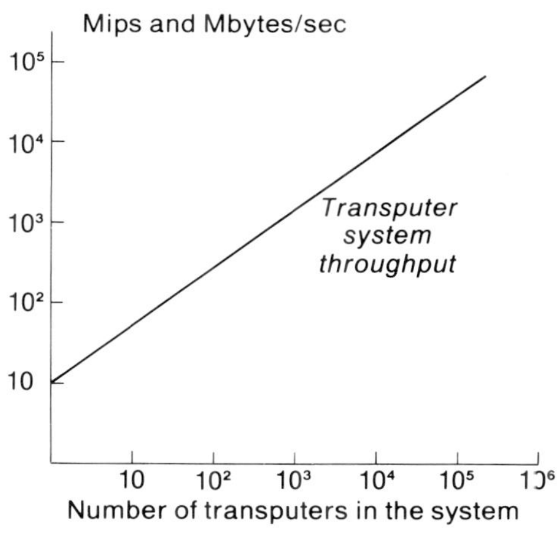

processing and communication rates increase linearly as the number of transputers in the system increases. Inmos (the manufacturers) make this claim, and theoretically this would appear to provide an infinitely powerful computing system.

The transputer processing model

The transputer provides an implementation of the **process** model of concurrent processing. This is essentially the model which requires the programmer to describe an **algorithm** in **sequential** form. Parallelism is achieved by creating separate 'chunks' of sequential code and executing these in parallel. The definition of what can be executed in parallel and where a sequence must be enforced has to be defined 'explicitly' by the programmer.

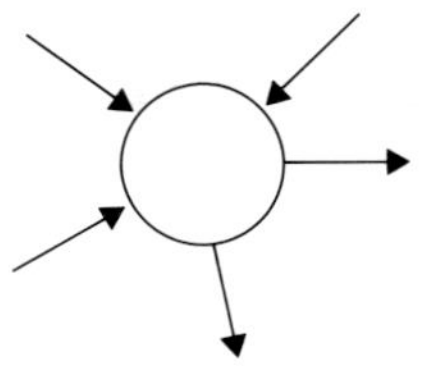

A process is a single 'black box' which receives inputs, produces output and does some processing. In other words we don't care what goes on inside the box. (A single transputer may be one process.)

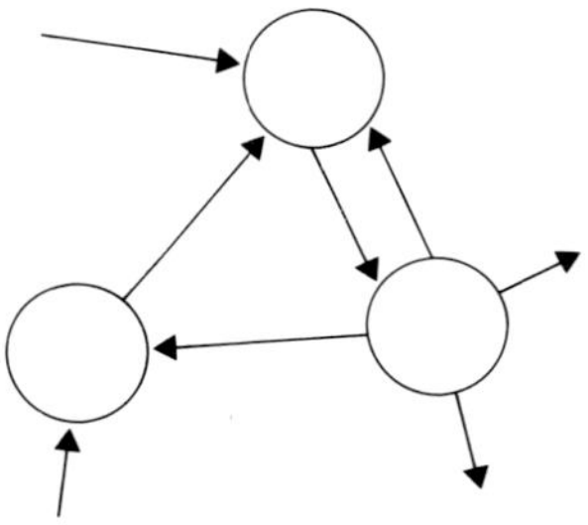

Processes may be linked together to build more complex and truly parallel systems.

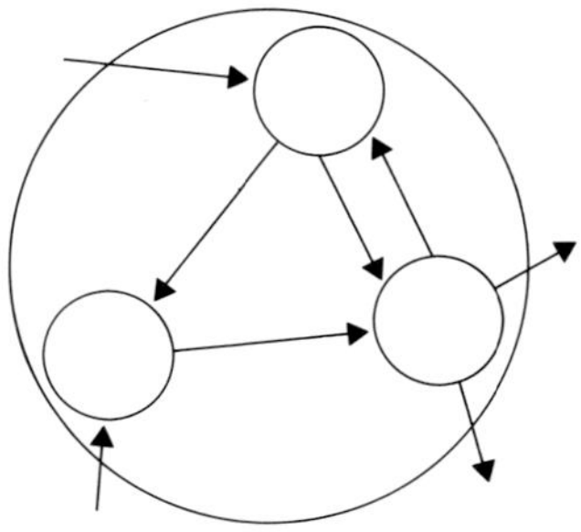

A collection of processes is itself a process (ie. A black box containing several transputers). Processes may have internal concurrency. In this way a **hierarchical** approach may be taken to designing and building a system.

A single transputer may run an OCCAM program with PAR (ie. run in parallel) constructs and channel usage. The concurrency is apparent, each transputer is provided with a 'hardwired' program which **timeslices** the processor between processes described as executing in parallel. Communication channels are **simulated** in the local memory.

In this way a single transputer may be programmed in the same way as many. A program may be developed on a single transputer and transported almost directly to a system of many transputers.

The communication links

Transputers communicate by means of **point-to-point** communications links. The advantages of this are:

There is no **contention** for the communications mechanism. For example, a **communication bus** with many links to it becomes overloaded as more links are added.

The communications capacity increases as processors are added.

By using local memory at each processor the overall **bandwidth** increases as processors are added. With a **global memory**, extra processors reduce the effective memory availability.

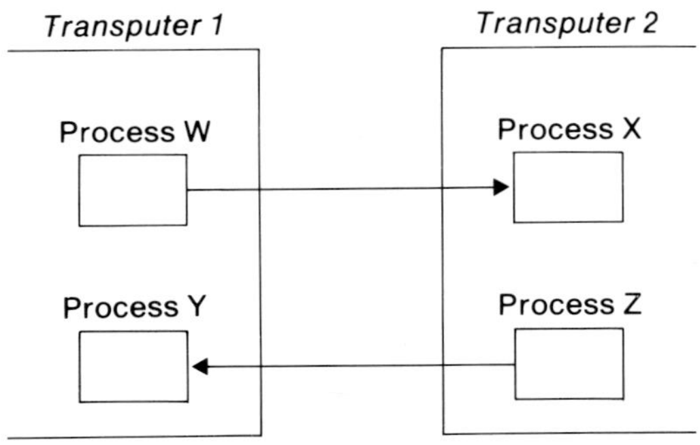

Each transputer is provided with 4 communication links. Each link provides 2 OCCAM channels, one in each direction.

Each link consists of a **serial input** and a **serial output** channel. A **message** is transmitted as a sequence of bytes. A message is passed as follows:

The sender process sends a data byte to the receiving process.

The sender waits for an **acknowledgement** from the receiver, signifying that it is to receive another byte. This continues until all the bytes are transferred.

The receiver starts to send an acknowledgement as soon as it starts to receive a byte, therefore transmission may be continuous.

In this way **synchronisation** is provided down to **byte** level and the communicating processes may run at different speeds.

Programming languages for the transputer

OCCAM is the language provided with the transputer. This language was developed alongside the transputer to avoid the traditional 'now we have the hardware lets think about programming it' syndrome. The language may be regarded as a **high level machine language**.

Other high level languages are available, such as FORTRAN, PASCAL and C. However, it would be interesting to see whether the compilers for these languages allow exploitation of the parallelism available.

The transputer general specification

The transputer chip has the following general specification:

A **32 bit** processor capable of running at **10 mips**.
On board **2k RAM** with a maximum data rate of **80 Mbytes/sec**.
This memory is directly accessible by the processor and by each of the 4 links.
Each link provides a **full duplex 10 Mbits/sec** data communications line.
It provides a direct address space of up to **4 Gbytes** via the **memory interface** at a data rate of **25 Mbytes/sec**.
Provides linking facilities for external peripherals, byte wide or memory mapped.
On board software handles the **communication protocols** for the channels and **timeslicing** of the processor when necessary.

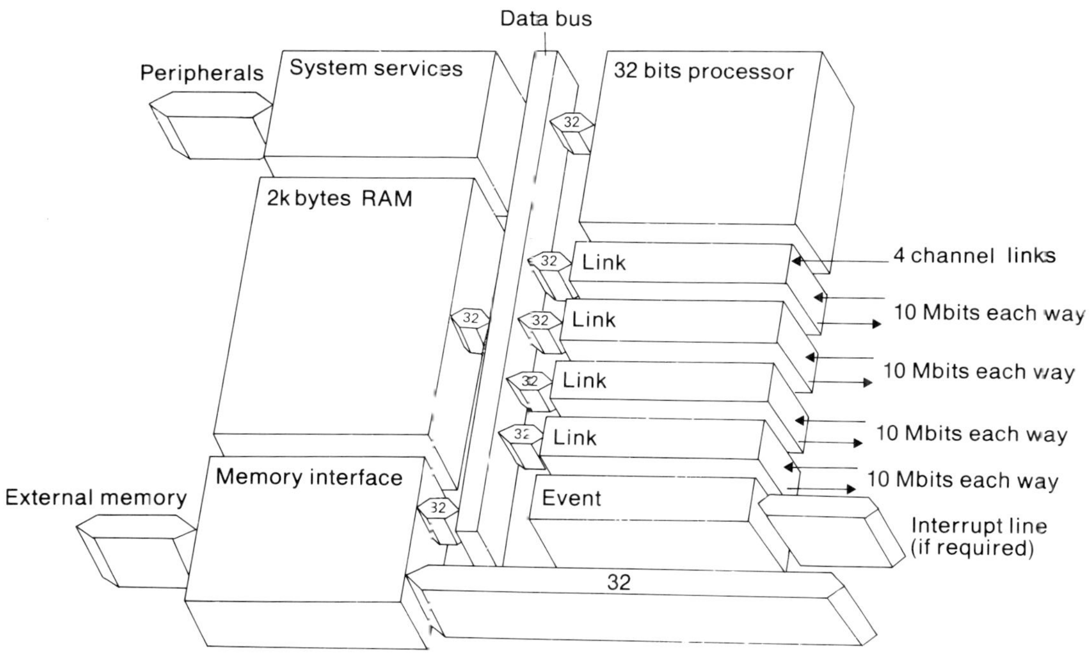

General schematic of a transputer

Questions

1 How does the transputer provide the increase in power described in the reader?

2 Why does the communication bandwidth increase as processes are added?

3 By referring to Chapter 5, describe a process and how a scheduler 'timeslices' a single process between other processes.

CHAPTER 7

Data Transfer and Communications

INTRODUCTION

The CPU and memory in a computer carry out the processing required to execute program instructions and manipulate data. But to be useful a computer must be able to **communicate** – to accept input and to produce output. Computers communicate by transferring data via input and output **peripherals**.

Increasing use of data **communications** is also being made, linking computers over short and long distances and transferring data between them. This may be done to **distribute** information in rapid and inexpensive forms, or to distribute processing of data, allowing for more than one computer to be processing the data at the same time.

This chapter looks at the techniques used in handling the transfer of data between computers and peripherals and over **computer networks**.

HANDLING INPUT AND OUTPUT

The CPU executes instructions which transfer, calculate and compare data. The running program may also input data from, or output data to, peripherals. A peripheral could be:

a keyboard – input

a printer – output

a disk drive – input or output

a VDU screen – output.

These are examples of peripherals that are commonly connected to general purpose computers. If the CPU is part of a **computer-controlled** system (for example, in the Kew Gardens case study) then the peripherals may also be:

a temperature sensor – input

a pressure sensor – input

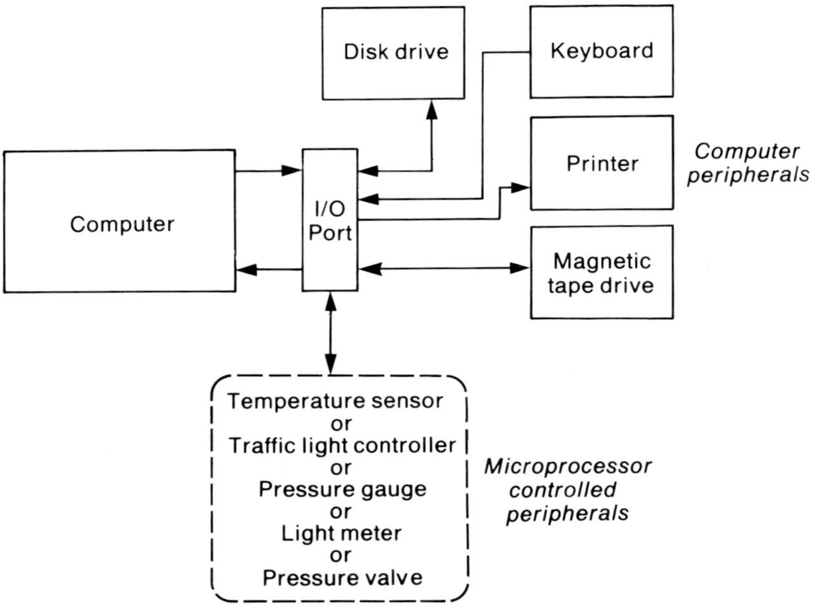

Figure 1 A computer may be connected to a variety of peripherals

a switch on a motor – output

a humidity sensor – input

a water valve – output.

The examples are endless, the actual input and output devices depend on the system being controlled. Fig. 1 shows the general arrangement of computer and peripherals.

■ Input/output bus and the input/output interface

Usually a computer has several input/output (i/o) devices connected to it. To allow the computer to select a device for a particular task, the devices are connected to the computer via an **input/output bus (i/o bus)**.

Fig. 2 illustrates a set of devices connected to the bus, which in turn, is connected to the computer.

The i/o bus is similar to the internal CPU bus system described in Chapter 6. Connected to the wires which form the i/o bus are **registers** – the **peripheral interface**. Each device connected has one of these peripheral interfaces containing its own set of registers. These are outside the control of the CPU.

The i/o bus consists of three sets of lines used for the transmission of address, data and control signals. When the CPU wishes to send data to or receive data from a particular i/o device it places a unique identity code, or **address**, on the address line. This is used to identify which i/o device is required. For example, the CPU may want to send data to device 1 in Fig. 2. The **identity code** on the address line will ensure that only that device will respond. It will respond according to the command placed on the control line, taking the data from the data line. Once the CPU has initiated or started the action in the relevant i/o interface it no longer has control over the operation.

To read data from one of the peripheral devices, the following sequence is followed:

1 Transfer data from device to i/o interface.

2 Transfer data from i/o interface to a register in the CPU over the i/o bus.

3 Transfer the data from the register to the memory.

Writing data to a device is the reverse of this process.

The interface is the **communication link**. It includes three basic elements:

▲ **A control bit** – a **one-bit register** (flip-flop) which when turned on generates a start command to the device to begin its input or output.

▲ **A flag bit** – set to 1 when the transmission between the device and its interface is complete. It may be tested or cleared under program control. (The program may repeatedly test to see if the transmission is completed.)

▲ **A buffer register** – the register in which the data is to be written, or which has been read is stored.

When a start command is generated, one character is transferred between the interface buffer register and the device or vice versa.

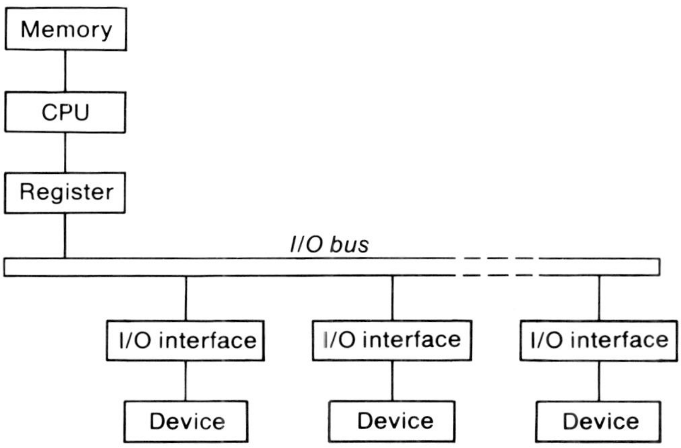

Figure 2 The i/o bus

■ Programming for input and output

Any input and output will be controlled by a program running in the CPU. The program will want to output to or input from a device. The program may be a **control program** which needs to respond to an input received following an **interrupt** (see Chapter 6). In all cases it is the responsibility of the running program to handle the i/o.

Following is a description of some techniques and the characteristics of approaches to programming i/o.

● *Input/output using 'Wait for Flag'*

The simplest way to program for i/o is to command the i/o operation to start and then wait for it to complete. Remember that the interface contains a flag bit which is set to 1 when a transfer is complete. By starting the transfer and then repeatedly testing the flag bit until it is set to 1, the program execution can be delayed until the transfer is complete. The **pseudocode** (see Chapter 4) and example code in Fig. 3 illustrate this for input and output.

So, why does the executing program have to wait for the transfer to be completed? To answer this we need to consider the relative speeds at which the CPU and memory, and peripherals operate. Most peripherals contain mechanical elements which operate at speeds which are very slow compared with the time taken to execute a program instruction. To allow for the device to complete the transfer of a character, the program must 'wait' for the transfer to be completed. If it didn't then it would be attempting to send the next character to the device before the previous one had been dealt with. If the device is a keyboard then the program is also dependent upon the rate at which a person types – which varies enormously from person to person.

The **loop of code** shown in Fig. 3 is often referred to as a **delay** or **idle** loop. The computer effectively does nothing until the i/o device is ready to receive or send the next character.

The disadvantage of this is that the computer spends more time 'waiting' (ie. doing nothing) than it does actually transferring data. The CPU is made to operate at the speed of the i/o device. This may result in the CPU spending up to 99% of its time doing nothing!

```
INPUT

Set control bit on I/O interface to 1
Start to transfer a character
Repeat
  do nothing
Until transfer is complete (i.e. flag bit set to 1)
Load contents of interface buffer into the
accumulator


OUTPUT

Load contents of the accumulator into the I/O
buffer register
Set control bit on I/O interface to 1
Start to transfer a character
Repeat
  do nothing
Until transfer is complete (i.e. flag bit set to 1)
```

Figure 3 Pseudocode for input and output using "wait for flag"

● *Input/output using interrupts*

Interrupts and **interrupt handling** are described in Chapter 6. Using interrupts removes the need for repeatedly testing the flag bit to detect when the transfer is complete. The i/o transfer is initiated by the computer, which may then continue processing. When the i/o device has completed the transfer it issues an interrupt to the computer. This in turn causes the computer to execute an **interrupt service routine** (as described in Chapter 6). This transfers the character from the i/o buffer register to the computer. The i/o transfer for the next character may then be initiated as before, and the computer may continue processing until the next interrupt, and so on.

With this approach, we can see that the computer is doing useful work for more of the time. It is not being continuously put into a delay-loop. The only time wasted is the time taken for transfer of control to and from the interrupt service routine. Fig. 4 opposite shows a flow diagram for this processing when inputting a string of 20 characters.

● *Input/output using Direct Memory Access (DMA)*

With the two methods described above the transfer of each character has to be dealt with by the CPU. This causes no problems if the i/o transfer rate is reasonably slow and if the number of characters to be transferred is small.

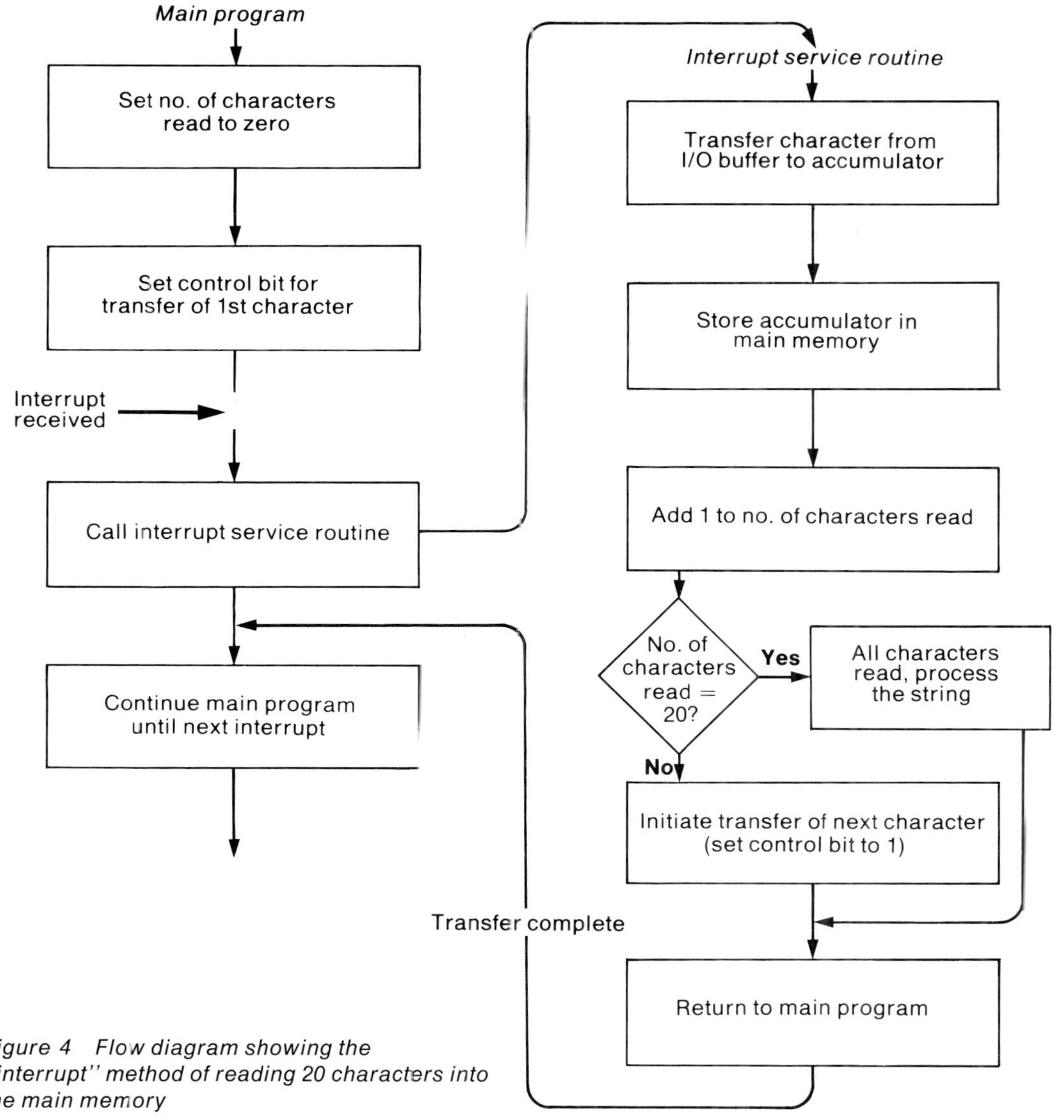

Figure 4 Flow diagram showing the "interrupt" method of reading 20 characters into the main memory

However, for i/o devices such as disk drives, those methods are too slow. Transfers to and from disk drives usually involve large volumes of data and the transfer is at high speed. The speed of transfer may be such that the CPU would not have time to process an interrupt before the next transfer was ready. To avoid these problems a technique which doesn't use the CPU at all is required. **Direct Memory Access (DMA)** is a technique which uses a separate **controller** for handling data transfers between i/o devices (usually disk drives) and memory. The controller is a hardware device which is programmed to carry out the data transfers.

Fig. 5 overleaf illustrates the layout of a computer incorporating a **DMA controller**.

The DMA controller hardware consists of:

- a register for generating the required memory address
- a register for the **word count**
- a register for instructions from the CPU
- a register to act as a data buffer register between the i/o device and the main memory.

Notice that the DMA controller is connected to the CPU. This is so that it may receive instructions from a running program to initiate data transfers.

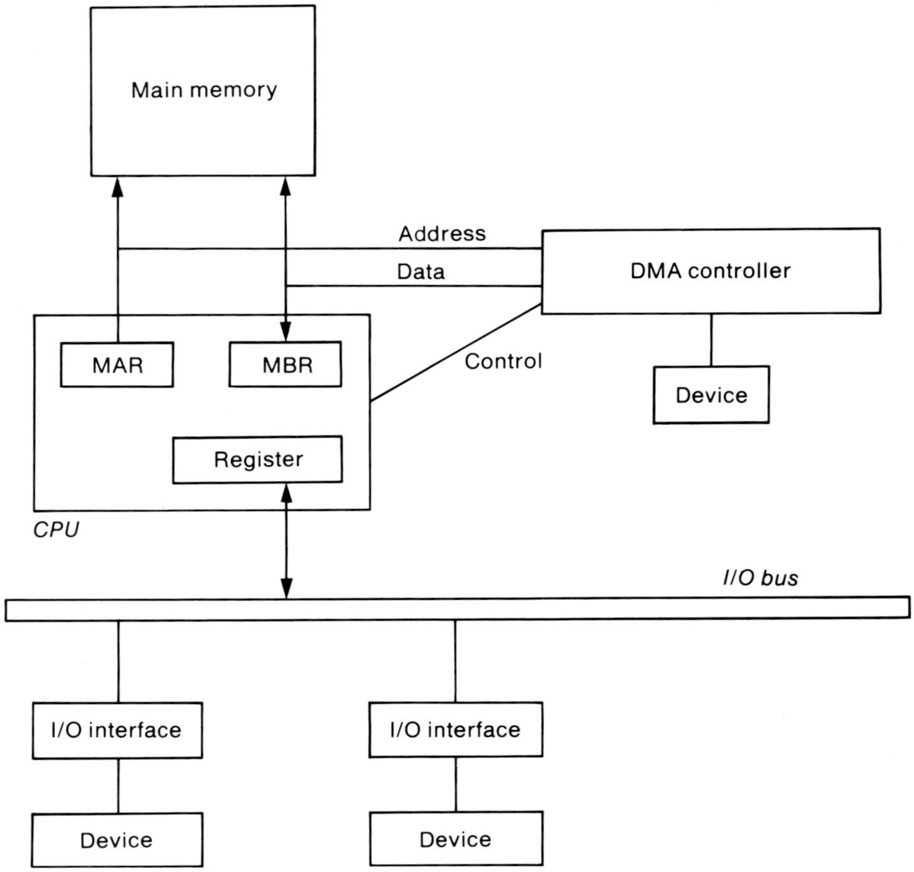

Figure 5 A computer incorporating a DMA controller

To start an i/o transfer using DMA, the following sequence is executed:

- ▲ Load the initial memory address to receive the data or take data from.
- ▲ Load the count of the number of **words** to be transferred.
- ▲ Load a control word to indicate read or write (input or output).
- ▲ Start the transfer.

Once the transfer is started the CPU may continue processing, allowing the DMA controller to handle the data transfer.

With devices such as disk drives, the data transfer will usually transfer a large number of **words** in one read or write operation. When the transfer is complete, the data will be stored in memory in an area available for access by the running program.

■ Summary

There are various approaches to programming for i/o. The requirements of the approaches taken depend upon how much data is transferred at each transfer and the speed of the i/o device, relative to the speed of the computer.

'Wait for Flag' is the simplest approach for single character transfers, but is very wasteful of processing – the CPU spends a lot of its time 'waiting' for transfers to complete. Using interrupts allows the CPU to do more work by allowing it to respond to an interrupt when the transfer is complete. However, even with interrupt processing the CPU has to be involved directly with each data transfer and this may not be adequate for high speed and large volume transfers. Direct memory addressing relieves the CPU of the need to be involved in data transfers by allowing the i/o device to communicate directly with the main memory.

DATA COMMUNICATIONS

Computer systems are increasingly becoming **distributed**. That is, computers are connected over some form of **communications mechanism**. This provides the following advantages over **centralised** computing, where all processing is done in one place. It provides:

- ▲ Shared processing – reducing the overall time taken to do work by sharing it out.
- ▲ Remote access to data – data may be extracted from, or input to data files via terminals sited long distances away from the files.
- ▲ Computing power in convenient locations – organisations may provide individuals with their own computer with links to other users and central data files.

Fig. 6 illustrates some of the possible ways that distributed computing is used, including the possibility of 'working from home'. The study of Data Communications includes:

- ▲ Looking at the detail of how data is **transmitted** and handled in **communication systems.**
- ▲ Considering how **distributed systems** are used in organisations.

We'll start by looking at the detail.

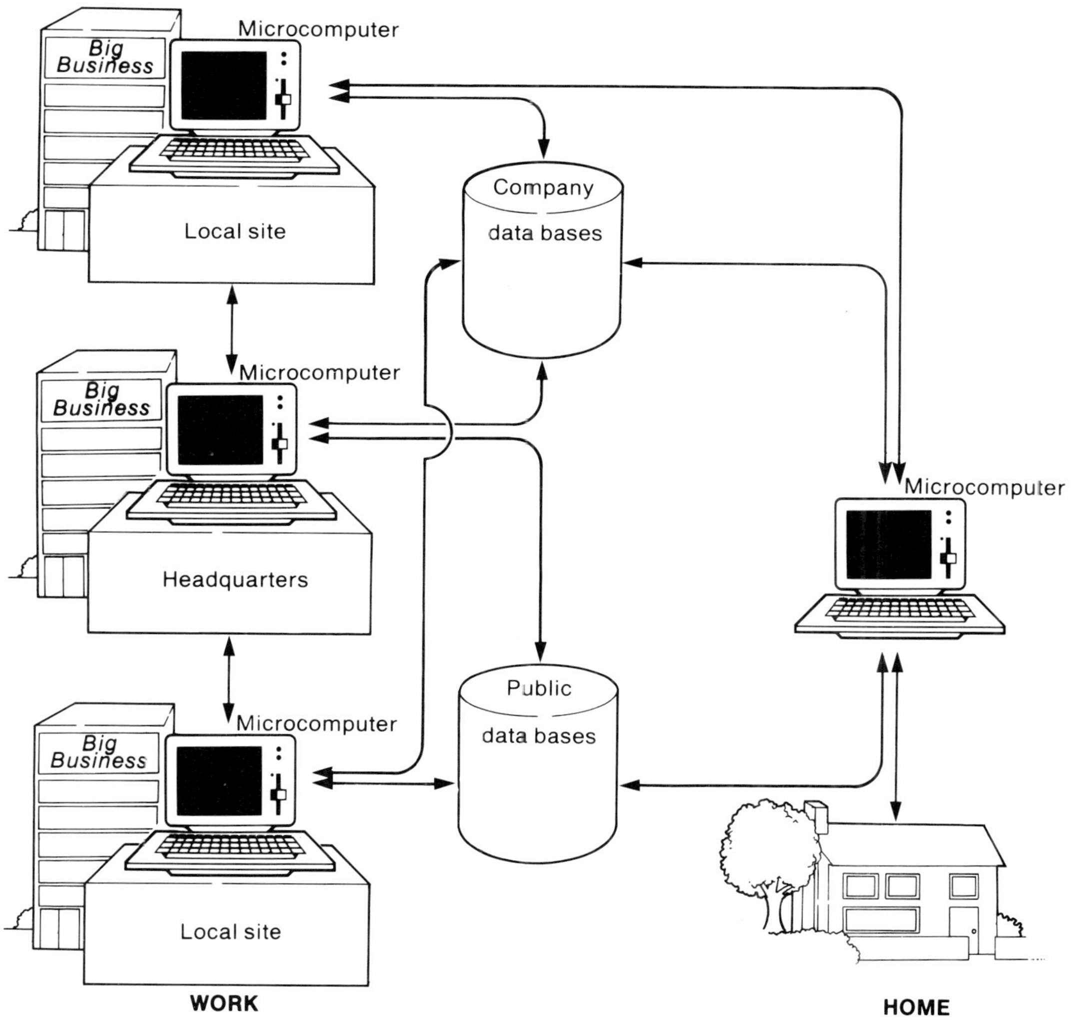

Figure 6 Data communications link companies and homes with information

■ Data transmission

Data is transmitted as a **stream** of **binary digits (bits)** over a line connecting two devices. The data is transmitted as a sequence of **characters**. As described in Chapter 6 the characters are represented by **patterns of bits**, according to a **coding system**. Chapter 6 described the **ASCII** coding system (American Standard Code for Information Interchange). This is now accepted as the standard coding system to be used when transmitting data. A standard is needed because a receiving device must understand the same meaning for a stream of bits as the sending computer. The letter 'A' converted into 1000001 for transmission will be converted back to 'A' by the receiving computer because 1000001 is the ASCII equivalent of the letter 'A'.

There are other coding systems. **Morse code** uses dashes and dots to represent letters. **Baudot code** uses a pattern similar to ASCII and is used in older telegraphy and telex transmission systems. **EBCDIC** (Extended Binary Coded Decimal Interchange Code) is a coding system, again similar to ASCII, used on older IBM (International Business Machines) mainframe computers. Figs. 7 and 8 show tables of codes for the Morse and Baudot coding systems.

A	·—	N	—·
B	—···	O	———
C	—·—·	P	·——·
D	—··	Q	——·—
E	·	R	·—·
F	··—·	S	···
G	——·	T	—
H	····	U	··—
I	··	V	···—
J	·———	W	·——
K	—·—	X	—··—
L	·—··	Y	—·——
M	——	Z	——··

Figure 7 The alphabet in Morse code

1	2	3	4	5	Lower case	Upper case
●	●				A	–
●			●	●	B	?
	●	●	●		C	:
●			●		D	who are you?
●					E	3
●		●	●		F	
	●		●	●	G	
		●		●	H	
	●	●			I	8
●	●		●		J	Bell
●	●	●	●		K	(
	●			●	L	)
		●	●	●	M	.
		●	●		N	,
			●	●	O	9
	●	●		●	P	0
●	●	●		●	Q	1
	●		●		R	4
●		●			S	!
				●	T	5
●	●	●			U	7
	●	●	●	●	V	=
●	●			●	W	2
●		●	●	●	X	/
●		●		●	Y	6
●				●	Z	+
					Blank	
●	●	●	●	●	Letters shift	↓
●	●		●	●	Figures shift	↑
		●			Space	
			●		Carriage return	<
	●				Line feed	≡

Figure 8 The Baudot code

	Most significant digits							
	000	001	010	011	100	101	110	111
0000	NULL	DC0	ƀ	0	@	P		p
0001	SOM	DC1	!	1	A	Q	a	q
0010	EOA	DC2	"	2	B	R	b	r
0011	EOM	DC3	#	3	C	S	c	s
0100	EOT	DC4	$	4	D	T	d	t
0101	WRU	ERR	%	5	E	U	e	u
0110	RU	SYNC	&	6	F	V	f	v
0111	BELL	LEM	'	7	G	W	g	w
1000	BKSP	S0	(	8	H	X	h	x
1001	HT	S1	)	9	I	Y	i	y
1010	LF	S2	*	:	J	Z	j	z
1011	VT	S3	+	;	K	[	k	{
1100	FF	S4	,	<	L	\	l	|
1101	CR	S5	—	=	M	]	m	}
1110	SO	S6	.	>	N	↑	n	ESC
1111	SI	S7	/	?	O	←	o	DEL

(Rows: Least significant digits)

Least significant digits

NULL	Null/Idle	BKSP	Backspace	DC0–DC4	Device control
SOM	Start of message	HT	Horizontal tab	ERR	Error
EOA	End of address	LF	Line feed	SYNC	Synchronous idle
EOM	End of message	VT	Vertical tab	LEM	Logical end of media
EOT	End of transmission	FF	Form feed	S0–S7	Separator information
WRU	'Who are you?'	CR	Carriage return	ƀ	Blank
RU	'Are you . . .?'	SO	Shift out	ESC	Escape
BELL	Audible signal	SI	Shift in	DEL	Delete/Idle

The following meanings may be assigned to the Code labelled DC0–DC4 and S0–S7.

SOH (Start of heading)	Used to indicate start of control information at the beginning of a block of data.
STX (start of text)	Indicates the end of the heading and the beginning of a block of data.
EXT (end of text)	Used to indicate the end of a message text which started with an STX
EOT (end of transmission)	Signifies the end of a transmission.
ENQ (enquiry)	Used to request a response, such as the address or status of the receiver.
ACK (acknowledge)	Positive acknowledgement usually indicating a successful reception.
BEL (bell)	Character used to activate a visible, audible alarm at the receiving terminal device.
NAK (negative acknowledgement)	Indicates unsuccessful reception.
SYN (Synchronous Idle)	Used to identify a sequence of synchronizing bits.
ETB (end of transmission block)	Used to indicate the end of a physical block of data where this may not coincide with the logical format of the data being transmitted.
CAN (cancel)	Used to signify that all preceding data in the block or message should be ignored.

Figure 9 The complete ASCII code with some data transmission control codes defined

Fig. 9 gives the complete ASCII coding system, including those codes used to **control** data transmission (in the table these codes are labelled DC0–DC4 and S0–S7). For example, STX (start of text) indicates to a receiving computer that a message is to be transmitted, so that the receiving computer may prepare itself for the message. EXT (end of text) may be used to indicate that the message is complete. ACK (acknowledge) may be used by the receiving computer to indicate to the sending computer that a message has been successfully received. NAK (not acknowledge) would indicate that the message has not been successfully received. Successful transmission means that the message sent is the same as the message received. But how do the two computers know whether this is true? This may be checked by the use of **parity bits**.

- *Parity bits*

Parity bits were mentioned in Chapter 6. A **parity bit** is a bit added to the seven-bit ASCII code, making the code eight bits in all. The value of the bit is set such that the sum of the binary **ones** in any character is an odd number (**odd parity**) or an even number (**even parity**).

Fig. 10 illustrates the checking of an odd parity code.

	Parity bit								
A	'1'	1	0	0	0	0	0	1	(a 1 added)
C	'0'	1	0	0	0	0	1	1	(a 0 added)
M	'1'	1	0	0	1	1	0	1	(a 1 added)
Z	'1'	1	0	1	1	0	1	0	(a 1 added)

Figure 10 A parity bit – a "I" or "O" added to give odd parity

Checking the parity would show if a 1 had got changed to 0 or vice versa in the transmission process. However, the method is not foolproof, since if more than one bit got changed the parity might be correct but the data wrong. Fig. 11 illustrates this point.

Using a standard coding system for information exchange, using methods for checking for the success of a transmission, and providing codes such as **ACK** and **NAK** gives the ability to **program** for distributed systems. But what about the transmission **medium**, the means by which the messages are transmitted? The following section gives definitions of some of the characteristics and terms concerned with data transmission media.

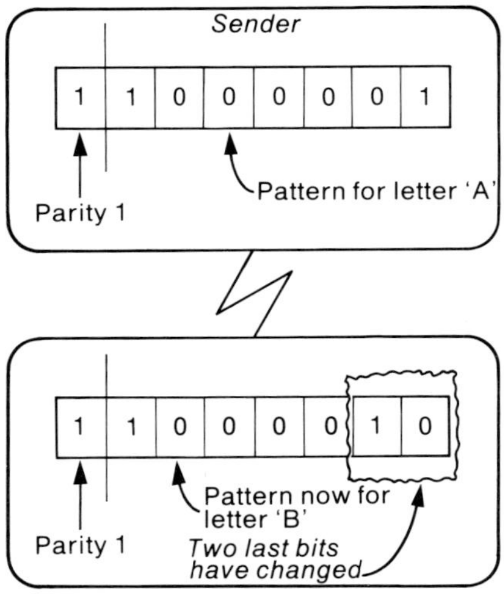

Figure 11 Parity checking is not foolproof

■ Modulation

When data is transmitted the line used to carry the data is often a telephone line. This is because telephone lines already exist and there is a very large **network** of connections. Telephone lines are designed to carry an **analogue** signal. The analogue signal is in the form of regular alternating electrical current, usually represented as a **sine wave** (see Fig. 12).

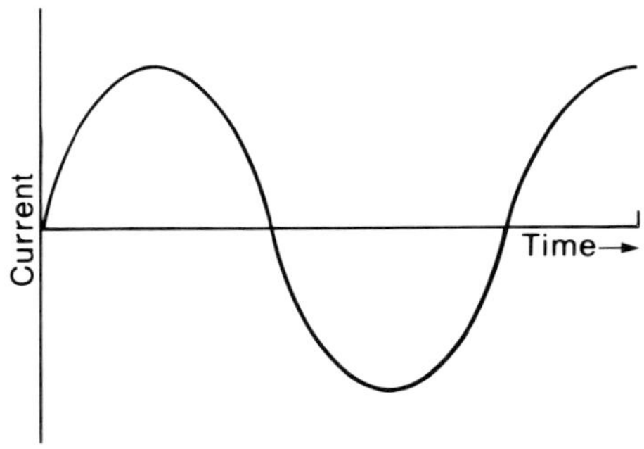

Figure 12 The alternating current sine wave form

The waveform has three characteristics:

Frequency of pitch

Amplitude or loudness

Phase or timing.

Any of these characteristics may be altered to indicate a 0 or 1 bit. Remember, the data to be transmitted is a **stream of bits**. By varying the waveform to represent a 0 or 1, data may be transmitted in an analogue form.

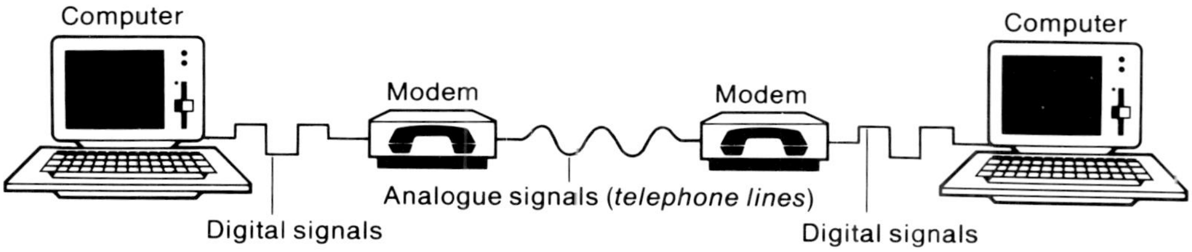

Figure 13 Computers connected using modems

The transmission line has a MODulator/DE-Modulator (**modem**) at either end. The modem at the sending end of the line converts the binary data into analogue signals, the modem at the receiving end converts the signal from analogue form back into digital form. Fig. 13 illustrates this.

Fig. 14 illustrates the different types of **modulation** and the binary signal being transmitted. Notice that the binary signal has a 'square' waveform, it switches from positive to negative instantaneously.

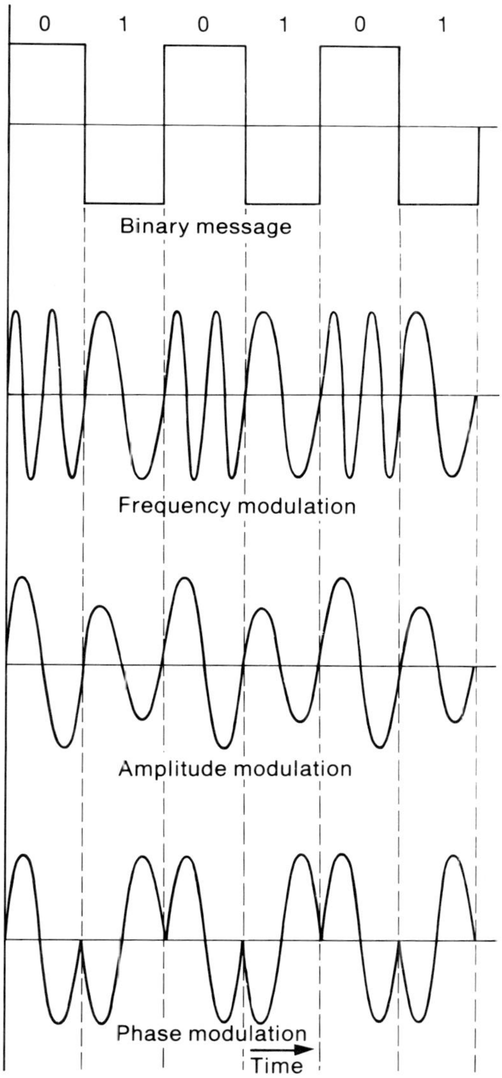

Figure 14 The different forms of modulation of an analogue signal

■ Transmission methods

Different devices communicate data at different speeds and volumes. The wires and cables used to carry the data have varying **capacities**. The difference between the lowest and highest transmission frequency capabilities of a particular wire/cable medium is called **bandwidth**. Network transmission capacities may be categorised into two ranges of bandwidth: **baseband** and **broadband** transmission.

- *Baseband transmission*

Baseband transmission carries a single electronic signal and dedicates the entire cable to one function eg. transferring a **wordprocessed** letter from one office to another. It is intended for use over short distances and is limited in the number of devices it may support.

- *Broadband transmissions*

Broadband transmissions carry **multiple** information **channels** ie. the transmission cable can carry many signals at once. This allows the cable to carry data from or to many devices at the same time. To achieve this a **multiplexer** is added to the system. The multiplexer is connected to each device wishing to communicate with a computer. It is connected to the computer using one cable, as shown in Fig. 15.

To keep the signals separate the multiplexer uses one of two different techniques. These are **Frequency Division Modulation (FDM)** and **Time Division Modulation (TDM)**. With FDM, the signal for each device is assigned a unique frequency for transmission. The line may then carry a signal for each connected device at the same time. The difference in frequencies allows for the signals to be kept separate.

TDM is achieved by transmitting blocks of characters. Each device is allocated a character position in the block. Any device which is not ready to transmit has a null inserted in the block at the relevant position. Fig. 16 illustrates the difference between FDM and TDM.

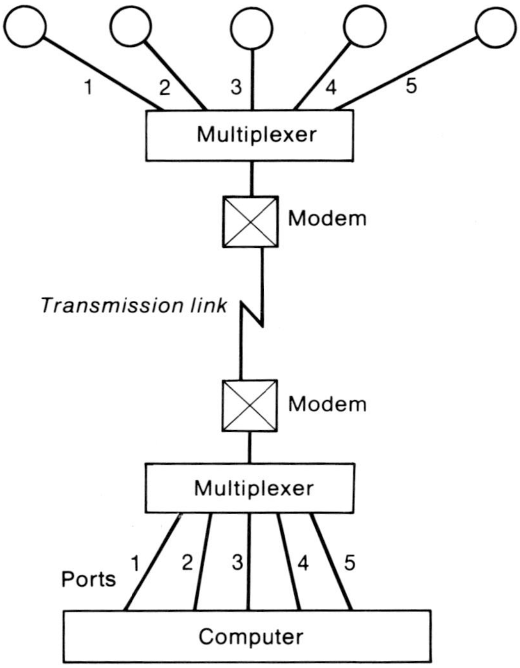

Figure 15 Many devices may be connected to a remote computer using a multiplexer between the modems and the terminals or computer

Broadband transmission allows for higher transmission rates than **baseband** simply because its capacity is greater. Baseband may transmit at rates of one million to 30 million bits per second (bps). Broadband may transmit at rates of ten million to 400 million bps.

The other major factor affecting the transmission rate is the **transmission media** used.

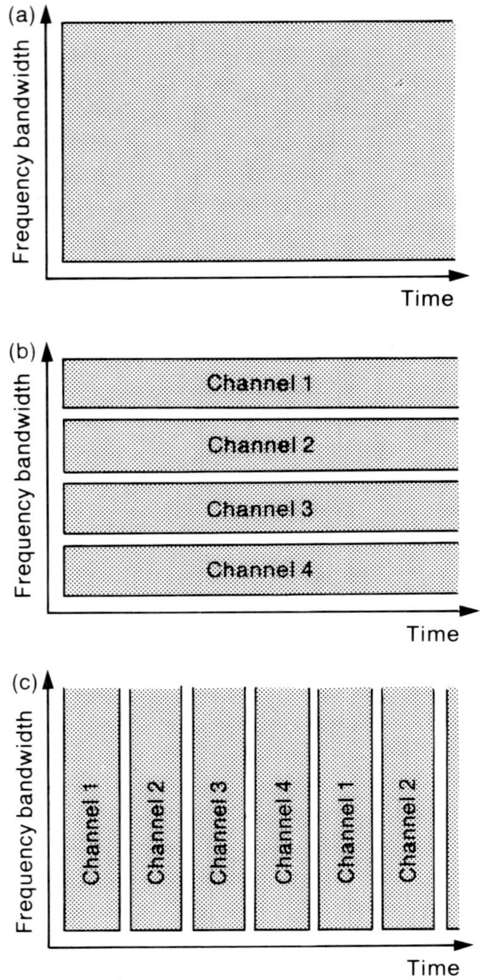

Figure 16 (a) Frequency against time
Figure 16 (b) Frequency is divided into channels ie. FDM
Figure 16 (c) Each channel is given a time division ie. TDM

■ Transmission media

Different transmission media have different capacities: that is, the number of channels they may support at the same time. The most common media are:

twisted pair copper wiring (baseband only)

co-axial cable (baseband and broadband)

fibre-optic cable (broadband only).

Telephone networks also include **microwave** transmission and the use of **communications satellites** in orbit around the earth.

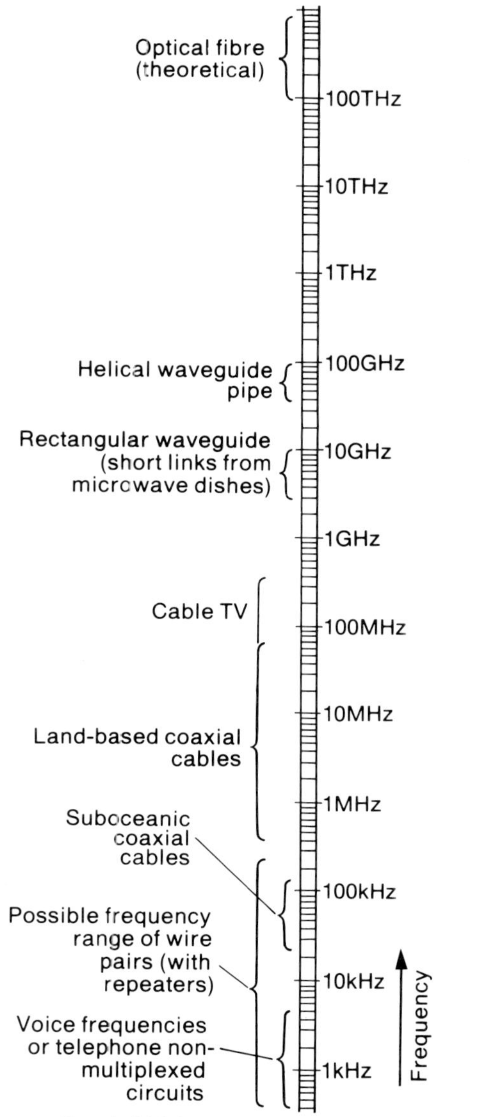

Bandwidth is measured on a scale of frequencies, expressed in hertz (Hz)

1kHz = 1 thousand hertz
1MHz = 1 million hertz
1GHz = 1 thousand million hertz
1THz = 1 million million hertz

Figure 17 Relative transmission capabilities of various transmission media, expressed in hertz

All of these media may carry voice and data messages. Broadband may carry voice and data channels at the same time. Twisted pair copper wiring has low capacity because it is capable of carrying baseband only, but it is cheap. It may be used to connect computers and peripherals over short distances where the volume of data to be transmitted is low and the number of devices is small.

Co-axial cable is the type of cable used in ordinary telephone networks (and also television) and may carry a far greater volume of data transmissions because of its ability to transmit using broadband techniques.

Fibre-optic cable uses **light pulses** rather than **electromagnetic pulses** to carry signals. It has the broadest bandwidth of all the media and has a higher transmission speed. It is capable of carrying about 1000 times more information than electrical communications media.

Fig. 17 shows the relative transmission capabilities of the different types of media. Because of fibre-optic cable's obvious advantages it is rapidly becoming the medium being used to 're-cable' the telephone network.

COMPUTER NETWORKS

A computer network may be generally described as a computer system which has:

- a geographical spread of equipment
- a geographical spread of computing ability in the system
- communication facilities between the computing elements in the system.

A network may have all its elements within a small geographical area: for instance, in the same office block, hospital, school etc. This is often called a **Local Area Network (LAN)**. Alternatively, the elements may be very widely dispersed with elements in different continents. This is called a **Wide Area Network (WAN)**. Fig. 18 overleaf illustrates the different types

The major difference between the two types is in the complexity of the communication mechanisms required.

Computer networks are becoming increasingly popular because they provide computing power where it is required – the computer moves to where the user is, rather than the user moving to the computer. Data may be shared conveniently by **distributed users**. For example: in a hospital, information about a patient may be available to the ward sister and the admissions department at the same time. Network systems are generally more reliable than **centralised** single computers because if one computing unit fails, another one may be used.

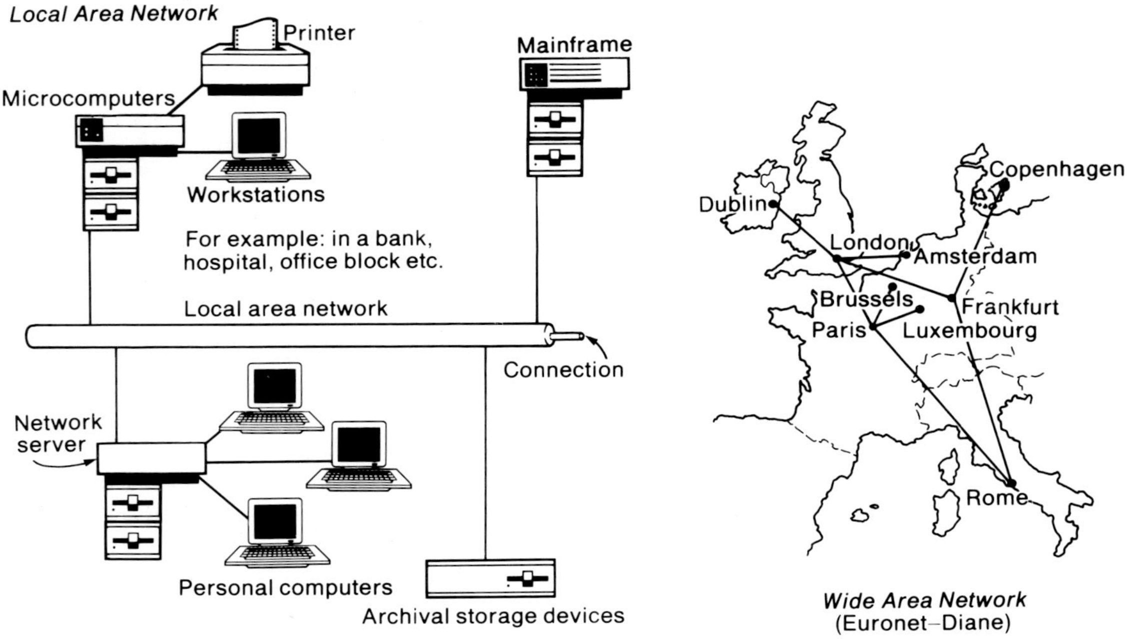

Figure 18   Local area and wide area networks

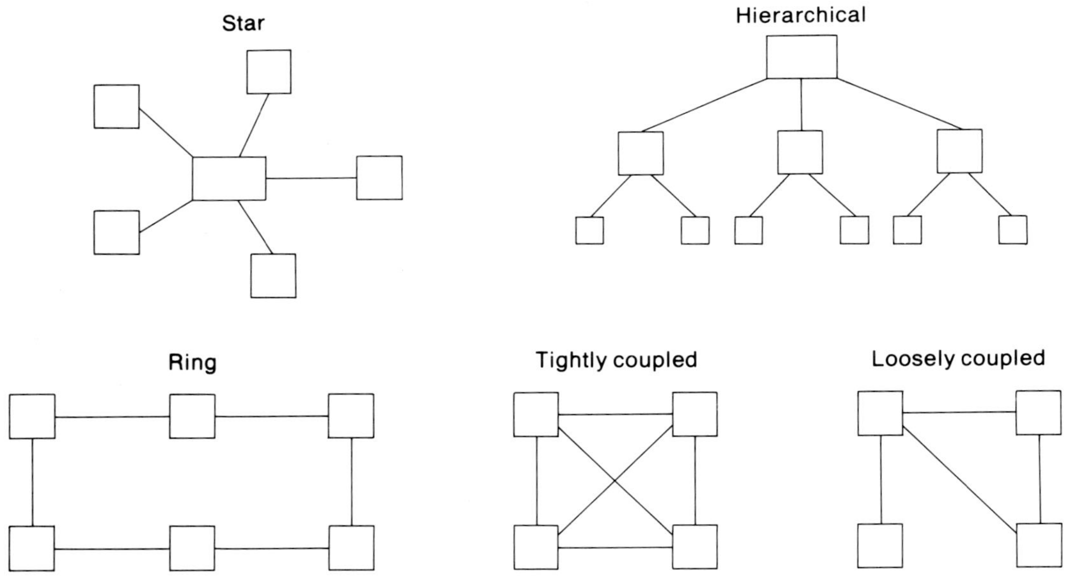

Figure 19   Some network configurations or topologies

■ Network configurations

Fig. 19 shows some common **network configurations**. That is, the organisation of the computer network. These different configurations have different characteristics.

Designing the configurations is as important as choosing the right equipment for each of the **nodes** on the network. Following is a brief consideration of each of the configurations shown in Fig. 19.

- *Star*

The central node is the most important, since if it fails the connected nodes can't communicate with it, or with each other. Such a configuration may be used where there is a central activity which provides information for the connected nodes. An example may be a central warehouse with **distributed outlets**.

- *Hierarchical*

This structure resembles the structure of many organisations. At the top of the '**tree**' is the headoffice or headquarters. The next level down represents branch offices, with departments at each lower level. This structure may best represent the information needs of the organisation; control information is passed between branches and head office, operational data is kept within branches. The Sainsburys case study is an example of this type of organisation.

- *Ring*

In a ring there is no central or hierarchical control, each node has equal status. Any shared data must pass around the ring. If any node fails, the ring is broken. This configuration is more suitable for systems where information is passed around (eg. a word-processed document) but not shared from a central source.

- *Tightly coupled and loosely coupled*

These configurations are similar to a **ring** in that there is no **central** or **hierarchical** control. The difference is that by providing extra connections, there is more than one **route** around the network. This has advantages over the basic ring. If a node fails data may be **re-routed** to **bypass** the failed node. If a communication line becomes very busy and another is less busy, the second line may be used for transmission. This allows for **load balancing** on the network. The **national telephone network** is a very large example of this type.

Note that a networked system may contain a mixture of **configurations**. For example, a large organisation may organise its network as a star or hierarchy, but each node in the star or at the department level may be a ring. Additionally, the overall network may be a mixture of wide area and local area networks. Head office may communicate with divisions over the telephone network. Each divisional office may contain one or several local area networks. Fig. 20 shows an example of this.

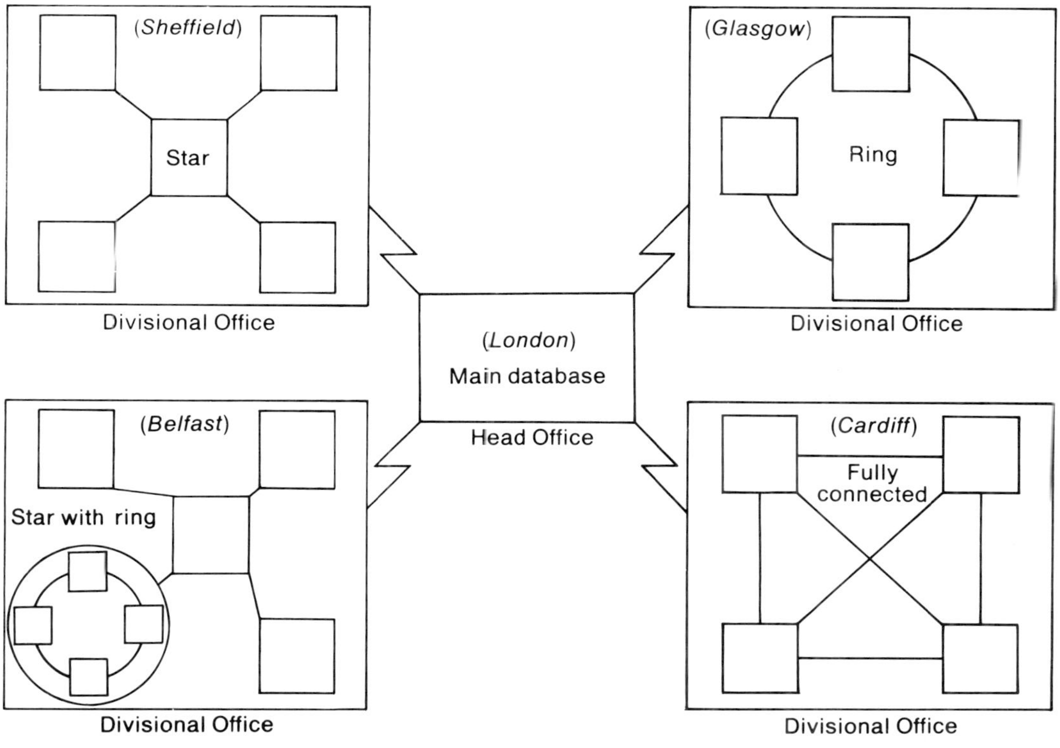

Figure 20 Network configurations may be mixed – each division is a node in a hierarchy, with the headoffice at the top

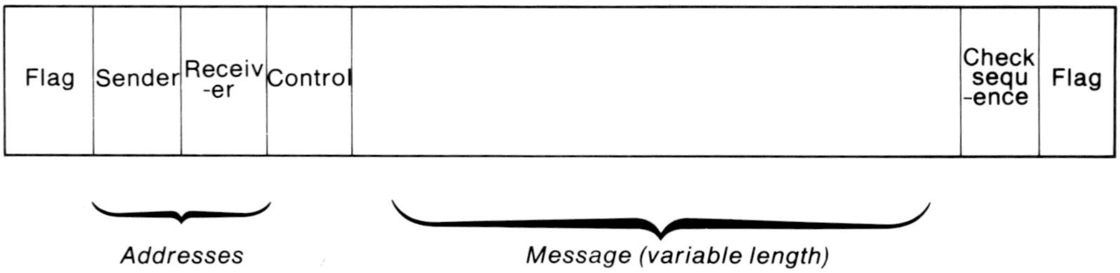

Figure 21 A typical message frame

■ Protocols

Computer networks consist of many different types of devices and possibly many different types of communication media. To ensure that data which is sent by one device is understood by the receiving device, rules and **standards** must be applied as to how the data is to be handled. The data is actually transmitted as **streams of bits** in one form or another and each connected device has to be able to make sense of these '**streams**'. **Protocols** give definitions of the **format** of data as it is sent and received and handled through the communications mechanism.

We have already discussed one standard – the **ASCII** standard for characters. This standard ensures that individual characters are recognised by communicating devices. However, the standard does not cater for messages, ie. collections of characters put together. What is also required is a means of ensuring that devices know which messages are intended for them, when a message starts, when a message finishes, and so on. This is especially important in systems sharing communications lines; ie. where **multiplexing** takes place.

In all protocols **control information** is associated with the data being transferred. This information is placed before and after the data being sent and is known as **framing**. The total information being sent is a **frame** or **packet**. The framing is done, within the computer sending the frame, according to the rules specified by the **protocol**. Each device handling the frame or packet does so according to the protocol and the message eventually arrives and is **decoded** at the receiving end. Fig. 21 gives an example of a typical **data frame**.

■ Network standards

There are several organisations whose responsibility it is to define the **standards** for **data transmission protocols**. They define the standard and a manufacturer may then consult the standard when designing a piece of equipment. Some of the standard setting organisations are listed here:

Institute of Electrical and Electronic Engineers (IEEE)

International Standards Organisation (ISO)

Consultative Committee for International Telephony and Telegraphy (CCITT)

American National Standards Institute (ANSI).

The IEEE and ISO are perhaps the most important of these bodies concerned with networks. The ISO has defined a standard called the Open Systems Interconnect (OSI). This attempts to define a standard for seven levels of communication. These levels are listed below. The first four levels of these define protocols as they relate to physical connections and system design (the hardware). The last three levels relate to user applications.

Level 1 – The physical level: establishes the physical/electrical connection between devices, including the proper voltages, signalling schemes, and **frequencies**.

Level 2 – The data link level: handles the access strategies for how different devices share information on a single cable. These are the **protocols** that acknowledge the presence of a transmission, and perform error detection and timing of signals. (Use of **ACK**, **NAK**, checking **parity** etc.).

Level 3 – The network level: controls the physical **routing** of information between devices. This level is concerned with finding the most efficient means of transmitting information from point A to point B across the network.

Level 4 – The transport level: provides reliable transmission of information. This is another level of insurance for providing end-to-end transmission quality. It deals with variations in the physical quantities of information transmitted, and it establishes protocols for entry and exit on the network.

Level 5 – The session level: defines and controls an actual **information exchange** between users. It is concerned with identifying the locations of individual **nodes** on the network, and controlling the starting and stopping of information sent.

Level 6 – The presentation level: implements data conversion protocols which control **formatting**, **editing** and display of information.

Level 7 – The applications level: provides **end-user interfaces** that allow completion of a given task. These protocols control such applications as **file transfer** programs, **electronic mail** and printer output. The functions of level 7 are supported by the functions of all other levels.

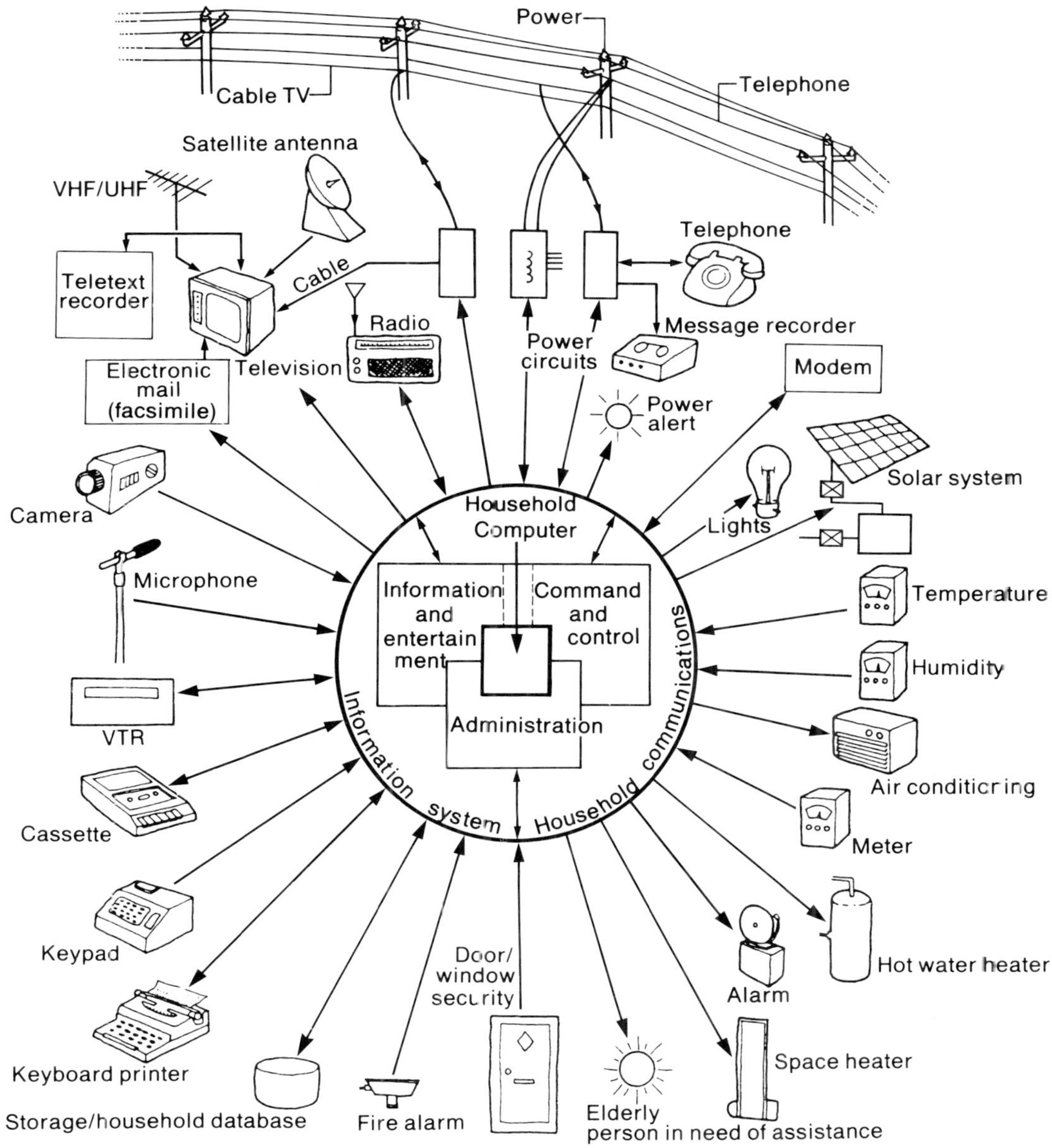

Figure 22 A computer-centred view of the home information ring mains

Although in an ideal world manufacturers would always design systems according to the standards, the truth is that they often don't. Manufacturers will often add 'enhancements' to give themselves a market edge or to protect their market. This can cause problems for users when choosing equipment. However, at least the existence of standards provides a measure of control in what could otherwise be a chaotic environment.

■ Summary

The subject of data communications is very large and could constitute an A-level subject in its own right. This chapter has covered the major aspects of **data transfer** and **communication**.

Transfer of data and data communications may be considered at several levels. At the lowest levels the programming of input/output, the **transmission techniques** and the **protocols** associated with **formatting** data for transmission are considered. The different types of transmission methods and media must also be considered to understand system capabilities.

At the highest levels the design of computer networks should also be considered. **Information requirements** in organisations are important at this level and the organisation of a network may be very closely related to the structure of the organisation in which it is being used. **Standards** for transmission protocols are important because of the variety of equipment and suppliers.

Finally, the increase in the importance of **information processing** is pushing the requirements of networks to new limits. New technologies such as **fibre-optic cable** and **communications satellites** have been developed and are being used to cope with these demands. Fig. 22 illustrates the variety of forms of information being transmitted over communications networks. It is also one author's view of how homes in the future may have 'Information Ring Mains', supported by developing communications technology.

QUESTIONS

1 Describe briefly *local area network* and *wide area network* with reference to digital communications systems.

Discuss the advantages to an organisation of using networks.

Discuss briefly why software is needed to enable devices connected by a network to interwork with one another. Also explain why standard protocols are desirable to enable a variety of machines to interwork.

[*OLE 1989*]

2 (a) A large company has need for all its constituent parts to have access to its centrally held computerised data. Describe the differences in the transfer of parts of the data to:

(i) workstations in a local area network (LAN), placed within the company's main computer system, situated at the Head office.

(ii) another computer system, attached to a wide area network (WAN), situated at a different site.

(b) A national supermarket chain has 80% of its outlets in the North of the country but other sale points scattered throughout the South and West. Differentiate between the types of data that need to be transferred to and from its head office computer, its four regional depots and its outlets. Suggest suitable transfer arrangements for these data.

[*COSSEC 1989*] *AS 8420/1*

3 A computerised monitoring system has been designed for use with an incubator. One of its functions is to monitor the baby's body temperature with a view to controlling the heat output from a heating element.

The system uses the following devices:

temperature sensor:
- operating temperature range 34–38°C
- output voltage range 0–5 volts

heater:
- input voltage 0 or 5 volts
- state of heater OFF or ON

(a) What is the function of the transducer used as a temperature sensor?
(b) What interfaces will be required?
(c) Describe the format of the information at each stage of the process.
(d) The baby's temperature should be maintained at 37.0°C, plus or minus 0.2°C. If the temperature drops to 35.8°C or below an alarm should sound.
Design the structure of the controlling software such that it maintains the baby's temperature within the given values and sounds the warning alarm when required.
(e) What might be the main concerns of medical staff if such automatically controlled incubators were to be introduced into a hospital? How might these concerns be answered?

[*SCE Higher 1990*] *Specimen paper*

4 A company with its head office in town A and branches in towns B, C and D has a computer system in each office. It now wishes to link the four computer systems together. Two ways of doing this are being considered.

Method 1 involves connecting the head office to each of the three branch offices as shown in Fig. 1.

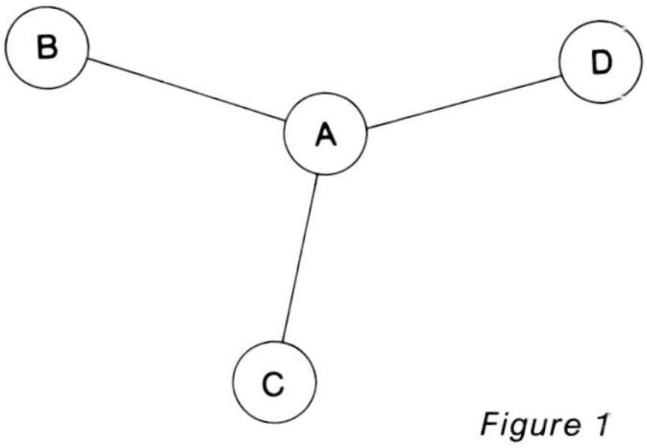

Figure 1

Method 2 involves connecting each office to two other offices to form a ring as shown in Fig. 2.

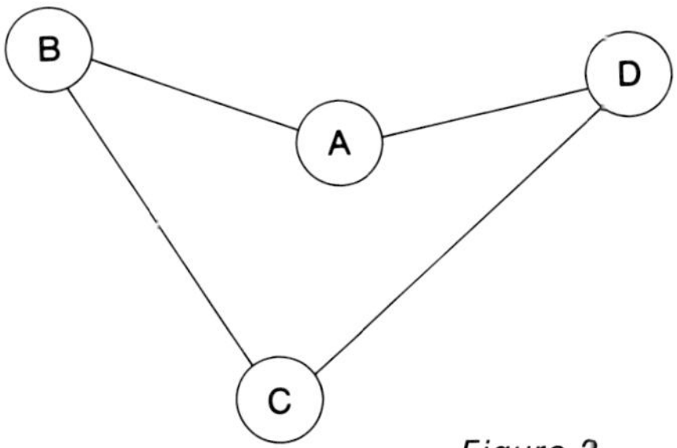

Figure 2

(a) Why is method 2 more satisfactory than Method 1 if

(i) a communication line breaks down between two computers?

(ii) one of the computers in the system breaks down?

What advantages has Method 1 over Method 2?

(b) When transferring a file of data from one computer to another it is important that the computer receiving the data should be able to check that the data it receives is the data that the transmitting computer actually sent.

(i) Describe the checks that you would expect to be performed during the data transfer, and explain what sort of error each check is designed to detect.

(ii) If during the transfer of a file no errors are detected, can one be sure that the file has been transferred correctly? Give reasons to support your answer.

[*COSSEC 1990*] *AS Specimen paper*

5 Many city centre buildings are nowadays used as offices. Millions of people travel daily between their homes and their offices. Many office workers make extensive use of computers. Some people have already found that using a home microcomputer linked to the office computer enables them to work from home. In the future there is the possibility that home could be the office for many people.

(a) Describe the technology which would need to be used to bring this about.

(b) Discuss the consequences which the widespread use of homes as offices would have on society. In your answer you should mention possible benefits and disadvantages to those who work in offices and their families, the companies and organisations they work for, and others who might be affected by the changes described. Indicate also the possible effects of such changes on city centres and the rest of the environment.

[*UCLES 1988*] *9345/2*

CHAPTER 8

Hardware Selection

Introduction

This chapter discusses the capabilities and characteristics of different **hardware** devices, with examples of organisations who use the equipment and why they selected it. We refer back to the case studies in this book and use additional examples where appropriate. We hope that this approach will help you to understand why certain equipment is selected for particular tasks.

To help us relate hardware to types of application we look at three broad categories of computer system:

large data processing systems

microcomputer-based systems

specialised systems (graphics and control systems).

Selecting hardware

There is no point in buying hardware that is unsuitable for the job it is required to do. The system will not work properly and replacement will be costly. It would be like a cyclist buying a mountain bike for the Tour de France; the gears are designed for going up steep hills and not for going fast on roads. The mountain bike would cope with the course but would be unlikely to win the race.

The choice of hardware also depends on the software available. The hardware has to be able to run the software that the company has chosen for their new computerised system.

There are two stages of hardware selection:

deciding on the **configuration** and making a 'shopping list' of items needed

assessing and choosing specific makes of equipment.

The 'shopping list' is likely to include the following: **Central Processing Unit (CPU)**; **memory**; **backing storage**; **input devices**; **output devices**; **communications** equipment; specialised equipment for **monitoring** and **control**. Hardware selection is part of the **systems cycle** (Chapter 1).

Large data processing systems

■ Networked computers

Large organisations such as Sainsburys and the Post Office, banks and building societies have **networks** of computers. They need these to communicate data between head office and the branches all around the country. A network often links different types of computer – **mainframe**(s), **minicomputers**, **workstations**, **microcomputers**. The **configuration** of the network depends on the specific needs of the organisation. Chapter 7 describes different network configurations.

These days it is difficult to draw a line between the different categories of computer; some minicomputers are as powerful as some mainframes and there is no longer a clear distinction between microcomputers and minicomputers.

Mainframe computers are used as the central facility for large organisations. The name 'mainframe' came from the original computers which had large banks of circuit boards and valves, all mounted in a huge steel frame. Although modern mainframe computers are more compact they are still large and often require air conditioning to keep them cool. (The heat output from the computers at the University of Manchester Regional Centre provides heating for several buildings.)

Mainframes are also large in memory capacity, both the main memory and backing store, and are very powerful; they can process large volumes of data at high speeds. Processor speed is measured in millions of instructions per second (MIPS). Many companies operate their mainframe 24 hours a day, with computer operators working shifts to load disks and tapes, collect printouts and organise the jobs the computer has to do. A mainframe is an expensive investment for a company to make.

Mainframes are good at **batch processing** (where large amounts of data are batched together for input and processing) which is what they were originally used for. But they also provide **multi-user** access, allowing many users to share the resources of the machine at the same time. (See Chapter 5.)

Minicomputers, introduced in the 1960's, are smaller in size and are often used as a local rather than a central computing resource. They were designed for sharing data and resources between a number of users but are also used for real-time systems and communications. They range from a small computer with a few terminals to a powerful supermini servicing a large number of users and costing hundreds of thousands of pounds.

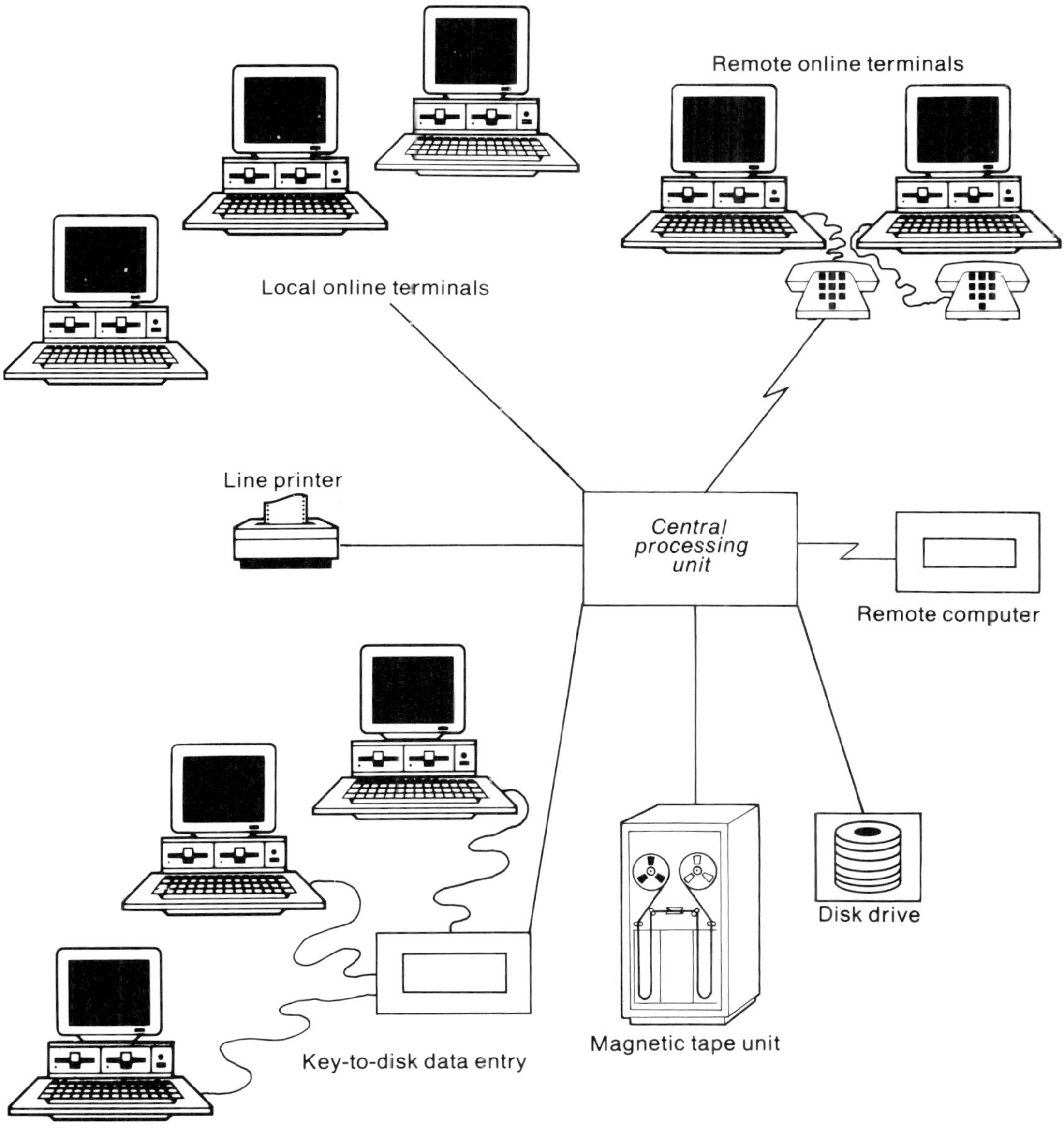

Figure 1 A mainframe computer system

Minicomputer

■ **Data capture for batch processing**

● *Keying data versus direct capture*

Large organisations process and store large amounts of data, which have to be input into the main computer. There are two methods of capturing that data. One method is to type in the data from a **source document**, which is time consuming and therefore costly. The second method is to capture the data directly from shop tags, barcodes or computer-readable documents.

Source documents are widely used for capturing data. We complete forms to obtain a driving licence or passport, to order goods, answer questionnaires, etc. Employees of electricity and gas companies fill in meter readings on special cards. Cheques are also source documents where we fill in the money payable and the date. Some of this data can be captured directly but most of it has to be entered manually.

● *Direct data capture using barcodes*

Systems like Datapost and Sainsburys need to identify objects (parcels and products) as they pass through the parcels office or checkout. Similarly, manufacturers need to identify their products for stock control and libraries need to identify their books and customers. One of the most common means of identification is **barcoding**.

There are two reasons for identifying items rather than just counting them. The first is operational: a parcel needs to be traced; goods can be priced automatically and the stock needs to be replaced; a book is loaned to someone. Recording items on the computer helps make these processes more efficient. The second is to do with management information. Analysis of the data provides management with information that is vital for fast and effective decision making. For example, in supermarkets, which products sell best? Does altering their position in the shop make a difference? There are seasonal variations, etc.

Barcoding is used because it is relatively cheap; the codes are easily printed on labels for parcels, products, books and on borrowers' cards; they can be read easily by devices which tolerate wide margins of error. A barcode is fairly compact (it needs to contain only the object's identification number) and can be used for quite small objects. The Article Numbering Association (ANA) has standardised barcodes for products in shops and supermarkets and there are international barcodes for parcels.

Barcode

The ANA uses a 13-digit number which uniquely identifies each product and its size and colour, if applicable. The barcode consists of a series of bars and spaces of varying width. The first two numbers identify the number bank which issued the number (this often coincides with the country of origin). Numbers issued by the British ANA start with 50. The next five digits are allocated to the company manufacturing or marketing the product. The next five are the particular size, colour, etc. of the product. The last digit is a **check digit**. Goods which are very small may carry a special short number with only eight digits. This is also true of some retailers' own brand goods.

Barcodes can be read easily and a variety of readers are in use. The reader passes a light beam over the bars and reflects it back on to a photoelectric cell. The black bars are detected because they reflect less light than the white background.

Libraries often use **wands**, which are cheap and simple. They are not always able to read the barcode if the label is creased or crumpled, but this is not often a problem on books. If the code can't be read, the operator types in the code number. Books are flat and so do not present the same problems as bulky or awkward shaped purchases and parcels.

Some supermarkets use wands, but others have moved on to **laser scanners**. These are more expensive than the wands but much easier to use. The scanner works in a frame which, by deflecting laser beams in all directions, detects and reads the barcode, whatever angle or position the article is in and even when the label is crumpled. The checkout operator simply moves the article over the scanner. There is no need to: turn the article; find the barcode and draw a wand along the code, all of which takes two hands and more time.

Supermarket scanner

Scanners in a 3-D frame are used in some mail order warehouses. You can throw a barcoded frisbee through the frame and the scanner will read the barcode!

Parcels come in all shapes and sizes and labels can get torn or crumpled. Datapost chose laser scanners for reading the barcodes. However they are not like the supermarket ones. Parcels can be very large (eg. a computer) and it is not practical to pass them across a supermarket scanner. So they use handheld laser guns to scan the parcel barcodes. Laser guns are also used by manufacturers to read the codes on large cases of supermarket products.

- *Direct data capture with merchandise tags and labels*

Kimball tags have been used for some time and are still in use in clothes shops. The tag is punched with small holes which represent data about the garment (id, size, colour and possibly price). When the garment is sold, the tag is removed and provides a record of the sale. Tags are either sent to shop's head office to be input, in batches, directly to the central computer or they may be read at the sales terminal and the data transferred, in a batch, over communication lines to the central computer at the end of the day. (See Fig. 2.)

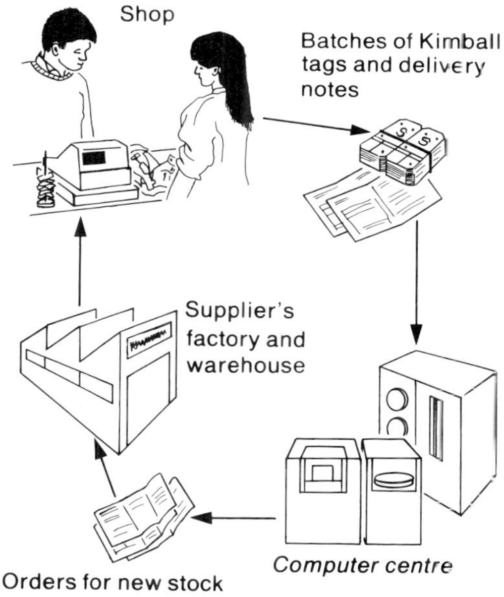

Figure 2 Tag system

Recording automatically what's sold saves time for staff and speeds up customer service as they don't need to write down the sale or take a daily stock check.

Magnetic stripe labels are read with a hand held reader attached to the shop terminal. They are similar to tags except that a small strip of magnetic material is used instead of punched holes. Up to 2K characters can be stored on the strip.

The disadvantages of tags and labels are that they are easily damaged by creasing or tearing; new ones are needed if customers return the item or if the price is altered.

- *Character recognition on source documents*

It is very convenient if the computer can simply read in all the data directly from a **source document**. Any data which is fixed can be preprinted on the document. The preprinted data is then captured directly and doesn't need to be keyed in, saving time. It is useful if the characters can be read by both humans and the computer input device. So ordinary characters are used and a special **character recognition** device or reader is needed to distinguish the shapes of characters. There are two ways this can be done: by magnetic ink and by optical means.

Banks use **magnetic ink character recognition (MICR)**. On cheques the customer's account number, the cheque number and the bank branch are preprinted in magnetic ink. When the bank receives a cheque, an operator keys in the amount of money which is also printed on the cheque in magnetic ink. The cheque is then read automatically by a special machine which recognises the shape of each magnetised character. Data is validated, using **check digits** and **batch totals**.

There are two MICR character sets (founts): the E13B fount comprises the ten digits and four special symbols; the CMC7 fount has ten digits, the alphabet and five special symbols. E13B is used on cheques as shown below and is recognised by its shape. CMC7 characters are made up of vertical bars and it is the spacing of these which defines the character. You will see CMC7 used on postal orders.

MICR requires specialised equipment which is expensive. However, it is fast (readers operate at up to 2000 documents per minute – a million or more per day). It is also accurate, which is vital when dealing with cheques. The equipment only recognises certain character founts but this is not a problem if all cheques or all postal orders use the same fount.

Optical character recognition (OCR) also reads preprinted characters on documents. The characters are recognised optically by reflected light. The reader shines a light at the paper (or other medium) and the light is reflected back on to a photoelectric sensor. The process is similar to reading barcodes.

High and medium speed OCR systems tend to read a limited range of founts. Slower systems read whole pages of text, aiming to recognise a wide range of character founts. In the past few years there has been a dramatic improvement in the price versus performance, particularly at the lower end of the market. OCR readers and **scanners** can be attached to a microcomputer. However, in large data processing systems where accuracy and speed are crucial, specialised, more expensive machines are used.

Pre-printed cheque

Receiving Cashier's Stamp

BANK GIRO CREDIT

Please write any change of address overleaf.
Cheques should be made payable to ACCESS.
Please do not fold credit slip or cheque.
ENTER AMOUNT IN TOTAL BOX.

Paid in by:

Date

3 62-00-58

National Westminster Bank PLC
HEAD OFFICE
H.O. Collection Account
Card Services Department

Fee

No. of Cheques

Notes £50
£20
£10
£5
Coins £1
50p
20p
Silver
Bronze
Total Cash
Cheques
TOTAL £

27080 5224 002431590404 2800 56582 A.N.Y. PERSON

PLEASE DO NOT WRITE BELOW THIS LINE

002431590404 X ⑈62⑈0058⑆ ⑈73

Pre-printed bank giro

There are two approaches to distinguishing individual characters; by the hardware or the software. The hardware method uses a grid of photoelectric cells and a technique called 'matrix matching'. Grid patterns of all the characters in various founts are stored in memory and matched against the character being read. This method is very fast and accurate but the readers are expensive and can only read the stored founts.

The second method uses hardware to convert the character image into data (an array of numbers representing black, white and levels of grey). The software takes this image data and applies tests to detect various shapes. For example a full length vertical bar indicates a B, D, E, F, I, etc. Similarly horizontal lines, curves, angles and enclosed spaces are used to narrow down the possibilities. However, poor print quality, unusual founts and smudges on the paper can cause problems.

The software method has the advantage that it can read almost any fount and a mixture of founts on a page. In theory it should read anything, even handwriting! But its success rate varies. Also it is slower than the hardware method because the shape tests take more time than just comparing a character's grid pattern with patterns in memory. Therefore the software method is less suitable for applications where accuracy and speed are important.

As well as preprinted characters, some readers can recognise handwritten characters. Because people's handwriting is so varied, it is difficult for a machine to read it. There are some devices for recognising writing but they are not very advanced; you have to write in a certain style to get them to work.

However, numbers are easier to recognise. Because meter reading cards consist of a pre-printed customer number and a few figures, it is possible to enter them directly through an optical character reader which recognises preprinted characters and handwritten numbers. Any cards that can't be read by machine are referred to the operator.

OCR is also used for sales order forms (the article number and customer number are pre-printed). Giro credit transfer forms are preprinted with customers' details and often with the amount due. Stock sheets have preprinted parts numbers and handwritten stock quantities for stocktaking.

MICR and OCR readers are expensive but for large numbers of documents they save a great deal of typing time and speed up the data entry process.

- *Optical mark recognition*

An alternative way of reading numeric data from a source document is by **optical mark recognition** or **mark sensing** where people mark small boxes to indicate digits/letters. The reader senses the mark and knows what it represents by its position on the document. Mark sensing is suitable for multiple-choice tests, questionnaire replies and pupil-profiling.

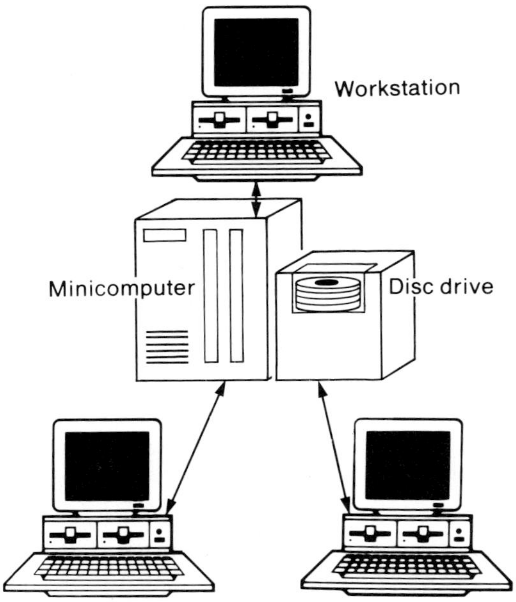

Figure 3 Key-to-disk

- *Key-to-disk*

A mail order company receives many order forms each day and the orders have to be entered and processed so that the goods can be sent out to the customers. The data is keyed in at **terminals** (sometimes called keying stations).

The terminals can be linked directly to the central mainframe and each order transmitted directly. But if there is a lot of data, passing messages and data to and from the terminals ties up a significant part of the computer's time, and slows down the other tasks it is required to do, such as answer enquiries. Also the key operator has to wait while the computer validates and accepts each order. So the mail order company is more likely to choose a **key-to-disk** system (see Fig. 3). Here the terminals are linked to a minicomputer (or microcomputer) which stores the data entered on disk. At regular intervals (usually at the end of the day), the data is sorted into batches and transferred to the mainframe to be processed.

The minicomputer also checks the data for obvious errors as it is entered (eg. customer number check digit, valid item numbers, sensible date) and mistakes are corrected. Another function performed by the minicomputer is to give the supervisor information on operator performance and how much data has been entered. A key-to-disk system offers greater control over the input and its accuracy, but it is expensive.

• *Single user key-to-store*

Where companies have salespeople working for them who take orders from customers, they can write the orders on forms and take or send them to the computer centre to be keyed onto disk. However there is a quicker method. Each salesperson has a small terminal or microcomputer which he or she takes to the customers. The order is keyed in and stored. Some information (eg. prices) can be permanently stored in the terminal to help the ordering.

At the end of the day the salesperson transmits the orders over the telephone by connecting the terminal or microcomputer via a **modem**

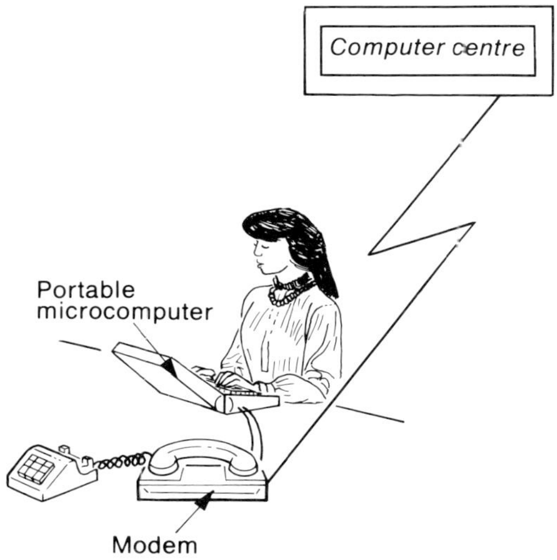

Figure 4 Salesperson sending orders

■ Online data entry

Data is entered and processed **interactively**. There are many applications, for example airline bookings, the NOAH enquiry system and Prestel.

• *Terminals*

A terminal allows one of a number of users to interact with a minicomputer or mainframe. The computer shares its time among the users; this is called **timesharing**. For example, students developing and running their programs share a Polytechnic mainframe with others who are using packages. The travel agent in the case study uses a terminal to communicate with the holiday booking systems. Libraries have terminals for online bibliographic searches.

There are many public information systems you can access with a terminal, a modem and a telephone. A microcomputer can act as a terminal if it has appropriate communications software and a modem is connected.

A 'dumb' terminal consists of a **VDU** (visual display unit) and **keyboard**. Each line the user types is sent to the central computer and processed, which makes the system slow if it's busy. An 'intelligent' terminal has local processing power. This means that it can handle some tasks itself and take some of the pressure off the central computer. A microcomputer is an intelligent terminal.

• *Special terminals*

Some applications need special types of terminals. For example, **point-of-sale terminals** are designed for use in shops. **Cash card machines** (sometimes called **automated teller machines**) are special terminals, connected either to the local branch or regional computer or to the bank's central computer, depending on the transaction. The keyboard has a numeric pad and keys for options such as withdrawing cash and getting a statement. The machines are equipped with specially designed readers to read the information coded on the magnetic stripe on your cash card. The card can be read by the machine but not by the human eye.

An **optical stripe card** can also be used to identify a person, but the optical stripe can store far more data than a magnetic one, up to several megabytes. It is possible to put a person's whole medical record on an optical stripe card.

Cash card machine

• *Home banking terminals*

Some banks and building societies provide a home banking service for which you need a terminal. For example, one building society lends a customer a special numeric keypad; no other equipment is needed. The customer dials the number of the central computer and holds the keypad over the telephone receiver. Messages to the customer are spoken. For example, the voice says 'Please enter your customer identification number'. When a key is pressed, a tone is sent down the telephone line to the central computer.

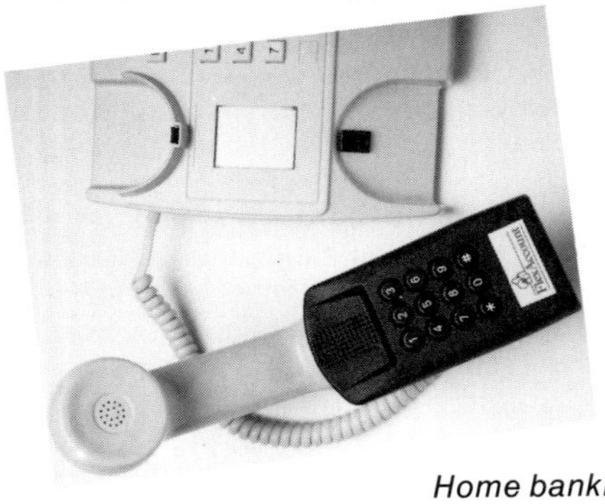

Home banking

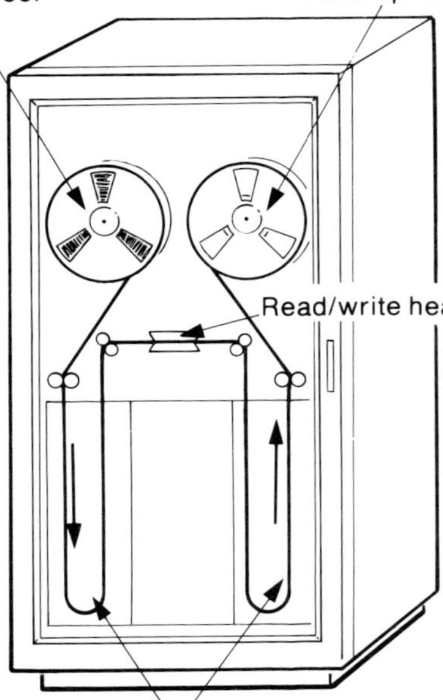

Figure 5 Magnetic tape drive

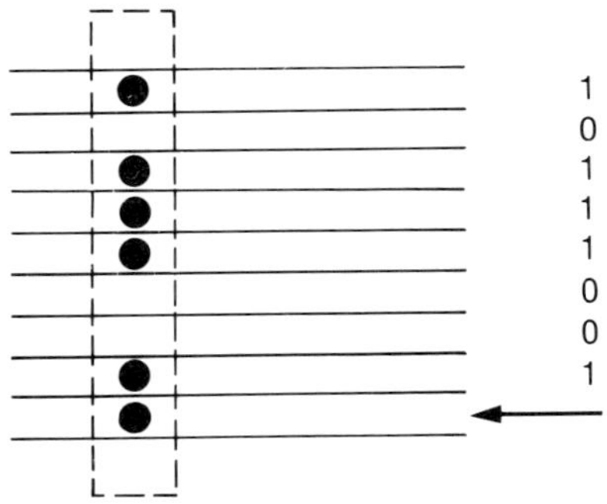

Figure 6 Data stored on a magnetic tape

■ Backing storage

Backing storage is used to store programs and data while they are not being used by the computer. The most common forms of backing storage are **magnetic tapes** and **disks**. Tapes can only be read serially, by moving through the tape to find the data required. Data on a disk can be accessed directly which means that finding an individual piece of data is much quicker. The same comparison can be made with audio tapes and records.

• *Magnetic tapes*

Tapes are often used for **backup** of data; the contents of a disk are dumped onto a tape in case the disk goes wrong. Tapes are also used for **archiving** data and for transferring data, for example, sending a bank's transactions to the central clearing bank. Tapes are cheaper than disks and easy to store as they are less affected by varying temperature. A reel-to-reel magnetic tape drive is shown in Fig. 5. The vacuum columns allow for the rapid acceleration and deceleration of the tape, otherwise the tape would snap.

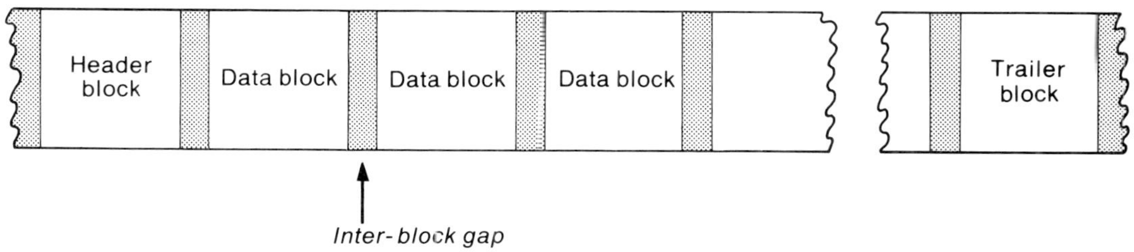

Figure 7 Layout of a magnetic tape

A reel of tape holds about 1000 metres (1 km) of 13 mm wide tape. It can store about 100 million characters (100 megabytes). The tape itself is similar to an audio tape; it is plastic, coated with magnetic material. Data is stored in nine parallel tracks (Fig. 6).

Each magnetic spot represents a binary digit, 0 or 1, and a frame across the tape stores an eight-bit character plus a **parity bit**. This is used to check the character in case there is an error when the tape is read. Our example shows even parity; the character code has five 1's and the parity bit is set to 1 to make an even total of 1's.

Data is stored in **blocks** on the tape, separated by gaps called **inter-block gaps** (see Fig. 7). The computer reads a block of data at a time into a special buffer in its memory. While the block is being processed the tape is stopped and it is restarted when the computer is ready for the next block. Data can only be read from or written on the tape when it is moving at a constant speed so the inter-block gaps are needed while the tape is speeding up and slowing down.

A block can contain one or several records. Block size can be varied and the bigger the block, the fewer the gaps and the fewer the stops and starts. A bigger block means faster processing, but it needs a larger **buffer** in memory. Each tape has a header label, to say what data is stored and its expiry date, and a trailer label which marks the end of the data and contains check data such as a record count.

A **tape streamer** is a newer form of magnetic tape storage, with the tape in a cartridge. It is not designed to stop and start to access pieces of data. It is normally used to dump the whole contents of a disk as backup.

- *Magnetic disks*

Disks can access data very quickly, given the address of the data, because the read heads go directly to where the data is stored; there is no need to read through all the data as is necessary on tape. Large computer installations usually have a number of **disk packs**. These may be fixed in the disk drive or exchangeable, ie. they can be loaded and changed as required. The pack consists of several disks fixed together on a central shaft. Data is recorded in concentric **tracks** by one of a set of read/write heads that move together across the disk (see Fig. 8).

The heads don't actually touch the disk surface; they 'float' just above it to avoid surface wear. The disks spin very fast (3600 rpm) and touching the surface damages them. People often call this a 'head crash'.

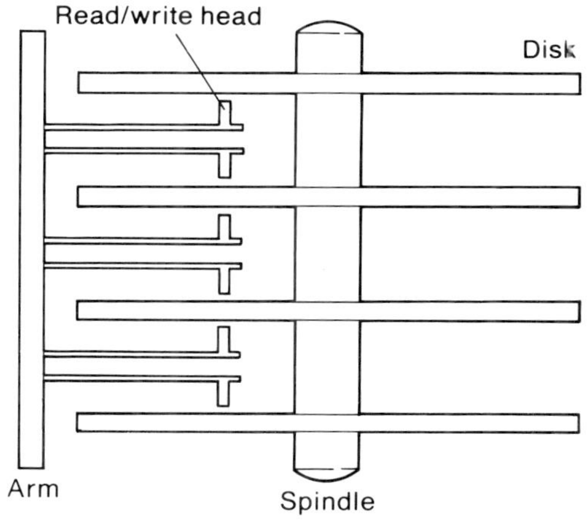

Figure 8 Accessing a disk pack

To find data the arm moves in and out while the disk spins. In our example, it can read the data from six surfaces without moving across the disk. If we wanted to access the data sequentially, it is efficient to store data on these six tracks and they are called a **cylinder**. If our pack has disks with 100 tracks on each, there are 100 cylinders. Data on a track is often divided into **blocks** and a disk is divided into **sectors** as shown in Fig. 9. The full address of a piece of data is the cylinder, the surface (or track) and the block.

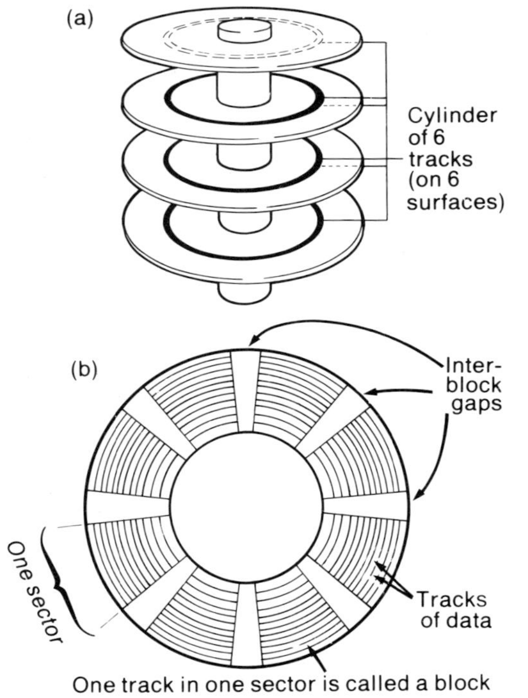

Figure 9 (a) A cylinder and (b) blocks and sectors

■ Output

● *Printers*

Most computer systems need to produce printed output (**hard copy**). Some companies produce large volumes of printout. For example, a mail order firm prints invoices for customers, orders and payment cheques for suppliers, personalised 'junk mail' for advertising, payroll slips for its employees and accounts and sales reports for its directors.

A lot of the mail we receive is printed by a computer printer: bills, statements, insurance policies, driving licence, reminders, advertising. The envelope is addressed by computer and the letter or bill is put into the envelope by a machine as well.

Most of the printing is done by high speed printers at the site of the company's central computer. Data for printing is **spooled** to the printer and waits in a queue to be printed. As well as printers, large companies often have decollating machines to separate continuous stationery, sheet cutters, machines for sorting printout and for folding and putting papers into envelopes. Staff are needed to control the printing, to load different types of stationery and to distribute the output.

Line printers have traditionally been used for high speed printing. They work by hammering the ribbon and paper onto letters embossed on a cylindrical drum or on a chain. The principle is similar to a typewriter except that a line of characters is printed at a time. As the drum or chain rotates, it prints all the A's on a line,

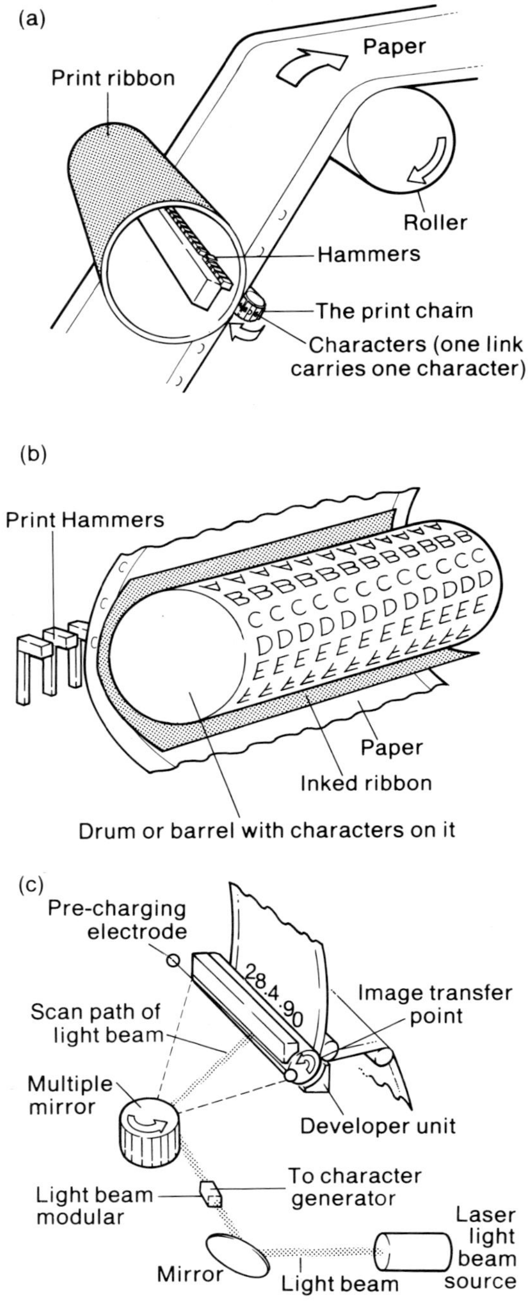

Figure 10 (a) A barrel printer; (b) a drum printer and (c) a laser printer

then all the B's, etc. Line printers are fast (up to 100 lines per second) but because they work mechanically they are noisy.

Laser printers have generally come down in price and are gradually replacing line printers. The fast laser printers, used to print large volumes of data, are still expensive, but they have several advantages. They are less noisy; they are page printers, meaning that they print a whole page at a time; the quality of print is very good and different founts and different sizes of characters can be mixed on a page; pictures can be mixed with text. A line printer, on the other hand, is limited by the characters embossed on the drum or chain.

A laser printer works by giving an electrical charge to the surface of its cylinder. A laser beam 'writes' on this surface by using its concentrated light to remove the charge from parts of the cylinder. The cylinder then picks up charged ink and transfers it to the paper.

An **electrostatic printer** is another type of page printer which uses special paper. An electronic print head forms dot-matrix characters as tiny spots of electrostatic charge on the paper. The paper is then passed over a cylinder carrying charged ink, which is attracted to the charged areas of the paper.

Within companies which have a network of computers there is a move to decentralise printing. This means that some output is printed centrally and some is transmitted to the local branch where it is printed. Some output needs to be printed locally, for example, Datapost sends each local office a list of parcels due to arrive shortly. There would not be much point in printing this information centrally and then sending it to the local offices.

Some data can be printed either centrally or locally, for example, bank statements. Some banks print and post statements locally; it takes the pressure off the central computer printing facilities and also it means that the local branch know what they've sent out to their own customers. Local branches do not need expensive high speed printers, they can use smaller, cheaper laser printers or good quality dot matrix printers. Usually the volume of data to print is relatively small and speed is therefore not important.

- *Computer output on microfilm*

Printers are the common output device for hard copy, but paper is not always the most appropriate medium. For example, the computerised catalogue of a large library could be printed on paper for people to use. It would take up a lot of space and would be awkward to use. A better solution is to condense the output and print it onto **microfiche** sheets. They take up less space, are easily viewed using a microfiche reader and are fairly durable. When the catalogue is updated, a new set of microfiche sheets are printed and the old ones discarded.

Other organisations such as building societies and insurance companies also use microfiche or **microfilm** as a convenient means of storing printed data.

- *Output to disk or tape*

Output data is not always needed in printed form. It may be output to disk or tape to be transferred to another computer system. Data is also output to disk or tape for backup or archiving purposes.

MICROCOMPUTER-BASED SYSTEMS

■ Single-user or network?

In the early 1970's, miniaturisation made it possible to put the **Central Processing Unit** on a single chip and soon microprocessors started to be used for washing machines, calculators, etc.

Microcomputers, or **Personal Computers (PCs)** can be 'stand alone' for the single-user or linked to a **Local Area Network (LAN)**. A typical microcomputer system is shown in the photograph below. The box contains a central processing unit and a hard disk drive, neither of which is visible, and one floppy disk drive. The **keyboard** is used for input and the **VDU** for display. A printer would be connected for printing.

Microcomputer

Many people now have a microcomputer at home, which may be used for word processing, storing names and addresses, doing accounts, running educational packages or playing computer games.

Networks are often used in education and in offices. A network of microcomputers is an alternative to a microcomputer with several terminals, though it is not the same thing. (Chapter 7 describes networks in detail.) The idea is to share data and to share resources between several users. For example, in a sales office people might share a database of contacts' names, addresses, telephone numbers and company details and word-processed reports about their sales. In a school, the network could store the data for a school magazine with articles and pictures. Sharing resources means sharing software packages and hardware (disk and printer).

■ Microcomputers in business

In the early 1980's, when microcomputers were new and before they became very popular, many large organisations relied on a mainframe for all their computing. The mainframe was distant and users didn't feel they had control over their own data. Some users complained that in busy times response was slow. When microcomputers became available many departments bought them, hoping that they would solve some of their problems. However, the microcomputers often remained unused because busy people didn't have the time, or the expertise, to use them properly. People also bought different types of machine and found that they couldn't share data.

To help solve the problem, many organisations set up microcomputer centres, with computer staff who advised departments on the purchase and use of microcomputers. They helped departments set up small applications using packages such as databases and spreadsheets. **Local Area Networks** became popular for sharing data and resources; links between microcomputers and the mainframe enabled users to download data stored on the mainframe for use in their department.

■ Input

• *Keyboards*

Most data input to a microcomputer is entered directly via a **keyboard**. The layout of alphabetic keys is similar to a typewriter and is often called a QWERTY keyboard. If you look at the top row of letters on a keyboard, you'll see why. Computer keyboards often have a separate numeric keypad for quick entry of numbers and a set of function keys which can be programmed to give special commands to the computer. For example, some wordprocessors use different function keys for underlining text, bold text, marking the start and end of a block of text, etc.

Special keyboards have been designed for particular uses with microcomputers. One example is the **concept keyboard** which is used in education. It does not have keys, but has a flat surface which is sensitive to touch. A sheet of paper (an overlay) with words, symbols or pictures, is placed on the surface and the user selects an object by touching it. The concept keyboard then sends two numbers, the co-ordinates of the area touched, to the computer, through the **user input port**. The software takes the two numbers and acts accordingly.

This simple input method is suitable for young children and handicapped people who can't use an ordinary keyboard. Some packages have also been developed for secondary schools, using the concept keyboard as an extra input device.

• *Joysticks and touch pads*

You'll probably be familiar with the joysticks used for playing computer games. This type of device can also be used by people who aren't able to use an ordinary keyboard for input to an educational package. For different handicaps, all sorts of other devices are used: switches, touch sensitive pads. An example of the latter is a package developed for use by physiotherapists for helping people to regain the use of their hands after suffering a stroke or an accident involving injury to the spine.

• *Touch screen*

Touch screen

A touch screen provides a very natural interface between the computer and the user. A menu of options can be presented on the screen and the user simply touches the one they want. There is no need to use the keyboard and it keeps the user's attention focussed on the screen display. It is ideal for people who are not used to using a keyboard and who might be put off using a system if they think it is difficult to operate. Touch screens are therefore useful for large public systems such as library catalogues or tourist information services.

They are also suitable in situations where a quick response is needed, for example, in computer-based training of medical students where the student is presented with information about the condition of an imaginary patient and has to make decisions about how to treat the patient. The student is presented with a menu of options and is timed on the response. Touching a screen is much quicker than looking down at the keyboard and finding the right key, then looking back at the screen again.

Some touch screens have an array of wires carrying high frequency signals embedded in a glass or plastic sheet. The change of frequency on a pair of wires caused by the contact of a human finger detects the touch and determines its position coordinates. Another technique uses sensors positioned round the edges of the screen.

- *Speech recognition*

Wouldn't it be convenient if we could simply talk to the computer and give it verbal instructions? For a computer to recognise natural language, it must be able to do two things: recognise the words spoken and understand their meaning.

Syntax and **semantics** are explained in more detail in the Audiocalc case study. Both areas have kept researchers busy for many years and will continue to do so. Here we look at devices which recognise words.

Speech recognition devices exist, but their capabilities are limited. Devices usually have a limited vocabularly that they can recognise and they have to be trained to recognise each user's voice. The user reads the list of words provided with the software and the device records the pattern of speech. It can then recognise that person speaking those words by comparing the speech patterns.

Voice recognition is particularly useful where a person is operating a machine and needs to give the computer instructions at the same time.

- *Optical character recognition (OCR)*

The best OCR devices are people, they can read a variety of shapes and sizes of letters and can use their intelligence to guess at a misspelled ward. You probably noticed the deliberate error but assumed it was 'word' not 'ward' because of the context of the rest of the sentence.

Earlier in this chapter we discussed the use of optical character recognition and its uses in large computer systems. OCR readers can also be connected to microcomputers for reading pages of text, for example to put into a word-processor. It saves typing in the text. Some errors may occur but the text is usually edited and checked anyway. It is different from using OCR as data entry for data processing applications which require a high level of accuracy, such as reading bank cheques.

A **scanner** can be used for OCR if it has good resolution and the appropriate software for recognising characters.

■ Backing storage

- *Disk drives*

Disks are the most common form of storage for microcomputers. Cassette **tapes** can also be used but they are very slow compared with disks and not suitable for storing large amounts of data. As we discussed earlier, tapes can only be accessed serially but disks are accessed directly.

- *Floppy disks*

In 1973, IBM produced a system which used **floppy disks** instead of punched cards; one floppy disk replaced 3000 cards. It was then realised that this would make an ideal medium for storage on the emerging microcomputer.

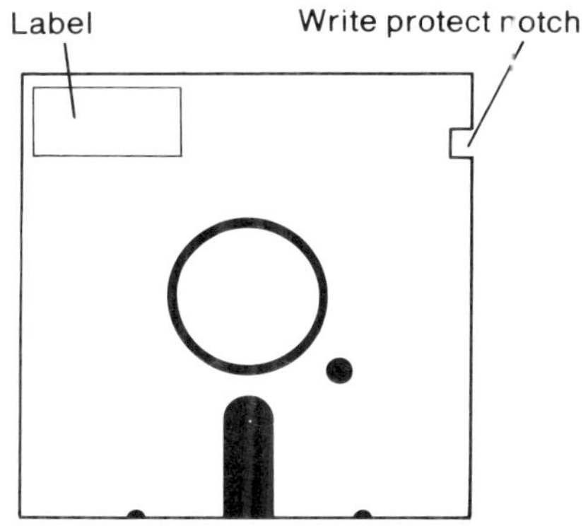

Figure 11 A floppy disk

Disks come in several sizes and can be hard or soft. Floppy disks are made of flexible plastic coated with ferrous oxide and come in various sizes, the most common being 5.25 inch (13 cm). The disk is kept in a plastic jacket for protection, with a cutout slot through which data is read. The jacket is lined with a special material which wipes clean the surface of the disk and absorbs dirt. The small notch allows writing to the disk unless it is covered with a write-protect tab. The small hole in the jacket is for correct positioning of the disk inside the jacket. If you turn the disk inside the jacket you'll see the two holes line up.

Like records, disks need to be carefully handled. They do not like heat, dust, coffee, or being bent or scratched. Inside the disk drive is a head that reads and writes data from or to the disk. The head moves across the disk along the slot. The drive also spins the disk.

A blank disk is simply a flat surface of magnetic material which must be formatted before it can be used. During formatting the disk drive numbers tracks from 0 to 39 (40 tracks) or from 0 to 79 (80 tracks) and marks sectors. It also sets up a directory, ready to store details of files (data and programs) such as the filename and its start address (track and sector).

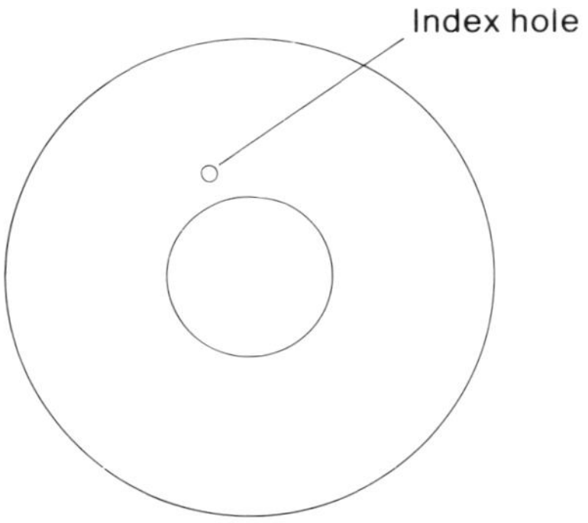

Before formatting

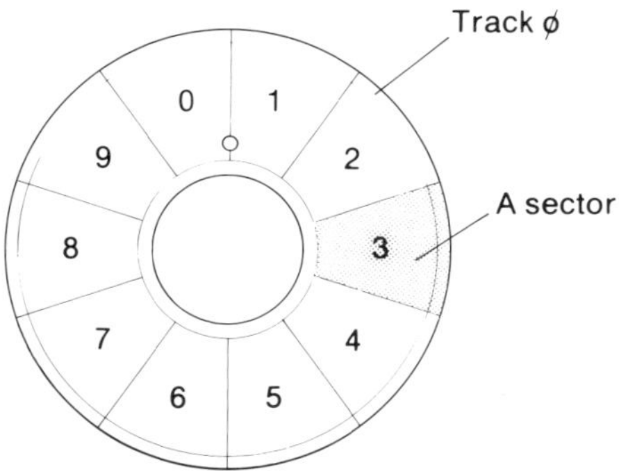

After formatting

Figure 12 Formatting a floppy disk

Different **operating systems** format their disks and organise their directories in different ways. This is why you can't use BBC microcomputer disks, for example, in an IBM personal computer; the operating systems are different. Another difference is the way they name the disks. The BBC microcomputer gives each side a number; the IBM PC counts both sides of the disk as A or B as shown in Fig. 13.

BBC micro IBM PC

Figure 13 Disk surface numbering

BBC disk drives were originally only single sided and had 40 tracks. The 80-track drives were introduced later. Switchable drives, which can read both disk formats, were produced to help overcome the problems in schools where both types of format were used. Switchable drives can write 40 or 80 tracks, but problems can occur if an old 40-track disk is used.

As technology advances, more and more data can be stored on a disk. At the time of writing this book, a high density disk can store a megabyte of data.

- *Mini disks*

Some microcomputers use small disks (7–9 cm) that are less flexible than floppies and protected by a hard plastic case so that they are less prone to damage.

- *Winchester hard disks*

Hard disks used on microcomputers are smaller versions of those used on mainframes. Now that the cost of these has come down significantly, many microcomputers are sold with a Winchester as standard. The disk is built into the machine and stores from 20 megabytes of data up to 100 megabytes or more.

As well as storing more data than floppies, hard disks are faster. With a hard disk computer there is not much need for floppies, but they are useful for backup and for transferring data or software from or to another machine.

- *Optical storage devices*

Optical disks come in various sizes and have several names. Basically they are all read by a laser beam which detects light and dark spots on the disk. You may have seen the Doomsday system which stores maps, photos, sound and text on its optical disks. The data for the local disk was gathered by school children throughout Britain and special software was written to help the user find information, either via the maps or by entering keywords. **Interactive video** systems are used by companies for training their employees and, more recently, in some schools. Video sequences and text are stored on the optical disk.

Compact disks (called **CD-ROM**) are used for record catalogues; they mix reviews, colour graphics and snatches of music and can store 600 megabytes of data. Another example is Whittakers Bookbank which contains a list of everything in print and is sold to libraries and bookshops.

You may see optical disks referred to as **WORM** (write once read many). Organisations buy blank worm disks and store their own data on them. For example, hospital medical records could be stored on WORM disks instead of keeping a lot of paper records. As well as patients' details, the disks could store X-rays and doctors' notes and all the information would be easily accessible.

The advantage of optical disks is that they store about ten times as much data as magnetic media. They are therefore useful for archiving large amounts of data. The data can be directly accessed, like magnetic disks, although optical disks can be slower than magnetic disks because the read head contains a laser and is slow moving across the disk to access data.

Optical disk systems usually include the laser disk drive, a microcomputer with high quality graphics and software to operate the drive. They display data from the drive and communicate with the user.

The examples above use 'read only' disks, which is not a problem in applications where a disk is produced and people simply need to get information from it. However when the data needs changing, this is not possible on 'read only' disks. To cater for this, 'read and write' disks are available but it is a more complicated process as the disk needs clearing before writing.

■ Output

- *Voice output*

Most computer output is either displayed on a screen or printed. However there are circumstances where these methods are not appropriate. For example, Audiocalc, the spreadsheet for the blind, uses **voice output** for users who can't see the screen. Voice output is also useful, sometimes necessary, for safety when our eyes should be looking elsewhere, for example when driving or operating machinery. The remote banking terminal described earlier could not operate without a voice; there is no other way the central computer can communicate with the user. Voice output is also more 'user friendly'.

- *Printers*

Dot-matrix printers are the most popular type of printer used with microcomputers. Characters are formed from an array of dots and are printed by a matrix of tiny wires, some of which come forward to press the ribbon onto the paper

When dot-matrix printers were first introduced, the quality of printing was not very good and it was obvious to the reader that characters were made up of dots. Advances in the technology provide us with 'near letter quality' (NLQ) printing, where the dots are hardly noticeable. Most printers are capable also of producing graphics by printing many tiny dots.

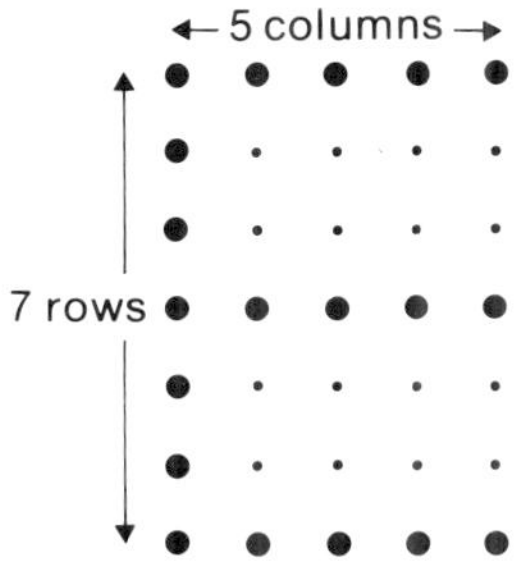

A 5 × 7 dot matrix forming the letter 'E'

Figure 14 Dot-matrix printer and output

Dot-matrix printers are cheap and fairly reliable. With most printers, the more expensive ones are usually faster, produce better quality print and better graphics.

Daisy-wheel printers have become less popular as dot-matrix printers have improved in their print quality. They work by spinning a wheel with the letters embossed on the spokes until the letter required is in the print position. It is then hammered against the ribbon and paper to produce the character. Daisy-wheel printers are very slow and are limited to the letters on the daisy wheel. The wheel can be changed but printing has to stop while this is done. Some people found that the wheels were not very robust and would break if a lot of printing was done.

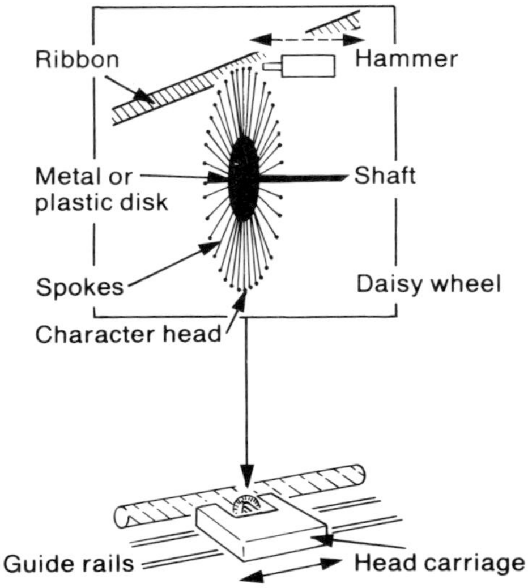

Figure 15 Daisy wheel printer

Dot-matrix and daisy-wheel printers are impact printers and are therefore quite noisy. An alternative is the **ink jet printer**. The idea actually dates back to 1951, but problems with clogging jets, correct thickness of ink and drying out of the ink have stopped it from achieving its full potential. A new approach, using solid ink, appears to have solved the problems. The solid ink comes in a cartridge which is easy to fit. The ink is warmed in the printer and squirted through a matrix of tiny jets onto the paper, where it cools and solidifies.

The ink jet method produces high print quality and is very good for colour printing. It can print on very high quality paper which has variations in thickness, on cardboard or plastic. A laser printer has difficulty handling these as it prefers a flat page.

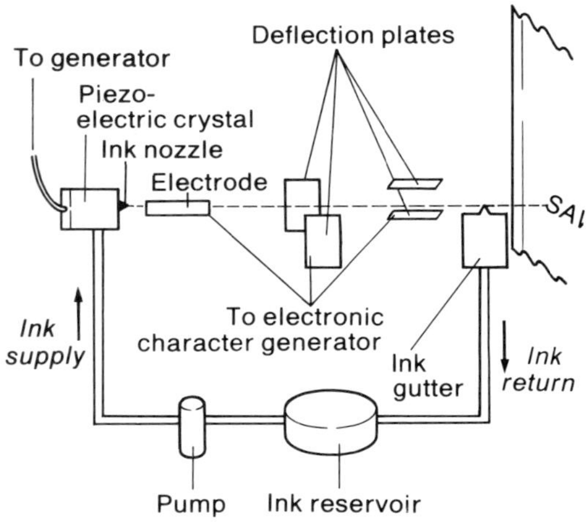

Figure 16 Ink jet printer

- *Laser printers*

Now that small **laser printers** have come down in price many offices are using them because they are quiet and produce excellent print quality. They are similar to the large laser printers described earlier, except that they are much slower. They are very useful in **desktop publishing**, where different founts and pictures often appear on the same page.

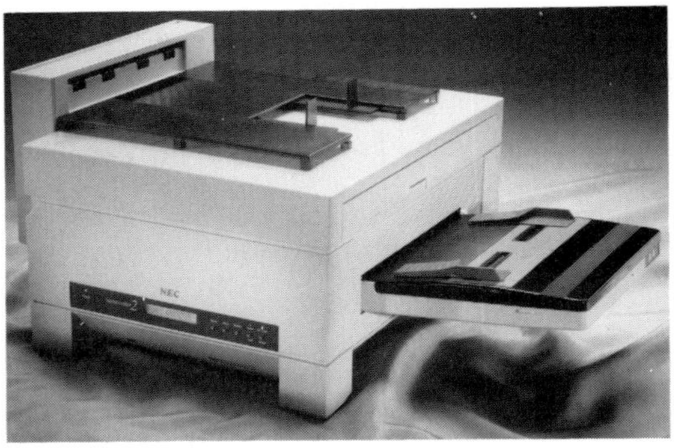

LASER WRITER PLUS

Figure 17 Laser printer and output

SPECIALISED SYSTEMS

■ Monitoring and control

The Kew Gardens system requires **monitoring** devices (**sensors**) to measure environmental factors in the greenhouse and **control** devices to make adjustments, to turn machines on and off and to warn staff of any problems. In the same way, data in industrial situations is collected automatically from pressure and temperature gauges, flow meters, position sensors, etc. The computer analyses the data received and outputs data which can control machines used in car manufacturing plants, chemical plants, steel mills, etc.

The sensors produce analogue signals in the form of a voltage or current of a certain strength. The signals are converted to digital form, suitable for the computer, using **analogue-to-digital converters (ADCs)**. Analogue devices measure data continuously, whereas digital devices reduce the data to a discrete scale, as illustrated in Fig. 18. To control machinery the reverse process is applied (digital-to-analogue conversion).

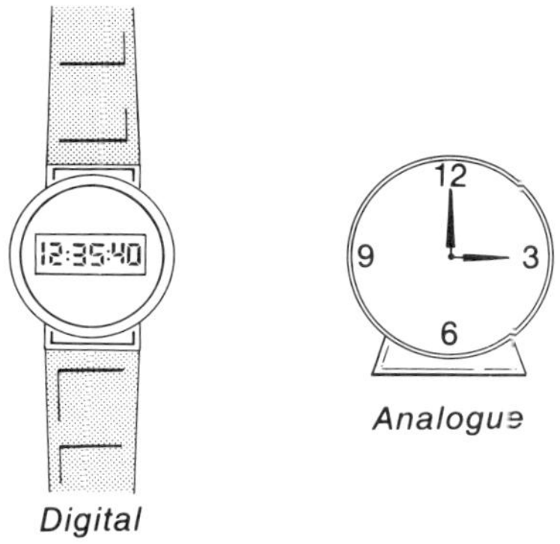

Figure 18 Analogue and digital measurement of time

Most computers are digital, though analogue computers do exist and are used for special applications such as flight simulators A system with a mix of analogue and digital parts is called a **hybrid** system.

■ Graphics systems

Many applications involve **computer graphics**; for example, art and design; computer aided design and manufacturing (**CAD** and **CAD/CAM**); film making; desktop publishing; simulations and computer games. The hardware required for these applications varies from a home computer to a sophisticated multi-user system for CAD/CAM.

• *Visual Display Units*

The screen is often the most prominent piece of equipment in a graphics system. The standard visual display unit (or monitor) is based on a cathode ray tube and works similarly to a television. Most screens work on a **raster scan display**. An image is created by displaying a large number of tiny dots called **pixels** (picture elements) in varying brightness levels on a monochrome screen or in colour on a colour screen. In colour each pixel is a triad of dots in the three primary colours: red, green and blue. Different combinations and intensities create different colours.

Vector graphics displays also use the cathode ray tube but display images differently, producing solid lines, rather than lines made of dots. Vector displays are therefore suitable for high quality diagrams, but not for pictures with large coloured areas nor for animation.

Liquid crystal displays, originally used for calculators and watches, have been developed as flat screens for microcomputers, particularly portable microcomputers. They are much lighter than the ordinary monitor and use little current, but they are more expensive.

• *Screen resolution*

For text applications such as wordprocessing, the screen image is stored as an array of **character codes**. The memory required is therefore small, for example, a typical 80 by 25 text screen in black and white needs approximately 2 kilobytes. For graphics applications, data about each pixel must be stored.

For many applications (eg. CAD) the **resolution** of the screen is important for displaying complex diagrams or pictures. Screens are referred to as low, medium or high resolution. The smaller the pixels and the more there are, the better the resolution is.

The resolution depends on two things: the capabilities of the monitor and the computer software. High resolution monitors are more expensive. The software stores the image of the screen in memory and higher resolution requires more memory. The image is stored as an array of pixel data. The simplest method is to use one bit per pixel; 0 for black, 1 for white. Using three bits for each pixel allows up to eight colours and six bits allows 64 colours. As an example, a screen of 640 by 350 pixels needs about 28 kilobytes for black and white and needs 84 kilobytes for eight

Low screen resolution

A 3-D drawing using CAD

High screen resolution

colours. There are more complicated techniques for compressing the data and storing large numbers of colours, and for using a palette of certain colours, but the principles are the same.

- *Processing power and storage*

Consider the typical facilities provided by a fairly simple drawing or design package: drawing lines and shapes; rotating shapes; moving, copying or enlarging parts of the drawing; zooming in on a certain part of the drawing. Most CAD packages also allow 3-D drawings; from simple wire-frame and surface models to complex shaded solids. A **library** of parts of drawings can be built up (some may already be supplied with the package); for example an architectural picture library may contain trees, street lamps, windows, furniture items etc.

Producing a complex design or drawing involves many calculations and therefore requires fast processing if the user is not to be kept waiting. Also, the data associated with the design or model must be stored (for example, all the measurements of the building which the architect is designing).

Although many graphics packages are available on ordinary microcomputers, the facilities provided are often limited and many people prefer to use **workstations**. First used for CAD, they are now being used for many graphical applications, such as art and fashion design, film creation and desktop publishing. Workstations (manufacturers include Sun, Apollo and DEC) are very powerful microcomputers, with fast processors, plenty of memory and high resolution graphics screens. They are often connected in a local network.

- *Input devices*

Most graphics packages have a **WIMPS** environment, with a **mouse** (Chapter 2) for selecting from menus and for moving objects. A useful device for drawing is a **digitising tablet**, a computerised drawing board. The user moves a special pen or a mouse across the board and the movement is duplicated on the screen. Alternatively a **light pen** can be used to point at the screen and control the movement of the drawing cursor.

Pictures, diagrams and drawings can be input directly using a **scanner**, which acts rather like a photocopier but sends the image to the computer in digital form.

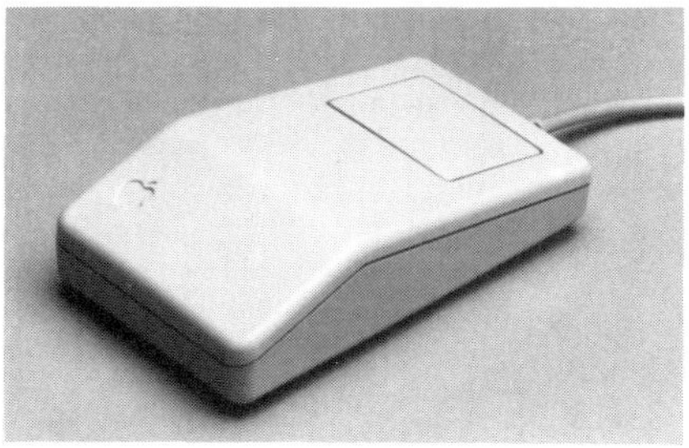

Mouse

Image scanner

Graph plotter

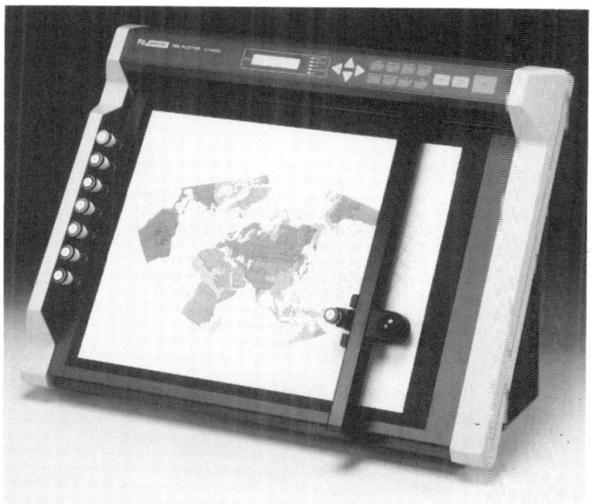

Pen plotter

- *Output*

Plotters are widely used in engineering and industrial or architectural design. They are specially designed for graphical output, though printers can be used as well. Plotters are available in several sizes, including very large ones for certain types of CAD drawings. They are slow compared to printers but produce very high quality drawings.

There are two types of graph plotter. A **flat bed plotter** consists of a drawing surface over which is suspended an arm carrying a pen. The arm can move backwards and forwards and the pen can move along the arm. It also moves down to draw a line and up when it is moving to its next position. The computer software controls these movements and can produce drawings and graphs and annotate them with text. Some schools have this type of plotter.

A **drum plotter** has a fixed arm and the paper moves underneath it. The pen moves from side to side on the arm. These plotters allow large drawings and diagrams to be produced without the need for a large drawing table.

■ Summary

As technology advances, existing computer hardware and peripherals are improved and new techniques are developed for storing, processing and communicating data. Most of the hardware described in this chapter will remain in use for some time, but there will also be many new developments, which will improve the performance of computer systems and extend their range of applications.

QUESTIONS

1 What methods of data capture or collection would you recommend for each of the following computer applications:

(a) stock taking in a supermarket
(b) recording the time of arrival and departure of employees
(c) extracting money from a bank automatic cash dispenser?

Describe briefly the main features of each method that you have mentioned.

[*ULSEB 1989*]

2 A national opinion research organisation intends to distribute questionnaires to about 10 000 households. The recipients are to be asked to put their views on each of 30 statements into one of the five categories shown below.

Strongly agree
Agree
Not sure
Disagree
Strongly disagree

Completed questionnaires are posted back to the research organisation.

(a) Describe two different methods by which this data could be entered into the computer. Comment on the relative merits of each.
(b) Select one of your methods in (a) above and design the form which you would recommend the research organisation to use if it adopted your chosen method of data entry.

3 (a) Most computers have both immediate access memory and backing store. Explain why two such levels of storage are desirable.
(b) Describe and explain the use of a buffer when data is transferred to or from a peripheral device.
(c) Explain what is meant by the *spooling* of printed output.

[*AEB 1989*]

4 (a) Before a floppy disk can be used for the first time it must usually be *formatted*. Explain briefly what this involves, and why it is necessary.
(b) A disk is formatted and has files written to it using a particular computer system. Why may it be difficult to read the contents of the disk using a different make of computer?
(c) What are the main benefits of having two floppy disk drives on a microcomputer system which has no other forms of backing storage?

[*UCLES 1988*]

5 Suppose you are asked by a sports centre manager, who commissioned the development of a computer system (see Chapter 1 questions) to recommend a suitable printer. What criteria would you use for selecting a printer? Obtain details of several different printers and write a short report for the manager, discussing the advantages and disadvantages of each.

6 Choose *one* industry in which graphical information is used widely, and investigate the use of computer-aided techniques in this industry. Discuss the relevance of standards for graphical information.

7 A graphic designer wishes to use a computer to assist in the design of regular patterns. These patterns may be used for tiling a floor, or for wallpaper or fabric designs.

(a) Discuss suitable forms of communication between the user and the system, including examples of the different kinds of data and the devices used.
(b) Describe the types of operation that the graphic designer could expect the computer system to perform.
(c) Explain why this kind of system would normally be based on a standard software package.

[*UCLES 1989*]

8 Technology is constantly being developed and updated. Find out about the latest developments in computer equipment.

9 Consider the possibility of a computer system able to accept directly the input of ordinary human speech. Describe briefly one way in which such a speech recognition system could be of benefit to an individual and one way in which it could be damaging to society.

Readers

Reader 1

Bedside manna

Reader 2

IT gets set to save the world

Reader 3

A robot by any other name

Reader 4

a) Tied to the phone
b) Marketing the facts of our lives

Reader 5

a) Lulled into a false sense of security
b) Law Commission gives hackers five years
c) IT crime squad calls for reinforcements

Reader 6

a) Flying blind to reality
b) Citibank

Reader 1 Bedside manna

IT IS THE year 2000. As the surgeon works, a patient lies unconscious on an operating table. Suddenly an alarm sounds, and the clinician's eyes dart to a computer screen.

The system, based on artificial intelligence (AI), warns of a combination of changes in the patient's physiological condition, and taking into account her medical record, suggests the administration of a certain drug. At the touch of a button, the clinician checks both the real-time and background information on the patient, and safely administers the dosage.

It sounds simple, but to produce a system capable of analysing both past and real-time data for individual patients, and which can work out when clinicians should be alerted to changes in a particular patient, is a problem scientists have been working on for years.

Existing monitoring systems can provide invaluable basic information on the patient's condition, such as blood pressure, heartbeat and temperature, and can sound alarms when these pass pre-set limits. But the difficulty lies in setting these thresholds to match the conditions of a patient at a given time—what may be dangerous for one person may be perfectly safe for another—and in putting any changes into context.

Expert systems can now be used to store basic advice, such as the likely cause and treatment of certain symptoms, but again the problem lies in adapting such advice to individuals, each with a unique medical history. It is here that AI-based systems may hold the answer.

Expert system software can achieve good levels of competence on specific tasks, using rules elicited from human experts. About 2,000 such expert systems have been developed, but their practical value is often limited.

AI research goes further, and often aims to produce systems which reason "intelligently," as humans do. However, only a handful of working AI-based medical systems exist in the US and France. None were developed commercially, and scientists disagree over whether or not many of them are simply expert systems.

But enormous funds are now being ploughed into the development of medical AI systems around the world. The European Society for Artificial Intelligence in Medicine— a group of doctors, scientists, health service managers and other interested parties, set up in 1986 to help disseminate experience—has attracted 550 members.

The European Community has also set up a £12 million pilot research project to look at the whole field of computers in medicine, with about a quarter of the research devoted to AI.

Bill Sharpe is director of Hewlett-Packard's information management laboratory in Bristol.

"If you ask clinicians the state of a patient, they will describe it in fairly broad, qualitative terms—of things rising and falling, rather than specific measurements. If you can provide this sort of reasoning in a machine, then you can replace numerical alarms with those based on qualitative changes," he says.

Sharpe stresses that such research can only be carried out in close conjunction with clinicians. "We need to understand their tasks, and what information they use at present to reach decisions. Is it purely numerical data, or do they use visual information too? These are questions we are attempting to answer."

Their first step was to construct a workbench. Clinicians are given ranges of computer-based information about a "patient" and asked to note their thoughts. This helps the researchers discover what information is relevant and what, if any, is missing when there is no visual contact with the patient.

The AI system will have to "reason" in real time while storing only data that is, or will become, relevant. "You have to keep multiple possibilities on the go, and obviously this causes many computational problems," Sharpe adds

Dr Jeremy Wyatt, a lecturer in medical informatics is also developing prototype AI-based medical systems.

He worked on the development of an expert system to help doctors identify the cause of chest pains in casualty departments, which in 12 per cent of cases are wrongly diagnosed. The system, called Acorn, uses a Toshiba laptop PC, and was tested in a year-long pilot scheme funded by a charitable research grant at Westminster Hospital's casualty department.

However, although doctors judged it to be helpful in 75 per cent of cases, and agreed with the advice it gave in 78 per cent, the trial was judged a failure. The system proved to be less accurate than in the laboratory, was often used too late, and its advice was not always acted on. Acorn has since been adapted; further trials are now under way.

All those working on the development of AI systems stress that it will be some years before such products are in widespread use, and their coming may create difficulties. Wyatt is concerned about the future legal implications. He wonders if, in the future, doctors could face claims for negligence if they fail to use the available technology, and whether similar charges could be brought against health authorities who fail to supply it.

Questions

1 Explain how artificial intelligence systems may be able to achieve the 'year 2000 scenario' described in the first paragraph of the article.

2 What are the difficulties involved in developing such systems? What knowledge is required?

3 Discuss whether artificial intelligence systems might eventually replace human experts, such as hospital consultants.

Reader 2 IT gets set to save the world

Computers processing satellite data obtained high above the Himalayas can determine the depth of snow cover and predict the run-off when it eventually melts. The same technique may soon be used to give early warning of impending disaster in the densely populated, flood-prone Ganges Delta.

Vast populations and many industries are to benefit from a global programme for the development of computer techniques for disaster prevention and management.

Mounted by the Commonwealth Science Council, the project focuses the work of many industrial research establishments, universities and government departments around the world.

The programme has just been launched at a meeting of specialists in London, and aims to exploit the rapid recent development of electronic data processing and telecommunications to make the world a safer place. It follows a series of devastating disasters this year which struck several member countries of the Commonwealth.

The United Nations has already designated the 1990s as the international decade to combat natural disasters through co-ordinated research, data gathering and information sharing.

Both programmes offer big business opportunities to the computer industry.

The Commonwealth technology programme is intended to help member countries to deal with natural disasters as well as those caused by human activity. It will focus on large scale transport and industrial accidents, floods, hurricanes, landslides, earthquakes and drought.

Data processing and management, telecommunications and remote sensing are to play an important part.

As a first step, the programme will provide an information base on the vulnerabilities and needs of high risk areas. There are also plans for a handbook on disaster prevention and management intended for public administrators in transport, health, welfare, education and other fields, training and research institutions and voluntary organisations.

The study may well prove to be of particular interest to the computer, electronics, shipping, navigation and marine construction industries.

A spokesman for the Commonwealth Secretariat describes the programme as a response to "a series of horrifying disasters during the past few months".

"In October and September, Bangladesh experienced the worst floods in history, and the Caribbean and Central America were struck by their worst hurricane in this century. In August, an earthquake killed 800 in India and Nepal. In July, Lesotho was cut off by snow."

Cyclones, floods, volcanic eruptions and other natural disasters have claimed millions of lives and caused an estimated £50 billion damage to property since the late 1960s. But the UN Centre for Science and Technology in New York comments, "The world community has learned a lot about climatic and other forecasting. A global focus on measures to predict, if not prevent, dramatic natural phenomena is long overdue."

Both the Commonwealth and the UN programmes will explore a range of spectacular recent developments in potent but relatively inexpensive data processing, navigation, communication and detection channels.

Other areas under study are preparation for disaster, embodied in risk assessment and planned responses to emergencies, as well as disaster mitigation, ranging from good planning and construction codes to tax reform and insurance incentives.

Computers have an enormous potential role in disaster prediction and management. The increasing power of supercomputers like the Cray 2 and the ETA-10 models has enabled climatologists to break more and more complex and sophisticated numerical models to study the behaviour of the climate.

Current interest focuses on studying the behaviour of the deep oceans, often the source of climatic disasters.

Studies range from large scale ones on general circulation of the ocean and its climate, through intermediate studies of the ocean eddy field and equatorial current systems to small scale studies of individual eddies and the flow of ocean currents through narrow channels.

One area in which ocean modelling has proved particularly promising is the study of El Nino—a change in the atmospheric circulation pattern which occurs at irregular intervals of up to eight years.

The present El Nino is blamed for the floods in Bangladesh and the Sudan.

The same phenomenon is responsible for such disasters as the recurring monsoon failures hitting South-East Asia, floods in Central and South America and the collapse of fisheries off the South American coast.

The southern oscillation associated with El Nino is an oceanic phenomenon involving big changes in atmospheric pressure across the Pacific between Australia and Latin America.

Thus the 1982–83 El Nino wiped out crops and ravaged the western seaboard of the Americas with persistent storms, destroying much of the global anchovy harvest. In Australia, the associated southern oscillation led to severe drought, furious bushfires and duststorms which carried away 200,000 tonnes of topsoil.

But computer scientists at the UK's Institute of Oceanographic Sciences cooperating with colleagues in the affected Commonwealth countries have now been able to model the El Nino phenomenon. They may soon be able to predict future occurrences of the pattern.

This will make dependable, very long range weather forecasting possible.

As a result, comments a recent discussion paper from the World Bank, specialists can be expected "to provide at least a few months' advance notice of increased risk of climate-related disasters, such as a poor south-west monsoon in India, drought in East Africa, Indonesia or the Brazilian Amazon or serious flooding on Peru or Ecuador.

"Advance information on seasonal climate fluctuations will make planning for the distribution of fertiliser or food relief more efficient. Construction projects could be timed to avoid flooding ..." All of which make the Commonwealth and UN studies in early warning and disaster management a very realistic exercise.

The UN study was announced earlier this year after at least 17 national professional groups, including the Royal Society of Canada and the Science Council of Japan, had called for a co-ordinated worldwide research and training programme to combat natural disasters.

Their case was supported by many concerned global organisations such as the International Council of Scientific Unions, the International Union of Geological Sciences and the International Association of Earthquake Engineering.

"Data processing backed by remote sensing offers the first and vital early warning," explains a specialist located at the UN science and technology centre.

"Flood control technologies, safer building techniques and land surveying give planners the option to resettle populations in less vulnerable areas."

He adds that land-based and airborne instrumentation can pick up the warning signs with great accuracy.

Communications technology and micro computers have been scaled to such convenient size and cost that it is almost criminal to leave poor and vulnerable populations defenceless in the face of predictable disasters.

"If humanitarian concerns will not suffice, then the cold hard cost of cleaning up after floods, earthquakes and tidal waves should convince politicians at home and in donor capitals that a satellite dish antenna and a small computer in high risk communities would be cheap insurance."

The Commonwealth initiative may well be overdue. Computer models plotting the climate change of the planet predict a rise in the sea level of up to 3.5 metres in the next century, devastating coastlines and, in the absence of proper preparations, even drowning cities.

Much of London and the Thames estuary may well be engulfed by tides overwhelming all flood defences, according to recent projections published by Ulster University's Department of Environment Studies.

"In Bangladesh alone, 15 million people will have to move or drown within 30 years," says a specialist for the UN Environment Programme.

The process of change is irreversible, fuelled by the "greenhouse effect"—the concentration of manufactured carbon dioxide and other gases trapping heat in the earth's atmosphere, melting the ice-caps and raising the sea level. Climatic change cannot be prevented.

But it may be possible to limit its extent, delay its onset and institute measures designed to mitigate its worst effects—given global accord on co-ordinated action.

QUESTIONS

1 In what ways does the article suggest that IT may 'save the world'?

2 How is 'remote sensing' used to make forecasts of impending problems?

3 Discuss the organisational aspects of enabling IT to help in limiting the results of natural disasters.

Reader 3 A robot by any other name

In April 1923 a play opened at St Martin's Theatre in London; a play that was to have a profound impact, not because of any social or political message that it carried, but solely because of its portrayal of an ancient idea in modern guise and described in one simple word. That word was 'robot'. The play was 'RUR' (Rossum's Universal Robots) by the Czech author Karel Capek.

At $150 each, Rossum's robots were cheap; so cheap in fact that, as their advertising proclaimed, 'Everyone should buy his own robot'. These were creatures of synthetic protoplasm made from a secret chemical formula, unlike the legions of 'mechanical men' and automatic devices that were named after them. In fact, in the decade or so following the play's London production, anything automatic was almost inevitably labelled a robot; traffic lights for instance were often called 'robot policemen'.

Nowadays, ideas about robots are even more confused. The term has been applied to everything from simple radio-controlled toys to artificial intelligence techniques providing natural language interfaces to databases, and from computer numerically controlled machinery to 'smart' weapons.

The late Doctor Christopher Evans attempted to clarify the meaning of the word by defining three basic categories of machine: simple machines directly controlled by human beings: programmable machines whose behaviour was completely controlled by a pre-set program; and program controlled machines that also received relevant information from the outside world, in response to which they could alter their behaviour.

This last category he considered a true robot. Applied literally, these definitions would mean that the vast majority of industrial robots are nothing more than complicated computer numerically controlled devices, whereas a fairly unsophisticated (and seemingly less intelligent) central heating system would qualify as a robot. And what of the first category; can a fly-by-wire aircraft, for instance, still be considered nothing more than a technologically advanced simple machine?

With the ever increasing amount of computer technology to be found in everything from an electric kettle to a nuclear power station, the subject of what is or is not a robot appears reminiscent of the search for the ultimate answer to life, the universe and everything. 'The Hitch-hiker's Guide to the Galaxy' suggests that the answer (42) is meaningless because the question itself lacks meaning. That could also be true of the question of robots. One should ask, perhaps, not is it a robot but rather how robotic is it?

Contemporary simple machines of the type mentioned by Evans, such as motor cars, certainly didn't meet his definition of a robot. They were, to use his phrase, 'nothing more than powerful mechanical muscles'. That's no longer an adequate description. Nowadays, anything containing a motor is quite likely to have a microprocessor or two in the control system. Motive power with a motive, as it were, but nevertheless under human control.

At first sight, tele-operated devices such as those used to handle radioactive materials, are more robot-like. But stripped of their modern technology, they're essentially remote manipulators.

In recent years tele-operation has become a fairly common way of working in hazardous environments. A much publicised use is that of bomb disposal 'robots'. Less well known perhaps are the considerably more sophisticated remotely operated vehicles for oil rig inspection and maintenance, for instance. However, the recovery of the flight recorder of the crashed Air India Boeing 747 in 1985, and the discovery of the Titanic in 1986 brought them briefly into the limelight. Despite their considerable use of computer technology, they are still operated by humans.

A completely different kettle of submersibles includes the autonomous submarines proposed for the Autosub undersea research and exploration project. They'll be programmed to act independently of their mother ships, and carry out long-range oceanographic surveys. This puts them squarely in Evans' second category, although they may have sufficient intelligence to satisfy partially the requirements for category three.

Warfare is yet another hazardous area of human activity where intelligent machines are increasingly being employed. Fire-and-forget weapons such as cruise missiles certainly qualify as category three machines, and there are plans to make them even smarter by adding automatic target recognition.

Even more ambitious is the US autonomous bomber project proposed by the Defence Advanced Research Agency. This unmanned aircraft would be capable of taking off independently, flying to its target, taking evasive action, employing countermeasures, dropping its bombs, and flying back to base—everything a human crew would be required to do.

The market for intelligent weapons is likely to be very large. The American Electronic Industries Association has suggested a figure of $6 billion over the next five years for the unmanned air vehicles market alone.

Ground vehicles with intelligence are also being developed. Martin Marietta has been working on another idea from the Defence Advanced Research Agency, the autonomous land vehicle. It's already able to follow roads, and should eventually be able to travel across country.

Although having nothing like the autonomous road vehicle's intended capabilities, mobile security robots have appeared in recent years. One such is the Programmable Robot Observer With Logical Enemy Response. The Prowler was first demonstrated in 1984. It's based on a six-wheeled vehicle, and is not so much a robot as a programmable free ranging automatically guided vehicle to patrol a given path.

It's designed to be a semi-autonomous tv camera, sensor and weapons platform that can act as a perimeter guard. Although its patrol function is largely automatic, and its possible complement of sensors and weapons formidable, it is, in the last resort, still under human control.

Almost friendly by comparison are the diminutive security guards intended to patrol inside buildings. Sandia National Laboratories, for instance, has developed the Sandia Interior Robot, and Denning has produced the Denning Sentry. Equipped with infra-red and microwave sensors, tv cameras and obstacle avoidance sonar, these robots are designed to wander about outside office hours, and report anything unusual.

Work in the US seems to have progressed further than in the UK. However, the idea of small domestic robots does seem to be catching on here. Personal Robots of Henley, for instance, has received DTI backing to develop a household security robot.

Another part of the program involves the development of robotic fire-fighting equipment. But such machines will probably have only limited autonomy.

Atomic energy appears to be yet another hazardous area where robotic devices are likely to be used in increasing numbers. Inside the Central Electricity Generating Board's Oldbury nuclear reactor, for instance, there's a maintenance and inspection system known as Warrior. It's not truly autonomous, since overall control is exercised by human operators, but in 1986 it was the first of its kind to allow welding to be carried out inside a live reactor.

A greater degree of autonomy is exhibited by Sandia's Remote Radiation Survey and Analysis System in the US, although it doesn't have to work inside a reactor. Developed to check nuclear waste, it can locate specific containers, pick them up, determine their contents, check for physical damage and test for radiation leaks.

Also in the US, Hanford Engineering has developed the nuclear equivalent of a robotic bonded warehouse for radioactive materials, to control their use.

In the next 30 years, more than 350 reactors worldwide will have to be taken out of service. According to the US-based Worldwatch Institute report, the technology to deal with this particular problem has yet to be developed. The countries principally involved all have robotic projects of one kind or another but it's still very early days. However, with costs put at anything from \$50 million to \$3 billion for a reactor, it looks like it could become a boom business.

By contrast, the explosive growth predicted for manufacturing robots (more precisely, category two) seems, in the UK at least, rather to have fizzled. A number of reasons have been given for this, including overselling in the 1970s and early 1980s, selling the wrong machines for the wrong job, saturation of the market and high cost.

On this last point, Howard Moraff of the US National Science Foundation has compared present-day robotics with the computer industry 25 years ago, when computers were large expensive machines that required complicated programs to perform simple tasks. Speaking at the Second International Conference on Robotics, he said the real market for robots will open up when they become small enough and cheap enough to allow their widespread application.

Moraff's extrapolation is, with all due respect, a simple one, and he may well be wrong. But interestingly, he suggested a critical price tag of \$200 that would set off the robot revolution. That's just \$50 more than one of Rossum's.

Questions

1 Describe in your own words the different categories of robots identified, in the article, and the uses to which they are put.

2 (a) A current area of industrial research work is concerned with the development of an automatic or robotic vehicle. The vehicle is intended to move along a number of predetermined routes or paths within a factory. The vehicle is required to carry a number of stackable objects from one loading bay to another, where it will deposit them. A computer will be used to control the movements of the robotic vehicle.

(i) Explain carefully how the robotic vehicle could be designed and tested. Indicate any assumptions that you make.

(ii) What are the possible benefits and drawbacks of using such a robotic vehicle rather than conventional manned vehicles in a factory?

(b) Describe one other distinct use of computers in industry with which you are familiar.

[WJEC 1988]

3 Discuss the advantages, disadvantages and limitations of using robots in

(i) industrial and
(ii) social and domestic situations.

[UCLES 1989] AS

Reader 4(a) Tied to the phone

ARE WE seeing the development of an Orwellian police state, or a humane and economic way to cut down prison overcrowding? This debate is now raging over the electronic monitoring of criminals under computer surveillance during house arrest.

The program has generated considerable argument in the UK since the Home Office began studying it as an alternative to incarceration. Like many high-tech law enforcement techniques, the idea began in the US where a number of experiments in computerised house arrest have been run since the early eighties.

A Spiderman comic book, in which the hero used small electronic "tracers" to keep track of the bad guys, was the inspiration for a New Mexico law-enforcement official who initiated the first formalised use of monitoring technology in criminal justice in 1983. Since then over 60 similar pilot programs have been tried across the US, and a small high-tech industry dedicated to "controlled activities" has emerged.

That industry has produced a variety of devices, most of which can be broken down into "active" and "passive" systems.

Both systems use a central computer connected via the telephone line to a monitoring device in the prisoner's home. With an active system, the computer randomly telephones the detainee during the hours he is required to be in his house. Depending on the set-up, the detainee identifies himself by voice or by inserting an electronic ID strapped to his wrist into the computerised monitor.

In the more popular passive system a radio transmitter, strapped to the detainee's ankle or wrist, sends a continuous signal to the monitoring device attached to the phone. Whenever the detainee steps in or out of range of the monitor, a signal is sent to the computer at police headquarters. The computer writes out a daily report of the detainee's schedule, noting any time he has violated his curfew.

"We have tended to be very conservative in our application of this technology," says George Baldwin, probation officer in a Boston area court district where electronic monitoring was tried on a limited basis for six months. "I don't know of any cases in the US where violent criminals, or people who represented a threat to society, like repeated drunk drivers, were allowed to participate in this type of program.

"In our case, we dealt with first-offence drunk drivers or non-violent parole violators who were on their way to jail. The judge offered them the option of participating in the computerised house arrest experiment, in which they were allowed to continue working but had to remain at home during all non-work hours. Our acceptance rate was 100 per cent.

"Our success rate was pretty good as well: only three people out of seventeen violated their curfew. In a standard parole setting, violation rates can be as high as 50 per cent." Those who clearly violated the rules of their sentence were given their original jail sentences, minus the time they had already spent under house arrest.

"There have been technical problems with the equipment," says Baldwin. "One fellow lived in a mobile home park where the presence of all those sheet metal houses interfered with the radio signal to the computer. We were able to correct that by shortening the receiver's range to two hundred yards.

"Another fellow—our first case, actually—had broken the strap holding the transmitter to his leg. Apparently his wife had caught one of her spiked heels in his anklet. We were sceptical, but when he produced hospital records and a wife on crutches we decided the man deserved the benefit of the doubt. It was quite a way to start the program."

Civil libertarians are less hostile to the program in the US than they seem to be in Britain. Most American personal freedom activists see computer monitoring as a humane alternative to a six-by-eight-foot prison cell.

Extended monitoring systems using video cameras or breath analysers attached to the monitoring system have raised some eyebrows, but law enforcement agencies have shied away from such controversial and complex technology.

Programs which charge prisoners \$7–\$10 (£5 to £8) a day to help defray the cost of the equipment have caused objections since fees prevent lower income prisoners from participating. So have telephones, as only people who can afford them can choose home over jail. These objections are being taken very seriously, but will most likely defy satisfactory solutions. The issue of fines versus jail sentences raises similar questions of fairness in today's judicial system.

The Prison Reform Trust is one independent group which objects to the use of this technology in the UK. They feel monitoring technology represents an intrusion into private lives which can lead to family stress and social stigma.

A government study of programs in the US looked into those same issues and found stress was indeed present, normally in cases of long house arrest. While some people have been kept under house arrest for over six months, sentences are generally short, averaging between four and eight weeks.

Also, for every detainee who reported stress and hardship brought on by computer monitoring, another found the temporary enforced structure to his life to be beneficial.

For the vast majority, however, the computer was simply an annoyance. Given a choice, they would rather have a small plastic device strapped to their leg for a few weeks than suffer the stress and stigma which accompanies the same amount of time spent behind bars.

Reader 4(b) Marketing the facts of our lives

YOU CAN automate car production," said the American trade unionist Walter Reuther, "but you cannot automate production of customers." Reuther died in 1970 and his maxim died shortly after, for computers are automating the customer production by cross referencing swathes of personal trivia into coherent personality profiles that indicate what we might be persuaded to do next.

Fact gathering was the problem, and while other junk mail artistes sneaked up on consumers by aggregating the electoral roll, credit histories, postcode analyses, guarantee cards and other customer records, International (ICD) has leapfrogged them all. Its Facts Of Living database has pulled a marketing coup which will soon have filed a million names.

"Give us your opinions and we'll make it worth your while" promise forms inserted into colour supplements and TV listings magazines. In return for entry into prize draws, two per cent of the population is revealing everything from politics to bra size, credit card, income, investments and whether they'd buy wine, prints, or porcelain through mail order.

John English of ICD talks of charity marketing to explain how it's done. 86 per cent of those on his database say they are charity donors. Of that majority, 68 per cent have credit cards. He knows more. "They are predominantly male homeowners—married male homeowners who are high earners." Push a couple of buttons and out pops a list of those most likely to respond to a postal charity appeal.

For commercial clients, where the rule is that four fifths of business comes from a fifth of the customers, the sales aim is usually to get them to change brands. "Switching," says English, "is the most important part of selling."

But who will switch? ICD finds out by using personal tit-bits in less obvious ways. With tools borrowed from academic psychology, it weights the strength of reactions to some of the questions to separate the "restrained" from the "venturesome" and "leaders" from "followers". Venturesome leaders, so the theory goes, are more likely to switch brands of soapflakes. Psychographics is the buzzword for this alliance between scholastic personality sketches and brute computing power.

ICD expects a two per cent response to its 25 million questionnaires. However, mailings done on the basis of its data get up to 15 per cent response, and ICD is confident enough to charge customers largely on this basis. Analysis of half ICD's probing can be bought by anybody, but the other questions are sponsored by companies, like the AA and Austin Rover, that pay between £10,000 and £70,000 depending on numbers of questions asked and the eventual response to mailshots.

The 15 sales from every 100 unsolicited letters is why English claims suspicion of the junk mail trade, even though ICD's 400 clients sent out 38 million letters last year. For English the junkiest thing about modern marketing is its reliance on "outmoded social groupings" which classify us crudely as A, B, C1, C2, D or E.

"Occupation is no longer a reliable indicator of wealth," says English.

What has emerged from the ICD database are categories defined when "the computer was programmed to select groups of people" who had answered the most questions in common. What excites ICD is that "clusters" leave old socioeconomic bands far behind and even pinpoint different buying habits in single households.

Rather than the old A-to-Es there are 16 groups from "active families on the way up" to "stay-at-home working class". And overlaid on these are "forced cluster groups" which, rather than plundering the database for blocks of commonest answers, used the psychographic patterns to sweat yet more marketing information from survey respondents.

English has other expansionary schemes and whispers of plans to merge Facts of Living with details on "more than 11 million UK households". These come from electoral rolls, a register of 250,000 recent house movers culled from estate agents' records and from the investors' list which got ICD going in 1987. The cleverness knows no bounds and ICD was an early subscriber to the Smee and Ford Inheritance Database, a new computerised record of recent deaths. "A good source for potential legatees," English notes. "Data enhancement," ICD calls it. "Inferring what we don't know from what we do."

One questionnaire includes a snapshot of Cherie Brooks who won a holiday to Ibiza. "Interesting to fill in," says Ms Brooks, "as you learn so much about yourself." Not half so much as ICD! And although the form, which was vetted by the Data Protection registrar, is frank that "answers will form part of database about consumers", it doesn't reveal the extent to which Ms Brooks' frankness is used.

It's perfectly conceivable to automate the production of voters as well as consumers. A block of questions on ICD's recent form sought "your opinions", graded five ways on levels of agreement about Government policy. What better way of finding floating voters than to target the "neither agree nor disagrees" who live in marginal constituencies and then to run them through some psychographics to find who might, to lapse into market-speak, be switchable? A candidate would only need a thousand such prospects and a rich party could canvass them in harmony with their smallest predilections.

Questions

1 Discuss the pros and cons of computerised criminal tracking as described in the article.

2 Some people are worried about the computer acting as 'Big Brother', controlling our lives. Explain why people might have this opinion and discuss the issues involved.

3 Debate the line: Sophisticated computer-based market research – is it a good or a bad thing?

Reader 5 (a) Lulled into a false sense of security

THERE has been considerable media coverage recently of computer security issues, focusing on the twin aspects of the Friday the 13th "trigger" date for viruses and the Law Commission's report into computer crime. This undoubtedly has helped raise general awareness of computer security concerns, in some cases to a frantic level.

In an attempt to combat the virus crisis—computer viruses will indiscriminately and arbitrarily invade any organisation—and protect their markets, some companies, especially manufacturers, have released programs that "scan" for invading code, searching for the tell-tale signs that a parasite is in hiding, ready to pounce.

Organisations rush to install such protection software on their computers, mistakenly believing that a defence has been found. But such scanning programs are fundamentally flawed and result only in the delusion of safety, with serious implications for the future.

Almost all scanning programs include a disclaimer admitting that they can only detect known computer viruses. The reason for this potentially devastating limitation is easy to understand, and is often explained in the documentation itself: the scanning program will search the suspect program for a known sequence of data that is the "fingerprint" of a specific virus. If the virus has a different fingerprint, then it cannot be detected by a scanning program until it is much too late.

Mistakenly, there is a belief that this is the only limitation of scan programs and that with rapid updates damage can be limited. This is not so. I foresee the possibility of "self-mutating" or "designer" viruses.

If a programmer has access to an existing virus then it is a comparatively simple matter to reverse engineer it, to rebuild the original program code. Two of the main tools that dedicated programmers use are the disassembler and the debugger. Using these, any program can be decoded and understood, given sufficient time.

Alternatively, the persistent virus writer could buy a widely-available textbook that gives not only complete virus listings, but all sorts of destructive ideas to try out. The revealed code can then be altered slightly and a newly-mutated virus released out into the world again.

Encryption techniques have already been used to hide the larger portions of program code in some viruses, so the chances of detection are reduced even further. Adding some disguising code to the beginning of the virus would reduce suspicion at finding a "jump" instruction at the beginning of a program, which is still reasonably common amongst first generation viruses. A complex block of code, possibly performing some arithmetic calculations or resembling data, could be used to "hide" virulent instructions.

Regardless of source, a brand new mutant or "species" of virus can be created from existing code with minimal effort. Even more advanced will be the inevitable second generation virus which deliberately modifies itself—the designer virus. Every time a program is infected, the virus would change slightly. Each infected program would be subtly different, making search programs useless.

Given the possibility of unique viruses, detection programs that scan for known parasites become impotent—non-solutions to a very serious problem. The only plausible technique for users to detect viruses is to notice any kind of change in a host file.

Unfortunately, virus writers can easily avoid more obvious changes, such as differences in length: either the virus code could be placed elsewhere on the disc; or else standard and well-publicised compression techniques could be used to reduce the required program space, subsequently adding extra virus bytes to keep the same file size.

A more effective detection technique involves checking the internal structure of files, but this is a time-consuming task if it is to be done well, and is often impractical in reality.

Common advice regarding computer viruses is to scorn the problem, claiming that it is overhyped and will go away with careful planning. But computer viruses will never be totally eradicated. Viruses are symptomatic of fundamental security weaknesses, and the heady rate of improvement of system performance will make the problems worse.

The predicament would have arisen within mainframe computers eventually, but it was the success of PCs that caused the early growth of PC viruses. PC user culture is different from mainframe user culture, but with the use of PCs in mainframe environments, spread of disease is inevitable. Mainframes will be next. The long term benefits of such systems must now be questioned.

There is increasing but unspoken recognition of the fact that any one PC in a data processing environment can imply reduced system integrity and, importantly, data validity. A resource that was once an opportunity is now a risk.

Modern organisations cannot exist without the PC: there is no possibility of returning to the days of centralised mainframes accessed by dumb terminals. Such a move would be unrealistic and unacceptable. In any event, unless the terminals are themselves secured, the dangers of invalid/erroneous data are again introduced.

Technology alone cannot guarantee a defence against computer viruses. The only realistic approach is to improve user knowledge, and enforce stringent physical and managerial security measures, limiting those with access to machines, and then granting access only for specific purposes.

Security techniques must move away from the misconceived emphasis on technological half-measures, and instead focus on defending against the actions of the ultimate computer virus: homo sapiens.

Reader 5(b) Law Commission gives hackers five years

Hackers and virus writers face five years in prison following the Law Commission's recommendations for three criminal offences to fight computer misuse.

In its report published on Tuesday, the commission aims to combat the growing problem of computer hacking which the employers' organisation, the CBI, says is costing UK business £400m a year.

After a year long study of computer misuse, the Law Commission has identified two main problems not properly covered by existing criminal law.

The costs of disruption and uncertainty caused to the owners and users of computer systems by hacking is covered along with the loss and damage caused by unauthorised alterations to computer held data or programs whether by simple alterations or by the use of viruses, worms or computer discs.

The commission recommends the creation of three crimes to make hackers and virus writers accountable for their actions, whether carried out in fun or for devious reasons.

This is preferred to patching up existing criminal law which the commission says would be an inadequate deterrent.

The first deals with the unauthorised entry to a computer system for fun or to interfere, carrying a three month prison sentence.

The second covers the more serious offence of unauthorised entry to a computer system with intent to commit or assist the commission of a serious crime, carrying a maximum penalty of five years in prison. This would apply to anyone entering a bank system to divert funds.

Thirdly, a further serious offence, covering viruses, of intentionally and without authorisation, altering computer held data or programs, is dealt with, again carrying a five year prison sentence.

Reader 5(c) IT crime squad calls for reinforcements

Top computer police officers have admitted they are badly under-resourced to beat the growing wave of computer crime.

Detectives Christopher Pierce and Noel Bonczoszek of the crack Computer Crime Unit claim police forces throughout the UK are still unaware of the dangers of computer-related crime.

'We have cases where officers search a premises, take out everything in the filing cabinet but ignore the computer,' said Pierce. 'Or worse still, an officer unplugs the computer and takes it away with him.'

The claims come amid widespread calls to outlaw hacking and make computer-related fraud a crime punishable by up to five years' imprisonment. Last week, MP Emma Nicholson criticised the Government for not including a bill on hacking in the new parliamentary session.

But Pierce admitted the force will be dependent on British Telecom's computer crime unit for equipment and expertise if these measures come into effect. He said the London-based police unit cannot pay computer consultants for the time they spend helping on a case.

'An investigation can be extremely expensive and time-consuming,' said Bonczoszek.

Both officers lecture at the police Bramshill Staff College on computers. Just 50 police have attended the four-week course on computer crime, said Pierce.

'It's not a great deal but better than nothing,' he said.

The computer crime centre where the detectives are based is the only police unit in the UK to deal exclusively with computer-related crime.

Questions

1 Describe the nature of the various forms of computer crime. Discuss reasons why the incidence of computer crime might have increased and explain why its total extent is hard to estimate. What types of people are involved in computer crime and what steps have been taken to attempt to curb its increase? At what point does society become aware of the effects of computer crime?

[*WJEC 1988*]

2 Explain what is meant by a computer virus and why 'antidotes don't kill all known bugs'.

Reader 6 Flying blind to reality?

The unscheduled arrival of a light aeroplane in Moscow's Red Square last May resulted in a considerable amount of egg landing on the faces of senior Soviet military personnel. Through their oversights, the pilot Matthias Rust managed his "impossible" flight.

Just as easily, flawed methods for ensuring that software functions reliably can "let in" tiny mistakes which (unlike the Red Square incident) can cause limitless physical damage to people and property. The dangers are obvious in programs controlling aeroplanes, dams and nuclear reactors.

Perhaps the phrase "functions reliably" is misleading: the software might run faultlessly in terms of the specifications detailed by the user.

But those in turn might contain oversights or inaccuracies. Clearly, the results could be catastrophic.

This argument has come up again over a larger aircraft than Rust's: the A320 passenger plane, built by the Airbus Industries consortium, which will have "fly-by-wire" controls entirely run by software.

Airbus Industries sees itself as a software buyer and contends that it is up to the suppliers of the systems to ensure they meet the Airbus specifications. But software reliability experts contend that the specifications themselves could be at fault – and remain untested until they fail unexpectedly.

In fact the chief problem facing designers of safety-critical systems lies not so much in the writing and testing of the programs as in the way specifications are drawn up by users, according to Barry Daniels, manager of software engineering at the National Computing Centre (NCC). He believes too much attention is devoted to the software at the expense of the system as a whole.

Janusz Gorski from the Institute of Informatics in Gdansk, said it was vital that designers concentrate on the physical environment in which the system is operating.

"Catastrophes happen in the physical world, not the logical world," he asserts.

"If you are designing a system controlling a railway crossing you have to ask whether drivers will observe light signals."

To tackle the specifications problem, Daniels says UK software houses are trying to train users to create special diagrams illustrating the situation the software is meant to deal with.

There are two prevalent formal (ie. mathematical) methods at the moment for influencing the design of the system, says Daniels. They are the Vienna Development Method (known by its initials, VDM) developed by IBM in the 1970s at its Vienna laboratories; and Z, from Oxford University, which Systems Designers uses.

One software house that swears by VDM, however, is Cambridge Consultants, which develops systems for nuclear reactors, air traffic control and railways.

"It's no good testing after development," says John Bromwell, who is a senior software engineer with the company.

"Reliability has to be built in during the development process. Formal methods are the best for this. VDM encourages you to define what part of the program should do what – but doesn't tell you the 'how'," he explains.

His firm is using Pascal as the final implementation language for the nuclear reactor protection system, combined with a toolset development at Southampton University called Spade.

VDM has its own notation, so there is an added problem when it comes to translating into Pascal.

"We aim to translate VDM into Pascal as mechanically as possible for speed and reduction of errors," according to Bromwell.

Bromwell says you can get round the problem that formal methods can only be applied to relatively short sections of code simply by partitioning programs into subsections of about 2,000 lines.

Having introduced methods for both specifying and writing, designers of safety-critical software are faced with a range of options for doing external tests.

An alternative is a method called static analysis.

Rather than trying to execute the software, it uses mathematical means to take the software apart, showing its structure and its internal relationships.

These are then compared with the specification to make sure the program does what it has been told to do.

Citibank paid out £2 billion in 30 minutes by mistake. The error was attributed to a software design flaw. Application software defaulted to an incorrect system date and allowed payments from the previous day to be duplicated. The bank says it has recovered all its funds. Has it recovered from the publicity?

Questions

1 Over the past decade many industrial, medical, financial and military organisations have become heavily dependent on complex computer systems. By making reference to an application that you have studied, discuss the consequences of a system failure. What measures have been incorporated to protect the individual and society from such failures? To what extent should the computer industry accept responsibility for the problems created by such failures?

[*ULSEB 1989*] *Specimen paper*

2 A worthwhile computerised control system must be secure, reliable and resilient. Nevertheless, failures in a system can occur. By considering an example such as an air traffic control system, show how the effects of failures in the system can be minimised.

[*UCLES 1989*]

FURTHER QUESTIONS

1 A concert hall has 2000 numbered seats. 1200 seats are reserved for season ticket holders. A season ticket entitles its holder to use the same seat for all events throughout the season. During the season people may buy tickets for any available seats from any one of four ticket selling points. The management is proposing to computerise the sale of tickets, printing out each ticket as it is sold.

(i) What hardware would be required for each station?
(ii) What files would be necessary for the system and what information would each file hold?
(iii) What safeguard should be included in the system to stop two selling points issuing the same ticket simultaneously?
(iv) What benefits might be expected from the implementation of such a system?

[*ULSEB 1989*]

2 An electronics firm manufactures video recorders to order. It produces several different models using a computerised manufacturing process. As the orders are received they are input into the system and the parts for each model are placed by the automated warehouse into boxes for assembly by the workers. Each worker is responsible for assembling a small number of parts. The box of remaining parts and the partially assembled video is passed onto the next worker and so on, until the video is completed. At four separate stages it is necessary to test the video recorder electronically to check that each circuit has been correctly fitted. This testing is done by computer. The completed video recorder is boxed and addressed ready for sending to the customer along with the receipt.

(a) Describe how the progress of a video recorder along the assembly line could be monitored by computer.
(b) What are the advantages of having the completed video recorders tested by computer?
(c) Describe the main files which would be required by the system.
(d) What problems are the company likely to have had to solve in implementing a fully computerised system?

[*ULSEB 1989*]

3 An enterprising nurseryman runs a successful business selling a wide range of bedding plants, trees, flowering shrubs, and seeds for both flowers and vegetables. He also offers a consultancy service to provide advice and plans for the landscaping and layout of gardens. The nursery occupies a site of approximately two thousand square metres and has about ten large greenhouses and an office. The site holds substantial stock and a security system is in operation. Customers visiting the site are able to park their vehicles nearby. The nurseryman approaches the computer science teacher at the local school seeking advice on how a microcomputer system might support and enhance his business activities.

Assuming that you were the teacher, describe how you would tackle this task. Indicate any assumptions that you would make and explain how you would gather any additional information that was needed. Supposing that a microcomputer system was recommended, suggest a viable configuration and list possible benefits to the nurseryman and his customers.

[*WJEC 1988*]

4 The Sellitall Trading Company keeps stock of about 2000 different products. It supplies shops with miscellaneous items.

The company currently uses a batch stock control system where stock records are updated at the end of each week from hand-written forms. It intends to introduce an on-line system.

(a) Describe in outline the nature and benefits of this type of online system.

(b) The adoption of an online system to replace the batch system has significant implications for:

(i) hardware;
(ii) systems software requirements.

By making reference to the hardware and systems software requirements of the present and proposed systems, discuss the differences between them.

[*UCLES 1988*]

5 A large company has for some years made use of a centralised computing facility run by specialists who were alone allowed direct access to the files and database. It is now intended to install a new system that will place a workstation on every desk, allowing much wider access to the data both for interrogation and update purposes. However, much data remains both commercially and personally sensitive.

(a) Describe briefly what measures would have to be taken to maintain both a consistent and secure system, accessible only to those with permission.
(b) Discuss what changes the new system will have on the attitudes and work of, firstly, the existing specialists and, secondly, the employees in the company who will be using extensive computing facilities for the first time.
(c) What should the management do to ensure the workforce meet the challenge of the new system?

[*UCLES 1989*]

6 The life expectancy of a typical mainframe multi-access system is about 10 years. Some systems may have several hundred users, who make extensive use of all the software and hardware facilities which are available. For example, some users may use packages available for word processing, information storage and retrieval, statistical analysis and graph plotting. Sometimes, special hardware facilities such as laser printers and plotters are required. Other users may develop programs in various high-level languages, and a range of utility software, such as editors, compilers and debuggers would be available. Most large systems provide a considerable amount of online disk storage, and magnetic tape facilities would also be available.

(a) Discuss the problems which users may face when an existing mainframe is replaced by a new mainframe system. In what ways can the computer staff help to ensure a smooth changeover from one system to the other?
(b) In many organisations, mainframe computers are being replaced by several smaller computers linked together to form a computer network. Describe the advantages which such a system has over a single mainframe computer, and explain, from the users' point of view, how the network might function.

[*UCLES 1988*]

7 (a) Outline the reasons that have led to the widespread use of electronic mail in business, industry and education.
(b) Discuss the security problems that have arisen with electronic mail systems and indicate what steps can be taken to overcome them.
(c) Describe the user interface that is provided by a system such as Telecom Gold.
(d) Discuss developments to electronic mail systems which might occur in the future.

[*UCLES 1989*]

8 In the next few years there are likely to be major developments in the capacity and capabilities of communications systems of various kinds and in the sophistication and performance of expert systems, largely through the exploitation of parallel processing hardware and techniques. (Expert systems make use of artificial intelligence, and are sometimes known as intelligent knowledge-based systems.)

Discuss the nature of these developments and describe, with the aid of examples, possible applications for which they would be suitable, or in which they could make a contribution.

[*UCLES 1989*]

9 The customer services manager of a large chain of supermarkets wishes to ensure that the number of available checkout points is generally adequate to avoid long queues developing. The number of checkout points which need to be staffed will vary at different times of the week. In order to help make suitable plans, a software package is to be produced to simulate the progress of customers in the queues for the checkout points. The package will need to provide information from the simulation, such as the mean and maximum queue lengths over any given period of time, the amount of time that there is no queue at a checkout point, and the range of times that customers need to wait in a queue before they are checked out.

(a) Explain what information would be needed to allow the simulation package to carry out these tasks, and indicate how this information could be gathered.
(b) Describe the steps which would be involved in the design, implementation and testing of the simulation package.
(c) Comment on the reliability and usefulness of the results obtained from a simulation such as this.

[*UCLES 1989*]

INDEX